C. S. Lewis—
On the Christ of a Religious Economy

C. S. Lewis—
On the Christ of a Religious Economy
I. Creation and Sub-Creation

P. H. Brazier

Foreword by Judith Wolfe

SERIES: C. S. LEWIS: REVELATION AND THE CHRIST

www.cslewisandthechrist.net

PICKWICK Publications • Eugene, Oregon

C. S. LEWIS—THE WORK OF CHRIST REVEALED
I. Creation and Sub-Creation

Series: C. S. Lewis: Revelation and the Christ 3.1

Copyright © 2013 Paul H. Brazier. All rights reserved. Except for brief quotations in critical publications or reviews, no part of this book may be reproduced in any manner without prior written permission from the publisher. Write: Permissions, Wipf and Stock Publishers, 199 W. 8th Ave., Suite 3, Eugene, OR 97401.

Pickwick Publications
An Imprint of Wipf and Stock Publishers
199 W. 8th Ave., Suite 3
Eugene, OR 97401

www.wipfandstock.com

ISBN 13: 978-1-61097-720-3

Cataloging-in-Publication data:

Brazier, Paul.

C. S. Lewis—on the Christ of a religious economy : I. creation and sub-creation / P. H. Brazier, with a foreword by Judith Wolfe.

Series: C. S. Lewis: Revelation and the Christ 3.1

xx + 298 p. ; 23 cm. Includes bibliographical references and index.

ISBN 13: 978-1-61097-720-3

1. Lewis, C. S. (Clive Staples), 1898–1963—Religion. 2. Lewis, C. S. (Clive Staples), 1898–1963—Theology. 3. Creation—History of doctrines. I. Wolfe, J. E. (Judith Elisabeth), 1979–. II. Title. III. Series.

BX5199.L53 B639 2013

Manufactured in the U.S.A

All royalties from this series are donated to the University of Oxford C. S. Lewis Society

Typeset by P. H. Brazier, Ash Design
Minion Pro 10.75pt on 14pt

SERIES PREFACE
C. S. LEWIS: REVELATION AND THE CHRIST

This is a series of books that have a common theme: the understanding of Christ, and therefore the revelation of God, in the work of C. S. Lewis. These books are a systematic study of Lewis's theology, Christology, and doctrine of revelation; as such they draw on his life and work. They are written for academics and students, but also, crucially, for those people, ordinary Christians, without a theology degree who enjoy and gain sustenance from reading Lewis's work.

Book One
Revelation, Conversion, and Apologetics

Book Two
The Work of Christ Revealed

Book Three
On The Christ of a Religious Economy

A fourth volume, consisting of an in-depth bibliography, plus an introductory essay on Christology as the study of Christ, and a glossary, completes the series:

C. S. Lewis—An Annotated Bibliography and Resource

There is a website to accompany (www.cslewisandthechrist.net) that provides material and downloads to complement these books. Those who feel somewhat bemused by the concepts in Christology (the study of Christ) may gain understanding from browsing the site, which will give an introduction to the series. In addition a full detailed contents, including all sections can be downloaded and printed as an aide-memoire and guide to each book in the series.

This series has been many years in the making. The serious writing of it started in 2007; however, sketches relating to some of the topics go back much further. With writing the work grew. Lewis was not a systematic theologian, nor did he attempt to write a systematic theology (though the aim of *Mere Christianity* gets close to it). What this work attempts is to present a systematic study of what Lewis understood about Jesus Christ, and the revelation of God, who is at the heart of orthodox, traditional, theology.

For Hilary

Contents

List of Illustrations / xi

Foreword / xiii

Acknowledgments / xvii

Introduction / 1

PART ONE
THE FALL, ORIGINAL SIN, AND AN EXISTENTIAL CRISIS

1. Creation and The Fall I: C. S. Lewis—A Doctrine of Creation / 17

2. Creation and The Fall II: Lewis's "Augustinian" Account / 47

3. Creation and The Fall III: Innocence and Sin, Re-Interpreted / 67

4. Creation and The Fall IV: The Human Condition Before God / 97

PART TWO
CHRIST REVEALED THROUGH ANALOGICAL NARRATIVE

5. Analogical and Symbolic Narratives I: Narrative Theology, Supposition and Genre, Mythopoeic Theorizing—Imagining The Christ / 123

6. Analogical and Symbolic Narratives II: Christology and Christlikeness—Hiddenness and Multiple Incarnations / 141

7. Analogical and Symbolic Narratives III: Christology and Christlikeness—Trinitarian Considerations / 167

8. Analogical and Symbolic Narratives IV: Salvation, Encounters and Judgement—the Work of the Aslan-Christ / 203

9. Analogical and Symbolic Narratives V: Father Christmas in Narnia?—Intimations of Atonement and Salvation / 239

Bibliography / 267

Indexes / 275

Sectional Contents / 293

List of Illustrations

PART ONE
Figure 1 (Chapter 1)
A Systematic Structure to Lewis's Doctrine of Creation / 21

Figure 2 (Chapter 4)
Joseph Nuttgens, "Christ Teaching the People," Stained Glass Window, King's College London, Chapel, Strand Campus. Photograph P. H. Brazier / 101

PART TWO
Figure 3 (Chapter 5)
Salvation History and a Christocentric Religious Economy in the Narniad / 135

Figure 4 (Chapter 7)
Ἀγάπη: the Love of God / 171

Figure 5 (Chapter 7)
Sammons' identification of Christian Concepts in the Narniad / 177

Figure 6 (Chapter 7)
A Narnian Trinity / 185

Figure 7 (Chapter 8)
Faith-Faithlessness . . . and the neo-Kantian, Feuerbachian Dwarves / 231

Figure 8 (Chapter 9)
A Comparison of Salvation History in Narnia and on Earth / 251

Figure 9 (Chapter 9)
The Gift-Bearer, the work of the Holy Spirit / 265

Foreword

In the third book of his *Revelation and the Christ*, Dr. Brazier turns from the preceding study of God as he is "immanently" or within himself, to consider God in relation to his creation, that is, the divine "economy." This brings Brazier to the heart of the title of his series: the work of Christ wrought and revealed. The first question of the present book, then, is what this work of Christ consists in. Traditionally, Christian thought—although recognizing the role of each divine person in each aspect of God's work—has tended to associate the work of creation most closely with God the Father, the work of salvation with God the Son, and the work of sanctification with God the Holy Spirit. Dr. Brazier keenly notices that although C. S. Lewis does not undermine this traditional ascription, his reflections on Christ are grounded in a shift of perspective away from an isolated emphasis on salvation, towards an understanding of the work of the Son as a single whole that begins with creation: "the universe created by and through the Christ."

Consequently, this entire first half-volume of *On the Christ of a Religious Economy*, the third book of *Revelation and the Christ*, is concerned with the Son as creator rather than as redeemer. This approach is of immense importance not only because it reveals a stage or aspect of Christ's work that is not usually given much attention, but also because it re-frames the more familiar work of Jesus as mankind's redeemer. As we will see, C. S. Lewis's vision of the world as created by and through Christ means that his incarnation—his birth, death, and resurrection for mankind—are not merely a response to humanity's fall and consequent need of salvation—a divine Plan B after a part of creation has gone wrong—but a *continuation* of the work of creation itself, which was always by and through Christ.

But what exactly does "creation by and through Christ" mean? Centrally, it means that when God resolved, "Let us make mankind in our image" (Gen 1:26), this decision must be understood as relating man especially to God the Son, who is "the image of the invisible God, the firstborn over all creation" (Col 1:15). Consequently, the incarnation of the Son of God as a human being was not an arbitrary divine act, but the unveiling, in the fullness of time, of the image after which all humans had been fashioned: the revelation of what it is, or should be, to be human. This does not mean that the death and resurrection of the Son should not be understood as providing what Ignatius of Antioch calls the "medicine of immortality" for a humanity sick and death-bound with sin. However, it means that this is not merely a medicine that is necessary because we are diseased, but would have been of no use to us had we remained healthy.

On the contrary, the incarnation, death, and resurrection of Christ are also the true nourishment of our desires and aspirations, the foretaste of our destiny. "God became man so that man could become god," as St Athanasius famously put it.

It is in this understanding of Christ's involvement not only in salvation but already in creation that C. S. Lewis' famous theory of christological prefiguration—that is, premonitions of Christ contained in pagan mythology—finds its theological context. Because all humans are made in the image of God, which is Christ, all humans carry within themselves a natural longing for, or intuition of, their archetype and exemplar. To C. S. Lewis, it is no surprise, then, that this intuition or longing, however tarnished by sin, should find expression in myths and stories about gods who die and rise for the salvation of their people. Even if, as the great modern anthropological chroniclers of myth suggest, these myths arise not from a spontaneous religious imagination but from an observation of the cycles of nature (P. H. Brazier himself cites the haunting English folksong of John Barleycorn as a clear example of this), the principle of creation in Christ holds: If the incarnation was, from the beginning, to be the culmination of the creation of mankind in Christ, then it should be no surprise that its contours should be etched into nature itself.

This vision of a natural desire for Christ has implications for another important area of Christian thought, namely the question of the fall and human sinfulness. It is this question which occupies the first four chapters of the present book. Protestant thought traditionally regards the fall of Adam and Eve into sin as an event so cataclysmic—a fall from such height to such depth—that the sacrifice of the Son of God himself was necessary to overcome its damage. Its effect on humankind, according to this tradition, therefore cannot be overestimated: sinful and unredeemed mankind is so corrupt in both reason and will that people are no longer capable of forming any idea of God or of so much as desiring him. C. S. Lewis is very attentive to human sinfulness (indeed, he writes that Christianity has nothing to say to those who do not recognize themselves as sinful[1]). However, as should be clear from what has been said so far, he does not think that the fall corrupted mankind—or the image of God in mankind—so much that humans are no longer capable of reasoning about God or desiring him. Although Lewis believes that both human reason and human will are impaired by sin, he also thinks that they are still capable of apprehending and pursuing not only natural ends, but also, to some extent, the things of God.

This conviction is not peripheral to the rest of Lewis's thought, but underpins his entire Christian authorship—apologetics as well as imaginative literature—in both content and form. It probably has its biographical roots in Lewis's own experience of coming to faith through the pursuit of an innate desire (or "joy") which he came to recognize at last as a desire for communion with God. The pursuit of this desire is the subject of both *Surprised by Joy* and *The Pilgrim's Regress*. But it is not only the subject matter but also the authorial principle of his narrative writings: *The Chronicles of Narnia* and *Perelandra*, for example, are "didactic" not only in the sense that they tell

---

1   See esp. *Mere Christianity*, book 1.

Christian stories but also in the sense (expounded in *The Abolition of Man*) that they educate their readers' emotions, awakening and sustaining in them that desire for God which Lewis regards as perhaps man's most precious endowment.

Similarly (and this harks back to the first two books in Dr. Brazier's series), Lewis's conviction that the fall has impaired but not obliterated mankind's capability to know and desire God informs his apologetic writings in both content and strategy. This is particularly clear in two areas: First, C. S. Lewis's argument that practical reason is innate and ineradicable; in other words, that people cannot fail to know the basic tenets of the divinely given moral law.[2] Secondly, in Lewis's contention that human rationality must be rooted in a supernatural Reason, not merely in unguided evolutionary processes.[3] These arguments could not get off the ground without a very strong sense of the continuity between creation and salvation. (Though to avoid the impression that C. S. Lewis's theology is a simple "theology of glory," I should also note that he holds that people's natural sense of moral right and wrong must, if they are honest with themselves, lead them to recognize that they are constantly placing themselves in opposition to the very moral principles that sustain them—in other words, that they need salvation from themselves.)

The two theological concerns—creation in Christ and the problem of human sinfulness—converge in C. S. Lewis's *narrative* presentation of Christ, which is the subject of the second half of the present book. As Dr. Brazier argues, C. S. Lewis's preferred ways of talking about Christ seem to be what Brazier calls analogical and symbolic narratives: stories that "draw people into an understanding of God's salvific purposes" not by simply re-telling the story of Jesus, but by transposing the shape of the Christian story into other, imaginative contexts, be they an alternative world (such as Narnia) or a different planet in our own universe.

This literary form can be seen as a direct response both to humanity's creation in the image of God in Christ, and to the tarnishing of this divine image in humans through the fall. I have already touched upon the relation of Lewis's narrative writings to the latter, the problem of sin. Lewis thought one of the effects of sinfulness was an endemic suppression or distortion of people's inborn desire for God. He regarded it as one of the chief tasks of the Christian writer to help rekindle this desire or re-direct it to its proper object. Consequently, his depictions of the Christ-like Aslan, Maleldil, and God of the Mountain were meant to evoke the glory, beauty, terror, and attractiveness—the *mysterium tremens et fascinans*—of Christ to readers for whom the figure of Jesus had become overlaid with associations of stale piety, hypocrisy, obligation or guilt.

But C. S. Lewis's analogical and symbolic narratives of Christ are also an expression of his belief in creation by and through God the Son. This can be seen in two ways. First, being made in God's image means that God may best be understood the way human beings are best understood, namely through the story of his life with us, culminating

---

2   See esp. *The Abolition of Man*, "The Poison of Subjectivity," and "*De Futilitate*."
3   Expressed in technical philosophical terms, naturalism is self-referentially incoherent; see esp. *Miracles*, chapter 3.

in the story of Christ. As Dr. Brazier rightly points out, this theological approach has recently gained considerable popularity under the title "narrative theology," and C. S. Lewis must be seen as an important forerunner of that movement.

Secondly, being made in God's image means, among other things, to be made in the image of him who creates—and thus, being in a certain measure called, like him, to create. C. S. Lewis famously shared this sense with his friend J. R. R. Tolkien, who termed the vocation, perhaps somewhat infelicitously but certainly memorably, "sub-creation". Chapters 6 to 9 of the present book are case studies in some of the particular narrative and theological puzzles, questions, and challenges that arise from the pursuit of sub-creation on the theme of Christ.

The present book thus reveals C. S. Lewis's narrative writings as informed by a profound and coherent theological perspective. It is my hope that it will lead readers to a deeper understanding not merely of C. S. Lewis as an author, but also of the Christian vision that motivated and inspired him from first to last.

Judith Wolfe
Fellow, St John's College, Oxford

Acknowledgments

My initial interest in C. S. Lewis started with a Sunday afternoon TV serialization of *The Lion, the Witch and the Wardrobe* in, I think, 1967. Crude by today's CGI standards, and in black-and-white, I only saw the first episode amidst a chaotic time of my life, yet a seed was sown, thoughts which I could not get out of my mind. Credit should also be given to a fellow student, Debbie Gould, when I was at art college, who commented pointedly to me that I should read Lewis's works. Something I started to do seriously when I became a Christian in 1980. Acknowledgment must be accorded to Dr. Murray Rae and Dr. Brian Horne (both formerly of King's College London) for engendering in me studious interest in Lewis from 1999, which culminated in this work. Thanks must also be given to Dr. Pat Madigan S. J. (Editor of *The Heythrop Journal*), for encouragement—and for publishing articles generated by this research), Judith and Brendan Wolfe (The University of Oxford C. S. Lewis Society), and also to John Field, a well-read Christian, for advice in reading early drafts. My thanks go to N. T. (Tom) Wright, for discussions (conducted by e-mailed message) on the nature of *the Christ* as presented in this work. My deepest thanks must go to Robin Parry (editor, Wipf and Stock) for countless ideas and advice, and his unrivaled expertise as a biblical scholar, particularly in his editing of this series. But ultimately acknowledgment and thanks must go to Hilary, my wife, without whom I would not be the person I am, and this work would never have existed.

Acknowledgment and thanks is given to the Dean, the Revd. Professor Richard Burridge, and the Chaplain, the Revd Tim Ditchfield, for permission to use the photograph of the DNA window in the Chapel, Strand Campus, King's College London.

Acknowledgment and thanks is given to the C. S. Lewis Co. Pte., for permission to quote from the following works.

Correspondence
C. S. Lewis, *Collected Letters, Vol. II: Books, Broadcasts and War 1931-1949* (2004). Extracts by C. S. Lewis, copyright © C. S. Lewis Co. Pte. Reprinted by permission.

C. S. Lewis, *Collected Letters, Vol. III: Narnia, Cambridge and Joy 1950-1963* (2007). Extracts by C. S. Lewis, copyright © C. S. Lewis Co. Pte. Reprinted by permission.

C. S. Lewis, *Letters to an American Lady*. Extracts by C. S. Lewis, copyright © C. S. Lewis Co. Pte. Reprinted by permission.

Single Volumes
C. S. Lewis, *Mere Christianity* (1952). Extracts by C. S. Lewis, copyright © C. S. Lewis Co. Pte. Reprinted by permission.

C. S. Lewis, *Broadcast Talks. Reprinted with some alterations from two series of Broadcast Talks 'Right and Wrong: A Clue to the Meaning of the Universe' and 'What Christians Believe' given in 1941 and 1942* (1942). Extracts by C. S. Lewis, copyright © C. S. Lewis Co. Pte. Reprinted by permission.

C. S. Lewis, *The Great Divorce* (1945). Extracts by C. S. Lewis, copyright © C. S. Lewis Co. Pte. Reprinted by permission.

C. S. Lewis, *Miracles* (1st ed., 1947). Extracts by C. S. Lewis, copyright © C. S. Lewis Co. Pte. Reprinted by permission.

C. S. Lewis, *Miracles* (2nd ed., 1960). Extracts by C. S. Lewis, copyright © C. S. Lewis Co. Pte. Reprinted by permission.

C. S. Lewis, *Letters to Malcolm: Chiefly on Prayer* (1964). Extracts by C. S. Lewis, copyright © C. S. Lewis Co. Pte. Reprinted by permission.

C. S. Lewis, *Beyond Personality: the Christian Idea of God* (1944). Extracts by C. S. Lewis, copyright © C. S. Lewis Co. Pte. Reprinted by permission.

C. S. Lewis, *The Problem of Pain* (1940). Extracts by C. S. Lewis, copyright © C. S. Lewis Co. Pte. Reprinted by permission.

C. S. Lewis, *A Grief Observed* (1961). Extracts by C. S. Lewis, copyright © C. S. Lewis Co. Pte. Reprinted by permission.

C. S. Lewis, *Christian Behaviour* (1943). Extracts by C. S. Lewis, copyright © C. S. Lewis Co. Pte. Reprinted by permission.

C. S. Lewis, *The Screwtape Letters* (1942). Extracts by C. S. Lewis, copyright © C. S. Lewis Co. Pte. Reprinted by permission.

C. S. Lewis, *Perelandra* (1943). Extracts by C. S. Lewis, copyright © C. S. Lewis Co. Pte. Reprinted by permission.

C. S. Lewis, *Out of the Silent Planet* (1938). Extracts by C. S. Lewis, copyright © C. S. Lewis Co. Pte. Reprinted by permission.

C. S. Lewis, *The Pilgrim's Regress: An Allegorical Apology for Christianity, Reason and Romanticism* (1944). Extracts by C. S. Lewis, copyright © C. S. Lewis Co. Pte. Reprinted by permission.

The Chronicles of Narnia
C. S. Lewis, *The Chronicles of Narnia—The Magician's Nephew* (1955). Extracts by C. S. Lewis, copyright © C. S. Lewis Co. Pte. Reprinted by permission.

C. S. Lewis, *The Chronicles of Narnia—The Lion the Witch and the Wardrobe* (1950). Extracts by C. S. Lewis, copyright © C. S. Lewis Co. Pte. Reprinted by permission.

C. S. Lewis, *The Chronicles of Narnia—The Horse and His Boy* (1954). Extracts by C. S. Lewis, copyright © C. S. Lewis Co. Pte. Reprinted by permission.

C. S. Lewis, *The Chronicles of Narnia—Prince Caspian: The Return to Narnia* (1951). Extracts by C. S. Lewis, copyright © C. S. Lewis Co. Pte. Reprinted by permission.

C. S. Lewis, *The Chronicles of Narnia—The Voyage of the Dawn Treader* (1952). Extracts by C. S. Lewis, copyright © C. S. Lewis Co. Pte. Reprinted by permission.

C. S. Lewis, *The Chronicles of Narnia—The Silver Chair* (1953). Extracts by C. S. Lewis, copyright © C. S. Lewis Co. Pte. Reprinted by permission.

C. S. Lewis, *The Chronicles of Narnia—The Last Battle* (1956). Extracts by C. S. Lewis, copyright © C. S. Lewis Co. Pte. Reprinted by permission.

Poetry Volumes
C. S. Lewis, *Poems* (1994). Extracts by C. S. Lewis, copyright © C. S. Lewis Co. Pte. Reprinted by permission.

Volumes of Essays
C. S. Lewis, *Undeceptions: Essays on Theology and Ethics* (1970). Extracts by C. S. Lewis, copyright © C. S. Lewis Co. Pte. Reprinted by permission.

C. S. Lewis, *Transposition and Other Addresses* (1949). Extracts by C. S. Lewis, copyright © C. S. Lewis Co. Pte. Reprinted by permission.

C. S. Lewis, *Screwtape Proposes a Toast* (1965). Extracts by C. S. Lewis, copyright © C. S. Lewis Co. Pte. Reprinted by permission.

C. S. Lewis, *Of Other Worlds. Essays and Stories* (1966). Extracts by C. S. Lewis, copyright © C. S. Lewis Co. Pte. Reprinted by permission.

C. S. Lewis, *Of This and Other Worlds* (1982). Extracts by C. S. Lewis, copyright © C. S. Lewis Co. Pte. Reprinted by permission.

C. S. Lewis, *Christian Reflections* (1967). Extracts by C. S. Lewis, copyright © C. S. Lewis Co. Pte. Reprinted by permission.

Single Papers in Journals/Periodicals or as Guest Writer
C. S. Lewis, "It All Began with a Picture . . ." *The Radio Times, Junior Section* (No. CXLVIII, 15 July 1960). Extracts by C. S. Lewis, copyright © C. S. Lewis Co. Pte. Reprinted by permission.

Acknowledgment and thanks is given to Houghton Mifflin Harcourt for the U.S. right for permission to quote from the following works:

Excerpts from REFLECTIONS ON THE PSALMS, copyright © 1958 by C. S. Lewis, renewed 1986 by Arthur Owen Barfield, reprinted by permission of Harcourt, Inc.

Excerpts from SURPRISED BY JOY: THE SHAPE OF MY EARLY LIFE, by C. S. Lewis, copyright © 1956 by C. S. Lewis and renewed 1984 by Arthur Owen Barfield, reprinted by permission of Harcourt, Inc.

Excerpts from LETTERS OF C. S. LEWIS (2ND ED.), copyright © 1988 by C. S. Lewis, renewed 1986 by Arthur Owen Barfield, reprinted by permission of Harcourt, Inc.

Excerpts from THE WORLD'S LAST NIGHT AND OTHER ESSAYS, by C. S. Lewis, copyright © 1960 by C. S. Lewis and renewed 1984 by Arthur Owen Barfield, reprinted by permission of Harcourt, Inc.

Extracts from the Bible used with permission:

Revised Standard Version of the Bible, copyright 1952 [2nd edition, 1971] by the Division of Christian Education of the National Council of the Churches of Christ in the United States of America. Used by permission. All rights reserved.

New Revised Standard Version Bible, copyright 1989, Division of Christian Education of the National Council of the Churches of Christ in the United States of America. Used by permission. All rights reserved.

New Revised Standard Version Bible: Anglicized Edition, copyright 1989, 1995, Division of Christian Education of the National Council of the Churches of Christ in the United States of America. Used by permission. All rights reserved.

THE HOLY BIBLE, NEW INTERNATIONAL VERSION®, NIV® Copyright © 1973, 1978, 1984, 2011 by Biblica, Inc.™ Used by permission. All rights reserved worldwide.

Introduction
C. S. Lewis—On The Christ of A Religious Economy
I. Creation and Sub-Creation

This is a book about Jesus Christ.

Jesus of Nazareth, the Christ, is of central importance to humanity.

Jesus Christ is considered by orthodox Christians to be the unique revelation of God, the God above all gods, the God beyond all gods.

These are strong, dynamic, and assertive claims. There are various ideas and interpretations of who or what this Jesus of Nazareth, the Christ, was and is; these theories vary across the churches. However, down the centuries there has been a constant and steady seam of knowledge and understanding as to who Jesus Christ is, how he is God, and how this affects all of humanity.

To talk about Jesus Christ is to speak of revelation—God's self-revelation, God's revealedness to humanity. Therefore, God is the one who initiates both in our knowledge and understanding about these most important of matters, but also, crucially, in our salvation.

1. WHO OR WHAT IS *THE* CHRIST

This is one of a series of books entitled *C. S. Lewis: Revelation and the Christ*. Like many ancient names that had cultural or religious meanings, the name Jesus—in Hebrew, *Yeshua*, given to Mary by Gabriel, the angel at the annunciation—was known to those who heard it as signifying "God is savior," or "Jehovah is savior"; Christ means "anointed one," messiah. The word Messiah was commonly used in the era between the two testaments, Old and New (i.e., the intertestamental period), the concept of messiahship having developed in later Judaism (from the early Hebrew *Mashiach*, the anointed one, derived from the ancient Hebrew tradition of anointing the king with oil). Messiah was not necessarily a name, but a label, an attribution, an office, a role, essentially a title. By the time of Jesus of Nazareth the title "Messiah" was often attributed to someone the people liked, whom they believed could fulfill, they hoped, a role for them. However, *the* Messiah was to be the one anointed at the end of days. Jesus is therefore taken by those around him to be *the* Messiah; hence the early attribution that he is the Christ. The word Christ is simply a translation from the Greek (χριστός, *Christos*) and the Latin (*Christus*) for messiah. Therefore Jesus Christ, in name and title, was God's salvation, the anointed one. This did not necessarily imply that he was the second person of the Trinity. The trinitarian perception is part of the dawning realization in the early church, with ample pointers and examples of Jesus's trinitarian nature in the books that became the New Testament (texts produced by the earliest church in the years after the resurrection and ascension).

Around the time of Jesus's birth messiahship carried expectations. Some saw the coming messiah as a political leader who would expel the Romans; others expected a messiah who would be a partisan revolutionary whose aims were unclear; to yet more the messiah would return the Temple religion back to a happier time, he would oversee the restoration of Israel. To an extent these can be seen as purely human offices. During the intertestamental period there were many false messiahs, men raised up to realize a revolutionary, political, or religious role supported by a group or sect to save Israel in some way or other. However, false messiahs lapsed, disappeared, or were killed by the Romans or the Jewish religious authorities. The Jews were left still hoping.

The idea of redemption, salvation, was part of these multitudinous expectations of a messiah figure during the intertestamental period—but saved *from what*, redeemed *to what*? The answers to those questions were as varied as the messianic expectations of these false messiahs. As a redeemer figure, expected and foretold, Jesus does not necessarily live up to the expectations of his fellow Jews. However, on reflection, the clues were there all along in Jesus's life and ministry, and crucially in the Old Testament. The ancient Hebrews priests and kings were anointed, they were messiahs (Exod 30:22–25); later, this messiahship entitled one anointed by God as a leader, a king from the line of David. Therefore, Jesus of Nazareth was perceived by many who saw and heard him to be *the* long awaited Messiah, with different and often subjective expectations as to his role. What is important is that *a posteriori*, after the event, the proto early church interpreted this messiahship in the context of Jesus's role as God descended to earth to judge and forgive humanity, hence the use of the Greek word χριστός (*Christos*), Christ, by the writers of the New Testament. Jesus is then *the* final Messiah of messiahs.

Messiah, Christ, is then revealed to be trinitarian: God anoints God to descend to save his chosen people, in potential, along with all humanity, reascending with them into the divine life. Only in the fullness of the incarnation-cross-resurrection and the ascension is messiahship finally defined by Jesus. Then his life and ministry, his sayings and actions, take on new meaning, a significance and understanding veiled to many during his lifetime. Whatever the expectations of messiahship, Jesus of Nazareth is *the* Messiah (therefore, *the Christ*), not a messiah, political or otherwise. It is fair to say that some of the Hebrew expectations were blown away by God's revelation; whatever people expected, it fell short of what was given by God in this Jesus. People couldn't see or fully understand what Messiah was to be, even though the evidence was there in the Old Testament.

The witness of the apostles, disciples, and the early church is then a form of revelation equal to Scripture. The early church tradition replaces the old Hebrew categories of messiahship; the expectations of Jesus's contemporaries were fulfilled by God's revelation, but not necessarily in accordance with what they desired or expected. This divergence also extended to the interpretation of messiahship that the Jewish religious authorities held to in Jerusalem. For many years the Western church concentrated only on the early church tradition and the conclusions of the church councils in the fourth and fifth centuries, often, in effect, ignoring the Hebrew tradition that Jesus of Nazareth was born into. In recent years many theologians and Bible scholars, for example the orthodox Christian N. T. Wright, derive most of their conclusions about Jesus of Nazareth from an understanding of the New Testament's Jewish background, a setting in the life of the times in some ways. Perhaps the answer is to hold in balance the Hebrew tradition and categories, the perceptions of the earliest church, and also the conclusions of the later church councils, about the person and nature of Jesus. This is how to see and understand the term Messiah, *the Christ*.

This is a work, in many ways, of Christology; that is, the work and person of Christ, Jesus of Nazareth. Christology is thinking about Christ; explaining using the faculty of reason, mostly in written form, so as to explicate who and what Jesus Christ was and is. Lewis's work was very much in the context of the developed understanding of who and what Christ was; an understanding that took shape in the first seven centuries of the Christian era. As with the Bible, this understanding became something of a compass as to what counts as sound doctrine about Christ and what does not. This body of understanding of what is a traditional and orthodox understanding of Jesus Christ developed gradually during the early church, and then through the following centuries, and was complete by around the year 750 AD. Christology is therefore seen to be the study of the person and work of Christ, fully human and fully divine, historical and universal, and his significance for humanity: this systematic study is therefore the doctrine of Christ, but it must always understand the Hebrew roots into which Jesus of Nazareth was born and lived.

2. WHY C. S. LEWIS

This is a book about one man's understanding of, and his encounter with, Jesus Christ. That man is Clive Staples Lewis—C. S. Lewis, Jack, at his insistence, to all he knew—who wrote many, many books to defend Christianity and the witness of the churches. Lewis's aim was to defend Christianity itself, not Anglican or Roman Catholic, not Methodist or Baptist, not Presbyterian or Evangelical. Why? He sought to defend what he famously called "Mere Christianity," which was not his own personal religion, or his own personal selection from Christian theology and church history, but the faith set out in the creeds and explained by the church fathers living more than fifteen hundred years ago, the faith that originated with the apostles who knew this Jesus of Nazareth. Lewis sought to defend the faith that the martyrs died for. Being a "Mere Christian" for him represented the distilled basics of the faith rooted in the God-man Jesus Christ. This was to be distinguished, for Lewis, from watered-down Christianity, from human-centered religion.

Lewis's "Mere Christianity" was, therefore, polemical in its assertiveness. This "Mere Christianity" was there to a greater or lesser degree in all the churches of Lewis's day, but had been compromised by disputes between the churches; indeed the very fragmentation of the church into so many denominations or groupings weakened the basic core of the faith. Games of one-upmanship and power politics between bishops from competing denominations, or arguments over the finer points of worship, or in some instances a wholesale rejection of the beliefs set out in the creed, this all weakened the gospel: that God became incarnate as a human being in Jesus of Nazareth and died for our sins to open up a way for us into heaven. This was at the heart of the Christian faith. This Jesus of Nazareth, the Christ, did not simply live two thousand years ago leaving us alone in the world: the Holy Spirit of this Christ is active, alive, presses on us, seeks to convert us, to save us.

Lewis believed strongly in a basic core to the faith, a "mere" Christian core. All else could be considered to be an embellishment, details that are to a greater or lesser degree important to individual denominations, and are valid to a greater or lesser extent before God, but nonetheless these details and differences are culturally relative, they are in many ways subjective religion. Lewis therefore distinguished what he called "Mere Christianity" from this subjective religion. Lewis was an Anglican; he saw this "Mere Christianity" in the Church of England of his day, that it was at its strongest in the Catholic and Evangelical wings, as distinct from the liberal, modernist, central ground, which he believed marginalized this core of "Mere Christianity": Lewis could therefore be fairly described as a Catholic-Evangelical, indeed he described himself as such.

This book then is written for students and theologians, but also general readers familiar with Lewis's works. Because Lewis was an Anglican this is a work written to be appreciated by Anglicans; however, it can also be appreciated by Roman Catholics who in recent years have developed an interest more and more in the writings of C. S. Lewis; it is also aimed at Evangelicals who have long had a love of Lewis's work, but have been selective about what they agree with and disagree with in Lewis's presentation of the basic core of the Christian faith. Evangelicals may not like the way Lewis subscribed to what can be considered a traditional Catholic position on the sacraments and on purgatory, but he held these beliefs for good reason. And Evangelical readers would do well to think why he did. Likewise Roman Catholic readers would do well to see how Lewis could get beyond the external structure of religion to appreciate the immediacy of relationship any believer can have with the Lord Jesus, which in some ways by-passes the structures and authority of the church(es).

3. AIMS AND OBJECTIVES

This series, *C. S. Lewis: Revelation and the Christ*, is a study of C. S. Lewis's Christology, and his doctrine as such of revelation: that is, his understanding of the person and the work of Jesus Christ, and how this is God's self-revelation. This study includes Lewis conversion, his acceptance of what Jesus Christ had done for him, but also his understanding of the church, which is to be seen as the body of Christ. Therefore this book is about how he put that understanding into words, but it is also about his encounter with Jesus Christ, how Christ revealed of Christ's person, Christ's self, to Lewis, and therefore brought him to the one true trinitarian God. This is, in effect, what this book is about: who and what Jesus Christ is, and what *he* does.

The aim of this book is to show what C. S. Lewis understood about Jesus Christ. The objective is to examine what he then wrote, but also how he came to know and to believe in the God behind and in the Christ. This book is–

- A systematic study of the person and work of Christ Jesus in the writings of C. S. Lewis, and the place this understanding has in the wider church, contemporary and historical.

- A systematic study of Lewis's understanding of revelation—God's self-revelation to humanity—and with it humanity's salvation.

- This is therefore a work about Lewis's doctrine of Christ (including his understanding of the church—the body of Christ), his doctrine of salvation, and his doctrine of revelation (including the respectful criticism he had for "religion").

- A presentation of the personal God in Christ, which is central to understanding C. S. Lewis himself, both child and adult, public and private, and how this relates to his work as a philosopher and theologian, and his personal salvation.

- A work that presents an understanding for thinking Christians and professional academics, which ranks Lewis amongst the more important theologians and philosophers of the twentieth century.

- An analysis of Lewis's method and technique (both theological and philosophical) in the way he re-presented the basic non-negotiable core of the faith in his apologetic, his analogical stories, and in his theological narrative.

- A study of Lewis's Christology that acknowledges the Catholic (for example, a high sacramental theology, a belief in purgatory) and the Evangelical (his acknowldgement of the need for personal conversion in the form of a direct relationship with the Lord) within his faith as a Catholic-Evangelical.

Many books relating to C. S. Lewis's theology assume that he was an amateur theologian who simply summarized Christian doctrine and ethics for his audience, that he was not an original thinker or a systematician on the scale of more noted professionals. This series of books, *C. S. Lewis: Revelation and the Christ*, demonstrates that this is *not* so, that such conclusions are spurious. Lewis may not have been employed as a religious professional but the same can be said for many theologians and apologists in church history. Lewis's work is original, underlyingly systematic, and orthodox (i.e., traditional).

Lewis excelled at a cohesive expounding of the essentials at the heart of the Christian belief, nonetheless he held to an understanding of the wider logical sweep of the faith, without becoming embroiled in the more controversial details that have bedevilled the churches, individual denominations, for centuries. Lewis's understanding of Christ was grounded in his conversion. This was a conversion that paralleled, in many ways, that of Augustine in his acceptance of what God had done for him in the incarnation and in his invocation of Christ as the light of the world, and was given its systematic edge by his daily reading of key works of theology and related philosophy from before the modern era (that is, works written prior to the Age of Reason and the Enlightenment in the eighteenth and nineteenth centuries, and the modernism-postmodernism of the twentieth century).

Revelation and salvation are all intertwined with what we know of and understand about Jesus Christ. Therefore we are dealing with three doctrines (that is, doctrine as a set of beliefs or principles held and taught by a group, whether the church, a political party, or academics, from the Latin *doctrina* "teaching, learning"). These three doctrines are closely related: a doctrine of *revelation*, a doctrine of *Christ*, and a doctrine of *salvation*. We cannot separate who and what Jesus is from what he came to achieve, and what this person reveals to us about God. This work is a systematic study of Lewis's presentation and understanding of Jesus Christ that, following his conversion, underpinned his work. It assesses the implications of what he wrote and how Lewis the philosopher/theologian—when writing on Christ—is to be seen in relation to the church. This is in regard to his reputation as a Christian theologian, but also how the person and work of Christ Jesus is central to the human that he was.

4. EXPLANATIONS, QUALIFICATIONS

Despite often being classified as an amateur, Lewis was a highly educated man. Although he had no formal training in theology, his intellect was confirmed in that he received, within four years of study, two BA Hons degrees from the University of Oxford, having passed all three required public examinations with first class honors. These degrees were in Greats (Greek and Roman Literature and Classical Philosophy) and in English. Despite the astute sharpness and strength of his intellect, Lewis tried to avoid specialized theological language (jargon). However, a few terms do need to explained before we proceed. Some readers familiar with Lewis's books may not appreciate the full meaning and use of the terms used here. Professionals familiar with these terms may still gain some understanding of the context in which they are used in this book. Many Catholics and Evangelicals are familiar with these terms derived from New Testament Greek, and from *ecclesial* (i.e., church) Latin—ironically it is often Lewis's Anglicans who are ignorant of them.

i. Revelation and Reason

Revelation is personal, as in the realization of perception and understanding many people will have—a eureka moment when one finds something, or when something is revealed to one. But it is also more than that, more than the personal and subjective. Revelation is about God's *self-disclosure* to humanity. Lewis understood and accepted how God had revealed of God's self to humanity in multifarious and diverse ways down the millennia and across vast geographical and cultural eons, but as an orthodox Christian he knew, both as fact and from personal encounter, that Christ was the unique, the highest, form of self-revelation of the one true living God. So to talk about Christ is to talk about God; to speak of Christ is to speak of revelation. Over recent centuries revelation has often been pitted against reason. Because of the confidence emanating from the Age of Reason and the Enlightenment, a confidence issuing from the belief that the human capacity to reason things out for ourselves was all that was needed, revelation became, in certain quarters, obsolete.[1] Lewis seeks to try to hold both revelation and reason in balance; as a trained philosopher he knew and understood the background against which he was writing.

ii. Patristic

The patristic era is from the time of Christ's resurrection through to the mid-eighth century. The church leaders and theologians of this period of over 700 years are called "patristic"—from the Greek for Fathers, πατήρ, *patēr*, *patros*—hence the theology of these centuries is patristic, formed by the early church fathers. The immediate years after Christ's resurrection is called the apostolic era—the era or period of the apostles, essentially the people who knew Jesus of Nazareth or were of his generation, all of whom had died by around the year 100 AD. We then have the sub-apostolic era, which is essentially the second century, then fully the patristic era.

iii. Platonism

Platonism is the name given to the philosophy of Plato (c.424/423BC–348/347BC), and his writings. The term also applies to systems of philosophy derived from Plato's work and ideas, for example, Neo-Platonism or Platonic Realism. Central to Platonism is the theory of forms. The forms are transcendent archetypes; what we take for reality is in some way a pale imitation of the forms—reality relates to the forms as an imperfect copy does to an original. The forms tell us that what we take for reality is *perceivable* but not *intelligible*, but that there is another higher reality that is *intelligible* but not *perceivable*. Lewis was a trained philosopher; indeed early in his career he taught philosophy. Platonism is a type of philosophy that he not only subscribed to but which characterized his work throughout his life. Most patristic theologians were Platonists, to varying degrees; Neo-Platonism was in many ways part of patristic theology. Many Protestant, Reformed or Evangelical supporters of Lewis's work today object strongly to his Platonism not realizing that it is fundamental to Lewis's interpretation of the Gospel and is at the heart of his understanding of revelation. The precise nature of Lewis's Platonism will be fully explained at the appropriate point in this work.

---

1 For an understanding of the relationship between revelation and reason in terms of the disciplines of theology and philosophy, see Gunton, *Revelation and Reason*.

iv. Apologist/Apologetics

C. S. Lewis is an apologist. Apologetics are defined by the Oxford English Dictionary as, *reasoned arguments in justification of a theory or doctrine*. An apologist is one who argues, who confronts the disagreements and divergences that are evident between different belief systems. The term comes from the Greek word ἀπολογία, *apologia*, meaning to speak *in defense*. Christian apologetics are written to defend the truth of the gospel against attack from atheists, scientists, philosophers, exponents of non-Christian religions, indeed anyone that denies the heart of the Christian faith. Christian apologetics are considered different to theology *per se*, because in apologetics the truth of the gospel is represented in such a way as possibly to change its content in reaction to a perceived threat; indeed the apologetic content may be defined by the threat. Academic theology is considered by some to be impartial, disinterested, and neutral—in theory—and therefore in some ways superior. Yet if the gospel is true we cannot hold to an impartial multi-faith position that regards all religions and philosophies as equal, more pertinently that regards the content of all world religions as equally valid. Lewis did not: he understood that the gospel stands in contrast to the world, was *against* the world in many ways. Most of the theological writings in the early church are considered to be apologetics because they were written against the background of pagan Roman religion and politics, and were therefore written under persecution.

v. Creation, Fall, Incarnation, Resurrection, Second Coming, and the Four Last Things

The heart of the Christian faith, the basics, are in some ways summarized by the creation and the fall into original sin set out in the Book of Genesis; by the incarnation, crucifixion, resurrection, and second coming of God in Christ, in the New Testament; but also the four "last things" from the Book of Revelation as well as the Gospels. This is Lewis's basic summary of the faith. Lewis believed in the traditional faith, set out by the apostles, the early church, and the early church fathers, which was biblical. At the centre of the Bible story, in some ways summarized by the creeds, is, as Lewis asserted "the Creation, the Fall, the Incarnation, the Resurrection, the Second Coming, and the Four Last Things."[2] Some of this may be obvious but it separates Lewis from many modern theologians and churchmen who have watered down the faith. First, whatever we may learn about evolution and the origin of the world and the universe, God created everything out of nothing and sustains it. Second, that humanity, through its own fault, disobeyed God and was infected by original sin; furthermore we brought this on ourselves, and the predicament we find ourselves in is perilous. Third, God became incarnated as a human being, Jesus Christ, who was crucified for our sins and was resurrected, all to atone for our fall into original sin and restore us to a right relationship with God. Fourth, that this same Jesus Christ will return to judge all at the end of the world, which will be, as Lewis terms it, the four last things: death, judgment, heaven, and hell. This is the *eschaton* (from the Greek, ἔσχατον, for last or final thing).

---

2   Lewis writing to *The Church Times*, Feb. 8, 1952. Lewis, *Collected Letters Vol. III*, 164.

Introduction

vi. Ontology

A concept that will come up often in this volume is ontology. Ontology is defined as a branch of philosophy (also metaphysics and theology) concerned with the very nature of being, of actual existence, and what there is to the intrinsic nature of entities. For example the human: is there a uniquely God-given human nature, and either way, what is it that characterizes the human as distinct from the rest of creation. Indeed what is the very nature of creation itself? Is the human as created, or changed by the *fall*? For example, is Jesus of Nazareth defined ontologically as merely human, or as fully human and fully divine—the very nature of his being is divine and human. The question of ontology also relates to the human capacity to know, to the very nature of language, and how we speculate about God: this involves the study of being or existence, of a thing's very nature.

vii. Liberal/liberal, Modernism

C. S. Lewis's writings are set against the background of liberal culture and society in Britain specifically, and the United States and Europe generally. "Liberalism" is often seen as a contentious and problematic word—often it appears to generate an emotional response, may be considered pejorative, and may also be invoked in an equally subjective manner. In this work the words "Liberal" and "Liberalism" with an initial capital letter are used strictly in the context of theological Liberalism in the church: this is a position that more often than not denies the incarnation and resurrection, seeking to promote Jesus of Nazareth as an ordinary human being, furthermore, a Liberal theological position may not believe in God (with a capital "G") but happily allow people to believe in "gods" of their own making, their own invention. Lewis often referred to this as a modernist tendency. Theological Liberalism since the eighteenth-century has claimed freedom not only from traditional dogmas and creeds but also in the analysis of and value accorded to Scripture. Such theology was to a large degree formulated in the light of what were considered advances in the natural sciences and philosophy—the spirit of the Age of Reason and the Enlightenment. In this work, when cited with a lower case initial letter ("liberal"), the term refers to liberalism in society and culture generally, in ethics and morality in the twentieth-century. This has often been to do with sexual behavior, but is also seen in culture, the media, entertainment, etc. Therefore a distinction needs to be drawn between Liberalism as a *theological* movement or belief system and what is often euphemistically called a liberal perspective in Western society generally. Today those who subscribe to ethical liberalism (particularly in the area of sexuality and marriage) may or may not to a greater or lesser degree subscribe to theological Liberalism. For example, there are East Coast American Episcopalians today who support the legitimization of homosexual behavior within Christian ethics yet who are strongly orthodox and creedal in their doctrinal beliefs; but then there are also those who subscribe to this ethical liberalism whilst simultaneously denying Christ's divinity and regarding him as just another ordinary man, therefore these two liberals (differentiated by an upper or lower case initial letter) cannot be seen as identical, or as completely separate from each other. Lewis uses the term "Modernism"/"Modernist" very much in the same context as Liberalism—he was often scathing about Modernist tendencies in the Church of England, tendencies that essentially were theological Liberalism, which argued that all our ideas about God were wrong, that there was no supernatural God beyond the ideas in our minds, our deepest desires, and wishes.

viii. Pagan

Lewis's theological writings, as indeed with his conversion, are played out against the backdrop of what is termed pagan religion or paganism. A pagan is essentially someone holding beliefs from outside of the world's main religions. "Pagan" therefore refers to this form of religion and religious myths from outside of, in our instance, the Jewish and Christian traditions. It is important to remember that the term "pagan" was used by Lewis, and is likewise used here, with no derogatory intent, nor as a term of abuse. Lewis used the term simply to refer to those peoples and cultures outside of the Jewish and Christian traditions: that is, Oriental, Middle Eastern, Indian, and European tribes and nations, but particularly in the ancient world (Greek and Roman philosophy and literature, religion, and mythology) and especially the religion and mythology of the North European tribes (Celtic, Norse, etc.), with whom the name pagan is most often associated. In comparison to the post-Christian world in the West today (Lewis was amongst the first to coin the term "post-Christian" at a time when Britain still perceived its civic pageantry and public religion, and its people as Christian, first using the term "post-Christian" publicly in an address on November 29, 1954[3]), where it often being asserted that Britain is "slipping," "descending," "regressing" into paganism, Lewis was quite adamant.

> When grave persons express their fear that England is relapsing into Paganism, I am tempted to reply, "Would that she were." For I do not think it at all likely that we shall ever see Parliament opened by the slaughtering of a garlanded white bull in the House of Lords or Cabinet Ministers leaving sandwiches in Hyde Park as an offering for the Dryads. If such a state of affairs came about, then the Christian apologist would have something to work on. For a Pagan, as history shows, is a man eminently convertible to Christianity. He is essentially, the pre-Christian, or sub-Christian, religious man. The Post-Christian man of our own day differs from him as much as a divorcée differs from a virgin. The Christian and the Pagan have much more in common with one another than either has with the writers of the *New Statesman*; and those writers would of course agree with me.[4]

When Lewis is talking about Paganism he is therefore speaking of the pre-Christian world of peoples and cultures diverse from the Christian but moving towards the fulfillment of some sort of understanding of the revelation of Jesus Christ. Essentially

---

3   Lewis's inaugural lecture at Cambridge, Nov. 29, 1954. C. S. Lewis, "*De Descriptione Temporum*," 9–25.
4   Lewis, "Is Theism Important?," 138.

Introduction

the difference between a pre-Christian pagan and the contemporary post-Christian pagan is one of movement: the pre was moving towards in his/her theistic beliefs, the post is moving away in his/her atheistic beliefs.

ix. Romantic

The term Romantic, with an initial capital letter, has nothing to do with cheap romantic novels or magazines, or romance! The term Romantic represents a movement in art and culture—poets such as Longfellow, Wordsworth, and Keats were considered Romantics, as were painters such as Constable and Turner, and composers such as Beethoven and, to a degree, Wagner. As an artistic and cultural term Romantic is to do with feeling, with expressing oneself, with responding to the innate beauty in landscape and the natural world. Romanticism was in some ways a reaction against the scientific rationalism of the Age of Reason. The Romantic Movement was often associated with the cult of the individual—of emaciated, troubled artists starving in garrets and producing works of genius entirely by themselves without any input and involvement from anyone else.

5. ". . . AND THE COLLECTED WORKS OF C. S. LEWIS"

Many people over the last one hundred and fifty years have tried to encapsulate the intellectual rigor, the cogency, and veracity of the gospel, while communicating it to an audience of ordinary people, often interested skeptics. The Bible scholar and bishop N. T. Wright, commenting on Lewis's writings, notes how "millions around the world have been introduced to, and nurtured within, the Christian faith through his work where their own preachers and teachers were not giving them what they needed."[5] Wright was a case in point; he notes how his tutors, when an undergraduate at the University of Oxford, "looked down their noses if you so much as mentioned him [Lewis] in a tutorial. This was, we may suppose, mere jealousy: He sold and they didn't. It may also have been the frustration of the professional who, busy about his footnotes, sees the amateur effortlessly sailing past to the winning post." But Wright, like other academics, raises questions about just how universal Lewis's work was—it was about the gospel, was a defense of the gospel, but it was not *the* gospel: "the Christianity offered by Lewis both was and wasn't the 'mere' thing he made it out to be . . . But above all it worked; a lot of people have become Christians through reading Lewis." There is, therefore, a universal appeal to Lewis's work that is lacking in many other apologists and academic theologians, whose work is often soon forgotten, being relative to and emerging from particular cultural, human, subjective positions. This has not been the case with Lewis's defense of the gospel. For example, the writer Joseph Pearce has noted how Joseph Fessio S. J. cited this universal appeal in comments at a theological conference in the mid-1990s. Quoting from an address given by the philosopher Peter

---

5 This and the following quotations are from, Wright, "Simply Lewis," 39–40. Online: http://www.touchstonemag.com/archives/article.php?id=20-02-028-f.

Kreeft, Pearce notes Fessio's comments, initially given somewhat tongue-in-cheek, which were roundly endorsed across all denominational divisions:

> Father Fessio made these remarks during a theological conference in the mid-1990s, which Peter Kreeft recalled in 1998 as "the most memorable moment of the most memorable conference I ever attended." Attending the meeting, says Kreeft, were "dozens of high-octane Roman Catholics, Anglicans, Eastern Orthodox and Protestant Evangelicals," who, despite their noted theological differences, converged near the end of the conference in a crescendo of agreement. Kreeft continues: "In the concluding session Father Fessio got up and proposed that we issue a joint statement of theological agreement among all the historic, orthodox branches of Christendom saying that what united us was 'Scripture, the Apostles' Creed, the first six ecumenical councils and the collected works of C. S. Lewis.' The proposal was universally cheered."[6]

Pearce notes how Protestants, Catholics, and Eastern Orthodox have managed to find areas of substantial agreement in Lewis's works. For example, Pearce notes, the centrality to salvation history of Christ's atoning death on the cross, the historical event of the resurrection, the authority of Scripture, and the unchanging reality of moral law. So despite flaws, despite Lewis's humanity, there is categorically, objectively, something to Lewis's work that transcends the relative, the fashionable and transient, the subjective, the slanted, prejudiced, and blatantly one-sided (i.e., denominational), in ways that other apologists and theologians have failed in.

6. THE CHRIST OF A RELIGIOUS ECONOMY

C. S. Lewis—On The Christ of a Religious Economy. I. Creation and Sub-Creation, consists of two parts, nine chapters in all. The first part (chapter 1–4) is about a fundamental component of Lewis's apologetics and philosophical theology: *the fall*, original sin. Speaking of the fall immediately invokes a doctrine of creation: how and what were we created for? What does Lewis have to say about the creation? If we have *fallen* we are not as created. What is Lewis's doctrine of creation—the universe created by and through the Christ? Lewis's understanding of creation is spread across all of his works, he did not write a doctrine of creation, as such. However, we can draw this understanding together from a multitude of his works and systematize into four axioms and four theological principles, explicated in detail by what Lewis wrote and said. Part two (chapters 6–9): creation leads into Tolkien and Lewis's understanding of sub-creation: Lewis's use of narrative—story, *The Space Trilogy* (1938–45), *The Screwtape Letters* (1942), *The Great Divorce* (1945), *The Chronicles of Narnia* (1950–56), and *Till We Have Faces* (1956)—underpinned by doctrine to convey the truth of the gospel and Christ's salvific actions. Lewis's mission and work (as a pre-modern orthodox traditionalist) is a precursor, in many ways, to Postliberal theology.

---

6   Pearce, *C. S. Lewis and the Catholic Church*, xiii–xiv. Joseph Pearce quotes from Peter Kreeft, "The Achievement of C. S. Lewis: A Millennial Assessment," unpublished address given at Boston College, 1998.

Introduction

At the heart of this book is Lewis's perception and understanding of the *economic Trinity*, as distinct from the *immanent Trinity*. The *economic* Trinity is our understanding of the action of the triune God in our reality, what we take to be the world, the universe; the *immanent* Trinity is God's "life", "existence" within God's triune self, the three persons of the holy and indivisible Trinity that subsist and persist in love. For example, the opening of John's Gospel is about the Trinity: it sets out the immanent—"In the beginning was the Word, and the Word was with God, and the Word was God. He was in the beginning with God" (John 1:1–2). This then proceeds into the economic—"And the Word became flesh and lived among us, and we have seen his glory, the glory as of a father's only son, full of grace and truth" (John 1:14). Hence, the economic Trinity is about how such a God interacts with humanity and this world, to redeem and raise us up in our *fallenness*. The action of God in this world—the will of the Father, through Jesus the Christ, through the manifestation of the Holy Spirit, though the churches—this is like the management of a household economy (from the Greek, οἰκονομία, *oikonomia*—"household management," "the rule or law of the house").

This results in a hierarchy—after death: the saved and the damned; the elect and the forsaken; with a myriad of variations between people in different "levels" of heaven and hell where their final end is decided by the judgment and righteousness of God, between the saints and the martyred and the ordinary Christian, and between the damned of varying degrees. This was demonstrated in Dante's *Commedia*, and in patristic art showing the hierarchy of heaven (Christ sitting in judgment, Mary, the apostles and martyrs, the saints, angels, the eschatological beasts from Revelation and Daniel, and so forth). This flies in the face of much modern and liberal, egalitarian and democratic concepts of equality (where personal self-definition is believed to lead to a republic of heaven); yet every human is ultimately responsible for the position they are in while alive, and pertinently *post mortem*: the saved, the elect, are those who are prepared to be changed by God in Christ (often, for Lewis, this would happen for the righteous after death).[7] From Cain and Abel, to Jacob and Esau, from Simon Peter to Judas Iscariot, from the teeming millions alive today explicitly or implicitly living for Christ or for themselves, governing all is the Christ who observes and assists humanity—if they will accept the Holy Spirit, and *his* righteous justifying judgment. This is characterized by the descent to reascend, with humanity, by Christ the second person of the Trinity: whatever it takes we will be changed we will be made perfect. It is this that underpins—often invisibly—religion, that is, all valid religion: God's love for us does not come and go—"It is not wearied by our sins or our indifference; and, therefore, it is quite relentless in its determination that we shall be cured of those sins, at whatever cost to us, at whatever cost to *him*."[8]

Thus we have the Christ of a religious economy.

---

7   "Listen, I will tell you a mystery! We will not all die, but we will all be changed, in a moment, in the twinkling of an eye, at the last trumpet. For the trumpet will sound, and the dead will be raised imperishable, and we will be changed." 1 Cor. 15:51–53.

8   Lewis, *Mere Christianity*, Bk. 3, "Christian Behaviour," ch. 9, "Charity," 133.

Part One

The Fall, Original Sin, and An Existential Crisis

"A new species, never made by God,
had sinned itself into existence."

"It [the creature] had turned from God
and become its own idol,
so that though it could still turn back to God,
it could do so only by painful effort,
and its inclination was self-ward."

"The guilt is washed out not by time
but by repentance and the blood of Christ."

Lewis, *The Problem of Pain* (1940).

1

Creation and The Fall I:
C. S. Lewis—A Doctrine of Creation

SYNOPSIS:
A fundamental component of Lewis's apologetics and philosophical theology is *the fall*, defined by original sin. These chapters explore what place it has in Lewis's theology generally and his Christology specifically. The fall is intimately intertwined with creation; therefore, we start with a doctrine of creation. The Judeo-Christian account is unique: a speech-act model (Gen 1:3), God speaks and things happen, the created world is not divine, objects in the world are inanimate—stars are not "gods," they are *created* objects—and creation creates, it "brings forth," (Gen 1:24). At the heart of creation is Christ, the λόγος (*logos*) as creator and redeemer of creation. As Lewis notes, creation is on-going; its fulfillment is in the future. Also, creation is a triune *act* and *event*, it is Christ who creates (Gen 1–3; Ps 104; and John 1), as the Holy Spirit hovers over the waters (Gen 1:2) and the Father looks on and declares that creation is good (Gen 1:25).

The origins of the world we live in cannot be seen separately from humanity's rebellion. As a systematic statement of axiomatic truth defined against contradiction and erroneous theories, Lewis's writing on creation does implicitly form a doctrinal whole, and concurs with orthodox Christian theology. Lewis did not write or publish a doctrine of creation, as such; however, spread across his multitudinous works is a sound doctrine of creation, which can be read from his apologetics, his philosophical theology, his analogical narratives (*Narnia*, etc.), and from his letters. In so reading we can systematize what Lewis wrote on creation into eight categories: four basic axioms and four principles: first axiom, creation was created (it has not always existed), by God the creator; second axiom, creation is an actuality, is knowable and understandable; third axiom, creation has a particular character, is observable and definable. Following on from these three axioms are four theological principles: a) creation involves separation and distinctiveness, b) the *origin* of creation is not directly knowable, and myth is essential in attempting an explanation of origin, c) humanity is in many ways the pinnacle of creation, a creature characterized by uniqueness and rebellion, d) humanity is given the responsibility of sub-creation and the custodianship of creation. Finally, leading from the three axioms and four principles is a fourth axiom: there is a new creation that issues from the incarnation-cross-resurrection; this event changes everything and is a response to the fall of humanity into original sin. Understanding a doctrine of creation allows us then to explicate Lewis's understanding of the fall.

ON THE CHRIST OF A RELIGIOUS ECONOMY. I. CREATION AND SUB-CREATION

1. INTRODUCTION

If a doctrine is a set of principles and beliefs taught by the church, and held against all contradiction, then a doctrine of creation is about the origin and conditions of the reality we occupy; it is also about the perception and truth of what we understand to be creation, and the extent to which we mere humans can understand the enormity of creation and how God creates and sustains all. There are certain fundamental axiomatic statements: God created the universe, the reality we live in; God created all that we sense and perceive, know and understand *ex nihilo*—out of nothing. Creation is good, God declared it good—not necessarily perfect, depending on what we mean by perfection, but good, purposeful, and suitable. Creation is *sustained* by God, he could at any moment cast it away, yet God is not *dependent* upon creation: God creates in freedom and loves creation in freedom. Humanity was in some ways the pinnacle of creation, created to reflect God's glory, to perceive and understand God, to reflect back to God the love *of* God, the love that is God. Humanity was created with the freedom to choose to love God and worship God, to put God in the center of its life. But humanity decided not to. This is the *fall*[1] whereby humanity chose to turn in on itself away from God: this is *original sin*. This affects the human, the creation, and thereby God's dealings with humanity, *in Christ*.

2. "AND GOD SAID . . ."

At the center of any doctrine of creation is the biblical account: The book of Genesis, the prologue to John's Gospel, and, for example, Psalm 104. The Genesis account tells us that, as Francis Watson has demonstrated, creation (if we acknowledge the centrality of the biblical account) is a speech-act.[2] This is quite different from many of the creation myths found in ancient religions: God speaks and things happen. (By comparison, the scientific theory of the so-called "big-bang" is merely a colossal and unimaginable act of violence, with evolution the accidental by-product.) Watson shows how the speech-act is crucial to creation: God conceives and speaks, and creation is created. But not in an instance. This is also a "fabrication model" for Watson: objects do not magically appear, complete, existence is not instantaneous, they are *constructed*. Genesis shows how God does initially create *instantaneously* by the speech-act and then through this fabrication model, but God *employs* creatures as the womb out of which the others proceed. Creation has a specific nature and it is not inherently divine, creation is separate and different from God: stars and planets are created objects, not "gods" as they were in Pagan and ancient Middle Eastern religions. What is more, the earth and the waters bring forth. Thus we find God's speech act creates heaven and earth—the speech is important—but then God also declares, "let the earth bring forth . . ." Therefore, at God's initiative creation creates: "And God said, 'Let the land

---

1   Lewis capitalizes the word as a proper noun, and to indicate the gravity of original sin. The OED capitalizes and states traditionally: "Fall: a defeat or downfall (the Fall of man) the lapse of humankind into a state of sin, ascribed in Jewish and Christian theology to the disobedience of Adam and Eve."

2   Watson, *Text, Church and World*, 137–53.

produce living creatures according to their kinds: livestock, creatures that move along the ground, and wild animals, each according to its kind.' And it was so" (Gen 1:24). God *enables* the creation to form something new.[3] The opening of Genesis and the first chapter of John's Gospel illustrate the close link between creation, the creative act, and Christ: the λόγος (logos). Watson comments that—

> If the act of creation is accomplished through speech, then speech and act are identified, and this results in what we may call the speech-act model of divine creativity. . . . [T]he first and best known is the command, "Let there be light," which immediately produces the desired effect—"and there was light" (Gen 1:3). In the second case, the utterance concerning the separation of sea and dry land is followed by the words, "and it was so." . . . In the third case, the same words announce the immediate fulfillment of the command that the earth should put forth vegetation (Gen 1:11). The specific speech-act implied in all three cases is that of the command, a strange command addressed to entities that do not yet exist and whose coming into being is their act of obedience to it: "For he commanded and they were created" (Ps 148:5).[4]

God has made known through Scripture what is conceivable for the human mind to comprehend about the creation of reality. What is important about the creation of reality is the election of Israel, and the incarnation, and the atonement: God allows us to know what is important for us to comprehend. There are limits, God-given limits: "the creator is known only insofar as he interacts with the creation."[5] The word of God in the speech-act is creation because it is the gift of God to humanity: "Ever since the creation of the world his eternal power and divine nature, invisible though they are, have been understood and seen through the things he has made" (Rom 1:19). Therefore, from the created order we can come to some knowledge of God, but not of the true nature of God or the necessity for our salvation: reality *reveals a creator*, but whether we can perceive of *the* creator is another matter, and given our state defined by original sin, we are left without excuse. Nonetheless, creation, as the Psalms assert, sings of God's glory because creations is a gracious act by the gracious God. To this extent there is a strong tradition, often associated with Roman Catholicism, that a doctrine of creation reflects a doctrine of universal grace: "It's the grace of creation: because the gracious God has created the world, the universe, simply reflects the marks of *his* creating grace."[6]

The world reveals God because reality is an actuality, and because of time's movement it is always a possibility: growth and change. This is at the heart of redemption: the incarnation and resurrection.[7] Therefore you can't conceive of creation separate from Christ.[8] As Maximus the Confessor (c.580–662) wrote, the one who is initiated into the infinite power of the resurrection knows the purpose for which God

---

3   Ibid.
4   Ibid., 140–41.
5   Gunton, *Revelation and Reason*, 22.
6   Ibid., 60.
7   Barth, *Church Dogmatics*, IV/3, §.72, 769.
8   Brunner, *The Mediator*, 262. See also, Gunton, *Revelation and Reason*, 249f.

knowingly created all things and loves all things.[9] However, as we will see from Lewis's doctrine of creation, it is important to get the right balance. If too much emphasis is placed on creation and not on salvation, the incarnation, cross, and resurrection is marginalized and your understanding of creation is flawed. Likewise if too great an emphasis is placed on salvation to the detriment of creation and the created order, then you will have a skewed understanding of humanity's importance over and above creation: "If you overweight the Incarnation and the cross at the expense of creation then you tend to have a conception of salvation out of the world, rather than in the world."[10] Therefore, and the resurrection and the potential of a new creation (Rev 21) bears witness to this, creation is on-going and its fulfillment is in the future: "To say that something is created is to say that it is on its way to being made; full knowledge will be granted at the end—this will be full revelation."[11]

So, what constitutes a doctrine of creation for Lewis?

3. LEWIS ON CREATION: THE WORK OF CHRIST

Lewis did not write or publish a doctrine of creation; however, spread across his multitudinous works is a sound doctrine of creation, which can be read from his apologetics, his philosophical theology, his analogical narratives (*Narnia*, etc.), and from his letters. At the center of Lewis's doctrine of creation is the Christ, the second person of the Trinity: Christ creates, Christ's sacrifice generates redemption, Christ judges, and Christ initiates the new creation. At the center is the Christ who is incarnated, crucified and resurrected all to atone for humanity's fall into original sin.

Understanding a doctrine of creation allows us then to explicate Lewis's understanding of the fall. Essentially this starts with the first axiom—that God is, and God creates; the existence of creation becomes the second axiom; the observable nature of an actual character to creation is the third. The rest flows from these three. Creation is circular: there is a new creation (Gen 1), reality and the human are created, humanity is pivotal, humanity falls, humanity is redeemed through the incarnation-cross-resurrection, which is a new creation (Rev 21—the new heaven and the new earth). Evolutionary time may be linear but salvation history is circular, the pivot point being the moment of the death of Jesus on the cross.

4. FIRST AXIOM: GOD THE TRIUNE CREATOR

The first, or primary axiom, is that creation was created. God is the creator. God is the first cause, the prime mover, and unmoved mover. God is the creator; creation was created, once it was not, once it did not exist. God created *ex nihilo* (out of nothing). But God is triune, so our understanding of creation is trinitarian: it is Christ who creates (Gen 1–3; Ps 104; and John 1), as the Holy Spirit hovers over the waters (Gen 1:2) and the Father looks on and declares that creation is good (Gen 1:25). Although biblical

---

9   Maximus the Confessor, *Centuries*, 1108A–B.
10   Gunton, *Revelation and Reason*, 29.
11   Ibid., 66.

A Systematic Structure to Lewis's Doctrine of Creation

If we take Lewis's hundreds of references to creation and structure them to give systematic order, we can see a doctrine of creation.

> **First Axiom: God the Triune Creator—**
> God is the creator, God is the first cause, the prime mover, and unmoved mover. God created, creation was created, once it was not, once it did not exist. God created *ex nihilo* (out of nothing).

> **Second Axiom: The Actuality of Creation—**
> Creation is an actuality, it is real, creation is knowable and understandable, creation is no illusion or the figment of our imagination, therefore this leads to a doctrine of creation.

> **Third Axiom: Purpose, Character, and Nature—**
> Creation has a particular character, creation is not everything; there is other than creation, and creation has an observable and definable nature.

Theological Principles

Theological Principle A: Creation as Separation:
Creation's distinctiveness is defined by separation.
Creation involves separation—God and creation are not synonymous.
Pantheism and Panentheism are simply wrong.

Theological Principle B: The Myth of Creation:
The *origins* of creation, the act of the creator God, are not directly knowable in the same way that the presence of creation is perceived and known. Reason and imagination form myth in explaining creation. The Jewish-Christian tradition uses the language of myth to present fundamental truths about the story of creation.

Theological Principle C: Humanity's Relation to God and Creation:
Humanity is a unique creation—the human is the pinnacle of creation.
The human is made in the image of God (*imago Dei*), specifically the *imago Christi*, and thus the human is defined by the Trinity (Jesus is the archetype, the new Adam, he is Son of God and Son of Man). But the human is also defined by rebellion.

Theological Principle D: Sub-Creation and Sub-creators:
Humanity is given the responsibility of sub-creation, and the custodianship of creation.

> **Fourth Axiom: The New Creation—**
> Finally, leading from the three axioms and four theological principles is a fourth axiom, distinct from what has gone before: there is a new creation that issues from the incarnation-cross-resurrection; this event changes everything and is a response to the *fall*

CREATION IS CIRCULAR: THERE IS A NEW CREATION, REALITY AND THE HUMAN ARE CREATED, HUMANITY IS PIVOTAL, HUMANITY *FALLS*, HUMANITY IS REDEEMED THROUGH THE INCARNATION-CROSS, WHICH GENERATES A NEW CREATION DEFINED BY RESURRECTION: A NEW HEAVEN AND A NEW EARTH.

Evolutionary time may be linear but salvation history is circular, the pivotal point being the moment of the death of Jesus on the cross.

Figure 1 A Systematic Structure to Lewis's Doctrine of Creation

in its triune acknowledgment, Lewis's doctrine of creation draws on his philosophical reading. As such, there is clear evidence, as we shall see, of him wrestling with the ideas of Aristotle and Aquinas in his use of language: God is the first cause, the prime mover, and unmoved mover.

It may seem obvious today that the universe had a beginning, indeed such a theory now forms respectable science, but in the mid-twentieth century, when Lewis wrote most of his theology, such an idea was considered questionable, even erroneous; the dominant theory was the steady state theory. Exemplified by the scientist and astronomer Sir Fred Hoyle, the steady state theory asserts that the universe has always existed and always will, *everything* was not created at a point from nothing, *everything* will continue into infinity. Christian theology has always acknowledged a point of creation, and a creator—the universe being created *ex nihilo* (out of nothing). Exponents of the steady-state theory, dominant in the post-war period, used their theory to mock religious belief, in particular a doctrine of creation. However, even then, the evidence and argument for a point of origin was gaining ground, as Lewis noted:

> If anything emerges clearly from modern physics, it is that nature is not everlasting. The universe had a beginning, and will have an end. . . . As Professor Whittaker said in the Riddell Lectures of 1942, "It was never possible to oppose, seriously the dogma of the Creation except by maintaining that the world has existed from all eternity in more or less its present state." This fundamental ground for materialism has now been withdrawn. We should not lean too heavily on this, for scientific theories change. But at the moment it appears that the burden of proof rests, not on us, but on those who deny that nature has some cause beyond herself.[12]

However, scientists may still claim this beginning was self-generated, also that it will go on expanding forever. Orthodox Jews and Christians will disagree: the universe was created and will at some point in the future end, and that it was not self-generated. Lewis wrote long and hard to refute the steady state theory, and to assert God as the creator, as first cause, as the prime and unmoved mover.[13] The universe *was* created. Those who subscribed to the steady state theory often subscribed to the myth of cultural progress, but they also denied the idea of catastrophe—evolutionary time with its gradual changes denied these sudden catastrophic events. In Lewis's time the dominant position was that change happened very, very slowly, over eons of unimaginable time; Christians by comparison expect and "reckon with sudden interruption from without—at any moment."[14] Scientists of all persuasions think differently now, the West is, to a degree, preoccupied now with the threat of sudden catastrophic events from asteroids to climate change.[15]

---

12   Lewis, "Dogma and the Universe," 18. Lewis is referring to Whittaker, *The Beginning and the End of the World*, 40.
13   See, for example, Lewis, "The World's Last Night," 93–113; Lewis, "Who was Right—Dream Lecturer or Real Lecturer," 4; Lewis, *Miracles* (2nd ed.), 160f; Lewis, *Reflections on the Psalms*, 5f.
14   Lewis, "The World's Last Night," 110–11.
15   Ibid., 100–101.

1. Creation and The Fall I: C. S. Lewis—A Doctrine of Creation

Therefore, for Lewis, there is but one God, not a panoply of "gods", and this one true God created everything *ex nihilo* (out of nothing). God is the creator, and *he* maintains and sustains creation. That God is the creator is absolutely at the heart of Christian doctrine; further that this is not some impersonal force but something *like* a "creative mind."[16] God conceives of, initiates, designs, and intends, he breathes into life *his* creation. This creator God is and always was, always existed. We compliment God by saying he is infinite, but this encourages us to think of God as formless, amorphous, everything (with the inherent dangers of pantheism);[17] and if everything God is *nothing in particular*, and all generalizations on God will be true.[18] Straight away Lewis knows he has to establish a sound framework of reference of what God is, and is not (God is not evil, God is not everything . . .), you cannot understand creation without a sound doctrine of God.

> God is a particular thing. Once *he* was the only thing: but *he* is creative. *He* made other things to be. *He* is not those other things. *He* is not "universal being:" if *he* were there would be no creatures, for a generality can make nothing. *He* is "absolute being"—or rather the Absolute Being—in the sense that *he* alone exists in his own right. But there are things which God is not. In that sense *he* has a determinate character. Thus he is righteous, not amoral; creative, not inert. The Hebrew writings here observe an admirable balance. Once God says simply *I AM*, proclaiming the mystery of self-existence. But times without number *he* says "I am the Lord"— I, the ultimate fact, have this determinate character, and not that. And men are exhorted to "know the Lord," to discover and experience this particular character.[19]

This does not necessarily obliterate the immeasurable difference between creation and God, it merely affirms God's creativeness, and God's ultimate authority as creator. And as creator he can be both infinite and finite (incarnated into *his* creation). The finite—the incarnate God—is not a denial of transcendence. This is what God is; God's transcendence means that he can become finite. If God's infinity means you can't become finite then God is not infinite. God's freedom to be transcendent includes, for Lewis, the capacity to be infinite and finite.[20] This relates to kenosis—the self-emptying of Christ the creator (Phil 2[21]); God comes to us in the form of a frail and vulnerable baby; how very finite! Lewis asserts that claiming particularity for God does not "obliterate the immeasurable difference between what *he* is and what all other things are but between the very mode of his existence and their existence."[22] So God is not inert, not self-contained, nor utterly infinite *if* to be infinite imposes restrictions on what God *is*. To be truly infinite is to be, as Lewis realized both finite and infinite. Both

16 Lewis, *Broadcast Talks*, 37, also, 10, 14, 24f.
17 Lewis, *Miracles* (2nd ed.), 91–3.
18 Ibid., 90f.
19 Ibid., 91.
20 See: Forsyth, *The Person and Place of Jesus Christ*.
21 "Christ Jesus: Who, being in very nature God, did not consider equality with God something to be grasped, but made himself nothing, taking the very nature of a servant, being made in human likeness . . ." Phil 2:5b–7.
22 Lewis, *Miracles*, 91.

are *particular* to God, and thus *he* is truly infinite. But if we argue that God exists and if creation exists, cautions Lewis, does this not conflate what God is into creation? Not so, asserts Lewis, waxing Platonic, for our existence is immeasurable tiny and hardly at all, in comparison to God's existence. The principle of creation is not in us—it is in God. We cannot exist without God, we are sustained moment by moment as the ongoing act of creation, yet we are separate, distinct.[23] Only when we realize this can we see, wrote Lewis, that the question of God's existence is spurious—it is impossible that God should not *be*.[24] This reflects the trinitarian nature of the creator. In *The Magician's Nephew*, Lewis presents the Aslan-Christ "singing" creation into existence The song, and the breath of the Aslan-Christ *is the Holy Spirit*; this is not modalistic, it is triune simultaneity.[25] The speech-act outlined by Francis Watson is re-imagined as music: the Word is sung, such as is the glorious *beauty* of God, for Lewis, which is then imbued into the beautiful goodness of the created reality. God, as *he* creates, sings poetically, orchestrates creation into existence, this contrasts with the mechanistic and violent imagery of scientific explanations (the so-called Big Bang).

Lewis is at great pains to stress how this question of particularity does not lessen the immeasurability we attribute to God. But to say that God cannot be incarnated, that God cannot be finite, is to place limits on his infinite immeasurability: *infinitum capax finiti*—God is infinite yet capable of being finite, God is boundless yet capable of limit. God's transcendence is boundless and infinite, unlimited, endless, yet *he* is fit and competent, has the capacity, to be contained, to be finite and restricted, defined, indeed must be also finite to be infinite. This issues from the *creativity* of a *creator* God! To propose that God is *infinitum capax finiti* is to assert God's freedom to be immanent in creation. God is and can be both immanent (existing or operating within) and transcendent (existing apart from and not subject to the limitations of the material universe). God is not so transcendent that he can't be within creation as the creator. If in asserting God's infinity you assert God cannot become finite, then God is not infinite. The key is Christological: God demonstrates to human minds his transcendence by being incarnated a human being in Jesus. The heart of creation for a creator God is the incarnation. Incarnation does not deny transcendence. It is humanity's projection of immeasurability onto God, which denies both immanence and transcendence, that creates false limits with which we compliment God. It is this compliment that denies revelation, so asserts Lewis: *infinitum capax finiti*—if God is truly infinite then God can encompass the finite without losing infinity.[26] Speaking of the Jews Lewis commented: "God, in their language, meant the being outside the world who had made it and was infinitely different from anything else."[27] Furthermore, God "is the opaque center of all existences, the thing that simply and entirely is, the

23   Ibid., 91f.
24   Ibid., 92.
25   Lewis, *The Magician's Nephew*, 97f.
26   Lewis examines this proposition, in a similar manner, which is central to his apologetics, in Ch. 14 of *Miracles* (2nd ed.) with little variance from the same principle in *Problem of Pain* (1940), 15, 42, 138, and in *Broadcast Talks*, See also, Lewis, *Beyond Personality*, 60–61.
27   Lewis, *Broadcast Talks*, 50.

fountain of facthood. And yet, now that *he* has created, there is a sense in which we must say that *he* is a particular thing and even one thing among others."[28] God is the creator, and *he* is glad; *he* inculcates value into all that *he* has created.[29] Those who have grasped the fact of creation and the particularity of God then, claims Lewis, find it impossible to deny that such a God is not the creator.[30] Praise is then the only legitimate response from the creature to the creator.[31]

5. SECOND AXIOM: THE ACTUALITY OF CREATION

The second axiom is that creation is an actuality, creation is knowable and understandable. That God—particular and universal—is creator implies the actual existence of creation: unlike some creation myths in ancient Middle Eastern and Oriental religions, the world is real, actual, in the Judeo-Christian tradition. Platonism makes it relative to eternity, but creation is an actuality. Lewis noted, "The total act of creation including *our own* creation . . . meets us, doesn't it, in every event at every moment."[32] To that extent Lewis will assert the simplicity and truism of Genesis: "In the beginning God made Heaven and Earth."[33] Unlike polytheistic ancient or pagan religions, God is not the product of creation. A Christian doctrine of creation is uncompromising in this regard: God, the persons of the Trinity, are not part of or issue from creation.[34] It is, for Lewis, in Judaism we initially find a doctrine of creation, which frames accurately the nature of creation and the relationship between God and the created order.[35] Such a belief, systematized into a doctrine of creation has unified Christians of widely varying beliefs the world over for Lewis.[36] A biblically-framed doctrine of creator and created is an essential part of Christian beliefs; it is not optional.[37] The story of creation is in fact a long, long, story, and we err if either through science or the Bible we think we know all there is to know about creation.[38] Neither the naive creationist worldview, nor the skeptical scientist's model can be proved beyond doubt: this is how we are before God.[39] "This act of creation . . . must always remain totally inconceivable to man"[40] Therefore, the burden of proof should fall to those who claim, without due evidence, that the universe has no primary cause.[41] The ground, for Lewis, of any doctrine of creation, should not be in some scientific theory but in *revelation*.[42]

---

28 Lewis, *Miracles*, 92.
29 Ibid., 172.
30 Ibid., 32–33.
31 Lewis, *A Grief Observed*, 73; Lewis, *Beyond Personality*, 61f.; Lewis, *Letters to Malcolm*, 91–2.
32 Lewis writing to Sheldon Vanauken, Apr. 6, 1955. Lewis, *Collected Letters Vol. III*, 592.
33 Gen 1:1, quoted, Lewis, *Miracles*, 34.
34 Lewis, *Miracles*, 7f. See also, Lewis, "Some Thoughts," 117.
35 Lewis, *Reflections on the Psalms*, 65–68.
36 Lewis writing to *The Church Times*, Feb. 8, 1952. Lewis, *Collected Letters Vol. III*, 164.
37 Lewis, *Broadcast Talks*, Series II, 39–41.
38 Lewis, *Miracles*, 12:7.
39 Lewis, *Broadcast Talks*, 12–13.
40 Lewis, *Letters to Malcolm*, 68. My emphasis.
41 Lewis, "Dogma and the Universe," 17–18.
42 Lewis, "Christian Apologetics, 67–68.

The same is true of apologetics: "Sentences beginning 'science has proved' should be avoided. If we try to base our apologetic on some recent development in science, we shall usually find that just as we have put the finishing touches to our argument science has changed its mind and quietly withdrawn the theory we have been using as our foundation stone: *timeo Danaos et dona ferentes*, is a sound principle."[43] However, the Trinitarian approach over the scientific at least regards creation as more than mere numbers and facts, this is demonstrated by the language used in the Psalms, where there is an animated liveliness, a freshness, to the *created* order, an order that issues from the design, will, and love of God not just from an impartial dissection.[44] But it is not simply a case of identifying the framework for a doctrine of creation in the Judaic-Christian tradition. Lewis identifies elements, relating to the fall, in North European Pagan religion, and evidence of an un-systematized doctrine in the Greek myths and philosophy:

> We find in Plato a clear "theology of creation" in the Judaic and Christian sense; the whole universe—the very conditions of time and space under which it exists—are produced by the will of a perfect, timeless, unconditioned God who is above and outside all that he makes . . . there is no question of self-existence or the timeless. Being is imposed upon them, as upon us, by preceding causes. . . . Plato fully understood this. His God creates the gods and preserves them from death by *his* own power; they have no inherent immortality.[45]

However, the elements of a doctrine of creation are for Lewis rare in the world's religions.[46]

In terms of basic principles for a doctrine of creation, Lewis notes that the beginning must have been outside the ordinary processes of nature (hence *ex nihilo*).[47] But what exactly do we mean when we say that the universe, creation, did not previously exist, that it was created out of nothing? What does Lewis comment?—

> I won't admit without a struggle that when I speak of God "uttering" or "inventing" the creatures I am "watering down the concept of creation." I am trying to give it, by remote analogies, some sort of content. I know that to create is defined as "to make out of nothing," *ex nihilo*. But I take that to mean "not out of any pre-existing material." It can't mean that God makes what God has not thought of, or that *he* gives *his* creatures any powers or beauties that he *himself* does not possess. Why, we think that even human work comes nearest to creation when the maker has "got it all out of his own head."[48]

There is, therefore, a paradox to creation. None of it was pre-existing, through—and here Lewis waxes Platonic—the very idea, the form of creation "existed" in the "mind"

---

43 Ibid., 67. Quoting: "I fear the Greeks even when they bear gifts." Virgil, *Aneid*, Bk. II line, 49.
44 Lewis, *Reflections on the Psalms*, 71–72.
45 Ibid., 68 and 70.
46 Ibid., 66–67.
47 Lewis, "Who was Right—Dream Lecturer or Real Lecturer," 4.
48 Lewis, *Letters to Malcolm*, 69.

1. Creation and The Fall I: C. S. Lewis—A Doctrine of Creation

of God (though to define what we mean by existing and God's mind is fraught with difficulties!).

The separateness of creation identifies it as distinct, created, and as subject to entropy. The randomness and decay in the universe is *the* rule in nature. This points to a beginning—as a clock can't run down unless it has first been wound up. We live, asserts Lewis drawing on scientific prediction, in a universe where organisms are always getting more disordered: irreversible death and irreversible entropy mean the whole of reality is winding down, echoing the Apostle Paul's vanity of nature, "her futility, her ruinousness . . . the movement from more order to less almost serves to determine the direction in which time is flowing. You could almost define the future as the period in which what is now living will be dead and in which what order still remains will be diminished."[49] Therefore such a doctrinal framework frames creation, even as it decays. To this the Psalms testify, writes Lewis: "creation is full of manifestations which show the presence of God, and the created energies that serve him."[50] In this the principle of creation remains: the creative act manifests in time yet is above time and is therefore timeless (Platonic). What is now decaying will be renewed, in particular the human,[51] because all that has been created has something of the *likeness*, writes Lewis, of God.[52] This is because of the unique purpose we find in a doctrine of creation: the universe was made *by* Christ and *for* Christ and everything is to be gathered together *in* Christ and by and through the action of the Holy Spirit for the Father: "It's even doubtful, you know, whether the whole universe was created for any other purpose. It says in the Bible that the whole universe was made for Christ and that everything is to be gathered together in *him*. I don't suppose any of us can understand how this will happen as regards the whole universe."[53] This is because Lewis asserts that creation is a work of art, prayerful poetry—"The great work of art was made for the sake of all it does and is, down to the curve of every wave and the flight of every insect."[54] This again echoes Lewis's narrative picture of the Aslan-Christ "singing" creation into existence (in this case a postulated parallel universe that Narnia is in).

6. THIRD AXIOM: PURPOSE, CHARACTER, AND NATURE

The third axiom is that creation has a particular character, is observable and definable. God declared that creation was good (Gen 1:31). This is the character and nature of the creation. What is more God *loves* the world: "For God so loved the world that he gave his one and only Son, that whoever believes in him shall not perish but have eternal life" (John 3:16). As Lewis notes, "it means creation—stars, trees, beast, men, and angels . . ."[55] The purpose of creation is, for Lewis, in communion, that there is

---

49 Lewis, *Miracles*, 160.
50 Lewis, *Reflections on the Psalms*, 70.
51 Lewis, *Miracles*, 187–90.
52 Lewis, *Beyond Personality*, 13.
53 Ibid., 43.
54 Lewis, *Letters to Malcolm*, 54.
55 Lewis writing to Mrs D. Jessup, Dec. 1, 1953. Lewis, *Collected Letters Vol. III*, 380.

the other, without of God: "In Pantheism God is all. But the whole point of creation surely is that he was not content to be all. *He* intends to be all *in all.*"[56] God is a giver; the nature of the "ontological continuity between creator and creature"[57] is what marks the character and nature of creation, and therefore its purpose. It is pure gift love from God, but God is free from creation, not contained or tied to creation; this is not a *need-love*. If God created the natural world it demands our respect. At the very least it demands our reverence if we are serious in our worship. The Psalms bear witness to this reverence and appreciation. To this end we must never cease to fight against death and decay.[58] We must also accept, asserts Lewis, that the intelligibility, purpose, and character of creation is not something imposed by a scientific mind on nature, but because the natural only becomes intelligible if God created it; the creation only exists at God's benevolence, creation has meaning at God's good will.[59] The creation of a reality displays a certain character, and that character and purpose issue from God's power in and through love for the creature.[60] Thus the laws of nature display God's love for us, even when they appear to work against us to our pain and suffering (Job 27–33).[61]

Humanity may be the pinnacle of creation (within earth, within the solar system, . . . within the universe?), we may be created to reflect back to God the love that *is* God but we are not able to truly know and understand the actual nature purpose and character of creation, *in total*. Neither are we in a God-given position to judge, to decide if the creation of the world was worth the suffering engrained in it. Therefore Lewis asks whether creating, with its potential of affliction and suffering, was acceptable rather than not creating.[62] This question also raises that of free will: would creation have been better if God have not imbued the human with free will, the capacity and capability to fall?

> Some comparison between one state of being and another can be made, but the attempt to compare being and not being ends in mere words. "It would be better for me not to exist"—in what sense "for me?" How should I, if I did not exist, profit by not existing? Our design is a less formidable one: it is only to discover how, perceiving a suffering world, and being assured, on quite different grounds, that God is good, we are to conceive that goodness and that suffering without contradiction.[63]

Does an orthodox doctrine of the fall endorse or refute such questioning:

> In the first place, I do not think the doctrine answers the question "Was it better for God to create than not to create?" That is a question I have already declined. Since I believe God to be good, I am sure that, if the question has a meaning,

---

56   Lewis, *Letters to Malcolm*, 68.
57   Ibid., 67.
58   Lewis, "Some Thoughts," 116, and 117.
59   Lewis, "Bulverism," 227f.
60   Lewis, *Problem of Pain*, 15–16.
61   Ibid., 15–16.
62   Ibid., 22.
63   Ibid.

1. Creation and The Fall I: C. S. Lewis—A Doctrine of Creation

the answer must be yes. But I doubt whether the question has any meaning: and even if it has, I am sure that the answer cannot be attained by the sort of value-judgment which men can significantly make.[64]

Lewis does go as far as postulating that the tragedy, the pain and torment, if we may call it that, may actually be woven into the character and purpose of creation and not *solely* be caused by the *fall*: there is "something tragic . . . inherent in the very act of creation."[65] The character of creation is on-going, unfolding, we won't know what creation truly is until the fulfillment, the completion. The purpose, writes Lewis, in the creation revolves to a degree around the teleological path the individual treads within creation, and its commission to relate to God.[66] The answer to the question of the nature, purpose, and character of creation for Lewis lies in one word: heaven.[67] The true nature and purpose of creation is Platonic: it exists in eternity and is *in fulfillment* in the here-and-now. Therefore the human rebellion to set up on its own, to call ourselves ourselves, will never work, the *fall* contradicts the nature, purpose, and character of creation—the *telos* of creation, where it is going, its aim towards fulfillment, such a *telos* contradicts the *fall*. The *fall* is a scar across creation [68]

The nature and character of creation, the universe, reflects, for Lewis, God's *desire* for what he terms "many-ness," that there was something other defined by "space and time and matter."[69] Creation is intimately intertwined with our observation and perception; we do see something of the character and purpose of the world, and God knew this would be so, and that it would give us intimations of the beyond, of eternity.[70] However, the primary purpose of creation, which defines its nature and character is simply presented in the Psalms, a theology we tend so often to overlook: "It seems to me appropriate, almost inevitable, that when that great Imagination which in the beginning, for *its* own delight and for the delight of men and angels and, (in their proper mode) of beasts, had invented and formed the whole world of nature, submitted to express *itself* in human speech, that speech should sometimes be poetry. For poetry too is a little incarnation, giving body to what had been before invisible and inaudible."[71] The poetic praise of creation in the Psalms, the joy in creation, this poetry is a reflection of creation and is part of creation. Creation is a joy and delight to God, it was *created* to be a joy and delight, and to reflect back to God, *his* glory. The human is especially endowed in so far as it has the gift of speech with which to reflect back to

---

64   Ibid., 52.
65   Lewis, *Letters to Malcolm*, 88.
66   Lewis, *Problem of Pain*, 123f.
67   Ibid., 119f.
68   Ibid., 61–62; but also, *Surprised by Joy*, 50–52, 132f., 177–78, 185f; *Screwtape Letters*, 81–84; and, Lewis writing to Mrs Johnson, July. 17, 1953. Lewis, *Collected Letters Vol. III*, 347–49.
69   Lewis, *Beyond Personality*, 32–33; these notes were comments added to the publication of the fifth talk in the series, which were then expanded in *Mere Christianity*, 152–53.
70   Lewis, *Miracles*, 102; referring to Sayers, *The Mind of the Maker*.
71   Lewis, *Reflections on the Psalms*, 5.

i. Theological Principle A: Creation as Separation

Theological principle A: creation involves separation—God and creation are not synonymous.

If Lewis is right, that creation is to reflect back God's glory, and to be a delight and joy to God, then this implies separation: there is distance and character, separateness, between God and creation (the opposite is true with Pantheism and Panentheism).

Creation as separation: God initiated, caused, matter-energy, the universe, and the creature to be; and in being there is distinctness. It is other than God, but in that separation the creation might turn and love God: "Once, before creation, it would have been true to say that everything was God. But God created: *He* caused things to be other than *himself* that, being distinct, they might learn to love *him*, and achieve union instead of mere sameness. Thus *he* also casts his bread upon the waters . . ."[73] Inanimate matter may be utterly obedient in its distance, and predictability, but it cannot turn to love the creator: "Even within the creation we might say that inanimate matter, which has no will, is one with God in a sense in which men are not."[74] Animate matter can be obedient, but only if it so chooses. Lewis noted how, "To say that God created nature, while it brings God and nature into relation, also separates them."[75] Creation and creator cannot be one.[76] In Pantheism God and nature are one, a deistic spirit infuses creation, is at one with creation, is creation. Pantheism is a belief that identifies God with the creation, or regards creation as a manifestation of God; as such pantheism relates to polytheism as the worship of many "gods," creation may not be just one "god." Panentheism is where God is not identical to creation, but is irrevocably and indelibly situated in creation, tied to the world. Or, perhaps better, the world is in God—a subset of God, as it were. From an orthodox and traditional perspective, endorsed by the book of Genesis, God loves in freedom, creates in freedom, but is not tied to the creation. God is Immanuel—leastwise, the second person of the Trinity is; the Father is not? An orthodox doctrine of the Trinity contradicts Panentheism and confirms the distinctness between creator and the creation. But we are not alone. The creature may be other then God, but God is in them, sustaining them. Yet in fallen humanity the creature can never be in another creature to the same extent. Our distinctness becomes isolation through original sin.[77] The condition of God being over

---

72 Lewis, *Problem of Pain*, 34–35.
73 Ibid., 125.
74 Ibid.
75 Lewis, *Reflections on the Psalms*, 69–70.
76 Ibid.
77 Lewis, *Letters to Malcolm*, 70, and 65f.

1. Creation and The Fall I: C. S. Lewis—A Doctrine of Creation

and against us, while sustaining us, is not the direct result of the *fall*, but original sin causes it to be paradoxical at best.[78]

But looking at creation in the abstract will give us only a limited understanding of this separation. At the heart of creation is the incarnation; the *cause* of the incarnation, in orthodox terms, is the *fall*. So we cannot look at the separation and free will that led to the fall as separate from the initial creation, and the *re-creation* post-resurrection. Lewis notes how "the more perfect the creature is, the further this separation must at some point be pushed?"[79] This is an explicit account for Lewis of the incarnation, God become man, Jesus the form of the divine. Jesus knew this separation only too clearly during his childhood as he grew up, then in his ministry, separated from the Father yet misunderstood by those around him, even the disciples, and finally in his passion whilst knowing the monumental significance for the world and for humanity *in his* passion and death. By being the creature, and by being separated Jesus shared our humanity and our human condition.[80] As Lewis noted, "For union exists only between distincts."[81]

ii. Theological Principle B: The Myth of Creation

Theological principle B: the origins of creation are not directly knowable in the way the presence of creation is; reason and imagination form myth in attempting an explanation of origin.

The biblical story of creation and the fall (for it is clear that the two cannot be regarded separately) meant more to Lewis as the truth about the human condition presented as myth than if these accounts are argued as complete historical and scientific fact. Lewis classified the material in the Old Testament as chronicle (essentially historical, though perhaps different to concepts of historicity today), poetry (Song of Solomon, Job, and the book of Psalms—but the Psalms also represent a different genre), moral and political diatribe (pietistic and spiritual teaching), and, crucially, romances and myths. The creation stories—for example, Genesis, and Psalm 104—are mythical by genre and nature.[82] This does not deny the truth that is inherent in the Genesis creation story, but this truth is phrased in the language of myth, essentially because the human mind cannot comprehend the vastness, the complexity, and the absolute truth of the origins of creation, this mythical language makes it comprehensible, to a degree, yet is framed in fact: that creation is, that God is creator, that creation stands apart from God, that parts of creation are inanimate objects and not "gods", that there is an order and givenness to creation, and that part of creation (the human) has rebelled and

---

78   Ibid., 67.
79   Ibid., 41.
80   Ibid., 40f.
81   Lewis, *Problem of Pain*, 125.
82   This raises profound questions about Lewis's doctrine of Scripture, these issues were dealt with in the second book in this series: *C. S. Lewis—The Work of Christ Revealed*, Pt. 1, Chs, 1–3

attempted to set itself up on its own, and so forth. Myth, for Lewis and for Tolkien, can be as real and more truthful than fact.

Creation stories can be found in the various religions and mythologies—Egyptian, Babylonian, Norse, and Greek are amongst those cited by Lewis[83]—but they have limited value and truth, more often contradicting the basic principles found in the Judeo-Christian story. The Genesis myth of creation generates the story of *true* creation by a *transcendent* creator.[84] The account in Genesis does owe much in terms of structure and genre to the creation myths found in the religious traditions of people surrounding the ancient Hebrews; however, Genesis conveys the reality of creation and fundamental truths of creation rigorously:

> No philosophical theory which I have yet come across is a radical improvement on the words of Genesis, that "In the beginning God made Heaven and Earth." I say "radical" improvement, because the story in Genesis—as St Jerome said long ago—is told in the manner "of a popular poet," or as we should say, in the form of folk tale. But if you compare it with the creation legends of other peoples—with all these delightful absurdities in which giants to be cut up and floods to be dried up are made to exist *before* creation—the depth and originality of this Hebrew folk tale will soon be apparent. The idea of *creation* in the rigorous sense of the word is there fully grasped.[85]

Therefore Lewis sees no problem in biblical studies that postulated that elements of the Genesis account are from earlier Semite stories, or from religious traditions without the Hebrews, pagan even.[86] The irony is that the truths within the Genesis story did not travel to these other creation stories to a greater or lesser degree. The essential truths of Genesis are, in relative terms, unique.

iii. Theological Principle C: Humanity's Relation to God and Creation

Theological principle C: humanity is, in many ways, the pinnacle of creation, characterized by uniqueness, but also by rebellion, and is thus trinitarianly defined.

Why did God create the human? What purpose is there in such a troublesome creature? What is the relationship between God's will, and ours. What does the fall do to the original intention in God's creation?[87] The human, as created, is defined by the *imago Dei* (the image of God), but then by rebellion; salvation is through the Christ,

---

83   Lewis, *Reflections on the Psalms*, 66f.
84   Ibid., 95.
85   Lewis, *Miracles*, 34–35. (Lewis's emphasis).
86   Lewis, *Reflections on the Psalms*, 95–96.
87   It is worth noting that Lewis does tackle, and refute, a philosophical system from the early twentieth century entitled Creative Evolution. Very few people take this belief system seriously now, or give it any value; however, it is worth noting that Lewis applies a rigorous logic in refuting it. See: Lewis, "Screwtape Proposes a Toast," 3–5; *Mere Christianity*, 35; *Screwtape Letters* 67f.; "Dogma and the Universe," 21f.

1. Creation and The Fall I: C. S. Lewis—A Doctrine of Creation

the indwelling of the Holy Spirit initiates the *imago Christi* (the image of Christ), thus the human is defined by and in relation to the Trinity.

Why the Human?

The human is created to be in many ways the pinnacle of creation, certainly the created order—above, and in many ways, master of the animals, but a little lower than the angels. However, Lewis is at great pains to deny anthropocentrism: the human is not at the center of the universe; creation's purpose was not solely for the human. Anthropocentrism can, mistakenly, be read from the Bible, and much in the medieval concept of the universe placed man and the planet earth at the center. What does Lewis have to say?—"Christianity is not wedded to an anthropocentric view of the universe as a whole. The first chapters of Genesis, no doubt, give the story of creation in the form of a folk-tale . . . and if you take them alone you might get that impression. But it is not confirmed by the Bible as a whole."[88] Lewis continues to note how the closing chapters of the book of Job should cure us of what we may call anthropo-egotism for we are "sternly warned against making man the measure of all things."[89] Lewis quotes selectively from the book of Job, God's reply to Job:

> 1a. Canst thou draw out leviathan with an hook?
> 4. Will he make a covenant with thee? wilt thou take him for a servant for ever?
> 9b. shall not one be cast down even at the sight of him?[90]
> KJV

God's reply to Job is the strongest denial of anthropocentrism in the Bible and the human condition confirms it; likewise, what is cautiously known about the universe, its sheer scale in terms of time and space. Furthermore Lewis notes how in Paul's epistles the skies often are hostile to the human. But what is important in endorsing or denying anthropocentrism is the *fall* and the incarnation: we cannot consider creation generally, nor the human specifically, without measuring God's love for humanity and how the problem of the human condition is solved, *in potential*, through the incarnation-cross-resurrection:

> It is, of course, the essence of Christianity that God loves man and for his sake became man and died. But that does not prove that man is the sole end of nature. In the parable, it was the one lost sheep that the shepherd went in search of: it was not the only sheep in the flock, and we are not told that it was the most valuable—save in so far as the most desperately in need has, while the need lasts, a peculiar value in the eyes of Love.[91]

Like God's rebuke to Job, the Parable of the Lost Sheep contradicts anthropocentrism. But, we may ask, does not the human condition defined now by the fall see the shepherd's concern for the one lost sheep as evidence of that sheep's greater importance

---

88 Lewis, "Dogma and the Universe," 21.
89 Ibid., 21.
90 Ibid. Quoting from Job 41:1a, 4 and 9b.
91 Lewis, "Dogma and the Universe," 21. Referring to Matt 18:12 and Luke 15:4.

than the rest of creation. Not so: God's love will seek that the lost are found, but that does not accord special status to the lost. A child in need of special help, in addition to the ministrations of the class teacher, so as to learn to read and write, may get a special needs assistant to help it learn on a one-to-one basis but this does not make that child more important than the rest of the class, or at the center of all decisions the head teacher may make for the school, or define education policy across all schools in a city! The special measures given to this child merely give it the opportunity of being on an equal footing with its class mates, its peer group; this is a right interpretation of the Parable of the Lost Sheep.

Therefore, Lewis considers the creation of humanity to be the raising-up of an *animal* to be something more than an *animal*.[92] We have importance with regard to the planet we live on, but we do not know our true position in the universe. Assigning anthropo-egotism to the fact God has moved heaven and earth, so to speak, to save us, is wrong. Humanity is therefore distinct from the other animals—creatures—in creation, therefore the Bible and church tradition does assert a distinctly, and unique, human nature. There are certain elements that are unique to the human. By contrast "Liberals"/"Moderns" often argue that there is no such thing as human *nature*. If there is a distinctly human nature then we must own to having marred it, transgressed, spoilt it. Lewis does speculate on the nature of Adam and Eve, concluding that they would seem much holier than us despite their triggering of the *fall*.[93] Asserting a distinctly *human* nature defines the parameters for how the human should be, and how it should behave and relate to God. And this human nature is qualified and modeled on the Trinity:

> The proper good of a creature is to surrender itself to its Creator—to enact intellectually, volitionally, and emotionally, that relationship which is given in the mere fact of its being a creature. When it does so, it is good and happy. Lest we should think this a hardship, this kind of good begins on a level far above the creatures, for God Himself, as Son, from all eternity renders back to God as Father by filial obedience the being which the Father by paternal love eternally generates in the Son. This is the pattern which man was made to imitate—which Paradisal man did imitate—and wherever the will conferred by the Creator is thus perfectly offered back in delighted and delighting obedience by the creature, there, most undoubtedly, is heaven, and there the Holy Ghost proceeds.[94]

Therefore, the good of the human animal, raised up to know the creator, is in surrender and worship, in this lies its contentment. The human was made for a specific purpose; and its relationship to God was defined by God—by the triune nature of God. The relationship between God the Father and God the Son is the model for our raising-up. This is a heavy compliment for God to pay to the creature. This raises questions about how real the *imago Dei* is within us, that God *is* in us—essentially the second person

---

92   Lewis, *Reflections on the Psalms*, 100f.
93   Lewis, *Problem of Pain*, 59–60. See also, Lewis writing to Sr. Penelope CSMV, Jan 10, 1952. *Collected Letters, Vol. III*, 156–58.
94   Ibid., 71–72.

of the Trinity, generated by the Holy Spirit, so the creature may turn in filial love to the Father. If people do not submit to this nature and model within them they will not be content, they will not be happy and will seek contentment in the passing fancies of this world.[95] Therefore, our creatureliness creates a commitment and responsibility to God as creator.[96] But this is not simply about subservience. It is also about praise: "But for our body one whole realm of God's glory—all that we receive through our senses—would go unpraised. . . . I fancy the 'beauties of nature' are a secret God has shared with us alone. That may be one of the reasons why we were made—and why the resurrection of the body is an important doctrine."[97]

It is important to remember that Lewis asserts a basic ontological feature of the human, and that is that we are always nearer to God (despite the spiritual blindness generated in us by the fall) than we are to other creatures in creation—even the angels.[98] This confirms Lewis's Protestant credentials, in that despite his belief in and respect for the communion of saints, we do have a direct connection to God through the indwelling of the Holy Spirit. This nearness is more real than any relationship with angels and saints. We are bound through Christ's sacrifice into the triune reality that is God: "For we are in one most blessed sense *nearer* to *him* than to them [angels]: partly of course because *he* has deigned to share our humanity, but partly, I take it, because every creature is nearer to its creator than it can be to superior *creatures*."[99]

Purpose

Lewis does note, particularly given how Jesus has sacrificed himself for us, how difficult it is to explain why we have such value before God.[100] But then the purpose in many ways of humanity is, for Lewis, for the human to be a "gift" that Christ offers to the Father.[101] Is this why we were created, is this our purpose? As the Son offers us to the Father, so the Father may love us: we are caught up in the Trinity, *in love*.[102] The relationship between the creator and the creature may seem special but this tells us more about God than we can glean from the world.[103] There is therefore a bond between creator and creature that is primary, and on it is built the repairing relationship between the human will and pneumatological grace.[104] Our utmost purpose and goodness is derived from God. It is this we denied in the fall, in our selfish demand for independence.[105]

---

95 Ibid., 37f., and 71–73.
96 Lewis, *Christian Behaviour*, 10–11.
97 Lewis, *Letters to Malcolm*, 15.
98 Lewis writing to "An American Lady," March 4, 1953. *Letters to an American Lady*, 13.
99 Ibid.
100 Lewis, *Problem of Pain*, 33f.
101 Lewis, *Beyond Personality*, 44. See also, *Mere Christianity*, 165.
102 Lewis, *Problem of Pain*, 34–35.
103 Ibid., 23–39.
104 Lewis, *Letters to Malcolm*, 69f.
105 Lewis, "Christianity and Literature," 6–7.

Relation and Obedience

It is important, notes Lewis, to remember that the human and all it stands for is not diametric to God. Sometimes we do get it right, we can be pleasing in our actions and decisions before God. Therefore human actions do not necessarily exclude a confluence with divine action; it comes down to the relationship between God's will, and ours.[106] The problem is in the human having access to and making a right judgment. Self-love is often a delusion in that it leads us to be convinced we are right when before God we are not. The love of the creature is, therefore, dangerous, not necessarily wrong or bad, or even primarily evil, but "small" and "insignificant."[107] We do, however, have the power gifted, awaiting our acceptance, by the Holy Spirit, to be more than the mess we have become through the fall.[108] Grace should give us the ability to focus once again on God, an ability that came naturally before the fall.[109] Grace is important, fundamental, because God is our only good, as *he* is the good of all creation;[110] as such all we can do is respond to God's love.[111] It is when we cease to acknowledge this that we most debase ourselves and convince ourselves that we are more than creatures whose existence is justified by the creator.[112] We err if we fail to see that we are, in Lewis's mechanistic terms, the creaturely machine, as God is the inventor.[113]

The Fall

Therefore, although Christ's sacrifice saves us, we need, on a daily basis, to consciously attempt to be obedient according to our human nature. However difficult this may be we begin to reverse the effects of original sin in us: "In obeying, a rational creature consciously enacts its creaturely rôle, reverses the act by which we fell, treads Adam's dance backward, and returns."[114] (This should read, if we are right to correct Lewis, "begins to return.") We were made with a capacity for "need-Love," which can only focus on God. Our fallen status makes this worse, more painful, *if* we refuse to focus on God.[115] If we make life more painful for ourselves by refusing the natural focus for this need-love, the implications are manifold because of original sin. The creature tries to go it alone, it is then faced by the problem of this independence, and in trying to solve the problem merely makes matters worse: "This sin has been described by Saint Augustine as the result of pride, of the movement whereby a creature (that is, an essentially dependent being whose principle of existence lies not in itself but in another) tries to set up on its own, to exist for itself."[116]

---

106   Lewis, *Letters to Malcolm*, 65–68, and, 69–73.
107   Lewis writing to Dom Bede Griffiths OSB, April 16, 1940. Lewis, *Collected Letters Vol. II*, 390.
108   Lewis, *Letters to Malcolm*, 46–48
109   Ibid., 70–72
110   Lewis, *Problem of Pain*, 37–38
111   Ibid., 35.
112   Lewis, *The Four Loves*, 127.
113   Lewis, *Beyond Personality*, 47.
114   Lewis, *Problem of Pain*, 80–81.
115   Lewis, *The Four Loves*, 124–26.
116   Lewis, *Problem of Pain*, 57. Lewis is referring to Augustine, *The City of God*, Bk. XIV, Ch. 13.

1. Creation and The Fall I: C. S. Lewis—A Doctrine of Creation

vi. Theological Principle D: Sub-Creation and Sub-creators

Theological principle D: humanity is given the responsibility of sub-creation and the *custodianship* of creation.

Sub-creation is the creation of subsequent or secondary worlds within the primary creation—God's creation is primary. God imbues the creation with the ability to create, to bring forth. This principle is enshrined early on in the Bible (Gen 1: where the earth and the waters *bring forth*). The subsequent or secondary creations will always relate to and derive their ultimate meaning from the primary creation, which in turn derives its legitimacy and ultimate meaning from God, from eternity. This is, in effect, Platonically, an echo from the mind of the creator, of the primary creation: God. Lewis's friend and professional colleague J. R. R. Tolkien wrote often of humanity as sub-creators.[117] Tolkien asserted that because there is an infinite potential variety within God and any creation derived from God, the meaning that sub-creations derive from God and from the primary creation is likewise imaginative, creative, and wondrous in scope, and not simply a pale shadow of the real. This is legitimate because the sub-creators were first created by God in God's own image, the *imago Dei*; God first creates, then we in God's image sub-create. Tolkien was thinking in terms of humanity, through the faculty of the imagination, creating myths and stories that complemented God's creation. But in some ways creation in itself has the freedom to sub-create. Is not sub-creation fundamental to any theory of evolution, or evolved development, whether through natural selection, or other agencies? A doctrine of sub-creation, applied to nature, acknowledges that creation creates, re-creates, changes, develops. Though it is pertinent to ask, in terms of sub-creation, what has humanity done to itself and to the natural world?

But what we are concerned with here is humanity's commission in sub-creativity. Do we truly invent and create out of nothing (*ex nihilo*), or are we, even in our sub-creation, channels? Lewis does note that applying the term creation, as in sub-creation, to human activities is in many ways a misnomer: do we not merely "rearrange elements" that God has already created?[118] Should writers believe they are bringing into existence out of nothing? Lewis extends this concept of merely identifying and rearranging by pointing out that originality is the prerogative of God alone in the Bible: beauty or wisdom is pre-existing.[119] Sub-creation as creativity, originality, spontaneity, issues from the prevenient action of the Holy Spirit in the fallen human, sub-creation is Platonic in that the originality of the ideas pre-exist in *form*, therefore, "[the] Human will becomes truly creative and truly our own when it is wholly God's, and this is one of the many senses in which he that loses his soul shall find it."[120] Therefore our

---

117 An account of sub-creation was presented by Tolkien in the Andrew Lang lecture given at St Andrews University in 1938: "On Fairy Stories", 38-89.
118 Lewis writing to Sr. Penelope CSMV, Feb 20, 1943. *Collected Letters, Vol. III*, 555. See also, Lewis, "Bulverism," 228.
119 Lewis, "Christianity and Literature," 6.
120 Lewis, *Problem of Pain*, 82

originality as sub-creators lies in re-combining elements from God's creation and from eternity.[121] On the act of creativity and invention, Lewis noted, "This act, as it is for God, must always remain totally inconceivable to man. For we—even our poets and musicians and inventors—never, in the ultimate sense, *make*. We only build. We always have materials to build from. All we can know about the act of creation must be derived from what we can gather about the relation of the creatures to their creator."[122] If our sub-creation is merely a channel of God's creativity, then this is important but relative and ultimately derivative. There is, therefore, an element of delegation in this: "Creation seems to be delegation through and through. *He* will do nothing simply of *himself*, which can be done by creatures. I suppose this is because *he* is the giver. And *he* has nothing to give but *himself*. And to give *himself* is to do *his* deeds—in a sense, and on varying levels to be *himself*—through the things he has made."[123]

If there is a weakness in the overall range of Lewis's doctrine of creation it is in the custodianship given to humanity—though this is not necessarily absent. Perhaps given the growth in understanding of environmental degradation and climate change, green issues, since Lewis's death we are now more aware of this God-given commission than in Lewis's day. Humanity's custodianship is rooted and grounded in the book of Genesis (Gen 1:27a, 28–30; 2:15; and 2:19–20). Lewis echoes the custodianship outlined in Genesis in *The Chronicles of Narnia: The Magician's Nephew*. In the creation of Narnia, responsibility for both the "talking animals," and the "dumb brutes," as well as the care and tending of the land and its defense, is given in solemn words by the Aslan-Christ to the London cabbie who has come into Narnia at its beginning, and who, with his wife, is now King Frank and Queen Helen: they are to rule and name these creatures, and rule with justice and protect them from evil.[124] Custodianship is the preserve of the human in our world, and also, hypothetically, in a parallel universe *at the will of Christ*. Whether we like it or not animals are our responsibility and are to be understood in relation to humanity as custodians;[125] furthermore, when people attempt to justify the sadistic treatment of animals, Lewis argues, they reduce themselves to the level of the jungle, to nature red in tooth and claw and abandon the rational nature God has given us which separates us from the animals.

Lewis does not really tackle this custodianship of the earth in his apologetics and his philosophical theology; however, he does focus often on the question of vivisection— the torture of animals in laboratories in the name of science and for human benefit.[126] Therefore, like Tolkien, Lewis is highly environmentally aware and relatively "green," even though such concepts did not really form a public awareness in mid-twentieth century Britain. In both *Narnia* and *The Lord of the Rings* the destruction of nature and the abrogation of humanity's responsibility before the LORD for looking after creation

---

121 Lewis, *Miracles*, 33
122 Lewis, *Letters to Malcolm*, 69
123 Ibid., 68
124 Lewis, *The Magician's Nephew*, 127–30
125 Lewis writing to "An American Lady," Nov 26, 1962. *Letters to an American Lady*, 110–11. See also, Lewis, *Problem of Pain*, 9:11.
126 See Lewis, *Vivisection* (a pamphlet for the New England Anti-Vivisection Society, 1947).

1. Creation and The Fall I: C. S. Lewis—A Doctrine of Creation

issues from the dark evil forces: Saruman's industrial destruction of the landscape and his genetic experiments in cross-breeding and creating mutant demonic species comes to mind, or the wasteland that is Sauron's Mordor, in Middle Earth;[127] then there is the White Witch's perpetual ice-age 100 year winter in Narnia,[128] or the Green Witch's industrialized slavery,[129] the Calormenes's destruction and despoiling of the Lantern Forest,[130] and so forth. As early as 1938 Lewis was acutely aware of the dangers to the biosphere that is the earth in our abuse of the commission of custodianship:

> How will the legend of the age of trees
> Feel, when the last tree falls in England?
> When the concrete spreads and the town conquers
> The country's heart; when contraceptive
> Tarmac's laid where farm has faded,
> Tramline flows where slept a hamlet,
> And shop-fronts, blazing without a stop from
> Dover to Wrath, have glazed us over?
> Simplest tales will then bewilder
> The questioning children, "What was a chestnut?
> Say what it means to climb a Beanstalk,
> Tell me, grandfather, what an elm is.
> What was Autumn? They never taught us."[131]

Margarita Carretero-González, through the biblical proposition of humanity as sons and daughters of Adam and Eve (and as "children of Aslan," children of God), examines an environmentalist perspective that can be read from *The Chronicles of Narnia*.[132] In effect this is part of a doctrine of creation. This necessitates considering animals, effectively sentient, conscious, rational animals, other than humans, in Narnia. (Those who balk at the concept of talking animals need to realize than man is in effect, and on a base level, a talking animal.) This consideration raises environmentalist questions about animal pain, and then questions of the analogical hierarchy in Narnia (dumb beasts, then talking animals, then a human monarchy), but not one where the higher can exploit the lower. As Carretero-González notes, it is the imported evil in Narnia that exploits and corrupts. Commenting on *The Magician's Nephew*, she notes:

> Polly and Digory find that the guinea pig is perfectly happy in the Wood between the Worlds, away from mad scientific experimentation but Digory is just acting responsibly toward this nonhuman form of life in a way Uncle Andrew cannot even understand. The same arrogant attitude toward any manifestation of the other—human or nonhuman—is displayed by Jadis. . . . Any type of supremacy, whether biologically or socially conferred, entails in Lewis's worldview a greater

---

127 See, essentially, Tolkien, *The Lord of the Rings*, Bk. 3, Ch. III, Bk. 6, Ch. II.
128 Lewis, *The Lion, the Witch and the Wardrobe*, 53–60, and 73–81.
129 Lewis, *The Silver Chair*, 114–25.
130 Lewis, *The Last Battle*, 17–26.
131 Lewis, "The Future of Forestry," 75 (extract from). Poem first published under the pseudonym of Nat Whilk in *The Oxford Magazine*, 1938.
132 Margarita Carretero-González, "Sons of Adam, Daughters of Eve, and Children of Aslan," 93–114.

degree of responsibility toward those who are inferior. Jadis's dictatorial ruling can only bring forth death, as seen in the dying world of Charn or in the perpetual winter that envelops Narnia during her illegitimate reign.[133]

This echoes with the environmental concerns, the abuse of creation, that can be read from Tolkien's *The Lord of the Rings*, an understanding of which is now only just beginning to be recognized as implicit in the work of many of the Inklings.[134]

The commission of custodianship is given to humanity *before* the fall; original sin therefore corrupts this commission and the results are self-evident. Lewis in many ways focused his concerns over the corruption of this commission of custodianship, and the inevitable and implicit environmental degradation, onto the character of Edward Weston in *The Space Trilogy*. Weston considers his perception of events and the world to be superior to all others, and to be in effect lord over all creation: Satan believed he could challenge God in divinity; Weston acts as if he were God. He exhibits and is proud of his racial superiority over all other beings, he is exploitative, will happily use, abuse and destroy for his own ends, and, faced by the potential for humanity to render the planet earth uninhabitable, his aim is that a scientific elite (similar to Nietzsche's supermen) must accelerate progress and scientific discovery so that an elite can travel to another earth-like planet to ensure humanity's survival—at whatever cost.[135] In Weston, who is representative of a certain group of people, who exercise influence out of all proportion to their place in society, sub-creation becomes un-creation.

7. FOURTH AXIOM: THE NEW CREATION

The fourth axiom is that there is a new creation that is formed through and from the incarnation-cross-resurrection. The new creation issues from the old creation; this event changes everything and is, in essence, a response to the fall (Rev 21:1–4). Therefore, we do need to consider this new creation in the context of Lewis's doctrine of creation.

i. Cause and Cross, Creation and Consummation

First, for Lewis, we need to balance the depravity and corruption of original sin with the new creation: if we focus too much on the fall (the cause) and God's response (the cross), creation (the original goodness of creation) and consummation (the new creation) are marginalized and we have an unbalanced picture of God's purposes for humanity: our *telos*, our ultimate objective, becomes destructive and the new does not replace or emerge from the old. According to God's loving purposes the new is a fulfillment of the old, the old is drawn up into the new through Christ's descent

---

133   Ibid., 101.
134   For further reading on these environmental issues, see, Dickerson and, O'Hara, *Narnia and the Fields of Arbol*.
135   See the first volume of the space trilogy, Lewis, *Out of the Silent Planet*, where the anti-heroes, Devine and Weston, assume all ideas that have gone before are inferior and flawed, even in relation to alien species on another planet, they represent the inevitable progress over a lesser species, and exhibit an amoral believe in their advancement.

1. Creation and The Fall I: C. S. Lewis—A Doctrine of Creation

and reascent. Death works backwards, entropy ceases. Lewis's Platonism is important here. The new exists in form; fulfillment comes through the resurrection. Most of our conclusions about our *telos* are tainted by original sin, therefore any conclusions about the nature of creation will be partial and flawed at best, inaccurate at worst, *if* we only look at the destructive side of human corruption, *if* we ignore or are ignorant of the new creation, *then* our understanding is wildly out of tune. The Anglican theologian Justyn Terry notes,

> We believe that Jesus is the Lord, and the resurrection of Jesus from the dead casts a whole new light on the challenges of this world. Death is not the end. And even if "survival of the fittest" is an accurate description of how you go from one species to the next, it's only a description in a fallen world. It won't be like that in the new heaven and the new earth, there'll be no entropy then, it won't be all gradually decaying away. You see so much of our current scientific thinking—magnificent as it may be—is describing a fallen world. And many of our scientists don't know that.[136]

If we are to consider in balance the new and the old creation, and if we are not to overemphasize the corruption of the old, then we need to have a clear understanding of the distinction between creation on the one hand and humanity on the other, with the incarnation as a third, key, factor.[137] This raises the problem of conflating the diversity of creation into a manageable concept for the human mind, and thus, the dangers of Pantheism. Lewis argues that in Pantheism God is everything, is all, whereas creation is because God did not want to be everything; creation is, as we have established, distinct, different: "*He* was not content to be all. *He* intends to be 'all in all.'"[138] Lewis continues

> One must be careful not to put this in a way which would blur the distinction between the creation of a man and the Incarnation of God. Could one, as a mere model, put it thus? In creation God makes—invents—a person and "utters"—injects—him into the realm of nature. In the incarnation, God the Son takes the body and human soul of Jesus, and, through that, the whole environment of nature, all the creaturely predicament, into his own being. So that "He came down from Heaven" can almost be transposed into "Heaven drew earth up into it," and locality, limitation, sleep, sweat, footsore weariness, frustration, pain, doubt and death, are, from before all worlds, known by God from within. The pure light walks the earth; the darkness, received into the heart of Deity, is there swallowed up. Where, except in uncreated light, can the darkness be drowned?[139]

The new is initiated by the incarnation and is defined by the resurrection, which starts with the moment of the death of Jesus of Nazareth on the cross. The fulfillment of the new creation is with the general resurrection, and thus the new heaven and the new

---

136 The Very Revd Dr Justyn Terry, "Recovering the Christian Mind: Educating the Anglican Ministry Today,":
http://anglican.tv/content/mere-anglicanism-2012-very-revd-dr-justyn-terry.
137 Lewis, *Miracles*, 67f.
138 Lewis, *Letters to Malcolm*, 68.
139 Ibid., 68.

earth. At the heart of the new creation, certainly for Lewis, is the resurrection, specific in Jesus, general in all humanity at the end of all things. Tom Wright notes, on the importance of the resurrection of Jesus in John's Gospel, "The resurrection matters for John because he is, at his very heart, a theologian of creation. The Word, who was always to be the point at which creator and creation came together in one, is now, in the resurrection, the point at which creator and new creation are likewise one."[140] This we will see later is so for Lewis.

ii. Lewis: Markers of the New Creation

Throughout Lewis's *corpus*, especially in his analogical narratives, are examples of the nature and character of the new creation. These examples of God's loving purposes for humanity. These are revelatory. They are intimations, moments of temporal paradox: this should not happen prior to the eschaton, the general resurrection, but they do! These are, in effect, Platonic markers: allusions and hints; inklings and rumors; suggestions, mentions and tip-offs—of eternity, the new heaven and the new earth. They are also warnings of pending judgment and the potential of damnation, as much as the potential of salvation. Therefore for Lewis human decision making is decisive: "All get what they want; they do not always like it."[141] This raises questions about the judgment of God as infernal voluntarism, which was a strong and assertive doctrine in Lewis's work, which will feature in the final part of this work and series. Lewis does not use the term "infernal voluntarism", but his understanding of heaven and hell, and the judgment of God is based on what is now identified as infernal voluntarism:[142] that humanity condemns itself to hell. Throughout our lives God waits for us to say to him, "Thy will be done." If we don't, then as we come before the judgment seat of Christ, *post mortem*, God simply says to us, "Thy will be done." ("Then I will tell them plainly, 'I never knew you. Away from me, you evildoers!'" Matt 7:23.) This is, in Lewis's words, the deep courtesy of heaven: all get what they want, but they may not always like what they get. The new creation may be defined by and as a new heaven and a new earth, but hell is as much a part of this new creation, once the old has gone. Or is hell a continuation, the remnant of the old, a corrupted fragment, perhaps even an echo of the evil of the old, for those who won't leave it? [143]

But what of the new creation, the resurrected? Jesus asserts categorically in his conversation with Nicodemus (John 3:1–21) that the old creation must die to live, to be born anew. We must be re-created in this life, *by the Spirit*, and then reborn in the general resurrection: "Jesus replied, 'Very truly I tell you, no one can see the kingdom of God unless they are born again, . . . no one can enter the kingdom of God unless they are born of water and the Spirit. Flesh gives birth to flesh, but the Spirit gives birth to spirit. You should not be surprised at my saying, You must be born again. The wind blows wherever it pleases. You hear its sound, but you cannot tell where it comes

---

140   N. T. Wright, *The Resurrection of the Son of God*, 667.
141   Lewis, *The Magician's Nephew*, 162–63.
142   See, Sickler, "Infernal Voluntarism and 'The Deep Courtesy of Heaven,'" 163–78.
143   See, Lewis, *The Great Divorce*.

1. Creation and The Fall I: C. S. Lewis—A Doctrine of Creation

from or where it is going. So it is with everyone born of the Spirit.'" (John 3:3b and 5b–8.) Lewis has markers throughout his analogical narratives as to intimations of the new creation. Perhaps the key one is Aslan: echoing the dry valley of bones in Ezekiel (Ezek 37:1–14) the Aslan's-Christ's breath brings those turned to stone back to life,[144] likewise Lucy's cordial—a gift from Aslan—heals those fallen in battle.[145] But crucially it is the sacrificial blood of the lionized-Christ that resurrects.[146] Whether the creatures in Narnia and the surrounding lands know of Aslan and believe in what *he* is, all will at some point meet with him and be faced with a decision that will seal their fate: born again, resurrected, in the new kingdom, or eternal damnation.[147] This is taken further in *The Great Divorce* by Lewis's ontological description of the solid realness of heaven as compared to the near-to-nothing of hell, where the condemned prefer to return to this world of the damned.[148]

In the gospel God descends to reascend, drawing-up humanity into the new creation. This is a familiar pattern in nature—all life must descend (i.e., a seed) to reascend. Cultures all over the world have death and resurrection myths woven into their perception and understanding of the natural world, many such myths are elevated to the status of corn kings, the king must die in the ground as a seed to reascend, to grow again, to rule again (this is echoed in the old English folk song/ballad, "John Barleycorn," which anthropomorphizes the barley seed/grain, which dies, is ground up, yet is reborn, metamorphosed). Lewis writes[149] that although the story of Jesus has remarkable parallels with the principle of descending and ascending within nature myths there is no suggestion in the Gospels of a self-awareness of this parallel in Jesus or his disciples. Lewis writes, "The doctrine of the incarnation, if accepted, puts this principle even more emphatically at the center. The pattern is there in nature because it was first there in God. All the instances of it which I have mentioned turn out to be but transpositions of the divine theme into a minor key."[150] Christ could be seen as simply another corn-king; Jesus was addressing an agrarian society, and although the metaphor of a seed falling and dying to rise again is used in his sayings as well as in other parts of the New Testament,[151] he draws no conscious parallel between this observable fact of creation and the reality of God descending to reascend taking fallen creation with him.[152] Lewis addresses this problem by asserting that the Christians are not simply claiming that God was incarnate in Jesus but that the one true God whom the Hebrews worshipped as Yahweh had descended. On the one hand, this is the God of creation—of nature—this is not a nature-god. This is the God for whom

---

144 Lewis, *The Lion, the Witch and the Wardrobe*, Ch. 16.
145 Ibid.
146 Lewis, *The Silver Chair*, 187–88
147 For example, Shasta's encounter with Aslan, echoing John 3, even though he knows virtually nothing about Aslan and what he represents. See, Lewis, *The Horse and His Boy*, 127f.
148 See, Lewis, *The Great Divorce*, essentially, 19–23, and, 103–4.
149 Lewis, *Miracles*, (1st ed.), 113–38.
150 Ibid., 118.
151 For example, Matt 13; 25; Mark 4; Luke 8; 13; 17; 1 Cor 15; 2 Cor 9:10; 1 Pet 1; 1 John 3.
152 Lewis, *Miracles*, 119.

the earth is his foot stool not his vesture—"Yahweh is neither the soul of nature nor her enemy . . ."[153] Therefore, writes Lewis, we must understand why Christ is at once so like the corn-king and so silent about him. He is like the corn-king because the corn-king is a portrait of him. Elements of nature-religion are strikingly absent from the teachings of Jesus and from Hebrew history, in particular the covenant, because of the unique calling of the Hebrew people to testify to the one true God, author and lord of creation, not merely a part of creation: "In them you have from the very outset got in behind nature-religion and behind nature herself. Where the real God is present the shadows of that God do not appear, that which the shadows resembled does. The Hebrews throughout their history were being constantly headed-off from the worship of nature-gods; not because the nature-gods were in all respects unlike the God of Nature but because, at best, they were merely like, and it was the destiny of that nation to be turned away from likenesses to the thing itself."[154] Hence, there is no internal evidence within the Gospels; likewise there is no direct parallel between the incarnation-resurrection narrative and these echoes and prefigurements (death-descent–rebirth-reascent), which are merely shadows because to Lewis the Christ-event is the reality beyond the shadows, a reality breaking in to redeem: hence Lewis at his most Platonic. Yet, this seed-death-to-rebirth, the "corn kings," are intimations of the wider picture, the worldview of humanity's salvation: in essence, *intimations of the new creation*.

Therefore, for Lewis, death and rebirth is a key principle in the move towards eternity;[155] this issues from a death-descent/rebirth-reascent paradigm and is inscribed into reality so that in death the secret of secrets is hidden.[156] The death-descent and rebirth-reascent paradigm in nature is for Lewis an echo, the theme transposed into a minor key, whereas we find the real theme, the real text or poem as he terms it, in the gospel;[157] this theme transposed into a minor key is also found in the myth of Adonis.[158] Therefore, the theme of death-descent and rebirth-reascent is the imitation of Christ, and is echoed in what is written into the natural world by Christ the creator: pointers to the new creation.[159] At its most explicit it is seen in nature in the myths, folk songs and ballads about the seed dying to be reborn, usually associated with corn/wheat—the seed buried in death to rise up anew the next year.[160] Through the pattern of death and rebirth Christianity transcends the limits of understanding in our conscious minds; the cross-resurrection is a theme unknown to virtually all religious people, especially the significance of it, however, it is the consummation of all religion.[161]

153   Ibid., 121.
154   Ibid.
155   Ibid., 112.
156   See, Lewis, *Mere Christianity*, 154–55; *Miracles*, (1st ed.), 125; also, *Screwtape Letters*, 147.
157   Lewis, *Miracles*, (1st ed.), 130.
158   Lewis, "The Funeral of a Great Myth," 82–93, specifically, 83.
159   Lewis, "Man or Rabbit," 82–84 and 86. See also, Lewis, *Reflections on the Psalms*, 106–7; also, Lewis, *Problem of Pain*, 149. Essentially these ideas can be found in, Lewis, *Miracles*, 1st edition, 98, 111–16, 125, 130 and 161.
160   Lewis, *Miracles*, (1st ed.), 113–15.
161   Lewis, "Religion Without Dogma?," 108–12, essentially, 110.

1. Creation and The Fall I: C. S. Lewis—A Doctrine of Creation

To be born again one must first die. To truly make alive God must kill the creation first. This is a paradox at the heart of the creation and the new creation. This is not just about a mechanistic correction to original sin. God's love desires our wellbeing, desires our recreation. We must accept the *desire* of God to delight in us, to change us, to remake us, to draw us heavenward to eternity. We know this desire of God in us:

> We do not want merely to see beauty, though, God knows, even that is bounty enough. We want something else which can hardly be put into words—to be united with the beauty we see, to pass into it, to receive it into ourselves, to bathe in it, to become part of it. That is why we have peopled air and earth and water with gods and goddesses and nymphs and elves.
>
> For if we take the imagery of Scripture seriously, if we believe that God will one day give us the Morning Star and cause us to put on the splendor of the sun, then we may surmise that both the ancient myths and the modern poetry, so false as history, may be very near the truth as prophecy. At present we are on the outside of the world, the wrong side of the door. We discern the freshness and purity of morning, but they do not make us fresh and pure. We cannot mingle with the splendors we see. But all the leaves of the New Testament are rustling with the rumor that it will not always be so. Someday, God willing, we shall get in.[162]

When we have become as perfect as possible in voluntary obedience, then God will confer that glory which is delight: this is resurrection. But, warns Lewis, the cross comes before the crown, and our neighbor now becomes a holy object presented to our senses, because Christ is hidden in him or her (Matt 25), and how we relate and care for our neighbor defines us in judgment.[163]

iii. Nature and Grace

Lewis noted that in Hooker's doctrine of creation there are few model universes more drenched, for Lewis, with Deity.[164] For Lewis, this relationship between nature and grace could not have a greater priority or importance: this is dialectical (though a supplementary dialectic not a complementary dialectic): revelation is set above reason, the spiritual is superior to the secular. The relationship stands, but the old creation is *subsumed* into the new; this is what resurrection is about, in part. Creation, nature, needs grace; but grace does not need nature, but has use for it. This is in keeping with Hooker's doctrine.[165] Creation prepares the way for grace: the new creation is the fulfillment of the graceful move into creation.

The working of the Spirit of God in the human heart is a marker of the new creation. This Lewis narrates in his three spiritual autobiographies, offering an account of the experience of grace.[166] This reveals, as does Lewis's apologetics, the *enchanted*

---

162 Lewis, "The Weight of Glory," 31.
163 This paradigm of death-descent/rebirth-reascent, and the question of the "corn king" and nature religion in relation to the new creation is dealt with in depth in the second book in this series, *C. S, Lewis—The Work of Christ Revealed*, Ch. 11, 258f.
164 Lewis, *English Literature in the Sixteenth Century*, Bk. 2, Ch. 2, 459.
165 Ibid., 460, quoting Hooker, *Of the Laws of Ecclesiastical Polity*, III. viii, 6.
166 Lewis, *The Pilgrim's Regress* (1933), *Surprised by Joy* (1955), and, *A Grief Observed* (1961)

nature of creation: nature reveals intimations of God. The creation reveals something of God (the Psalms) but this does not necessarily help us in our predicament. Is there value in this? The natural world can lead one way or the other: the world can point to God, or to nothingness, which is why atheistic scientists can read nothing of God from nature. The truth of God can be gleaned from observing and examining the ways in which God has chosen to order the creation? It is our *fallenness* that blinds us. But even then, reading God from creation, from the natural order, does not save us, as the apostle Paul demonstrated (Rom 1:20–32).

8. REBELLION

If *the Christ* is shown to be at the heart of creation, for as we have established, Christ creates, Christ redeems, Christ judges, and Christ initiates the new creation, this being so the rebellion that is the *fall* is equally defining. Creation is, as we have seen, circular: there is a new creation, as explicated in the first chapter of the book of Genesis, in this reality the human is created, humanity is pivotal and responsible, humanity falls, humanity becomes irresponsible, humanity is redeemed through the incarnation-cross-resurrection, which is a new creation (2 Cor 5:17), which will form a new reality: the new Jerusalem, a new heaven and a new earth. World history and evolutionary time may be linear but salvation history is circular, the pivot point being the moment of the death of Jesus on the cross. If the *fall* is so defining and has such profound cosmic implications then we need to examine, in depth, Lewis on a doctrine of original sin.

2

Creation and The Fall II: Lewis's "Augustinian" Account

SYNOPSIS:
Fundamental to Lewis's apologetics and philosophical theology is an orthodox doctrine of the fall. As representative of a doctrine of original sin, based on the biblical story of Eve and Adam's rebellion (Gen 3), we may ask, what exactly is a Christian theological anthropology and why is it relevant? What exactly does the biblical story tell us? We need to examine what exactly Lewis has to say about the *fall*, about original sin. Much of Lewis's doctrine of the fall is derived from his patristic reading—specifically Augustine. After examining the biblical account (Gen and Rom) we can explore Augustine's doctrine of original sin—*the fall*; likewise contemporary influences. What exactly is concupiscence and what role does it play? Acknowledging the fall raises a pertinent question, what was humanity created for and why are we no longer as we were? *Homo incurvatus in se*: humanity is turned in on itself, the human condition before God is now defined by this sin. But what do we understand of original sin? The answers lies in what Lewis wrote about the *fall*, and God's atonement achieved through *his* sacrifice on the cross. Lewis's comments are spread widely throughout his *corpus*, and it is an understanding that does not really change in any substantive manner between the early, middle, and later periods of his work. The *fall* is a foundation block in his apologetics and philosophical theology, consistently.

Lewis's account, and the theology we can read from it, invokes an important distinction between *prelapsarian* humanity, *postlapsarian* humanity, and *redeemed* humanity, defined by the centrality of the corrupting influence of original sin, but also the concept of the *unfallen*, that is, humanity before the fall. Lewis critically deconstructs a doctrine of total depravity, applying his training in logic, concluding that it cannot be so, or we would not be able to perceive it. There is therefore still, for Lewis, some goodness left in humanity, corrupt in manifold ways though the human is through the *fall*, this goodness, in relation to, indeed initiated by, prevenient grace, will give us some perception of what God has done for us: Christ has done all—all we need to do is turn, but can we? Can humanity *still* hold out against God?

1. INTRODUCTION

A fundamental component of Lewis's apologetics and philosophical theology is the *fall*. Central to Lewis, post-conversion, is the Christ: incarnated, crucified, resurrected, and ascended for our salvation. But saved from what? We are saved from *ourselves*. Why? A basic foundation block in Lewis's writings post-conversion, that consistently informs, is the story of humanity's rebellion against God, presented in Genesis 3. It is the reason and proof for the incarnation-cross-resurrection-ascension: Jesus's sacrifice heals and cures, restores humanity's relationship with God: atones. The cross-crucifixion is the answer to the *fall* into original sin. Why?—because only the sacrifice of an innocent individual uncorrupted by original sin will wipe the slate clean, atone, redeem. But what does this ancient mythological story really tell us about humanity? Can we trust it? Many from a scientific, philosophical, or New Atheistic background will dismiss it. So where does the story come from? It is clear that any remembrance generally in humanity of the fall is lost. The story is unique to Judaism. The answer lies in a doctrine of illumination and Scripture. The remembrance of what happened was *revealed*; the remembrance of the salient features of the fall were inspired, illumined, in the faculty of the *imagination*, by the Holy Spirit in the mind of the early Hebrew patriarchs. This understanding was then formulated into mythological language to communicate, and then codified into Scripture, *with the authority* of Scripture.

Therefore, any consideration of Christology generally, Lewis's understanding of *the Christ* specifically, in the context of God's revelation, will be worthless if it is not grounded in an orthodox reading of humanity's *fall* into original sin. Here we need to establish what Lewis wrote, and what he understood constituted a doctrine of the fall.

2. THE FALL: THE BIBLICAL ACCOUNT

The fall, encapsulated in a doctrine of original sin, defines the human condition before God: *prelapsarian* and *postlapsarian*.[1] Lewis subscribed to an orthodox understanding of the fall and original sin, indeed what he says is very much based on Augustine, though as a twentieth-century apologist he does diverge and digress. Why digress?—because he was all too aware that amongst "Liberals" the story of the fall was regarded as a fictional tale that bore no resemblance to humanity as it then knew itself. Furthermore, some regarded the story as simply invented by a ruling elite so as to exercise control over ordinary people (drawing on a Marxist and/or Freudian perspective). We need to examine what is the story in the book of Genesis, but crucially, what exactly a Christian anthropology is, and how this relates to the Christ, and therefore Lewis's Christology.

What is the fall? The fall was about the corruption of the will: the willful decision to eat, metaphorically, of the fruit of the tree of the knowledge of good and evil; the will and knowledge are therefore intertwined. What does Genesis say?—The Lord God *commanded* the creature not to eat from the tree of the knowledge of good and evil, for such would lead to death (Gen 2:16–17). But the creature is beguiled by personified evil—the serpent—which persuades them that death will not come, the eyes of the creature will be opened, they will be enlightened, and they will be like God, knowing good and evil (Gen 3:1–7). They eat. But the knowledge of the "gods" eludes them. The fall generates spiritual blindness, fear, enmity and a broken relationship with the Lord

---

1   The human condition prior to original sin (represented by the biblical picture of Adam and Eve in their pristine creation, obedient and a delight to God) is theologically described as *prelapsarian*, that is, *pre* (before) *lapsarian* (the *fall*, the *lapse*). The human condition after the fall, after original sin, is theologically described here as *postlapsarian*—that is, *post* (after) *lapsarian* (the *fall*, the *lapse*).

2. Creation and The Fall II: Lewis's "Augustinian" Account

God. And so they are banished (Gen 3:8–11 and 22–4). There are three characters in the fall: first, God; second, humanity—Adam and Eve; and third, the serpent (usually taken by Christians to be Satan, the fallen angel, evil personified). The fall is about a doctrine of creation: a creation that corrupts itself. But then the fall is also about a doctrine of redemption. Essentially, the fall was about *disobedience*, the fruit of the tree of the knowledge of good and evil is clearly analogical, a metaphor, which was a test— that humanity failed. The story of the fall tells us what has happened to humanity. We were tempted by evil, complimented and patronized by personified evil, until we gave in and decided to go it alone and try to be like God. The serpent complimented and flattered, beguiled Eve; she *fell*, and then tempted Adam, and he also *fell*. We now make bad decisions, selfish decisions, which we are convinced will be right and will cause affairs to work out right. But it is not just a self-inflicted spiritual corruption and blindness. God judged; and in his justice banished humanity from its previous state, its *prelapsarian* bliss. We were driven out: East of Eden! The names Adam and Eve suggest and refer to universal humanity. Indeed both are representative because the definite article is placed before their names in the Hebrew text (when grammatically the definite article is not used in Hebrew for personal names): hence "the Adam" is as representative of humanity as "the Eve" is in the opening chapters of Genesis. Eating of the fruit of the tree of the knowledge of good and evil represents disobedience, rebellion: don't go this way, says the Lord, go my way; don't decide for yourself. But once we have metaphorically eaten of the fruit of the tree of the knowledge of good and evil there is no stopping humanity. Once humanity develops this *habit* of going it alone it is forced to keep making the decisions for itself, it is forced to keep trying to find the right way through problems and getting it wrong, but defining the wrong way as the right way, *ad infinitum*. Humanity is therefore alienated from God, a situation that gets worse and worse in terms of society and culture, politics and religion, as the generations pass, though humanity on an individual basis remains unchanged—we are no better, no worse, than Adam and Eve's sons and daughters, than the first humans.

The other key scriptural passages in a doctrine of original sin are in the Paul's epistles; these establish the principle of transmission, inheritance: the sin entered through the creature, death dominated; but what was taken in disobedience is countered by God's free gift—Christ's sacrifice: "Therefore just as one man's trespass led to condemnation for all, so one man's act of righteousness leads to justification and life for all. For just as by the one man's disobedience the many were made sinners, so by the one man's obedience the many will be made righteous" (Rom 5:12, 14–19). Somehow the rebellion that was original sin *affects* all that come after. Some might say that this is by association—the children are guilty of the parent's sins—but there is something deeper happening here. The very nature of humanity is changed, thus we *inherit* the propensity for original sin whether we like it or not.

An often overlooked passage in defining the nature of original sin is also to be found in Romans. It concerns the relationship between law, ethics, and the will. Once, *prelapsarian*, we made the right decisions, we behaved appropriately, our will was at one with God, the LORD. We may believe we are master of our own fate that we are in control of our bodies and our lives, but that is something of an illusion. We may believe we have sound aims and objectives in our relationship with others and with the world but this is not so. We can recognize right and wrong, good and evil, but we cannot elect to do one or the other, worse, when we believe we elect for the good, we eventually realize that this was just a selfish charade. As the apostle Paul notes: "I do not understand my own actions. *For I do not do what I want, but I do the very thing I hate.* Now if I do what I do not want, I agree that the law is good. But in fact it is no longer I that do it, but sin that dwells within me. For I know that nothing good dwells within me, that is, in my flesh. *I can will what is right, but I cannot do it. For I do not do the good I want, but the evil I do not want is what I do*" (Rom 7:14–19, also, 7:20–25. My emphasis.)

3. AUGUSTINE'S DOCTRINE

i. A Judeo-Christian Anthropology

The term "fall" is attributed to Augustine of Hippo (354–430): it represents a fundamental change in the nature of humanity, a state of rebellion and disobedience in relation to God. The word "fall" is not in the biblical text; it was coined by Augustine.[2] But it does accurately explain what happened to humanity at some point in the past. Alienation and death result from the fall. But this is a spiritual death; we are no longer in the state we were created in, we are no longer how we should be. Augustine did not invent original sin, but he did codify it into a systematic doctrine, drawing primarily on the Apostle Paul, the book of Genesis, and the early church tradition he has been schooled in, framed by his pre-conversion training as a rhetorician and philosopher.[3] Through his interpretation of Paul's comments in Romans, Augustine asserts that there was a fundamental and irreversible change in the human so that all descendants are born *in sin*; redemption can only come through grace: through one all die (Eve, and Adam), however, all are reborn— *in potential*— through the sacrifice of the one (the Christ).

The understanding of transmission developed slowly during the early church. The Greek Fathers (second and third century, Eastern Mediterranean) asserted humanity was fallen but still had some freedom of will. Thus they did not subscribe to a doctrine of *total depravity*. In the Latin (Roman, Western) church, Cyprian (d. 258AD) and Tertullian (c. 160–225AD), and later Ambrose (c. 340–397), saw human generation as

---

[2] It is of no mere coincidence that the term "the fall" has precedence in the book of Revelation—the fall of Satan: "that ancient serpent called the devil, or Satan, who leads the whole world astray. He was hurled to the earth, and his angels with him" (Rev 12:9).

[3] Augustine's doctrine is reiterated throughout many of his works. The earliest example can be found in, *De Diversis Quaestionibus Ad Simplicianum* (*To Simplician—On Various Questions* 396–97 AD). The main or primary doctrinal analysis is in, *de civitate Dei* (*The City of God*, written after the sacking of Rome in 410 AD by the Visigoths), essentially Bk. XIII. For "original sin", see, Bk. XVI, Ch. 28, 688f. See for "The fall", Bk. XIII, Ch. 1–3, 510–13, Bk. XIII, Ch. 12–15, 522–24, Bk. XIV, Ch. 11–14, 569–75; for the effects of the fall on all mankind, Bk. 13, Ch. 16, 525; for the results of the fall, Bk. XIV, Ch. 14, 575.

the key: original sin was passed on through sexual intercourse. However, Augustine does not see sexual transmission as primary. He argues for a spiritual transmission of sorts. Human free will is compromised but not obliterated. Augustine focuses on, "the fall of the first man, or rather of the first human beings, and the origin and propagation of human mortality."[4] If humanity had continued in obedience they would have shared in the immortality of the angels, "an eternity of bliss."[5] The problem is that although the human soul is immortal it does have a kind of death, asserts Augustine, through sin. If it no longer draws its sustenance from and in God, then it suffers a kind of "second death."[6] Through original sin, the proto-humans are abandoned:

> When God abandons them, for their own life, in virtue of which they are immortal, [they] still persist, in however low degree. But in that last condemnation, although a man does not cease to feel, his feeling is not that of pleasure and delight, nor that of health and tranquility. What he feels is the anguish of punishment, and so his condition is rightly called death rather than life. The second death is so called because it follows the first, in which there is a separation of natures which cohere together, either God and the soul, or the soul and the body.[7]

This second death is where the soul is separated from the body, but cannot unite with God because of its sin, this "death has passed to all mankind through the sin of the first human beings."[8] After the first or original sin, we thereafter sin involuntary, we can no longer control ourselves, but the result is separation, divorce, from God, from the divine life of bliss—*post mortem* this is a grey diminished existence, the insubstantial nihilism of Hades or Sheol.

Augustine places the onus of transmission on the metaphysical; he does not subscribe to the body-mind, or body-soul, dualism, common in the fourth and fifth century. The body was not something to escape from as the Manichees and Platonists would have argued. Augustine may have been ambiguous at some points on the body but he rejected the dualism that declared the body evil. God had created the flesh as well as our minds, and they had been declared good, but were now fallen.[9]

ii. A Roman Catholic and Anglican Perspective

Augustine is considered the father of a doctrine of the fall and original sin. The catechism of the Roman Catholic Church codifies and presents Augustine's doctrine.[10] This is a neat summary of what we are dealing with, which Lewis's writings concur with in all salient points. The catechism asserts that humanity was created in the image of God as a spiritual creature who transcended the laws of creation and the

---

4   Augustine, *The City of God*, Bk. XIII, 510.
5   Ibid.
6   Ibid.
7   Ibid., 511.
8   Ibid., 511–13.
9   See Jenson, *The Gravity of Sin*, 15f.
10 *Catechism of the Catholic Church*, §. 396–402, 89–90.

insurmountable limits defined by its human nature as dependent on God.[11] Tempted by the devil, humanity "let his trust in his Creator die in his heart and, abusing his freedom, disobeyed God's command[;] . . . all subsequent sin would be disobedience toward God and lack of trust in his goodness."[12] Instead of living in a state of holiness whereby humanity would have been fully divinized by God in glory[13] humanity scorned God.[14] Seduced by the devil, the creature wanted to be like God, but without God."[15] Disgraced, Adam and Eve become fearful of God, and invented the image of a jealous god.[16] All are implicated in their sin,[17] leading to the universality of sin and death, countered by the universality of salvation in Christ.[18] This is in essence the doctrine of original sin, the fall, systemized by Augustine over fifteen hundred years earlier, which has stood in Roman Catholic doctrine and in many of the Reformation churches—notably adopted by Luther.[19] Lewis is noted for the influence of Augustine on his understanding of the fall, and how his position is close to that of the Roman Catholic Church.

In the case of Lewis's Church of England, the doctrine is stated succinctly in "The Thirty-Nine Articles." These articles of religion were established in the later sixteenth century during the reign of Elizabeth I, and are often considered to be part of the so-called Elizabethan compromise. As such they are considered to be the defining statement of the Church of England. They established Anglican doctrine and belief, as distinct from Puritanism, continental Protestants and Reformers, and specifically from Roman Catholicism, however, the three articles dealing with the *fall* differ in no substantive manner from Augustine. The Thirty-Nine Articles have been in the *Book of Common Prayer* since their publication,[20] and state that original sin "standeth not in the following of Adam (as the Pelagians do vainly talk), but it is the fault and corruption of the nature of every man that naturally is engendered of the offspring of Adam, whereby man is very far gone from original righteousness, and is of his own nature inclined to evil, so that the flesh lusteth always contrary to the spirit; and therefore in every person born into this world, it deserveth God's wrath and damnation."[21] This corruption continues in the regenerate—those who have turned to Christ.[22] The corruption is such that humanity cannot of its own volition turn: "we have no power to do good works pleasant and acceptable to God, without the grace

---

11   Ibid., §. 396, 89.
12   Ibid., §. 397, 89. Referring to Gen 3:1–11 and Rom 5:19.
13   Ibid., §. 397–98.
14   Ibid., §. 398.
15   Ibid., §. 398. Referring to Gen 3:5
16   Ibid., §. 398. Referring to Gen 3:5–10 and Rom 3:23.
17   Ibid., §. 402. Quoting Rom 5:12 and 19.
18   Ibid., §. 402. Quoting Rom 5:12 and 19.
19   In all but the smallest of details the Reformation churches adopted Augustine's doctrine.
20   For an online text see: http://www.churchofengland.org/prayer-worship/worship/book-of-common-prayer/articles-of-religion.aspx.
21   Ibid., §. "IX. Of Original or Birth Sin."
22   Ibid.

2. Creation and The Fall II: Lewis's "Augustinian" Account

of God."[23] However, we are righteous before God through Christ by faith, "and not for our own works or deservings."[24]

Augustine and the "Articles" concur: we willfully brought about our condition; this status is ontological, it has changed the very nature of our being. Further, we cannot save ourselves, we cannot undo the effects of original sin, we rely on prevenient grace to be able to do any good. Only by the sacrifice of Jesus Christ can we become acceptable before God. Perhaps here there is a difference given the pre-Reformation Roman Catholic Church's emphasis on works earning redemption (article XI).

iii. Concupiscence

Augustine places a heavy emphasis on the spiritual and how the spirit *drives* the flesh. Is this a form of dualism?—a separation of the spirit and the flesh? Jesus's conversation with Nicodemus would appear to concur, to a degree: "Flesh gives birth to flesh, but the Spirit gives birth to spirit" (John 3:6). Likewise, "The Spirit gives life; the flesh counts for nothing. The words I have spoken to you are spirit and they are life" (John 6:63). Drawing on Romans 8, The Church of England "Articles" refer to φρονημα τῆς σαρκός (*phronema tēs sarkos*), sensuality, fleshly desire, carnality (Rom 8:5–11). The mind-spirit that is set on the flesh, fleshly desire (not just carnality), which in some ways can be interpreted as the genetically-driven survival instincts, self-interest in many ways, such a mind-spirit characterizes and defines original sin. This notwithstanding Augustine does not condemn the flesh as evil, but corrupted by the spirit: sin is spiritual. Augustine's emphasis is not on human generation, sex, but on *concupiscence*. Augustine does not see sexual transmission as primary; he argues for a spiritual transmission of sorts: metaphysical concupiscence. The flesh born is corrupted by the human spirit. Concupiscence is *spiritual desire*, the aim and direction of the will. Certain behavior (often sexual practices) may be considered revolting to contemplate by some people, yet others regard them as holy and marvelous: a dark force, animated and conscious, beguiles and seduces, flatters and corrupts, whispers thoughts into the minds of men and women, a dark strength that willfully deludes. A person finds it can do something, an act or action that initially it might have regarded as repugnant, even abominable; then it finds it enjoys this act, then it realizes it can no longer stop doing it, such a person then develops justification for this act, even religious theories to justify such fallen willfulness: such an action is so often abuse or perversion, whether physically violent or sexual. Therefore, as sexual desire, concupiscence becomes lust, disordered and deviant, perverse practices (paraphilia). As with the body, concupiscence is not created sinful but becomes wrongly directed. To an extent, Lewis's use/misuse of *Sehnsucht*, prior to his conversion, was an example of this misdirection of spiritual energies, this longing, a yearning for somebody or something, for Lewis this was a sudden stab, a yearning, a craving, an ache, that caught him unawares, but the moment he recognized its presence *it* had gone, dissipated. He

---

23 Ibid., §. "X. Of Free Will."
24 Ibid., §. "XI. Of the Justification of Man."

wrote at length about how he tried to cultivate it, he sought it, tried to reproduce the circumstances of its brief appearance. *Sehnsucht* was, for the pre-conversion Lewis, a wounding disabling, a craving with almost mystical qualities where the experience of *Sehnsucht* itself replaces the object of desire. This was in many ways the Holy Spirit pressing upon Lewis to convict an individual of sin, where the Spirit begins to draw the person out of itself and into a new God-ward life in Christ; this would apply whether the person has access to explicit knowledge of Jesus Christ or not, and is the action of the Holy Spirit pressing on an individual. Lewis's response was painful, disabling and sinful, it was spiritual force and energies misdirected. Hence, *concupiscence*, spiritual desire, corrupted and turned in on itself.

4. *HOMO INCURVATUS IN SE*: WHAT DOES LEWIS HAVE TO SAY?

Before he commenced upon his career in apologetics, Lewis had spent much of the seven to eight years after his conversion reading widely and in-depth, essentially patristic theologians and especially, from 1937, Augustine's *The City of God* (*de civitate Dei*): "Lewis had Augustine's original Latin under his reading lamp several times between 1937 and 1944 when he wanted authority for his understanding of Christian beliefs. It may be said of Lewis's characteristically metaphorical and lucid explanations that no one before him ever translated Augustine into English so precisely, if by translation we mean not a crib or a full rendition, but a meaningful appropriation."[25] Lewis's understanding of the *fall* is orthodox. His main work on it—*The Problem of Pain*—was written early on, in the wake of studying Augustine's *Confessions* in 1936 and *The City of God* in 1937, both in the original Latin (then study-translating the latter from 1937–44). We can therefore identify and extract the salient details and material to constitute an orthodox doctrine of the fall and original sin from Lewis's writings, written by Lewis very much in an Augustinian framework: *homo incurvatus in se*—humanity, literally, curved in on itself, turned away from God, focusing on its selfish needs and defining reality in its own image.

i. *The Fall . . . and the Unfallen*

So what did Lewis have to say? The term *fall* is, for Lewis, the changeover, the alteration, characterized by a fundamental ontological[26] shift of the first humans into a state of guilt-driven insubordination, a condition of defiance, rebellion and disobedience, that is, *before* God, in relation to the divine creator. Prior to the fall humanity lived in bliss, in a state of innocent obedience *with* God. Derived from Genesis 3, but primarily from

---

25 Ross, "C. S. Lewis, Augustine, and Rhythm of the Trinity," 4–5. Lewis read in depth Augustine's *confessiones* (*Confessions*) in 1936, and *de civitate Dei* in 1937, both in the original Latin, returning to them over the next decade, as well as translating *de civitate Dei* himself. See, Lewis writing to Dom Bede Griffiths, April 24, 1936; and, Lewis writing to Dom Bede Griffiths, May 23 1936. Lewis, *Collected Letters Vol. II*, 187–90 and 191–95.

26 This is ontological because it is something that happens to the very nature of being that is humanity in and before God: essentially this is spiritual and physical.

2. Creation and The Fall II: Lewis's "Augustinian" Account

Paul's epistles, Lewis's doctrine asserts that an essential change in the very nature of humanity is that all people are now born with the sin of Eve, and Adam, they are born with the *result* of their sin. Redemption is through prevenient grace issuing from the cross; for Lewis, as with Augustine, Jesus was the innocent sinless victim: sacrifice equates with redemption. In the Augustinian tradition all mainstream churches assert that the *fall* corrupted not just the human but also the entire natural world, thus causing Eve and Adam's descendants to be born *in* original sin, thus denying them communion with God and eternal life in heaven: grace not so much restores as renews. Lewis draws heavily from Augustine, essentially through his reading of *The City of God*. Humanity is trapped between the fall and the unfallen: we fell *with* Adam and Eve, we suffer, we wallow, in our lapsed state, but we still have a glimmer of a memory of *prelapsarian* bliss, but also a realization that we should not be like this. We are held in a tension between the fall and the unfallen, between the *prelapsarian* and the *postlapsarian*, and as such there is an unresolved tension in us as the yet to be redeemed.

ii. postlapsarian: The Fallen

At the heart of theology and any understanding of the human condition is, as Lewis reiterates essentially from the creeds, "the Creation, the Fall, the Incarnation, the Resurrection, the Second Coming, and the Four Last Things."[27] One thing leads to another: created free will leads to the fall; the fall leads to the need for redemption and salvation—the atonement; the atonement leads to the second coming, to the *eschaton*: death, judgment, heaven, and hell. Humanity, through its own fault, and out of willfulness, *fell* through disobedience. The implications of the fall are universal, original sin affects all humanity, not just Eve and Adam.

Lewis notes how it is important to remember that the unfallen, the fallen, and the redeemed are not the same thing; the third is not a reproduction of the first; we may live in the *postlapsarian* state, but we do not live to reclaim the unfallen (*prelapsarian*) state but to move on to the redeemed stage.[28] Therefore Lewis notes how not everything that results from the fall is bad—after all, redemption issues from it.[29] Furthermore, however much the story in Genesis is couched in mythological language, this does not detract from the truth of the human condition, the turning of the fall into myth happened long after the initial event.[30]

It is important to note, wrote Lewis, that the fall is part of Christian beliefs; indeed it is central to Christian doctrine.[31] Science should have no objection to the fall being

---

27 Lewis writing to *The Church Times*, Feb. 8, 1952. Lewis, *Collected Letters Vol. III*, 164.
28 Lewis writing to Michael Edwards, Oct 20, 1956. Lewis, *Collected Letters Vol. III*, 799–800. Lewis uses the term "unfallen" for the prelapsarian human, but also, significantly, for the hypothetical sentient creatures in other worlds who resisted the temptation of original sin and are thus "unfallen". For example, the inhabitants of Malacandra (*Out of the Silent Planet*, 1938) and Perelandra (*Perelandra*, 1943).
29 Lewis writing to Michael Edwards, June 27, 1958. Lewis, *Collected Letters Vol. III*, 959.
30 Lewis writing to Wayne Shumaker, March 21, 1962. Lewis, *Collected Letters Vol. III*, 1324.
31 Lewis, *Broadcast Talks*, 37–40.

central to Christian doctrine; for Lewis the doctrine of the fall and the doctrine of evolution are not related in any important way:

> There is no relation of any importance between the fall and evolution. The doctrine of evolution is that organisms have changed, sometimes for what we call (biologically) the better . . . quite often for what we call (biologically) the worse. . . . The doctrine of the fall is that at one particular point one species, man, tumbled down a moral cliff. There is neither opposition nor support between the two doctrines[;] . . . evolution is not only not a doctrine of *moral* improvements, but of biological changes, some improvements, some deteriorations.[32]

Again, from a scientific perspective, Lewis notes that the question of whether the eating of the fruit in the story of the fall in Genesis actually happened is a spurious question. It is irrelevant. Eating tells us nothing of the reality of the human condition, it is the description of the fruit of the tree of the knowledge of good and evil that informs.[33] That the early, proto, human was different is without doubt: "We do not know how many of these creatures God made, nor how long they continued in the paradisal state. But sooner or later they fell. Someone or something whispered that they could become as gods—that they could cease directing their lives to their Creator."[34] So how important is this turning. We can judge by our present condition and by human history:

> This act of self-will on the part of the creature, which constitutes an utter falseness to its true creaturely position, is the only sin that can be conceived as the fall. For the difficulty about the first sin is that it must be very heinous, or its consequences would not be so terrible, and yet it must be something which a being free from the temptations of fallen man could conceivably have committed. The turning from God to self, this fulfills both conditions. It is a sin possible even to Paradisal man, because the mere existence of a self—the mere fact that we call it "me"—includes, from the first, the danger of self-idolatry. Since I am I, I must make an act of self-surrender, however small or however easy, in living to God rather than to myself.[35]

Therefore, asserts Lewis, in the face of nature and the condemnation of God for its fall, the will of man had no resource but to force back, to suppress, through sheer strength of will, the new thoughts and desires arising from the tidal wave of mere nature, simply to cope with being on its own: aloneness and the responsibility for itself, divorced from God, was overwhelming.[36] The effects of the fall are variable, as variable as human nature is, thus Lewis will assert that the fall did not deprave our knowledge of the law in the same degree as it depraved our power to fulfill it.[37] However, the fall became a

---

32   Lewis writing to Miss Breckenridge, Aug 1, 1949. Lewis, *Collected Letters Vol. II*, 962. See also, Lewis, *Problem of Pain*, 57.
33   Lewis, *Problem of Pain*, 61f.
34   Ibid., 60–61.
35   Ibid., 62.
36   Ibid., 65.
37   Lewis, "The Poison of Subjectivism," 79.

2. Creation and The Fall II: Lewis's "Augustinian" Account

manifestation of divine goodness and righteousness, painful though the moment of existence was for humanity in its rebellion.[38]

Lewis comments that the first sin is described by Augustine as the result of the fall: pride; which is where the creature tries to set up on its own.[39] Regarding Paul's Epistles and Augustine's doctrine, the story of the fall from Genesis is an example of a true account of humanity phrased in mythological language, which is then formulated into systematic theology. Both are true, but represent the truth in different ways.[40] Lewis is responding to comments about Milton, and is at pains to stress that the myth-making process (Genesis) through to the sophistication of Milton (*Paradise Lost*) happened in both cases long after the actual event. The Genesis story of the fall is written as a scriptural myth: the fruit of knowledge in Genesis (Lewis cites "magic apple") becomes "in the developed doctrine . . . simply one of disobedience."[41] The doctrine quite correctly asserts for Lewis that the fall of man happened because he tried to set up on his own.[42] The fall of man created conflict between spirit and nature which causes disintegration and death of the body; Christ's death is the remedy.[43]

Since the fall, because of the ontological nature of original sin, no organization or way of life has an innate propensity to be successful or true before God.[44] Lewis is a Christian realist on this count, and he sails against the pietistic popular religion of both Roman Catholics and establishment Anglicans in the mid-twentieth century:

> Since the fall no organization or way of life whatever has a natural tendency to go right. In the Middle Ages some people thought that if only they entered a religious order they would find themselves automatically becoming holy and happy. . . . In the nineteenth century some people thought that monogamous family life would automatically make them holy and happy; the savage anti-domestic literature of modern times—the Samuel Butlers, the Gosses, the Shaws—delivered the answer. . . . Both family life and monastic life were often detestable, and it should be noticed that the serious defenders of both are well aware of the dangers and free of the sentimental illusion[;] . . . domesticity is no passport to heaven on earth but an arduous vocation—a sea full of hidden rocks and perilous ice shores only to be navigated by one who uses a celestial chart. That is the first point on which we must be absolutely clear. The family, like the nation, can be offered to God, can be converted and redeemed, and will then become the channel of particular blessings and graces. But, like everything else that is human, it needs redemption. Unredeemed, it will produce only

---

38 Lewis, *Problem of Pain*, 65.
39 Ibid., 57–58.
40 Lewis writing to Wayne Shumaker, March 21, 1962. Lewis, *Collected Letters Vol. III*, 1323–24.
41 Lewis, *Problem of Pain*, 54.
42 Lewis, *Broadcast Talks*, Series II "What Christians Believe," 3rd talk, "The Shocking Alternative", Feb 1, 1942, 46–51.
43 Lewis, *Miracles*, 31–32.
44 Lewis, "The Sermon and the Lunch," originally written for *The Church of England Newspaper*, published on Sept 21, 1945. Reprinted with some variance in *Undeceptions* (1971). All references are to this subsequent edition.

particular temptations, corruptions, and miseries. Charity begins at home: so does uncharity.[45]

We are all fallen and thus find it difficult to live together, to co-exist, writes Lewis,[46] therefore turning to God is difficult and a hurtful experience after the fall, the move contradicts humanity's selfish tendency.[47] Lewis may therefore ask, was the fall in accordance with the will of God?[48] He is loath to go down the *felix culpa* ("happy fault") path even though this is at the heart of the Augustinian doctrine because of the pain and suffering that comes out of the fall; we should look to the future, the solution in the atonement. Lewis quite categorically sees the human in teleological movement, that is, where is it going, what is its τέλος (*telos*, its ultimate object or aim, the point aimed at). We cannot return to a state of *prelapsarian* innocence, there is no going back to the garden; there is no *apokatastasis* (from theological Greek: ἀποκατάστασις; there is no reconstitution or restitution, no restoration to the original condition, no homecoming to the primordial). We move forward, and the way forward and our τέλος is in Christ who has opened up the way ahead of us. The redeemed state will not be the same as the *prelapsarian*. Humanity's habitual gravitation away from God and toward self is a product of the fall and there is nothing joyous or good about this, asserts Lewis, quite correctly.[49] Fallen humanity is not only characterized by imperfection, "spoiled" is a word Lewis invokes, but also we are each a rebel "who must lay down his gun, his arms."[50] What Lewis concentrates on is the debilitating and corrupting effect of the fall. The fall generated pride and ambition, selfish admiration, envy driven insecurity.[51] It is important, notes Lewis, that the fall of humanity was not the result of sexual corruption; however, we are correct to interpret Genesis as insinuating that sexual corruption issues *from* the fall.[52] The inheritance bequeathed by the fall is spiritual death: true immortality becomes hopeless—Sheol, Hades, a diminished grey nihilistic existence is the spiritual death that the fall generates, *post mortem*, in humanity:[53] "According to the doctrine, man is now a horror to God and to himself and a creature ill-adapted to the universe not because God made him so but because he has made himself so by the abuse of his free will."[54]

---

[45] Lewis, "The Sermon and the Lunch," (1945), 235.
[46] Lewis writing to Mary Willis Shelburne, Nov 8, 1962. *Collected Letters Vol. III*, 1379.
[47] Lewis, *Problem of Pain*, 63.
[48] Lewis, *Mere Christianity* II 3, 39–40.
[49] Lewis, *Problem of Pain*, 63–65.
[50] Lewis, *Mere Christianity* II 4, 46–47.
[51] Lewis, *Problem of Pain*, 63.
[52] Lewis, *Mere Christianity* II 3, 40f. Is not all human sexuality perverted, to a greater or lesser degree, after the fall?
[53] Lewis *Miracles* (2nd ed.), 165–66.
[54] Lewis, *Problem of Pain*, 52.

2. Creation and The Fall II: Lewis's "Augustinian" Account

iii. prelapsarian: The Unfallen

The story of the fall is central to Christianity, to the Christian world view.[55] Take it away and, as we have established, the incarnation-cross becomes superfluous.[56] At the heart of the story of the fall is rebellion. But this is so because of a doctrine of creation: humanity was made, created by God, in a certain way, a certain characteristic human nature defined us. But no longer. We contradict creation. We are not as we were; and we do not look after creation as God intended us to.[57] This does not deny that God created, and looked on creation and decided it was good. A doctrine of creation is intimately intertwined with a doctrine of the fall. Lewis does not see a developed doctrine of creation outside the Judaist-Christian-Islamic religious tradition, which weakens any claim to the truth that other religions have. Paganism, for Lewis, includes a proto-doctrine of the fall, something of a realization that things are not right with humanity, that we are not as created, but this does not form a systematic doctrine.[58] What is more, many North European Pagan myths, which Lewis knew well, see the solution to the human condition in human self-strength (which merely makes the situation worse). There was therefore a time when we were unfallen, we were as God created, as God intended. Lewis will then ask if the fall of humanity is unique in the universe.[59] Speculatively, we may ask, are there sentient creatures, other rational beings, in the universe (or in other worlds, universes, creations, outside and beyond what we take for the universe), pertinently, the question is, are they fallen and how does redemption work for them, or does humanity's redemption affect them? Or perhaps they are unfallen, they resisted temptation, asserts Lewis.[60]

There is, for Lewis, no return to the original form. However, redeemed humanity is to be something more glorious than unfallen, *prelapsarian*, humanity had been.[61] Adam as the archetype, the form of humanity, *prelapsarian*, would Lewis argues appear as a savage, but also holier than all we know: "the holiest among us would soon fall at his feet."[62] Yet we inherit his, and Eve's, sin; we are intimately involved in their original sin . . . we are members of a "*spoiled* species."[63] As the archetypal humans turned from

---

55 Lewis, *Broadcast Talks*, 37–40.
56 There is a proposition in the early church that states that Christ would have come anyway, been incarnated as one of us even if humanity had not fallen. This proposition is often associated with Irenaeus (died 202 AD), and argues that Christ would have come to complete our humanity in relation to the divine.
57 Genesis 1:28. However, in our custodianship humanity has defiled and destroyed the earth—an ability that issues from the scientific and technological nature of the so-called Enlightenment. There are many of the more fundamentalist environmentalists who now regard humanity as a disease, a virus, which is destroying the world, the biosphere that is the earth.
58 Lewis "Some Thoughts," 117.
59 Lewis *Miracles* (2nd ed.), 128–30
60 Lewis, "The World's Last Night," 86–88. Lewis deals with this question in-depth in his Space Trilogy—specifically *Out of the Silent Planet* and *Perelandra*. This will be examined in the next part of this volume on Lewis's use of narrative.
61 Lewis, *Miracles* (2nd ed. 1960), 128. This is a development on from a sermon preached in the church of St Jude-on-the-Hill, London, published in The Guardian, April 27, 1945.
62 Lewis, *Problem of Pain*, 61.
63 Ibid., 66–67.

God to self we share this condemnation also.⁶⁴ Consideration of God came first in the thoughts and love of unfallen humanity, without, as Lewis terms it, "painful effort,"⁶⁵ for the service of God was the "keenest pleasure" of *prelapsarian* blissful obedience.⁶⁶ This characteristic self-surrender of *prelapsarian* humanity came naturally, it was what the human was created for, therefore there would have been no struggle for the unfallen, but only "a delicious overcoming of an infinitesimal self-adherence which delighted to be overcome."⁶⁷ Essentially the turning from God to self-interest, Lewis speculates, was the *prelapsarian* becoming aware of God as distinct from self: "From the moment a creature becomes aware of God as God and of itself as self, the terrible alternative of choosing God or self for the center is opened to it. This sin is committed daily by young children and ignorant peasants as well as by sophisticated persons, by solitaries no less than by those who live in society: it is the fall in every individual life."⁶⁸

iv. lapsarian: Original Sin

The decision to turn from God to self in proto-humans is termed original sin; but the name also applies to the inherited tendency and predilection to prioritize self above everything else, including God, in humanity today, a condition which is inherited and renders humanity true to type. Lewis deals with a doctrine of original sin in chapter 5 of *The Problem of Pain* (1940). He comments that, "If, none the less, I call our present condition one of original sin, and not merely one of original misfortune, that is because our religious experience does not allow us to regard it in any other way."⁶⁹ This clearly issues from free will, the creature was created with the ability to decide, thus it was possible to make the wrong decision, but the creature was not created inherently fallen. Lewis is right, other sentient creatures in creation *may not* have fallen, therefore, Lewis can comment, "I'm not saying . . . that evil is inherent in finitude. That would identify the creation with the fall and make God the author of evil. But perhaps there is an anguish, an alienation, a crucifixion involved in the creative act. Yet he who alone can judge judges the far-off consummation to be worth it."⁷⁰ The desires and abilities that the creature was created with do not necessarily point to evil, or lead inevitably to the fall. What was once good becomes corrupted: "Pleasure," wrote Lewis, "was then an acceptable offering to God because offering was a pleasure. But we inherit a whole system of desires which do not necessarily contradict God's will but which, after centuries of usurped autonomy, steadfastly ignore it."⁷¹ So, *prelapsarian*, there was no distinction between the pleasure of God's will, and the pleasure of our will in responding. However, *postlapsarian*, the will works differently. Lewis continues—

---

64 Ibid., 114–15. See also, for Lewis's speculation on the proto-human, ibid., 64–65.
65 Ibid., 59–61.
66 Ibid., 79–80.
67 Ibid., 62–63. For Lewis speculation about *prelapsarian* humanity see also, ibid., Ch. 5, esp., 59f.
68 Ibid., 57.
69 Ibid., 66.
70 Lewis, *Letters to Malcolm*, 42.
71 Lewis, *Problem of Pain*, 59.

2. Creation and The Fall II: Lewis's "Augustinian" Account

> If the thing we like doing is, in fact, the thing God wants us to do, yet that is not our reason for doing it, it remains a mere happy coincidence. We cannot therefore know that we are acting at all, or primarily, for God's sake, unless the material of the action is contrary to our inclinations, or (in other words) painful, and what we cannot know that we are choosing, we cannot choose. The full acting out of the self's surrender to God therefore demands pain: this action, to be perfect, must be done from the pure will to obey, in the absence, or in the teeth, of inclination. How impossible it is to enact the surrender of the self by doing what we like . . ."[72]

The key to original sin in humanity lies in an action being contrary to our inclinations and our will; to contemplate or do what is contrary to our fallen willful inclinations is, inevitably, painful, it is a form of mental anguish. It is our misuse of the gift of decision-making, free will, and not necessarily desire, that causes the fall and in consequence the hereditary nature of original sin, and this *postlapsarian struggle to overcome the wrong decision*. Though Jesus was sinless it was the sheer weight of this mental anguish, wrestling as he did over the will to run away from the path of martyrdom and self-sacrifice, that is most characteristic of Jesus's agony in the Garden of Gethsemane.

For Lewis any consideration of original sin in the contemporary context becomes complex, certain details are relevant to all, other details and beliefs are not. He notes how the doctrine of the immaculate conception (that Mary was born free of original sin) is peculiar to Roman Catholicism, and that it "does not concern us at all."[73] Original sin is ever present despite the atonement wrought for us by Jesus on the cross: "war cannot be eliminated until original sin is eliminated."[74] Original sin means that when we try to solve a problem we will so often make matters worse and seek to remedy one sin with a worse sin. For example, Lewis notes how, "It is certainly not wrong to try to remove the natural consequences of sin, provided the means by which you remove them are not in themselves another sin. (E.g., it is merciful and Christian to remove the natural consequences of fornication by giving the girl a bed in a maternity ward and providing for the child's keep and education, but wrong to remove them by abortion or infanticide.)"[75] When asked about whether original sin was simply a mythical explanation for bad thinking Lewis wrote back to one person that, "No. I don't think sin is completely accounted for by faulty reasoning, nor that it can be completely cured by re-education . . . our will is not necessarily determined by our reason. If it were, then, as you say, what are called 'sins' would not be sins at all but only mistakes, and would require not repentances but merely correction."[76] Speculation is not as important as many would think. Reasoning likewise will not cure us however well we understand original sin. What is important is that we move

---

72   Ibid.
73   Lewis writing to Genia Goelz, June 13, 1951. Lewis, *Collected Letters Vol. III*, 126.
74   Lewis writing to Jane Douglass, Dec 21, 1954. Lewis, *Collected Letters Vol. III*, 545.
75   Lewis writing to Mary Van Deusen, Feb 7, 1951. Lewis, *Collected Letters Vol. III*, 91.
76   Lewis writing to Elsie Snickers, May 18, 1953. Lewis, *Collected Letters Vol. III*, 329–30.

from an intellectual assent that Christ has forgiven us, to a realization that our sins are forgiven.[77]

5. A DOCTRINE OF TOTAL DEPRAVITY

Realistic though Lewis is about the inherently, and inherited, perilous state of humanity, Lewis does not necessarily subscribe to a doctrine of total depravity—for purely logical reasons. A doctrine of total depravity, often referred to as "total corruption" or "absolute inability," is derived from Augustine's understanding of original sin whereby we are all enslaved to sin and are incapable of choosing the good from our own state, fallen as we are: the only good we can do is through God's grace working in us. Humanity through original sin can no longer *wholly* love God, and so often what we define as the good is merely self-centered protectionism. Augustine countered a doctrine of total depravity with an understanding of the reality of prevenient grace: any true good that we do will issue from the graceful action of the Holy Spirit working in us, preveniently (prior) to our own selfish thoughts and intentions.

i. An Inverted Understanding

Lewis understood total depravity, and acknowledged the historical reality of the fall and its manifold ramifications on and in humanity, but he stops short of endorsing a doctrine of *total* corruption such as to blind humanity to its condition. Lewis commented that,

> On the other hand, if God's moral judgment differs from ours so that our "black" may be his "white," we can mean nothing by calling him good; for to say that "God is good," while asserting that his goodness is wholly other than ours, is really only to say "God is we know not what." . . . If he is not (in our sense) "good" we shall obey . . . an omnipotent fiend. The doctrine of total depravity—when the consequence is drawn that, since we are totally depraved, our idea of good is worth simply nothing—may turn Christianity into a form of devil-worship."[78]

Therefore, we must take care not to utterly condemn our concept of goodness, for if we do, we invert God: the word good in itself becomes meaningless, God's promises become cruelty, the reality of the intimations of heaven *become* hell.[79] However, if through our faith we have a relatively sound idea of God's transcendence, through our *reasoned* reception of *revelation* we can intimate something of the truth of God and God's dealings with us; if this is so then we need to temper a doctrine of *total* depravity. If we do not, then the risks lead to a flawed understanding of God, which contradicts revelation.

The comments quoted above were written at the beginning of Lewis's career as an apologist, published in 1940. Here, writing twenty years later and written only a few

---

77 Lewis writing to Mrs D. Jessup, 5 Feb, 1954. Lewis, *Collected Letters Vol. III*, 425. See also, Lewis writing to Mary Willis Shelburne, Apr 15, 1958. Lewis, *Collected Letters Vol. III*, 935.
78 Lewis, *Problem of Pain*, 23. Comments repeated by Lewis in "The Poison of Subjectivism", 79.
79 Ibid., 29f.

2. Creation and The Fall II: Lewis's "Augustinian" Account

years before his death, and in the light of his wife's death from cancer, his understanding is relatively unchanged. He comments—

> [Could one] seriously introduce the idea of a bad God, as it were by the back door, through a sort of extreme Calvinism? You could say we are fallen and depraved. We are so depraved that our ideas of goodness count for nothing; or worse than nothing—the very fact that we think something good is presumptive evidence that it is really bad. Now God has in fact—our worse fears are true—all the characteristics we regard as bad: unreasonableness, vanity, vindictiveness, injustice, cruelty. But all these blacks (as they seem to us) are really whites. It's only our depravity makes them look black to us.[80]

Simply recognizing and defining the perilous state of humanity that issues from the fall will not necessarily give a right judgment; secularists (Lewis cites Freudians in this context) can offer little if such ideology leads not to an acceptance in "Christian humility" of Christ's atoning forgiveness, but only to despair and a veiled hatred of self: "Even Christians, if they accept in certain forms the doctrine of total depravity, are not always free from the danger."[81] Furthermore we must not ignore what Jesus had to say relating to such a matter:

> I think the doctrine of the goodness of God is the more certain of the two. Indeed only that doctrine renders this worship of *him* obligatory or even permissible.
>
> To this some will reply, "Ah but we are fallen and don't recognize good when we see it." But God himself does not say we are as fallen as all that. *He* constantly, in Scripture, appeals to our conscience: "Why do ye not of yourselves judge what is right?"*—"What fault hath my people found in me?"+ and so on.
>
> Socrates' answer to Euthyphro is used in Christian form by Hooker. Things are not good because God commands them; God commands certain things because he sees them to be good.[82]

Lewis notes how much modern theology "protests against an excessively moralistic interpretation of Christianity,"[83] and that there is a degree of truth in this, as God's claim on us is "something more and other than the claim of moral duty."[84] But this observation can be used as an evasion; Lewis notes that "the road to the promised land runs past Sinai."[85] The moral law exists to be transcended. However, to transcend we must first admit the claim that natural law has upon us, and thereby acknowledge our failure to meet it: moral law equates with the will of God—what God wants for us, what we were created for. So-called badness is not an evolutionary hangover, asserts Lewis, from nature: "Now Christianity, if I have understood the Pauline epistles, does admit that perfect obedience to the moral law . . . is not in fact possible."[86] Is this yet

---

80   Lewis, *A Grief Observed*, 28.
81   Lewis, "Two Ways with the Self", 55.
82   Lewis writing to John Beversluis, July 3, 1963. Lewis, *Collected Letters Vol. III.*, 1437. Lewis is quoting, *: Luke 12:57, and, +: Jer 2:5.
83   Lewis, *Problem of Pain*, Ch. 4, 49.
84   Ibid.
85   Ibid.
86   Ibid., 50.

more evasion, for Lewis? Lewis does attribute a certain degree of moral responsibility, decision making, to the human. We need to recognize and accept that we are not what we were created for; we cannot act and be as intended. The moral law, natural law, is a measure of this. But this should lead not to desperation and self-hatred. We simply need to accept the grace and forgiveness offered by God in and through Christ—accept the *prevenient* action of how God will change us. This is sanctification, and it may be painful to our egos. If we still fall short we must ask ourselves why? In so doing Lewis quotes William Law: "If you ask yourselves why you are not as pious as the primitive [early] Christians were, your own heart will tell you, that it is neither through ignorance nor inability, but purely because you never thoroughly intended it."[87] There is therefore a degree of sound judgment about our condition that allows us to reason out and get a balanced view of the crisis of our existence, which should not—for the Christian—lead to despair. This reasoned-out, balanced, understanding is through revelation, through prevenient (prior) grace. Therefore Lewis is moving towards something of the reality of a doctrine of total depravity. He outlines this in the fourth chapter of *The Problem of Pain*—but not as a verbatim reaffirmation and endorsement of the doctrine from the Reformed-Calvinist tradition: "This chapter will have been misunderstood if anyone describes it as a reinstatement of the doctrine of total depravity. I disbelieve that doctrine, partly on the logical ground that if our depravity were total we should not know ourselves to be depraved, and partly because experience shows us much goodness in human nature. Nor am I recommending universal gloom."[88]

So who is right? Or is Lewis missing something even in his logic? Yes we are subject, as the Reformed-Calvinistic doctrine asserts, to a form of depravity that is *total*, we can no longer know truly what is right and wrong; but Lewis is right to assert that there is much goodness in human nature. So what generates this goodness if we have lost the ability through total depravity to make a sound judgment? Despite the fall, that goodness issues from the prevenient action (i.e., *prior* to any decision we take for the good, or any recognition of the good), the grace imbued often secretively into the human, *by the Holy Spirit*. Without prevenient grace that goodness that Lewis identifies would not exist. Is the prevenient action of the Holy Spirit universal? According to Lewis yes, it is *in potential* universal.

ii. A Doctrine of Limited, or Pseudo-Depravity

The Holy Spirit will act on us all, but people respond in different ways, in differing degrees. Lewis's atonement theory is inherently Arminian[89]—humanity can hold out

---

87 Ibid., 23. Lewis is quoting from the English cleric, divine, and theological and spiritual writer, William Law (1686–1761), his, *A Serious Call to a Devout and Holy Life and The Way to Divine Knowledge*, Ch. 2, 10.

88 Lewis, *Problem of Pain*, Ch. 4, 50. A Calvinist-Reformed understanding is grounded in Calvin,'s *Institutes*, Bk. II, Ch. 1, §. 8.

89 Jacob Arminius (1560–1609) professor in theology, University of Leiden, whose views on atonement became known as Arminianism.

against God. If humanity could not hold out against God, we would never have fallen in the first place! An analysis of Lewis's neo-Arminian atonement theory will be in the last part of this volume and series,[90] however, a brief understanding of Arminianism in terms of how it effects Lewis doctrine of limited, or pseudo, total depravity, and thereby his understanding of the fall and original sin, is needed. According to Classical Arminianism depravity is total, but atonement is intended for all because Jesus's death was for all people. Jesus draws all to him, through the Holy Spirit; the opportunity for salvation through faith is open to all because Jesus's death satisfies God's justice, however, grace is *resistible*: God takes the initiative in salvation, his grace then is open to all, but God respects human free will to respond or resist, election is therefore conditional: election justifies believers, in potential. Salvation is (to use modern terminology) universal, *in potentia*, in its potency, or its *potential*, because it has the capability or openness of actualizing the salvation of all, but is not yet in existence, actualized; however, human nature would appear to deny that all will be saved. And there is the reality attested to by Jesus of Nazareth, the Christ, in his sayings and parables that points to the reality of damnation—of heaven and hell. All are invited; not all come into the Kingdom. All are included; many choose to stay outside. All are invited; not all *accept*.

6. WHITHER ATONEMENT?

This raises questions about how the atonement works, how we are reconciled to God. Lewis asserts the total act of forgiveness, *in potential*, of Christ's sacrifice on the cross, yet we are still mired in sin and subject to God's judgment. What is happening here? Lewis subscribed, from his reading of Gustav Aulén's work on the atonement, *Christus Victor*, to the "classic" atonement theory.[91] In this context Lewis advocates a "debt" model in his apologetics, and a "ransom" model in his analogical narratives. These two models combine for Lewis in the "classic" model: humanity is in bondage to the devil through original sin. According to the "classic" model of atonement Christ's sacrifice releases humanity from its bondage to the devil, Satan, to the dark evil forces. In a sense this resets the human condition to its pre-fall state. It frees humanity to be for God, or against God, our beliefs and actions, our faith, ethics and morals, give away our loyalty and allegiance: the Last Judgment decides who we are for.

This is analyzed in depth in the final chapters of this work and series.[92]

---

90 Brazier, *C. S. Lewis—On The Christ of a Religious Economy. II. Knowing Salvation*, Pt. 3, Chs. 11–12.
91 Aulén, *Christus Victor* (1931). See. Lewis writing to Corbin Scott Carnell, Oct. 13, 1958. Lewis, *Collected Letters, Vol. III*, 978-98
92 See, Brazier, *C. S. Lewis—On The Christ of a Religious Economy. II. Knowing Salvation*, Pt. 3, Chs. 9–10, see specifically, Ch. 9, §§. 2, i–iv, 4, and, 5.

3

Creation and The Fall III:
Innocence and Sin Re-Interpreted

SYNOPSIS:
Lewis, like others, explores the story of the *fall*, re-told, trying to work out what exactly happened to proto-humans, and what exactly is meant by the fruit of the tree of the knowledge of good and evil, but pertinently how humanity comes to be in the state it is in now: how does our present state relate to something that the early proto-humans did? Is the *fall* merely a spiritual disease, or has it become physically embedded in us? Should we be distinguishing between spiritual and physical? Or for that matter eternal and temporal? To this end we can examine the retelling of the story of the *fall*—variations on a theme. Lewis undertook three forms of re-telling the story of the *fall*. First, where Lewis attempts to tease out the implications of what actually happened to humanity in the *fall* (*The Problem of Pain*, 1940), in a form of theological anthropology. This will lead into an examination and comparison with the fall re-told by such writers as Fyodor Mikhailovich Dostoevsky, John Milton, and William Golding, but also attempts to postulate the ideal society untainted by original sin, from Thomas More's *Utopia* (1516) to seventeenth- and nineteenth-century idealistic socialist communities. What do these writers tell us? Is a godly and holy life possible, after the *fall*? How do these re-tellings compare to Lewis's attempts?

Lewis's second form of re-telling the story of the fall is in his novel (*Perelandra*, 1943): a conscious, sentient, rational, creature, God-created, in another world, on another planet, is obedient and does not fall, despite manifold temptation. This is paradise retained. This shows us that the object of temptation has no intrinsic value; the risk is in a dialectic between obedience-disobedience, which Lewis explicates in *The Chronicles of Narnia: The Magician's Nephew* (1955); this is confirmed by biblical precedence: the healing of Naaman (2 Kgs 5). It is disobedience that taints and corrupts: "All get what they want; they do not always like it." By comparison Philip Pullman (*His Dark Materials*, 1995–2000) explicitly praises the fall—it is a worthy price to pay for self-awareness, knowledge, and freedom from God? In Pullman's inverted world of secular liberal humanism the fall is a moral good because through it humanity, in Pullman's inverted thinking, achieves self-awareness and control over its destiny.

Lewis's third form of retelling the story of the fall is in bearing witness to, in cataloguing the presence of sin every day and in every way in humanity: sin and sinners—acknowledging the fall is one thing, but when the human predicament is to live with or without knowledge of original sin, what does Lewis make of the human condition and its propensity to sin? Lewis was writing about life *in the shadow of the Christ*, steeped in the effects of the *fall*, corrupted by original sin. How accurate did Lewis see people's consciousness of sin? What does he tell us through Screwtape's inverted understanding? Orthodoxy and responsibility vie with desperation and delusions.

ON THE CHRIST OF A RELIGIOUS ECONOMY. I. CREATION AND SUB-CREATION

1. INTRODUCTION

Despite its manifold attempts to create its own heaven on earth, humanity is despairingly predictable: history is characterized by wars and empires, corruption and perversion, by the arrogance of political creeds, whose exponents are convinced of the utter rightness of their power and authority and "policies," which so often end in despair and confusion, this notwithstanding humanity simply cannot get it right—except to attempt to believe, and then to define the right in its own image. The story of the *fall* in the book of Genesis is short, concise, yet pertinent: humanity can reject this story, dismiss it as a fiction, but the reality of the human before God, defined by a Christian interpretation of anthropology, says otherwise: sin rules. When we try to do the good, we get it wrong. However marginalized the story may be in some circles, many have, down the years, tried to reinterpret the story of the fall so as to *remind* humanity of its truth. Lewis did. Lewis undertook three forms of re-telling the story of the fall:

- **First**, where Lewis attempts to tease out the implications of what actually happened to humanity in the fall (*The Problem of Pain*, 1940); this is in the form of theological anthropology.

- **Second**, is Lewis's re-situating of the story of the fall in the form of analogical narrative—a theological story (*Perelandra*, 1943): a conscious and sentient, a rational creature, created by God, exists in another world, on another planet, however, it is obedient and does not *fall*: paradise is retained.

- **Third**, Lewis retells the story of the fall in the presence of sin every day and in every way, in humanity: this analysis is throughout his apologetics and philosophical theology from 1940–63.

Across all three retellings is a form of theological anthropology: the human condition before God defined by original sin.

2. THE FALL: RE-TOLD

Lewis dedicates a whole chapter to the fall in his first work of apologetics, *The Problem of Pain*.[1] Within this Lewis offers his interpretation and version of the fall: what actually happened.[2] Lewis opens with a concession to the evolution of proto-humans, these are human-like simians that God evolves into *homo sapiens*—humans. Then God "caused to descend" upon these creatures a consciousness that made them a different species: through its psychology and physiology a new kind of consciousness was generated which could say "I" and "me," which could look upon itself as an object, which knew God, which could make judgements of truth, beauty, and goodness, and which was so far above time that it could perceive time flowing past. Lewis is unclear as to the *cause* and trigger of this new consciousness—is it physical, does it issue solely from

---

1 Lewis, *Problem of Pain*, 52–69.
2 Ibid., 59–66.

3. Creation and The Fall III: Innocence and Sin, Re-Interpreted

evolution? Is it triggered by the action of the Holy Spirit? What is the role of the Spirit that hovered over the waters (Gen 1:2b). Lewis leaves the questions aside. This new consciousness ruled and illuminated the whole organism, flooding every part of it with light, and was not, like ours, limited to a selection of the movements going on in one part of the organism, namely the brain. "Man was then all consciousness."[3] Lewis asserts that this creature, which lived in blissful communion with God, had some sort of control, power, over its physical bodily functions, further, that sleep was blissful awareness, restful not a stupor. This *prelapsarian* proto-man had "a mysterious power of taming beasts . . . this power the paradisal man enjoyed in eminence . . . for man was made to be the priest and even, in one sense, the Christ, of the animals—the mediator through whom they apprehend so much of the Divine splendor as their irrational nature allows."[4] Lewis admits that this is, in effect, biblically-informed speculation. He is attempting to marry-up Darwinian evolution with the Genesis account of creation.

> We do not know how many of these creatures God made, nor how long they continued in the Paradisal state. But sooner or later they fell. Someone or something whispered that they could become as gods—that they could cease directing their lives to their Creator. . . . They wanted, as we say, to "call their souls their own." But that means to live a lie, for our souls are not, in fact, our own.
>
> They wanted some corner in the universe of which they could say to God, "This is our business, not yours." But there is no such corner. They wanted to be nouns, but they were, and eternally must be, mere adjectives. We have no idea in what particular act, or series of acts, the self-contradictory, impossible wish found expression. For all I can see, it might have concerned the literal eating of a fruit, but the question is of no consequence.[5]

Therefore the fall, for Lewis, is an act of utter self-will by humanity, first one *fell*, then another, and so forth. The assumption is not the solitary Eve, and Adam, but one, then two, and so forth, among many. A pattern that has been repeated, *ad infinitum*, through human history: but it starts with the one. One person comes up with an idea that catches on, others join in, they will say that the idea has come to its time, come of age, when it is just another repetition of the fall, an idea—socio-cultural or political—that seems grand and marvelous, generous, and altruistic, but descends into the usual self-willed chaos. Humanity does not change, does not improve. We cannot improve through our own willful strength; we cannot survive and flourish sealed-off from God. Lewis noted in his spiritual autobiography *Surprised by Joy*, how in the atheistic pride of the apostate (circa fourteen to thirty-one years of age) he desperately desired this hermetic aloneness, this separation from God, the "gods", or from anyone. Lewis realized even at the age of eighteen years that there was no possibility of a treaty with this Christian reality: "there was no region even in the innermost depth of one's soul which one could surround with a barbed wire fence and guard with a notice, 'No

---

3   Ibid., 59.
4   Ibid., 60.
5   Ibid., 60 and 61.

Admittance!'"[6] This epitomizes Augustine's dictum of *homo incurvatus in se*. Is this the answer? Is original sin triggered by and defined by this inward turn? Was original sin entirely caused by self-will? Lewis acknowledges an external force, without of the human. However, he is surprisingly neutral with regard to the role of personified evil in this—referring to Satan in the guise of a serpent as someone or something. In so doing Lewis misplaces ownership. Fallen humanity belongs to Satan, personified evil; Satan *claims* rebellious humanity. There is no mention of this in Lewis's account. Humanity, yes, has turned in on itself (*homo incurvatus in se*, an Augustinian principle), but, for Lewis, there are just the two parties involved: God, and man; in his account the third party is too vague and undefined—"someone or something."[7] Lewis is here writing in 1940, his first attempt at apologetics; later, in *The Lion, the Witch and the Wardrobe* Lewis is prepared to acknowledge Satan's ownership over fallen humanity. Jadis, the White Witch (evil personified), claims Edmund as a traitor, he rightly belongs to her, not to the Aslan-Christ, even though once he is rescued from her clutches, Aslan speaks with Edmund, alone, and forgives him his treachery.[8] The offence, the sin—in this case treason—still stands after Aslan forgives Edmund: there is the question of ownership, Jadis claims ownership: a blood-price must be paid. Here we have the correct third party: evil personified in the form of the White Witch beguiles and seduces Edmund with the promise of greatness, to be king above all else, he "falls," a Narnian "fall" and thereafter, like the discussion between God and Satan in the early chapters of the book of Job, ownership is plain and obvious: Edmund must die, Aslan offers himself in exchange. Thus the fall-atonement is tripartite, as demonstrated by its cause and source in the book of Genesis: God, humanity, Satan. Through the cross, humanity can turn back to God (a turn initiated through the Holy Spirit acting preveniently, inviting people), which is likewise an essential part of the story (Aslan's sacrifice on the stone table).

However, this act of self-will, the fall, the turning from God to self, humanity curved and bent in on itself (*homo incurvatus in se*), changes, in minute details initially, the creature. Lewis continues in his account: it is now cut off from God and loses control over itself, its bodily function—it is cut-off from the source of its being. The creature separated from God no longer "knows" God; the creature is ruled, *thus God wills*, asserts Lewis, not by the Spirit but by nature, an external rule. The creature is ruled by desires, yet conscious of this lack of control; "the mind itself fell under the psychological laws of association."[9] Furthermore as time passes and the changes become more concrete, the creature loses the memory of this fall, and takes itself for itself: a meaningless serendipity takes over.

> It had turned from God and become its own idol, so that though it could still turn back to God, it could do so only by painful effort, and its inclination was self-ward. Hence pride and ambition, the desire to be lovely in its own eyes and

6   Lewis, *Surprised by Joy*, 166.
7   Lewis, *Problem of Pain*, 60.
8   Lewis, *The Lion, the Witch and the Wardrobe*, 127–31.
9   Lewis, *Problem of Pain*, 64.

3. Creation and The Fall III: Innocence and Sin, Re-Interpreted

to depress and humiliate all rivals, envy, and restless search for more, and still more, security, were now the attitudes that came easiest to it. It was not only a weak king over its own nature, but a bad one.... This condition was transmitted by heredity to all later generations, for it was not simply what biologists call an acquired variation; it was the emergence of a new kind of man—a new species, never made by God, had sinned itself into existence.[10]

Lewis is often criticized for being ignorant of genetics and DNA, yet as we shall see in the next chapter despite the vagueness of his account it does now have some degree of cogency, given a contemporary understanding of evolution, horizontal gene transfer, and the evidence for environmental and behavioral factors that can *alter* DNA. Whether "evolved" or "developed" (never has so much been loaded in one word) the human creature changes itself through its own actions and behavior. As we noted earlier, creation can sub-create, develop, and change. Lewis is orthodox here: this change is not willed by God, humanity has taken over control of its destiny, and there is no going back. It cannot help itself—in more ways than one. Lewis is orthodox, but in his fall re-told he has abstracted; the essential framework of the story is there, but it is characterless, colorless. It appeals to a (pseudo) scientific mind-set—whether atheistic or theistic, agnostic or Christian. But in its apologetic appeal it does, as we have seen, lose essential details. The crucial point here is, therefore, as the American philosopher Nicholas Wolterstorff point out in his criticism of Lewis's attempt to explain the fall, a new species is created out of the old—but self-generated, self-created.[11] This is the strongest point in Lewis's re-presentation of the fall. So, the fall does not just issue from the will, but also from humanity's God-given ability to sub-create, and be courted by personified evil.

3. THE FALL: VARIATION ON A THEME

Lewis is fascinated by the theological and eschatological implications of the fall; this issues essentially from 1937, following on from his reading and translating of Augustine's *The City of God*. Therefore, this attempt to re-tell the story of the fall (essentially in the context of pain and suffering), is to try to explain and elucidate what exactly happened, and how we come to be in the situation we are in. Lewis is not alone is postulating what might have happened, such is humanity's *postlapsarian* amnesia. The nineteenth-century Russian prophet and writer Fyodor Mikhailovich Dostoevsky likewise attempted a transposition of the story of the fall. Other attempts that relate to Lewis are Milton's *Paradise Lost*, among others, along with stories that complement the fall, for example, William Golding's *Lord of the Flies*, 1954 (even where the author's aims were not explicitly Christian).

---

10 Ibid., 64–65.
11 Wolterstorff, "C. S. Lewis on The Problem of Suffering," 9.

i. An Idealistic Inversion?

Some stories, we will see, actual promote the fall as a good for humanity, for example, Philip Pullman's, *His Dark Materials*. Ironically, Thomas More's *Utopia*[12] (1516—an early work, from his youthful confidence as a Renaissance Humanist) asserts that humanity can get it right, can organize itself politically and sociologically so as to, in effect, return to what appears to be the *prelapsarian* state. (Perhaps the first of these idealistic socio-political communal statements lies with Plato's *Republic*?) In many ways More's *Utopia*—the ideal society where everything is good and wholesome and well organized, with no glint of dysfunction, anarchy, or contradiction, let alone rebellion—can be described as generated by a pseudo-Pelagian "heresy." That is, the idea that the effects of the fall are not permanent or transmitted, and humanity can live the perfect godly life untainted by original sin, humanity can through its own efforts improve and define itself. Some critics argue that More's aim was to satirize English society by presenting the opposite, and the idealism was not his primary aim (the word utopia is from the Greek for "no place"). More's *Utopia* has been cited as an early example of idealist politics, often considered pseudo-socialist or communitarian, indeed many political groups attempted to found ideal communities. For example, the Diggers[13] during the period of the English Commonwealth in the mid-seventeenth century, or the work of the nineteenth century Welsh social reformer and founder of Utopian Socialism, Robert Owen (a belief system that in many ways contradicted the revolutionary and materialistic basis of much of the political creeds that followed on from Karl Marx, though it was in effect socialist communitarianism). All of these ideal communities failed, often from within, or failed to take seriously the existence of sin without (the diggers were often evicted from the land they sought to till, for they had no defense, no armed militia). A contemporary example of this sort of theological story that postulates the *possibility* of a perfect society is found in the work of the Anglican bishop and theologian John Austin Baker, in the imagined land of *Oudamovia*, which, like More's *Utopia*, postulates an ideal society, untainted.[14] Laudable though the aims are, all of these ideal communities are postulated *this* side of the *eschaton*. They are not predictions of the new creation, the new heaven and the new earth, even though some were promoted as heaven on earth in their time. The problem with all of these statements of idealistic communities is that they are not a solution to the fall, or even an attempt to confront humanity with the reality of the fall, they are an extension of the fall: humanity trying to solve the problem of original sin for itself.

---

12 More, *Utopia*, 2004 [1516].
13 The Diggers were a group of English Protestant proto-communists who from 1649 attempted social reform through the idealistic creation of small egalitarian rural communities: all dug (tilled the land), and grew all that they ate, all were equal, and equally "levelled."
14 Baker, *Travels in Oudamovia*.

3. Creation and The Fall III: Innocence and Sin, Re-Interpreted

ii. Dostoevsky: The Dream of a Ridiculous Man,

Lewis was wise enough to see that these communities were not going to be sustainable, or flawless.[15] The vanity, we might say, of these idealistic socio-political communities ultimately miscarried. In the context of a doctrine of original sin this is also presented by the Russian writer and prophet Fyodor Mikhailovich Dostoevsky—though from a critical and orthodox perspective. In a short story entitled, *The Dream of the Ridiculous Man*,[16] Dostoevsky focuses on the relationship between religious belief and theological anthropology—that is, the nature of humanity before God. Written in the form of a story/parable, and recounted as narrative by the "ridiculous man" the work deals with the state of humanity *prelapsarian/postlapsarian*, the nature of original sin as a decision (therefore existential), and it raises issues to do with the "invention" of religion by fallen humanity. The "ridiculous man" epitomizes, and is representative in detail, of the cultured, liberal and atheistic, progressive and humanitarian nineteenth-century intellectual whom Dostoevsky was as a young man before his conversion to Christ.

Innocence Corrupted

The alienated self-confessed "ridiculous man," who narrates the story, is on the verge of suicide but he falls into a deep sleep where he dreams he is dead yet conscious. He prays fervently to be released[17] and finds himself exhumed by a creature that transports him through the infinity of space till he then recognizes a star as the sun he knew from earth and then finds himself back on an earth-like planet, in the Aegean[18]—*prelapsarian*, that is, he is amongst people who are not subject to original sin. There is no sin in this world prior to the arrival of the "ridiculous man" with all his "Western inspired Petersburg sophistication."[19] This other world is created; the "ridiculous man" arrives, the people fall. These people are genuinely innocent. Dostoevsky goes into some depth in describing them, their virtue, kindness, but above all their freedom from deceit, jealousy and lying, from subterfuge and cruelty, barbarity and murder. They are as happy and frolicsome as children.[20] These people are not religious as such but they radiate holiness without affectation and exhibit an unconscious oneness with God:[21] "They had no shrines . . . they had no religious creed."[22] There is no sin in this world prior to the "ridiculous man's" arrival. In their *prelapsarian* state the holiness of these people is the result of innocence not the attainment of saintliness.[23]

---

15 See, for example: Lewis, "We Have No 'Right to Happiness'", 265 and 269; Lewis, "The Sermon and the Lunch," 235; and, Lewis, *Broadcast Talks*, 49.
16 Dostoevsky, *The Dream of the Ridiculous Man* first appeared in *The Diary of a Writer* in April 1877 with the subtitle, *A Fantastic Story*. The edition referred to here is published is in Dostoevsky, *A Gentle Creature and Other Stories*, 108–28.
17 Ibid., 115.
18 Ibid., 117–18.
19 Ibid., 111.
20 Ibid., 118–19.
21 Ibid., 121.
22 Ibid.
23 Ibid., 121–22.

The dream appears to lasts for millennia; however, little by little, gradually over immense periods of time these people were corrupted. The "ridiculous man" is the cause or trigger: "All I know is that I was the cause of the fall . . . like a pestilential bringing contagion to whole countries, I infected that earth, happy and sinless before my arrival. They learned how to lie, and grew to love lying and perceived its beauty. Oh it may have started off innocently, as a joke, in a coy way, as part of an amorous intrigue, perhaps a mere germ, but that germ of a lie penetrated their hearts and found a welcome."[24] This one man, the "ridiculous man," taught one individual to take the decision to lie. It may have seemed just a small step, a little thing but this decision bred other lies and so on—the germ of sin was sown. What followed? "[L]echery swiftly came into being,"[25] then jealousy, then cruelty, soon the first murder: blood was shed. They began to separate into groupings, classes, and eventually racial groups. "Alliances formed, pitted one against another;"[26] reproaches and upbraidings followed. They came to know shame, which led them to invent virtue. Honor sprang up, and flag waving nationalism. "The struggle began for separateness, isolation, for personal identity, what's yours and what's mine. They began speaking different languages."[27] They knew sorrow and loved it, even thirsted for it—eventually believing that truth could only be attained through suffering.[28] As time passed they forgot what they had been in their innocency. They refused to believe that they had ever been happy and innocent. They called it a dream; they lost all faith and invented the notion of legends to account for these memories. They crafted an idol of it, statues proliferated; they set up temples and worshipped this idea[29]—which they acknowledged as no more than their own projected desire. Thus they invented religion, including theories of religion to explain that it was really all nothing—however, this was a secret kept for the priestly caste, the ruling class.[30]

After a sojourn of millennia the "ridiculous man" realizing what he had caused was beside himself with grief and guilt He awoke from his dream and back in St Petersburg lived a changed resurrected life, honoring God and accepting God's righteousness.

Religion as the Result of the Fall

Lewis held to a balanced but critical view of the value of religion. Religion could lead to God or to the devil, as Screwtape knew! Religion could serve God or it could work against God. Chapter XI of the first edition of *Miracles* explicates this criticism. He opens the chapter with a quotation from the work of Thomas Erskine of Linlathen that encapsulates this dialectical approach to revelation and religion: "Those who make religion their god will not have God for their religion."[31] Like Lewis, Dostoevsky has

24   Ibid., 123.
25   Ibid.
26   Ibid.
27   Ibid., 124.
28   Ibid.
29   Ibid.
30   Ibid., 124–25.
31   Lewis, *Miracles*, (1st ed.), 99.

3. Creation and The Fall III: Innocence and Sin, Re-Interpreted

reservations at best, serious concerns at worst, about religion, *per se*. Although this criticism is implicitly presented, as with Lewis, in story form, we can codify it into a proposition: religion issues from the fall. The fall, for Dostoevsky, is transmitted among these people, proto-humans, though nurture, education and conditioning. If someone arose who tried to challenge the state of humanity, s/he was corrupted and absorbed. It is as if the germ was there in them from the start, all it took was one tiny incident to trigger the fall. Transmission therefore appears for Dostoevsky to be sociological, social interaction that exploits an inherited flaw. Were they born with this flaw (free will?) or does it appear in them after the fall, to be transmitted? Is Dostoevsky right to consider free will a flaw in creation?

Some religion did challenge people in their state of sinfulness; but it also patronized and complimented them. Whatever belief system these people came up with it did nothing to change the underlying nature, ontologically, of their original sin or the effect in the present, existentially, of their corrupt nature. So although there is no explanation of transmission, there is an hereditary element to Dostoevsky's story. But like Lewis's story from *The Problem of Pain*, nothing is spelt out: is this a physical transmission, with the human nature altered by inherited changes? Is the corruption spiritual and transmitted spiritually? In Dostoevsky's tale religion should have informed them. "Religions sprang up":[32] religious consciousness also arose outside of the officially sanctioned elite. Holy men and women came to these people, weeping, and talked to them of their pride, of their shame. But they never question, or reflect on, why they had become as they had (inherited original sin). These prophets were laughed at or stoned: "sacred blood was shed on the temple thresholds."[33]

The Dream is a portrait of humanity without God, humanity that has turned its back on God and deludes itself with all sorts of beliefs systems—religious, political, individualistic, socialist, nihilist. *The Dream of the Ridiculous Man* is a parable of the human race as another race on another earth-like planet who (unlike the human race on earth) have no name for God, that is, no revelation as in the Old Testament—"that merciful Judge who will judge us and whose name we know not."[34] Furthermore they have no real revelation of the nature of that God/Judge as in Jesus Christ (they only have natural theology and religious cults) and therefore there is for them no atonement—these people are truly lost.

In the context of Lewis's work on the fall, and his attempts at re-telling the story, there are two conclusions we can draw from Dostoevsky's Dream:

- **First**: the people in *The Dream* are left suspended with no forgiveness: what is missing, what they cry out for (though they do not realize it), is the grace and forgiveness bestowed from the God of love—tangibly revealed in Christ, in the atoning sacrifice of the Christ. As Lewis noted, "It is not

---

32   Dostoevsky, *The Dream of the Ridiculous Man*, 125.
33   Ibid., 125.
34   Ibid., 124.

enough to want to get rid of one's sins. We also need to believe in the One who saves us from our sins."[35]

- **Second**: if the ultimate origin of the trigger of the fall, amongst these people, is undefined, transmission is sociological. The "ridiculous man" *triggers* the fall in these people, but where is the serpent, personified evil? The fall for Dostoevsky is binary: the visitor (the "ridiculous man") and the people—two parties. But the biblical witness is tripartite: God, humanity, and the serpent.

The value in Dostoevsky's account is in his detailed analysis of how humanity continues to fall, piling sin upon sin, while believing they are improving the human condition, inventing multiple belief systems, defining righteousness in their own image.

iii. Milton, Paradise Lost

John Milton's *Paradise Lost* (1667) is an epic poem, a retelling of the story of the fall and its cosmic implications. The aim, stated by Milton, was to justify the ways of God to humanity. The opening verses of Book 1 states:

> Of Man's First Disobedience, and the Fruit
> Of that Forbidden Tree, whose mortal taste
> Brought Death into the World, and all our woe,
> With loss of EDEN, till one greater Man
> Restore us, and regain the blissful Seat.[36]

The framework of *Paradise Lost* is sound: the story from Genesis of humanity's fall through the temptation of Eve and Adam, by the fallen angel, Satan, and humanity's expulsion from the Garden of Eden, however, questions have been raised down the centuries as to how orthodox or heterodox the poem is (often arguments are around the multitudinous mythological figures Milton weaves into his epic, but also, on more conventional theological issues).

Paradise Lost opens with Satan banished to hell,[37] organizing his fellow fallen angels and outlining how he will contaminate the newly formed Earth and the most favored of God's creation, humanity. Travelling through hell, and the abyss and chaos beyond, the war in heaven that led to their expulsion is recounted and discussed: this is the angelic war over heaven where the final battle involves the Christ defeating the legion of rebels and expelling them. The story highlights how this purging is followed by the creation: the pinnacle and culmination of creation is to be Adam and Eve who are free agents, and rule over creation, a power and authority defined by the commandment not to eat the fruit of the tree of the knowledge of good and evil—on penalty of death. With the conclusion of this re-telling, and his final arrival on earth, Satan, disguised in the form of a serpent, secretes himself into the Garden of Eden

---

35 Lewis, "Cross Examination," 217.
36 Milton, *Paradise Lost*, Bk. 1, lines 1–5.
37 Rev 12:7–10. See also, Luke 10:18, Isa 14:12–14 and Ezek 28:12–18.

3. Creation and The Fall III: Innocence and Sin, Re-Interpreted

and successfully tempts Eve to eat of this fruit, beguiling her with his silver-tongued rhetoric, and flattering her. Adam's shock is soon placated and he likewise eats. Milton oddly presents Adam as the greater sinner than Eve, as he is considered to be much more aware of what he is doing than Eve. Both discover sexual lust and concupiscence, and initially believe the serpent was right—they are now like "gods." However, guilt soon follows. They realize the terrible act of disobedience they have committed against God thus, they argue over responsibility for the act, and descend into acrimonious and mutual recrimination. Eve is presented as the reconciler; she tries to placate Adam, and through her encouragement they approach God bowing and pleading for the grace of forgiveness. Adam receives a vision from the angel Michael where he sees everything that will happen to humanity—until the great flood and Noah. Adam is distraught and bereft at this vision, yet Michael then tells him about humanity's potential redemption through the sacrifice of the Christ, the King Messiah. Both Adam and Eve are then expelled from Eden: they are alone (apart now from God, who though omnipresent is now invisible and distant); they are adrift and fighting for survival in a hostile world, with nothing but the promise of potential redemption eons into the future.

As a *literatus* and a teacher of English literature at Oxford, and as a lay-theologian, Lewis published *A Preface to Paradise Lost* (1942),[38] which is still regarded as a standard introduction to the work for students of English literature. Lewis writes as an orthodox believer to a target audience either indifferent or skeptical to the theological reality Milton bears witness to. What is relevant to us and our developing discussion is how Lewis handles Milton's theology, and the question of heterodoxy. An analysis of what Lewis wrote is really beyond the scope or relevance of this work, save that he unravels the often contradictory and confusing *secular* literary comments from non-Christian academics as to what is questionable in Milton's theology, what is not, and what is heterodox in Milton's other works, but not in *Paradise Lost*. From a Christological viewpoint Lewis fairly identifies Milton's self-effacing heresy: that he is an Arian, in that he promoted the doctrine that Christ was pre-existing to creation, all creation and worlds, but was not co-eternal with the Father; but any Arianism in *Paradise Lost*, is veiled, and implicit, being read essentially from Milton's other works.[39] What does Lewis comment in conclusion on the theology of *Paradise Lost*? Lewis comments that Christian readers may find Milton's work unsatisfactory in many ways, not least as a religious poem (attributing some of its failures to Milton's heretical beliefs).[40] However, Lewis believes we should judge *Paradise Lost* on its qualities and virtues, because the poem is overwhelmingly Christian.[41] Lewis does correctly assert that apart from details *Paradise Lost* is orthodox, and is indeed deeply Augustinian in its respect for the doctrine of the fall. Lewis does note that Milton's version is "substantially"

---

38   Lewis, *A Preface to Paradise Lost*. Given by Lewis as The Ballard Matthews Lectures, delivered at University College North Wales on three consecutive evening, December 1–3, 1941, published by Oxford University Press in 1942.
39   Lewis, *A Preface to Paradise Lost*, 85–86.
40   Ibid., 92.
41   Ibid., 92.

Augustinian; furthermore this is the position, which is also "that of the Church as a whole."[42]

iv. Golding: Lord of the Flies

William Golding's, *Lord of the Flies*,[43] explores the deeply dark side of human nature and challenges the myth of human progress. This, inadvertently, promotes and endorses an orthodox doctrine of original sin. By exposing the reality of the fall lurking beneath the moral ambiguity, the fragility and insubstantial nature of human civilization, Golding exposes, the pretense, as Lewis noted of civilized society.[44] In Lord of the Flies a plane crashes; the survivors gather on an isolated island in the Pacific Ocean. The survivors are all boys aged seven to thirteen years, most of whom are choir boys. Despite their best efforts to organize themselves and to survive (organizing hunting parties, and a constant smoke signal from a high point) they descend into two tribes, fighting and preying on each other, they develop paranoia about a fearful beast or monster on the island, they invent "magic" religion, convinced of dark forces on the island. All the trappings of civilization slowly disappear from them, from their clothes to their possessions. They become savages. Certain members of the survivors are stigmatized, and then hunted as outcasts. What is initially playground teasing, then bullying, becomes tribal and violent. Then the first child is killed, and the aggressors invent theories to justify their actions, even pseudo-"religious" aims and objectives. They have already adopted a large sea shell, a conch, to be a totem, a symbol of authority and power, and the right to speak of the one who holds it. The "Lord of the Flies" is a severed pig's head on a pole stuck in the ground left as an offering to the monster, the "beast," the grinning head attracting scores of flies, all dancing attention, buzzing around it. The name "Lord of the Flies" is taken to be a literal translation of Beelzebub, a demonic manifestation of Satan. Eventually one tribe dominates, leaving two survivors to be hunted down. The hunters set fire to the forest, inadvertently drawing the attention of a passing ship. A landing party finds Ralph, the survivor, running from the savage tribe.

The shock in 1950s Britain that the publication of the book caused was in part due to the rapid descent into tribal savagery and violence, exploitation and hatred, in civilized middle and upper middle class boys who would surely have behaved in a polite civilized bourgeois manner. But worse, Golding has an English Cathedral choir amongst the survivors, who turn out worse than most of the others. The assumption was that respectable Church of England choirboys would certainly have known better, and would have been beyond such a descent into savagery. Golding refuted very successfully the myth of human progress, that we have become civilized and are becoming nicer people year-on-year. To Lewis, this was a delusion: it was a position that was characterized by the uncritical acceptance that whatever has gone out of date is on that count discredited because humanity has progressed towards an ever finer

---

42   Ibid., see, 66–72, quotation, 66.
43   Golding, *Lord of the Flies*.
44   Lewis, "The Sermon and the Lunch," 235.

3. Creation and The Fall III: Innocence and Sin, Re-Interpreted

and more superior civilized manifestation.[45] Original sin is therefore endemic and the savagery, the selfishness of the *fall*, lurks beneath each and every man, woman and child. Anglican choristers are no different. They may be in the paradise of an unspoilt South Seas island, with all they need to survive easily to hand, they may be far away from "modern" civilization, but well-educated privileged boys regress into the natural human state: *fallen*, selfish and willful. All humanity is the same when it comes to original sin.

v. A Hedonistic Paradise

In the genre of secular writings that implicitly bear witness to the reality of the fall, a latter day version of *The Lord of the Flies* is the novel and film, *The Beach*.[46] Various back-packing, free-wheeling, young men and women, cushioned by Western wealth, discover a secret ideal beach on a remote Thailand island and develop a hedonistic community living for indulgence: sexual freedom, casual drug use, swimming—beach culture. They jealously guard the secret of "The Beach" (in part because the island is used by a drug cartel to grow and harvest cannabis—tiny amounts of which they "take" to sell on the occasional boat trip to civilization so as to buy essentials). This is *postlapsarian* humanity going it alone, and believing it can create the ideal community, independent from God (though playing with occasion bit of Eastern religion and culture). Problems start when sexual partners are exchanged, one wanting to stay in a monogamous relationship. The crisis comes when two of the community who regularly fish in the lagoon are attacked by a shark. One dies shortly after the attack; the other is refused hospital treatment for fear that the secret of "The Beach" would be found out. His wounds are severe, and become gangrenous; his moans and screams disturb the indulgent lifestyle of the community, so they move him into a tent, sufficient distance from the beach so that his cries won't disturb them in their permissive hedonism, leaving him to die (though one member stays with him to try to comfort him, disgusted at the actions of the community). The author of *The Beach*, Alex Garland, acknowledged the criticisms of the story, but commented that his aim had been overlooked. In an interview the journalist Rom Glickman, quoting Garland, writes,

> A lot of the criticism of *The Beach* is that it presents Thais as two dimensional, as part of the scenery. That's because these people I'm writing about—backpackers—really only see them as part of the scenery. . . . To them, it's all part of a huge theme park, the scenery for their trip. . . . This book is anti-traveler in a lot of ways. That was absolutely my intention. The Beach was meant to be a criticism of this backpacker culture, not a celebration of it.[47]

---

45   See, Lewis, *Surprised by Joy*, 206 208.
46   Garland, *The Beach*, 1997; the film was released in the year, 2000.
47   From an interview with Alex Garland, by an American journalist: "More Postcards from the Beach:" http://www.gluckman.com/BeachGarland.html. The full interview was in *The Wall Street Journal, Weekend Journal* Feb. 19–20, 1999.

Like Dostoevsky's analysis of postlapsarian humanity, the community becomes riven by jealousy, rivalries and eventually breaks down when threatened by the drug cartel because others are coming to the island, and this impinges on and threatens their secret world of growing and harvesting cannabis. Humanity will ever try to solve the problems of *postlapsarian* humanity for itself, refusing to countenance God's solution. The writer of *The Beach*, like Golding, was not writing from an explicitly Christian perspective, yet bore testimony to the theological anthropology that can be read from the *fall*, and from a doctrine of *original sin*. Humanity ever searches for, or attempts to create, utopias, whether political systems or mysterious lost worlds, remote islands, thereby believing in self-defined and self-referential (and inevitably self-reverential) communities; though in this instance Garland is observing how Western humanity and culture pollutes and destroys the sanctuary sought and created, and cannot escape the reality of what orthodox Christians define as original sin.

4. LEWIS-PULLMAN: THE FALL RE-VISITED, OR RE-DEFINED?

Philip Pullman's, *His Dark Materials* (1995, 1997, and 2000) explicitly praises the *fall*—it is a worthy price to pay for self-awareness, for knowledge, it grants humanity freedom from, for Pullman, a dictatorial and overbearing "god." By contrast, Lewis's second form of re-telling the story of the *fall* is in his novel *Perelandra* (1943): a conscious, sentient, rational, creature, God-created, in another world, on another planet, is obedient and does not fall, despite manifold temptation. This is paradise retained. This shows us that the object of temptation has no intrinsic value; the risk is in a dialectic between obedience-disobedience, which, we will see, Lewis explicates in *The Chronicles of Narnia: The Magician's Nephew* (1955).

i. An Unholy Inversion

Philip Pullman's trilogy, entitled, *His Dark Materials*,[48] recasts the fall as good: original sin is no sin, but the awakening of human consciousness, self-awareness, and the defining of the self as the center of all. Pullman's aim was in part to contradict Lewis's *The Chronicles of Narnia*, indeed, in many aspects his work is essentially derivative. He simply borrows from established greats, and then inverts. The title, *His Dark Materials*, came from Milton's *Paradise Lost*;[49] like Milton original sin is central, but inverted. God is then dismissed as autocratic and oppressive. Pullman's trilogy is a reversal, an upturn, of values: God is evil, Satan is good, original sin becomes a heavenly grace, where hell becomes heaven, and the kingdom of God becomes a republic of heaven. Even this technique is derivative—Lewis invented such a literary inversion for *The Screwtape Letters*, where the senior devil refers to Satan as "our father below," and all

---

[48] Philip Pullman, *Northern Lights* (1995), *The Subtle Knife* (1997), and *The Amber Spyglass* (2000).

[49] For example, Bk. 2, line 916.

that is evil and will bring about the fall of individuals and their condemnation into hell is considered good—from Satan's perspective.[50]

Crucial to our developing understanding is that for Pullman the fall is not bad and disastrous, In Pullman's inverted world of secular liberal humanism, the actions of Eve did not trigger a disaster, it was an upward, heavenly, reaching to emulate, and in effect, transcend the "gods," and take over from the oppressive God. The *fall* is a moral good because through it humanity, in Pullman's inverted thinking, achieves self-awareness and control over its destiny. For Pullman, this is a *felix culpa*, a blessed or happy fall; humanity can take over from God, once it acknowledges the secret knowledge (discovered by an intellectual elite) that the "gods" do not really exist. The inversion is then complete, derived as it is from Lewis, Milton and T. S. Eliot, and projected as part of a liberal humanist rebellion against the Christian tradition. Pullman's self-confessed aim was to destroy and denigrate God and the church. Pullman—who is rated as one of the more fashionable media New Atheists (under the self-styled leadership of the Evangelical atheist, celebrity, cult figure, and media scientist Richard Dawkins)—wrote *His Dark Materials* as an explicit challenge to *The Chronicles of Narnia*: Narnia reveals to us something of God's reality, and Christ's loving purposes for humanity; by contrast, Pullman has commented that, "My books are about killing God."[51]

As the Revd Hugh Rayment-Pickard (parish priest and lecturer in philosophy) demonstrates in *The Devil's Account: Philip Pullman and Christianity*, the trilogy is either loved or hated: people are never indifferent to *His Dark Materials*. Ostensibly for children, literary research[52] has shown that a significant group of readers (and audiences at the Royal National Theatre's production of *His Dark Materials* in London) are young adults, twenty- and thirty-somethings who wander around the world creating an exclusively postmodern personalized belief system and morality, characterized by a disregard for organized religion, in particular doctrine and ethics, yet who often exhibit a glazed romantic expression reminiscent of evangelicals when they discuss Pullman's trilogy. A teenage schoolgirl's comment on the Royal National Theatre's production was, "So God don't exist and as long as we make up a good story we can do anything we like":[53] autonomous over heteronomous ethics? This comment is perceptive, for what Pullman has created for postmodernist Westerners (complemented by Richard Dawkins *The God Delusion*) is implicitly religious—essentially atheistic mythology for the children of secular liberal humanists? So how does Christian theology counter this? It is difficult to avoid seeing Pullman's work essentially as a neo-Gnostic heresy: the parallels between his imagery and iconography, his theology and ethics, the supernatural structure of the layers of god-like forces within his work, these are all comparable to a greater or lesser degree with patristic Gnosticism, a resemblance that

---

50 On Pullman's definition of sin, see, Rayment-Pickard, *The Devil's Account: Philip Pullman and Christianity*, 49, 62–65, 88.
51 See, Meacham, "The Shed Where God Died," *Sydney Morning Herald Online*, 2003.
52 For example, see, Williams, "Judas Betrayed his Brother with a Kiss," 38–39.
53 This was from a conversation amongst members of a school party of teenagers, overheard at a bus stop on Waterloo Bridge, next to the National Theatre, after a matinee performance.

is quite unnerving. And the structure, as we have seen, is derivative from past great writers.

ii. Paradise Retained

Lewis looks at the story of the fall differently to Pullman's unoriginal inversion. He may have attempted to rationalize in *The Problem of Pain* what actually happened—as we saw earlier in this chapter—but there is another aspect of Lewis's work where he re-situates the trial, the test, which humanity failed, leading to the ontological redefinition of humanity and its relationship with God. In the second novel of *The Space Trilogy* entitled *Perelandra*,[54] we find another sentient, conscious, species on another planet (Venus, named Perelandra), only here, although subject to a similar temptation to humanity's, this people (the first male and female) *do not fall*: we have a picture of paradise retained, not lost. Importantly they continue to live in immediate and close communion with God, yet distinct from God—Maleldil (a term that embraces God, yet is identifiable as triune). Elwin Ransom (a philologist, who exhibits Christlikeness) and Edward Weston (an evil scientist) have arrived on Perelandra, which seems to be a water world with floating islands of vegetation. They meet the Green Lady, a female humanoid, who exists in *prelapsarian* innocence: "Never had Ransom seen a face so calm, and so unearthly, despite the full humanity of every feature. This was a calm which no storm had ever preceded."[55] The Green Lady refers to herself as the mother, which puzzles Ransom, till he realizes she is an Eve, the first woman on that world. As such she cannot conceive of death, or disobedience, or how Ransom and Weston can be as they are (i.e. fallen, but she cannot find words to describe the concept, their *postlapsarian* state). Ransom explains evil to the Green Lady, to warn her, leastwise, he tries to; he describes evil as a clinging to a past or imagined good in the face of a new gift. In trying to explain, he prays to God that he may not corrupt the Green Lady and her kind with humanity's evil. By comparison Weston joyfully tries to corrupt her. The Green lady freely, innocently, talks to him explaining the central prohibition from Maleldil (in this instance, essentially God in Christ, the second person of the Trinity) that they must not live permanently on the dry land, only on the floating islands. There is a fearful battle between Ransom and Weston, played out as spiritual warfare, played out against the backdrop of the obedient innocence of the Green Lady amidst the floating islands and the mountainous dry land of Perelandra. Weston returns from the dry land with evidence of the two thrones there for the king and queen. So why, he taunts, don't they go and claim what is theirs, despite the prohibition, indeed why don't they disobey Maleldil? The Green Lady clearly has free will, and could choose. But she does not. She resists temptation. The battle between Ransom and Weston continues; the Green Lady meets the king, to be her husband; Weston is eventually overthrown and dies, defeated at Ransom's hands, but at great cost to Ransom. Obedient to their trial, obedient to the command not to dwell on the dry land, the Green Lady and her

---

54   Lewis, *Perelandra* (1943).
55   Ibid., 64.

3. Creation and The Fall III: Innocence and Sin, Re-Interpreted

husband ascend, with Maleldil's permission to the dry land, to their thrones, anointed king and queen.

> Up and up came the light from the mountain slope. It filled the whole valley. The shadows disappeared again. All was in a pure daylight that seemed to come from nowhere in particular. He knew ever afterwards what is meant by a light "resting on" or "overshadowing" a holy thing, but not emanating from it. For as the light reached its perfection and settled itself, as it were, like a lord upon his throne or like wine in a bowl, and filled the whole flowery cup of the mountain top, every cranny, with its purity, the holy thing, Paradise itself in its two Persons, Paradise walking hand in hand, its two bodies shining in the light like emeralds yet not themselves too bright to look at, came in sight in the cleft between two peaks, and stood a moment with its male right hand lifted in regal and pontifical benediction, and then walked down and stood on the far side of the water. And the gods kneeled and bowed their huge bodies before the small forms of that young King and Queen.[56]

The king and queen thank Ransom for his part in preserving Perelandra. Ransom is overwhelmed by the spiritual-physical appearance of the king, Tor, because of a sense in which he is like Christ. Like humanity they have the commission of custodianship of all the other creatures. They live on the dry land, the fixed land, with Maleldil's permission; that which once formed the prohibition, they are granted freely.

The order—you must not spend the night on the dry land—has been rescinded; in fulfillment they can dwell permanently on the dry land: this is a trial of obedience, but more than that, obeying the command is an assessment of commitment—putting God first, not self. Lewis's theme in *Perelandra* is intimately to do with the relationship between creator and creature—in freedom. Jerome Bertram, notes "The question is, how can a totally free person, without unfair manipulation by God, spontaneously carry out what God most desires, and find for herself a destiny which God fully intends[;] . . . the woman [the Green Lady] needs to make her own free and spontaneous choice to do the will of God, without being unduly influenced by God. . . . At one point Ransom himself asks why isn't Maleldil doing anything. . . . But we are not much wiser about the problem of grace and free will."[57] Humanity was subject to this test, but failed; humanity broke the command and as a result *fell*. So, if Lewis is right in his analogical narrative—*Perelandra*—would humanity, if obedient, have eventually been granted enjoyment of the fruits of the knowledge of good and evil, *with God's permission*? Such fruit, given by God, would not have corrupted as the taking of the fruit by our own *volition* did; original sin, the decision to eat of the fruit of the tree of the knowledge of good and evil, does above all else corrupt in its rebellion.

---

56   Ibid., 258–59.
57   Bertram, "In the Hall of the Fisher King: C. S. Lewis's Cosmic Trilogy as Arthurian Romance." Quoted in, Hooper, *C. S. Lewis: a Companion and Guide*, 222–23. Bertram notes the relationship between Perelandra and Wagner's Ring Cycle, Icelandic myth, and the work of William Morris.

iii. "All get what they want; they do not always like it."

Lewis explicates this in *The Chronicles of Narnia: The Magician's Nephew*. Digory and Polly, two children from London, have inadvertently brought a deeply evil witch-queen into the primeval Narnia at the point of its creation. To protect the fledgling peoples Aslan asks Digory to travel far within Narnia to collect a magic silver apple from a tree, the seed from which will grow into a tree of protection. But, warns Aslan, he must not eat one of the apples. When he gets there Jadis—the evil witch-queen (the White Witch of *The Lion, the Witch and the Wardrobe*)—is seen gorging herself on these apples, and telling Digory how they are the apple of youth, how just one fruit will cure all disease, all ills, and allow her to live forever. Digory's mother is dying of cancer and he is severely tempted to take a second apple: one for Aslan for planting the tree of protection, and one for his mother. He does not; he *resists* temptation. When he returns he confesses to Aslan of his temptation. Aslan comments that if he had taken one for his mother it would have cured her but turned her into a cruel evil person like Jadis. Aslan comments that the witch has now fled because the scent of the tree and its fruit is now despair, horror, death, to her. But, contradicts Polly, she has eaten many of the silver apples. Aslan replies, "That is why all the rest are now a horror to her. That is what happens to those who pluck and eat fruits at the wrong time and in the wrong way. The fruit is good, but they loathe it ever after."[58] Polly is puzzled and asks if it won't work because she took it in the wrong way. Aslan explain, and this applies to humanity's taking of the fruit of the tree of the knowledge of good and evil:

> "Alas," said Aslan, shaking his head. "It will. Things always work according to their nature. She has won her heart's desire; she has unwearying strength and endless days like a goddess. But length of days with an evil heart is only length of misery and already she begins to know it. All get what they want; they do not always like it."
>
> "I—I nearly ate one myself, Aslan," said Digory. "Would I—"
>
> "You would, child," said Aslan. "For the fruit always works—it must work—but it does not work happily for any who pluck it at their own will. . . . And the Witch tempted you to do another thing, my son, did she not?"
>
> "Yes, Aslan. She wanted me to take an apple home to Mother."
>
> "Understand, then, that it would have healed her; but not to your joy or hers. The day would have come when both you and she would have looked back and said it would have been better to die in that illness."[59]

But that is not the end of the implications. Such is when the trial of obedience is broken, we fail. Aslan explains further. And does this apply to humanity?—

> "That is what would have happened, child, with a stolen apple. It is not what will happen now. What I give you now will bring joy. It will not, in your world, give endless life, but it will heal. Go. Pluck her an apple from the Tree."[60]

---

58 Lewis, *The Magician's Nephew*, 162.
59 Ibid.
60 Ibid., 163.

3. Creation and The Fall III: Innocence and Sin, Re-Interpreted

So written into the very nature of the human creation is free will, complemented by a test of obedience: if we turn our will to God, obey and accept what is given to us, we will find our heart's content. It is the disobedience that corrupts, not necessarily the object used in our rebellion. If humanity *had not fallen* (like the sentient species on Perelandra), we would, according to Lewis's conjecture, have been given fruits of the knowledge of good and evil, *with God's permission*. And we would have used that knowledge wisely and to humanity's benefit, whereas Romans 5 and 7 shows us that try as hard as we can we will always get it wrong. This is the corrupting effect of the turn in on self, trying to go it alone away from God: *homo incurvatus in se*—humanity is turned in on itself, the human condition before God defined by original sin.

iv. Obedience-Disobedience: A Dialectic

This is a weakness, a flaw, in the theology of *The Chronicles of Narnia*. If the silver apple works wondrously when given freely by Aslan, yet when taken—stolen—in disobedience works horribly, demonically, then we may postulate that there is no inherent power in the silver apple to corrupt, to generate a fall, or to bless. We noted earlier how Lewis commented on the fall of Eve and Adam, "For all I can see, it might have concerned the literal eating of a fruit, but the question is of no consequence"[61] what was pertinent was the *willful* decision, which profoundly affected their existence. In *Perelandra* the dry land is neither good nor bad, it just is; and it is obedient to God's will in its creation. If Digory's mother took the silver apple from her son she would not have known the circumstances of its arrival (both Eve and Adam *knew* what they were doing was wrong). Therefore in relative innocency Digory's mother would have taken it and eaten it, and logically, it would have had no effect—neither to cure her, nor to condemn her; she had not eaten it with permission, nor out of disobedience. She was not subject to a command, either way, about taking and eating it; Digory was, but that is a different matter. So where is the power to consecrate or corrupt, bless or condemn, sanctify or despoil? The answer lies in Scriptural witness.

Naaman, commander of the armies of Ben-Hadad II in the time of Joram, King of Israel, a proud and powerful man was afflicted with *tzaraath*.[62] A Hebrew slave tells him of a prophet, a man of God, in Samaria who could heal him. After much political wrangling he does indeed travel to meet Elisha, with the equivalent, in today's terms, of a regiment of soldiers and tanks, expecting a personal audience with Elisha, indeed for the prophet to wait on him:

> So Naaman came with his horses and chariots, and halted at the entrance of Elisha's house. Elisha sent a messenger to him, saying, "Go, wash in the Jordan seven times, and your flesh shall be restored and you shall be clean." But Naaman became angry and went away, saying, "I thought that for me he would surely come out, and stand and call on the name of the Lord his God, and would wave his hand over the spot, and cure the leprosy! Are not Abana and Pharpar, the rivers of Damascus, better than all the waters of Israel? Could I not wash in them,

---

61   Lewis, *Problem of Pain*, 60 and 61.
62   Often translated today as leprosy.

> and be clean?" He turned and went away in a rage. But his servants approached and said to him, "Father, if the prophet had commanded you to do something difficult, would you not have done it? How much more, when all he said to you was, 'Wash, and be clean'?" So he went down and immersed himself seven times in the Jordan, according to the word of the man of God; his flesh was restored like the flesh of a young boy, and he was clean.
>
> 2 Kings 5:9–14

So what cured Naaman? Was there something magical about the waters of the River Jordan? No. It was God, the Holy Spirit that healed Naaman, in the context of his act of obedience. Obeying the prophet's command was an act of contrition and humility, a denial of his will. God could have healed him; God did so once Naaman's proud will had turned. The washing in the Jordan carried little if any actual value or medicine. If Naaman had heard of the idea of bathing in the Jordan, claiming it would heal him, and if he had then done so demanding a healing from the Lord God of Israel, there would have been no cure: God would not have healed him. Indeed in his proactive rebellion and pride the act of bathing in the Jordan, *of his own volition*, would have made him a worse person, merely strengthened his will and arrogance against God.

So what is Lewis saying, between *Perelandra* and *The Magician's Nephew*? An act or event given with God's permission is a blessing; an act or event taken against God's instruction corrupts and condemns (if an individual convinces itself that permission was given, where the instruction was to the contrary, then that person is either bad, or deluded; being mistaken doesn't really come into the question given the seriousness of the *fall*[63]). There is a dialectic here: a creation (humanity, or the species on Perelandra, or—speculatively—any number of sentient conscious rational species) is given the freedom to decide, but some decisions will be wrong, leastwise, the primary decision of a creation is to turn, in freedom, to God in obedience; disobedience always involves a turning away. The object of temptation has no intrinsic value; the risk is in a dialectic between obedience-disobedience, which Lewis explicates in *The Magician's Nephew*. It is disobedience that taints and corrupts. Pullman simply redefines paradise in his own image, and the image of his fellow Postmodern educated liberals: the republic of heaven is what he declares it to be, humanity takes heaven by storm and defines evil to its own advantage (which merely reflects Pullman's personal belief system). Lewis, by comparison (though we must not forget that Lewis was writing over half a century before Pullman) questioned the arrogance and narrowness of humanity's storming of heaven. Human history, for Lewis, is characterized by money and poverty, war and ambition, prostitution, the class struggle, empires and slavery. Original sin is the key to history: civilizations and cultures are raised up, seemingly founded on sound principles, apparently good laws are formulated, but things always go wrong, the fatal flaw from the *fall* leads to selfishness, cruelty, "and it all slides back into misery and ruin."[64]

---

[63] See Book 2 in this series: *C. S. Lewis—The Work of Christ Revealed*, "Part Two The Revelation of Christ—God, or a Bad Man," on the question of delusion and wickedness in human decisions.

[64] Lewis, *Broadcast Talks*, 49.

3. Creation and The Fall III: Innocence and Sin, Re-Interpreted

5. IN THE SHADOW OF CHRIST: SIN AND SINNERS

Lewis's third form of retelling the story of the fall is in the presence of sin every day and in every way in sinners, in humanity. Acknowledging the fall is one thing, but living today (with or without knowledge of original sin) what does Lewis make of the human condition and its propensity to sin? His comments are spread amongst his apologetic and philosophical theology, but pertinently in his analogical narrative (essentially, *The Screwtape Letters*). In terms of practical apologetics, Lewis wrote often about the reality of sin, about human attempts at acknowledging sinfulness, about the relationship between holiness and an awareness of sin: in effect he was writing about life *in the shadow of the Christ*; steeped in the effects of the fall, *corrupted by original sin*. People may, or may not, have been aware of Christ in their lives, and what the Christ had done for them on the cross, they may have committed themselves to Christ, or not—regarding him as a religious cultural "artifact." However, Lewis's consideration of sin and sinfulness in his apologetics is of humanity illumined by the light of Christ; this consideration is of people forced into the shadows either to contemplate and repent of their sin or wallow in original sin, in their sinfulness.

Sin is about a contradiction—the breaking of moral code, or law. While Lewis was only too aware that for some "Modern"/"Liberal" theologians, whom he repudiated, the idea of sin was imposed from without and in maturity of faith there was nothing that the religious individual could not do provided it felt comfortable with its behavior and thereby invented good reason for its actions. On the contrary, Lewis argued, although these,

> Modern theologians have, quite rightly, protested against an excessively moralistic interpretation of Christianity. The holiness of God is something more and other than moral perfection . . . but this conception, like that of corporate guilt, is very easily used as an evasion of the real issue. God may be more than moral goodness: *he* is not less. The road to the promised land runs past Sinai. The moral law may exist to be transcended: but there is no transcending it for those who have not first admitted its claims upon them, and then tried with all their strength to meet that claim, and fairly and squarely faced the fact of their failure.[65]

Facing the moral law, admitting failure, is then followed by turning to God in repentance. This is the Christian way; the devil's way is to constantly argue against repentance, indeed to revel in sin, in our fallenness.

---

65 Lewis, *Problem of Pain*, 49.

ON THE CHRIST OF A RELIGIOUS ECONOMY. I. CREATION AND SUB-CREATION

i. A Consciousness of Sin

Screwtape's Inverted Understanding

People are not born with a consciousness of the fall. This knowledge is *revealed* to them; it is a side-effect of original sin that we forget what is unpleasant to us.[66] Only after they have ceased to try to invent the moral law in their own image, and realized the existence of their own transgression of natural, moral, law external to them, will the fact of original sin make sense to them. It is then that a conscious realization of their own frailty and mortality, indeed their own sin, will begin to impinge on them. But this is the start of a supernatural battle played out in the mind: evil spirits will assail, angels will court—decisions are to be taken. This is best characterized by Lewis in the character of Screwtape,[67] the senior devil, who has an understanding of sin to rival that of the saints, and will use it to cause the continued fall of individual humans.

Screwtape comments that temptations to the sins of the flesh will yield results especially during periods of boredom and repetition, "trough periods of human experience," therefore weariness is to be encouraged.[68] Such a dreary weariness may steal away a life through the unconditional offering of tiny sweet sins, almost seen, by the sinner, as tiny consolations for the boredom, the greyness, and dreary repetition of a wasted life.[69] Screwtape's advice to the junior devil is to cultivate a self-centered concern with sin in the human, to turn her or his attention outward; however, the risk of charity must be avoided—charity may wipe away sins, and the devil wants humanity to sin![70] Anything, even a sin, which has the effect of moving the human closer to God works against the purpose of the devil: whispering an invitation to sin into the mind of a human is good (from Screwtape's perspective), but care must be taken over this advice, as certain sins may trigger clear repentance and move the human closer to God and out of the devil's clutches.[71] So what matters? Screwtape, in his advice to the naive junior devil, stresses:

> steal away a man's best years not in sweet sins but in a dreary flickering of the mind over it knows not what and knows not why, in the gratification of curiosities so feeble that the man is only half aware of them[;] ... [focus on a] dim labyrinth of reveries that have not even lust or ambition to give them a relish, but which, once chance association has started them, the creature is too weak and fuddled to shake off.
>
> You will say that these are very small sins; and doubtless, like all young tempters, you are anxious to be able to report spectacular wickedness. But do

---

66   We will often sublimate memories of our actions which we find uncomfortable to remember, but also, the memory of how we are sinned against may also be locked away (for example, the victims of paedophilia), attempts at recovering these memories through therapy usually end up with new memories being planted thus confusion ensures. The Holy Spirit will recover these memories for us if God sees fit, and at the right time for us.
67   Lewis, *Screwtape Letters* (1942) and "Screwtape Proposes a Toast," (1965).
68   Lewis, *Screwtape Letters*, 33f.
69   Ibid., 46.
70   Ibid., 55.
71   Ibid., 46–47.

3. Creation and The Fall III: Innocence and Sin, Re-Interpreted

> remember, the only thing that matters is the extent to which you separate the man from the Enemy [God]. It does not matter how small the sins are provided that their cumulative effect is to edge the man away from the Light and out into the Nothing. Murder is no better than cards if cards can do the trick. Indeed the safest road to Hell is the gradual one—the gentle slope, soft underfoot, without sudden turnings, without milestones, without signposts.[72]

Screwtape also recommends that humans are encouraged to believe that their sins are trivial and revocable, and often are simply wrong choices, which can be rectified by making a different choice.[73] Encourage people to adore celebrities, movie stars, and popular musicians, encourage them to see such people as role models and the epitome of a good life; this will lead them out of the custody of Christ: "almost every film-star or crooner—can now draw tens of thousands of the human sheep with him."[74] If the human creatures begin to perceive their sinfulness, advises Screwtape, then whisper into their minds despair: this will have a greater success than any of the sins which have generated the despair! It is despair and the utter condemnation of sinfulness which is the total opposite of the salvation wrought by Christ.[75] To this end it does no harm, recommends Screwtape, to generate a sense of guilt and pain, not to hide from the knowledge of their sins.[76] The important thing, counsels Screwtape the tormenter, hungering for human souls to torment in eternity, is to *blind* the humans to any understanding of Christ's salvation: repentance is to be avoided.[77] The most deplorable of sinners, Screwtape warns, are the same as the great saints, except they have not yet turned to God and repented—many have been lost at the last moment of life![78] The most appalling and debauched of sinners, if they are conscious of their sinfulness, are only moments away from actual repentance and salvation: "After you have played them for seventy years, the Enemy [God] may snatch them from your claws in the seventy-first. They are capable, you see, of real repentance."[79]

An Orthodox Teaching

Lewis comments that people will so easily justify sin by claiming good intentions.[80] Therefore a "recovery" of a traditional understanding of sin is critical to a right judgment, and to salvation.[81] A sin may appear nice but it is still a breach of the moral law.[82] For example, writes Lewis, the theft of an apple is wrong—but that does not deny the sweetness and enjoyment of the fruit.[83] That sin is a reality issues from God-given

---

72 Ibid., 47–48, also, 75f., 105f.
73 Ibid., 45.
74 Lewis, "Screwtape Proposes a Toast," 7.
75 Lewis, *Screwtape Letters*, 115.
76 Ibid., 121f.
77 Lewis, "Screwtape Proposes a Toast," 16–18.
78 Ibid., 6–7.
79 Ibid., 13.
80 Lewis, *Problem of Pain*, 40–41.
81 Ibid., 42.
82 Lewis, "Christianity and Culture," 21f. See also, *Broadcast Talks*, 45–46.
83 Lewis, *Letters to Malcolm*, 86.

free will.[84] The abuse of free will leads to original sin, and then, "Sin may recur because the original temptation continues; but quite apart from that, sin of its very nature breeds sin by strengthening sinful habit and weakening the conscience,"[85] writes Lewis. Yet grace abounds: sin remains sin even when God brings good out of the situation.[86] Sin relates to the will of God imbued into the human; what should concur and create a holy act ends up mutating through self-will into sin: "The only way in which I can make real to myself what theology teaches about the heinousness of sin is to remember that every sin is the distortion of an energy breathed into us—an energy which, if thus not distorted, would have blossomed into one of those holy acts whereof 'God did it' and 'I did it' are both true descriptions."[87] Drawing on Augustine, Lewis asserts pride as the cause and continuation of sin.[88] And if we look on and don't censure sin we are complicit,[89] even if these little sins seem innocent and obscure enough to start with. Sin issues from the fall: that is the pride "of putting yourself as the center instead of God,"[90] however, repentance leads to forgiveness:

> I certainly believe (now really, long since with a merely intellectual assent) that a sin once repented and forgiven, is gone, annihilated, burnt up in the fire of Divine Love, white as snow. There is no harm in continuing to "bewail" it, i.e., to express one's sorrow, but not to ask for pardon, for that you already have—one's sorrow for being that sort of person. Your conscience need not be "burdened" with it in the sense of feeling that you have an unsettled account, but you can still in a sense be patiently and (in a sense) contentedly humbled by it . . .[91]

But we must not allow the devil to deceive us with false guilt: repent and confess, don't believe that you are still guilty: "What the devil loves is that vague cloud of unspecified guilt feeling or unspecified virtue by which he lures us into despair or presumption."[92] Sins are forgivable precisely because they issue from the fall: "the gravitation away from God must be a product of the fall and sin, because it is unavoidable, it must be venial."[93]

Disorder and Responsibility

Disordered relationships, perversions of affection, are not an illness, a disease, requiring medical intervention; such are sins, Lewis is quite clear on this. In such cases the sinner needs spiritual guidance and absolution.[94] Sin is not something medical,

---

84   Lewis, *Miracles*, 128. See also, Lewis, *Problem of Pain*, 112–13, and, Lewis, *Broadcast Talks* 46f.
85   Lewis, *Problem of Pain*, 94.
86   Ibid., 89–90.
87   Lewis, *Letters to Malcolm*, 67.
88   Lewis, Problem of Pain, 19–20, 52, 57–59; Lewis, *Christian Behaviour*, VIa, "The Great Sin," 42–47.
89   Lewis, *Problem of Pain*, 94.
90   Ibid., 57–58.
91   Lewis writing to Mrs Lockley, Jan 8, 1952. Lewis, *Letters of C. S. Lewis*, (2nd ed., expanded, 1988), 416. See also, *Problem of Pain*, 45.
92   Lewis writing to Mary Willis Shelburne, Jul 21, 1958. Lewis, *Collected Letters Vol. III*, 962.
93   Lewis, *Problem of Pain*, 58.
94   Lewis, *The Four Loves*, 46, 52–53.

3. Creation and The Fall III: Innocence and Sin, Re-Interpreted

which, for Lewis, would make crime pathological; sin is not in need of "healing" or a "cure," sin deserves forgives, or divine punishment if the sinner does not repent.[95] We are responsible, we cannot evade guilt, sin does not issue from someone else—"I am rather sick of the modern assumption that, for all events, 'we,' the people, are never responsible: it is always our rulers, or ancestors, or parents, or education, or anybody but precious us..."[96]—Lewis continues, elsewhere, if I hurt someone I am responsible, if by injuring him I corrupt him further this worsens my sin and my guilt: sin feeds on sin.[97] This is why for Lewis humanity will persistently try to avoid recognizing and naming sin. Why? For in that recognition lies the demand for repentance, and repentance is only real if it is deep-rooted, where the person is inwardly shriven, and leads to change.[98]

Personal Responsibility

Lewis warns those who do not think much about their own sins, but speak incessantly about the sins of others, that their priorities are all wrong.[99] Contemplating our own sins is far more urgent: "Try not to think—much less speak—of *their* sins. One's own are a much more profitable theme! And if, on consideration, one can find no faults on one's own side, then cry for mercy: for this *must* be a dangerous delusion."[100] He counsels that we should identify our own sins, externalize them onto a list and consider seriously how to repent of each.[101] Instead of judging others for their sins perhaps we should consider how our own sins "infect" others who decide to follow our example,[102] especially when a refusal to contemplate and face one's own manifold sins can often be a contributory cause to an inability to pray.[103]

> Christian writers seem to be so very strict and finicking at one moment and so very free and easy at another. They talk about mere sins of thought as if they were immensely important: and then they talk about the most frightful murders and treacheries as if you'd only got to repent and all would be forgiven. But I've begun to see they are right. What they are always thinking of is the mark which the action leaves on that tiny central self which no one sees in this life but which each of us will have to endure.... One man may be so placed that his anger sheds the blood of thousands, and another so placed that however angry he gets he can't do much damage. But the little mark on the soul may be much the same in both. Each has done something to himself which, unless he repents, will make it harder for him to keep out of the rage next time he's tempted.[104]

---

95   Lewis, "The Humanitarian Theory of Punishment," 238 and 242–44.
96   Lewis, "Lewis to Mary Willis Shelburne, May 30, 1953." Lewis, *Collected Letters, Vol. III*, 333
97   Lewis, *Reflections on the Psalms*, 20–22.
98   Lewis, *Letters to Malcolm*, 60f.
99   Lewis, "Miserable Offenders," 94–95.
100   Lewis writing to Mary Willis Shelburne, Jan 9, 1961. *Collected Letters, Vol. III*, 1225. Lewis's emphasis.
101   Lewis, "Miserable Offenders," 94.
102   Lewis, *Problem of Pain*, 95.
103   Lewis, *Letters to Malcolm*, 108–9.
104   Lewis, *Christian Behaviour*, 26.

But it is not just *what we do*; we err if we forget, or dismiss as non-existent sins, what *we do not do*, what *we fail to act on*. In this context Lewis refers to Matt 25, the Parable of the Sheep and the Goats.[105] If we are not prepared to face our sins of commission and omission, if we are not prepared to acknowledge that sins exist in a public arena, then we may be eternally lost.[106]

"The more important sins"

Generally speaking Lewis asserts, and is quite right, that the world does not have the right priorities. What it considers to be important sins often issue from a distorted perspective. What is serious before God is often considered unimportant by humanity, where the human overfocuses on "the sins of the flesh," particularly in the media.[107] In further correspondence he extends this principle: spiritual evils which we share with the devils (pride, anger, and arrogance, also malice, malevolence, and spite) condemn us to a greater degree than the sensual incontinent flaws which we often share with animals.[108] But then those who know the depth of sin and find no satisfaction in it may be in a far greater position of accepting the need to repent than those entrapped by worldly success: "Prostitutes are in no danger of finding their present life so satisfactory that they cannot turn to God: the proud, the avaricious, the self-righteous, are in that danger."[109] Is not, continues Lewis, cruelty more evil than lust and the world as dangerous as the flesh?[110] It is always too easy, Lewis asserts, for people to be caught up, judgmentally, with the sins in the media—the public sins of government, crime waves, adulterous politicians—and ignore their own spiteful pride, envious greed, vain glorious conceit.[111] The sins of the flesh, bad though they are, are among the least of all sins, as Lewis noted in the wartime radio broadcasts:

> Although I've had to speak at some length about sex, I want to make it as clear as I possibly can that the center of Christian morality is not here. If anyone thinks that Christians regard unchastity as the great vice, he is quite wrong. The sins of the flesh are bad, but they are the least bad of all sins. All the worst pleasures are purely spiritual: the pleasure of putting other people in the wrong, of bossing and patronizing and spoiling sport, and back-biting; the pleasures of power, of hatred. You see, there are two things inside me, competing with the human self which I must try to become. They are the animal self, and the diabolical self. The diabolical self is the worse of the two. That is why a cold, self-righteous prig

---

105 Lewis, *Reflections on the Psalms*, 8.
106 Lewis, *Problem of Pain*, 45–46. see also *Screwtape Letters*, 123–24.
107 Lewis, "Lewis writing to Dom Bede Griffiths OSB, Jan 17, 1940," *Collected Letters, Vol. II*, 325–26.
108 Lewis, "Lewis writing to Mary Willis Shelburne, Nov 26, 1962." *Collected Letters, Vol. III*, 1383–84.
109 Lewis, *Problem of Pain*, 79.
110 Lewis, *Surprised by Joy*, 83–84, see also, "Lilies that Fester," 47–48.
111 Lewis is here writing about the often diametric difference between what the general public (whether self-confessed Christian or not) consider important as compared to the priorities of the saints of the Church. See, Lewis, "Christian Apologetics," 70f.

3. Creation and The Fall III: Innocence and Sin, Re-Interpreted

who goes regularly to Church may be far nearer to hell than a prostitute. But, of course, it is better to be neither.[112]

ii. Sinfulness and Desperation

Knowledge of original sin (characterized by the presence of individual sins) in the person is one thing; a general feeling and awareness of sinfulness is another. Many all over the world will have no knowledge of the *revealed* reality of the fall, yet may be steeped in an all-pervading sense of their unworthiness and sinfulness. But then, wrote Lewis, the gospel offers nothing to the human who has no awareness of its own sinfulness: "Christianity simply doesn't make sense until you've faced the sort of facts I've been describing. Christianity tells people to repent and promises them forgiveness. It therefore has nothing (as far as I know) to say to people who don't know they've done anything to repent of and who don't feel that they need any forgiveness."[113] Then, if the human responds, and not simply in the form of cultural spirituality and civic religion, but when the human truly takes on Christ, it will—more and more—come to recognize its sinfulness (this gradual recognition should be generated by the Holy Spirit), and will be turned, by degrees, into a Christlike human, which is what it should have been in the first place—*prelapsarian*.[114] The developing sense of unworthiness, sinfulness and corruption should not lead in this case to despair—providing it is balanced with repentance before God, either implicitly or explicitly in Christ (the Holy Spirit may intimate something of God's forgiveness into someone who geographically and culturally, even in temporal terms, is isolated from any knowledge of the Christ event). What Lewis is asserting is the paramount importance of the *revealed* fact that Christ's salvation works on the basis that humanity is bad, corrupt, "fallen," and lost:

> A recovery of the old sense of sin is essential to Christianity. Christ takes it for granted that men are bad. Until we really feel this assumption of his to be true, though we are part of the world *he* came to save, we are not part of the audience to whom his words are addressed. We lack the first condition for understanding what *he* is talking about. And when men attempt to be Christians without this preliminary consciousness of sin, the result is almost bound to be a certain resentment against God as to one always inexplicably angry. Most of us have at times felt a secret sympathy with the dying farmer who replied to the Vicar's dissertation on repentance by asking "What harm have I ever done *him*?" There is the real rub. The worst we have done to God is to leave *him* alone . . .[115]

Even then, Lewis asserts, our true sinfulness, the depth of our personal rebellion which seems so normal to us, is shielded from us by our self-will.[116] "We are deceived by looking on the outside of things. We suppose ourselves to be roughly not much worse than Y, whom all acknowledge for a decent sort of person, and certainly (though

---

112 Lewis, *Christian Behaviour*, 29–30.
113 Lewis, *Broadcast Talks*, 32.
114 Lewis, *Beyond Personality*, 160.
115 Lewis, *Problem of Pain*, 42.
116 Lewis, "Miserable Offenders" 92–94; see also, Lewis, *Problem of Pain*, 42–47.

we should not claim it out loud) better than the abominable X. Even on the superficial level we are probably deceived about this."[117] But then in the context of an awareness of our sinfulness the saint should not been seen with a halo around his or her head, the saint is saintly because s/he is more aware of its sinfulness than the unrepentant: "when the saints say that they—even they—are vile, they are recording truth with scientific accuracy."[118] We must be aware of our inherent sinfulness, but we must not wallow in this realization, there is a perverse pride in self-loathing: "In solitude, and also in confession, I have found (to my regret) that the degrees of shame and disgust which I actually feel at my own sins do not at all correspond to what my reason tells me about their comparative gravity."[119] Sinfulness in itself is not irrevocable. Lewis cites the Parable of the Unjust Judge to illustrate how no evil is so entrenched as to be unmovable.[120]

6. THE ANSWER: THE CHRIST

Contradicting original sin, *curing* selfish sinfulness, will inevitably be a painful process.[121] But we cannot do it alone, we cannot do it of our own strength. The answer comes from without. Acknowledging the crisis within us is, for Lewis, at least a first step. Often the unrepentant and therefore unregenerate is utterly lost, unable to identify this crisis. The voice of conscience is, however corrupted our interpretation and reception of this voice may be, nonetheless important. We must never cease to remember that "this too is for us the voice of Christ. For we have been taught that *he* who was without sin became sin for our sakes, plumbed the depths of that worst suffering which comes to evil men who at last know their own evil."[122] A cynical approach would be to decry *prayerful* repentance because God knows already what our sins are, but prayerful acknowledgment, regret, and repentance is crucially important because, "To put ourselves thus on a personal footing with God . . . by unveiling, by confessing our sins and making known our requests, we assume the high rank of persons before *him*. And *he*, descending, becomes a person to us."[123] In confessing and repenting we match God's will, to a degree, for *he* seeks that they are removed: *his* love for us is not diminished,[124] for, writes Lewis, God is the God of mercy and seeks our repentance, but not our submission and compliance to sin.[125] God is not the God of compromise. Ignoring sin, our sins, putting our life's busy-ness first won't help, believing that time heals and absolves does not reduce the magnitude of sins; believing we have matured, become decrepit in old age, does not write-off the sins of youth.

---

117   Lewis, *Problem of Pain*, 43.
118   Ibid., 51.
119   Lewis, *Letters to Malcolm*, 96.
120   Ibid., 102.
121   Lewis, *Problem of Pain*, Chs. 6 and 7.
122   Lewis, *Reflections on the Psalms*, 110.
123   Lewis, *Letters to Malcolm*, 18–19.
124   Lewis, *Problem of Pain*, 30–32.
125   Lewis, *Christian Behaviour*, 48f.

3. Creation and The Fall III: Innocence and Sin, Re-Interpreted

> We have a strange illusion that mere time cancels sin. I have heard others, and I have heard myself, recounting cruelties and falsehoods committed in boyhood as if they were no concern of the present speaker's, and even with laughter. But mere time does nothing either to the fact or to the guilt of a sin. The guilt is washed out not by time but by repentance and the blood of Christ: if we have repented these early sins we should remember the price of our forgiveness and be humble. As for the fact of a sin, is it probable that anything cancels it? All times are eternally present to God.... It may be that salvation consists not in the cancelling of these eternal moments but in the perfected humanity that bears the shame forever, rejoicing in the occasion which it furnished to God's compassion and glad that it should be common knowledge to the universe.[126]

Therefore, in an interview near the end of his life, Lewis commented that it is not enough to want simply to be rid of one's sins, what is important is "to believe in the One who saves us from our sins. Not only do we need to recognize that we are sinners; we need to believe in a Savior who takes away sin."[127] We may be wearied by our sins, or even indifferent, but God—who is all love—is not. "The great thing to remember is that, though our feelings come and go, *his* love for us does not. It is not wearied by our sins or our indifference; and, therefore, it is quite relentless in its determination that we shall be cured of those sins, at whatever cost to us, at whatever cost to *him*."[128]

---

126   Lewis, *Problem of Pain*, 45–46.
127   Lewis, "Cross Examination", 215–21.
128   Lewis, *Christian Behaviour*, 50.

4

Creation and The Fall IV: The Human Condition before God

SYNOPSIS:
We have invoked the doctrine of original sin, however, how does it have manifold and far reaching consequences for humanity, how does it actually affect us? What is the human condition before God? We are, for Lewis, the corrupted creation, we are the rebel stood before its maker and judge. What is the backdrop of twentieth-century theology that Lewis is reacting against—characterized by a form of neo-Pelagianism? A refutation of such "Liberal" skepticism lies in understanding the *transmission* of original sin, and how humanity is "true to type" (but not true to "form": platonically we are not as we should be). Lewis consistently argued for the transmission of original sin. Can science help or hinder in understanding the human condition and its manifold delusions in its rebellion? In addition to Augustine's proposition of spiritual concupiscence, can science help explain (DNA and horizontal gene therapy: do our behavioral decisions effect our genome)?

Turned in on itself humanity locks itself in and thereby protects itself from any saving grace God, through the Holy Spirit, might offer. Lewis uses story to present the truth of the manifold ramifications of original sin. Like the Russian writer and prophet Dostoevsky, Lewis identified how the human rebellion that is the *fall* works, and how the individual raises itself up above the common herd to redefine morality in its own image: *eritis sicut Deus* (Ye will be like God, to act as if you were God). Uncle Andrew and Queen Jadis, in *The Magician's Nephew*, voice the same "idea" as Raskolnikov and other characters in Dostoevsky's works. Why is this so?—because, claimed Dostoevsky (a claim Lewis implicitly concurred with), "I deduced from all of this the utter necessity of faith in Christ."

Lewis concluded his apologetic writing on sin by reasserting in the last year of his life natural, God-given, law, which defined human relations and behavior; even if we failed to obey, to act out and be obedient to this natural law, it still stood over and against us. Why, asks Lewis, does God not do more to control, restrict, and limit humanity?—this raises questions of what we may term ontological custodianship (which relates to theodicy). Should God restrict our freedom and change the nature of the human?

1. INTRODUCTION

Lewis's doctrine of creation frames the human story. It provides a worldview. It is orthodox and biblical. However, it does appear to fly in the face of much scientific theory, or more pertinently, Western socio-psychological theories about humanity, which attack the very idea of sin, let alone the *fall*, and are promulgated by people who are convinced that humanity can, does, and will improve itself, such is the aim of civilization. But are we really any different to so-called "primitive" peoples, thousands of years ago?

2. CREATION, NEO-PELAGIANISM, AND TRANSMISSION

i. Solving the Problem for Ourselves

The "Modern"/"Liberal" theological tradition dismisses Lewis's assertion that original sin is hereditary[1] and asserts that behavior is not transmitted down the generations; the changes, if any, caused in the proto-humans "Adam" and "Eve" are not written in stone. This "Modern"/"Liberal" tradition as a form of neo-Pelagianism, asserts humanity's right to raise itself up, improve itself, defining whatever it chooses as the good. As a very British heresy (originating in Pelagius c. 354–430 AD, a Romano-British churchman, orator, and ascetic who denied the doctrine of original sin and was declared a heretic by the church), Lewis saw Pelagianism in some quarters of the Church of England of his day as representative of a denial of the hereditary nature of original sin. Essentially Pelagianism taught that individuals could achieve salvation purely by their own efforts, through good works. Pelagius's teachings are essentially a contradiction of an Augustinian doctrine of original sin. Lewis, as we have seen, consistently argued for an Augustinian position and against the neo-Pelagianism of many "Modern"/"Liberal" senior Anglican clerics in the mid-twentieth century whom he had contact with in Oxford. According to Pelagianism, Eve and Adam's sin did not taint human nature; therefore people are still capable of choosing good or evil without the influence of God through the Holy Spirit in the form of divine grace: the sin of Eve and Adam was merely a bad example to follow. Augustine countered Pelagius with the concept of prevenient grace: God's Holy Spirit working in us, inspiring us, acting on our minds, *prior* to any good we believe we may do. Any real good is not of our own volition.

ii. Lewis: Grace and Free Will

Lewis tackles these issues in his final book, published posthumously. He asserts that causal thinking does not help. It has led to the "puzzle about Grace and free will."[2] It is, for Lewis, our presuppositions that make a nonsense of causal classifications: "You will notice that Scripture just sails over the problem. 'Work out your own salvation in fear and trembling'—pure Pelagianism. But why? 'For it is God who worketh in

---

1 See, for example, Pittenger, "Apologist versus Apologist: a Critique of C. S. Lewis as 'Defender of the Faith,'" 1104 and 1107, and, Lewis's response, Lewis, "Rejoinder to Dr Pittenger," 1369 and 1371; see also, Lewis, "Modern Theology and Biblical Criticism," 152–66. For the implications of Lewis's confrontation of "Liberalism" see Brazier, "The Pittenger-Lewis Debate: Fundamentals of an Ontological Christology," 7–23.

2 Lewis, *Letters to Malcolm*, 47.

you'—pure Augustinianism. It is presumably only our presuppositions that make this appear nonsensical. We profanely assume that divine and human action exclude one another . . . so that 'God did this' and 'I did this' cannot both be true of the same act except in that each contributed a share."[3] Lewis therefore postulates a two-way traffic. We may be created, where to be created implies a passive verb—once we were not, but now we are, yet, we are also "made to be agents, we have nothing that we have not received."[4] But we are more than mere receptacles, as our predisposition to sin demonstrates. Therefore, concludes Lewis, divine action (the forgiveness wrought by Christ) is subsequent to our behavior: "For God forgives sins. He would not do so if we committed none—'whereto serves mercy but to confront the visage of offence?' In that sense the divine action is consequent upon, conditioned by, elicited by, our behavior."[5] The incarnation is caused by the fall; Lewis is traditional and orthodox on this point. From a twentieth-century neo-Pelagian perspective the cross simply becomes an unfortunate accident, atonement through the blood of Christ is not necessary. All we need to do is follow Jesus's good example. Lewis parodied this approach in *The Great Divorce*. An atheistic apostate bishop who speculates on what Jesus would have been like had he not been crucified—had he not died he would have gone on to become a profound and wise religious philosopher, presumably equal to the Buddha or Socrates: atonement and salvation is therefore nothing to do with Jesus's life and mission, and pertinently his death. Lewis has this apostate bishop, who resides in hell, and is content with the grey thin near-to-nothingness existence of his damnation, comment that he has still been speculating:

> I'm taking the text about growing up to the measure of the stature of Christ and working out an idea which I feel sure you'll be interested in. . . . Jesus was a comparatively young man when he died. He would have outgrown some of his earlier views, you know, if he'd lived. As he might have done, with a little more tact and patience. . . . A profoundly interesting question. What a different Christianity we might have had if only the founder had reached his full stature! I shall end up by pointing out how this deepens the significance of the Crucifixion. One feels for the first time what a disaster it was: what a tragic waste[;] . . . so much promise cut short.[6]

The assumption here is that wisdom and maturity will lead to sinlessness. With education and maturity humanity can make the right decisions, leaving behind whatever sins the proto-humans indulged in. The pertinent question for these twentieth-century neo-Pelagians is about inheritance, legacy. The action of original sin did not, according to Pelagianism, have a changing effect on the rest of humanity— the very nature of humanity was not changed, corrupted, dis-graced, by the actions of Eve and Adam. The behavior and actions of those who explicitly believe in Pelagius's doctrine (or especially those who know not of this heresy but act in a self-contained

---

3   Ibid., 47. Lewis is quoting from Phil 2:12–13.
4   Ibid., 47–48.
5   Ibid., 48. Lewis is quoting Shakespeare, *Hamlet*, Act 3, Scene III, lines 48b–49.
6   Lewis, *The Great Divorce*, 40–41.

manner believing they are sealed off from God and can raise themselves up), are of little difference to today's secular atheists who reject God and create an hermetic world of values and beliefs to live in: both are corrupting any sound understanding of God, and God's salvific actions towards the human creation. The view of Pelagius is that Jesus is setting a good example for humanity to follow (therefore the sacrifice on the cross was not necessary; atonement is reached through being good). Therefore humanity has full control and therefore full responsibility for obeying or disobeying Jesus's teachings: explicit Pelagians believe they have the actual strength and soundness of mind to follow Jesus; others, whether they "know" of Jesus or not, believe they are acting right and proper, good and just (as the National Socialists in Germany, or the Marxist-Leninists did in Russia, in the twentieth century) and are thus improving the human lot. The central objection/argument against a doctrine of original sin cited by often closeted contemporary neo-Pelagians is the question of transmission. The objection states that the sin of Adam and Eve is their sin and their responsibility and that there is no way it can be transmitted; the infection is isolated, their descendants are immune.

iii. Born this Way?

If we accept orthodoxy then we need to ask a simple question: how is original sin transmitted? Pertinently, if behavior issues from the will, conditioned to a greater or lesser degree by reason, and if original sin is defined by a corrupt will, then we may ask, is there a hereditary element to behavior, in addition to the social interaction and nurture that influences how we behave. Further, is there a hereditary element to behavior, written into creation? Household cats are much more instinctive, wild, and undomesticated than most other domesticated animals, therefore they retain and display much of their natural behavior. North-West European wild cats (from which most of our household pets are descended) will move around in a tight circle one way, then the other, before settling down to sleep. This is commonly observed behavior. Why? It makes no difference to the chair or bed they choose to sleep on. Ethologists[7] tell us that this is because their wild ancestors circled around several times to tamp down the grass and weeds to make a bed to sleep on; they also (being ultimately descended from African and Middle Eastern wildcats) circled to remove any danger from the bedded down grasses (spiders or scorpions).[8] A kitten separated from its mother within days of birth, even if it remains in a house and never goes outside, will as an adult display this circling behavior: this is instinctive, it has been

---

7   Ethology is the scientific study of animal behaviour and as such is a sub-topic of zoology.

8   This relates to epigenetics, a branch of biology, as the study of heritable changes in gene expression or cellular phenotype caused by mechanisms other than changes in the underlying DNA sequence. It refers to functionally relevant modifications to the genome that do not involve a change in the nucleotide sequence. Experiments have been carried out that prove that the activity of genes can be turned on or off according to behavior. Therefore the manner in which a rat's offspring develop is not exactly, or exclusively, genetic, but *epigenetic*: environmental, also nurturing factors by the mother, turn on or off genes which affect the eventual creature, and its progeny and so forth. Is there a selfish gene that would not be so dominant but for *the fall*?

4. Creation and The Fall IV: The Human Condition before God

CHRIST
THE LOGOS,
THE WORD OF GOD,
DISCLOSING

**Figure 2
Joseph Nuttgens,
"Christ Teaching the People,"
Stained Glass Window,
King's College London, Chapel,
Strand Campus, 2000-2001**

Academics debate, led by Jesus, Christ the Logos, the Word of God, behind whose head is an atom, the book on the table shows the double helix of DNA genes and chromosomes, recalling the College's discovery of DNA through the work of Rosalind Franklin and Maurice Wilkins in the 1950s.

Photograph:
P. H. Brazier

bred into the felines. It is presumably passed on genetically. So, can modes of behavior be ingrained into synaptic pathways into the brain, which then determine the genetic encoding which will form the brain in subsequent generations? Can the way cats behave affect how this behavior is chemically, physically, manifested in our genome and over time change their feline nature. This takes place bit by bit over much time, and if the behavior suits a creature's adaptation to an environment it will survive. Such is the theory of evolution through natural selection: it would seem that it is not just limbs, fingers, night-vision, and so forth that can evolve and become fixed, but also certain forms of behavior. In subsequent generations, thousands of years from now, household "domestic" cats will probably lose this circling behavior.

iv. Inheritance?

But this is animals, and we are human, and Lewis is adamant about an inherited element to original sin. He is not just talking about Augustine's invocation of spiritual concupiscence, yet, he presumably knew virtually nothing about genetics. Can we help Lewis here? Original sin is about morals and ethics, which in turn is about behavior; behavior may often be the result of nurture; however, can our behavior actually alter the genetic inheritance we pass on to the next generation? If so, then there is an inherited behavioral element to original sin, specifically in the character of our decisions. A Darwinian theory of evolution through natural selection traditionally denies such a possibility. For Darwin random mutations give rise to changes in the creature that either increase its adaptability to survive, or not. It is no good looking at the simplistic presentation of Darwinian evolution through natural selection often presented in the media. Darwin's so-called "tree of life,"[9] which branches out for different species is too neat and simplistic; the "tree" is now to be seen as a human invention. Horizontal gene transfer (HGT) complicates matters infinitely: the idea of simple singular progression from one species to another (the "tree of life," branching out into species from a common ancestor in the primordial seas) is not how life developed. Sections of DNA swapped between species complicates matters infinitely. After 150 years there is no "missing link" to be found, linking humans to primates, *solely*. Evolution appears to be part of the answer, perhaps accounting for development within species, but accounts for only part of the wonder and mystery of creation.[10] Significant and highly important parts of the human genome have resulted not from random DNA mutation but from HGT. The scientist Graham Lawton comments:

> Cases of HGT in multicellular organisms are coming in thick and fast. HGT has been documented in insects, fish and plants, and a few years ago a piece of snake DNA was found in cows. The most likely agents of this genetic shuffling are viruses, which constantly cut and paste DNA from one genome into another,

---

9   For Darwin's sketch of the Tree of Life see: http://darwin-online.org.uk/EditorialIntroductions/vanWyhe_notebooks.html

10   For horizontal gene transfer and how it disproves Darwin's so-called Tree of Life, see, the primary statement: Doolittle, "Uprooting the Tree of Life," 72–77. Online (subscription access): http://www.nature.com/scientificamerican/journal/v282/n2/pdf/scientificamerican0200-90.pdf

4. Creation and The Fall IV: The Human Condition before God

often across great taxonomic distances. In fact, by some reckonings, *40 to 50 per cent of the human genome consists of DNA imported horizontally by viruses*, some of which has taken on vital biological functions."[11]

If 40–50 per cent of our genome is imported by horizontal gene transfer it is of no surprise that the so-called missing link has not been found, and in all probability won't ever be found: we are fearfully and wondrously made—*created by God*.[12] Clay in the potter's hands is a better analogy than atheistically driven random meaningless mutation. Lawton comments further, "The tree of life, one of the iconic concepts of evolution, has turned out to be a figment of our imagination."[13] The story is part of basic biological curriculum, where Darwin is reputed to have sat down in July 1837 in his study, and in his red notebook wrote, "I think" then drew a spindly sketch of a tree, of life, where different groups of life forms, species, evolve from one to the other, forming separate families. "The tree-of-life concept was absolutely central to Darwin's thinking, equal in importance to natural selection. . . . Without it the theory of evolution would never have happened. The tree also helped carry the day for evolution. Darwin argued successfully that the tree of life was a fact of nature, plain for all to see though in need of explanation. The explanation he came up with was evolution by natural selection."[14] What was once represented as the tree of life, the development of life on earth into ever more complex creatures in specific groups, characterized by linear evolution, isolated development along separate branches, is now considered by many scientists to be no more than a biological mish-mash, an impenetrable thicket. What is perceived now is a tangled *web of life*, and the web is of such a complexity with life forms swapping DNA on a vastly unimaginable scale so as to be impenetrable to the human intellect. If the human wants to try to see the whole picture, a picture so vast that the neat liner evolution of Darwin must, from a theological perspective, be regarded as a pseudo-religious myth, a neo-Gnostic figment of his imagination, then in humility the human must understand that any theories it comes up with—of its own volition—will be transitory and relative (here the baptized imagination of the theologian is superior to the supposed academic impartiality of the scientist). Life did not start in a single "creature" from which all others evolved; life is now considered to have started as a common ancestral *community* of primitive cells: once the conditions were right on the earth, life simultaneously started in a multitude of locations and developed, swapping DNA, and so forth producing an ever more complex web of life. Life is infinitely too complex in its ceaseless creative fecundity for such a neat simplistic linear evolved pattern: life simply started and then grew and developed at a phenomenal rate, the only limits or constraints being the relative boundaries of the earth as a biosphere. So what of Darwin's "Tree of Life:"

---

11   Lawton, "Uprooting Darwin's Tree of Life," 34–39, quotation, 38 [my emphasis]. See *New Scientist*, Aug 27, 2008. Online (subscription access): http://www.newscientist.com/article/mg20126921.600-why-darwin-was-wrong-about-the-tree-of-life.html.
12   Might viruses in this context be seen as God's "intelligent" agents of creation?
13   Ibid., 34.
14   Ibid.

> [T]oday the project lies in tatters, torn to pieces by an onslaught of negative evidence. Many biologists now argue that the tree concept is obsolete and needs to be discarded. "We have no evidence at all that the tree of life is a reality," says Bapteste. That bombshell has even persuaded some that our fundamental view of biology needs to change. So what happened? In a nutshell, DNA. The discovery of the structure of DNA in 1953 opened up new vistas for evolutionary biology. Here, at last, was the very stuff of inheritance into which was surely written the history of life. By the mid-1980s there was great optimism that molecular techniques would finally reveal the universal tree of life in all its glory. Ironically, the opposite happened.[15]

Bacteria, plants, and animals increasingly reveal that different species crossbreed, genes are not simply passed along individual branches of the supposed tree of life, they are *primarily* transferred between species on different evolutionary or developmental paths. "Microbes swap genetic material so promiscuously it can be hard to tell one type from another, but animals regularly crossbreed too—as do plants—and the offspring can be fertile."[16]

Spiritual concupiscence both directly and indirectly governs our behavior, which is will and desire; this therefore influences the corruption of human nature, and thereby the transmission of a state of original sin, of fallenness. We are born changed and corrupted in our humanity, our despoiled human nature, before God, and in the spiritual concupiscence that governs us as a creature. Can behavior changes be inherited? Darwinian evolutionary theory assumes that acquired traits, learnt modifications of behavior, cannot be inherited by the offspring. But horizontal gene transfer, based as it is on observable changes in DNA, complicates matters and points to the possibility. Why? If we expose ourselves outside of the graceful protection of God (represented, perhaps, by the "Garden of Eden") then we expose ourselves to a potential maelstrom of HGT, which will therefore change our genome and *pass on the conditions of our rebellion to our descendants*! The earth brings forth; this is the defining principle of sub-creation. Life within the biosphere that is the earth is interconnected. There is nothing in Scripture to deny this. But can we pin this hereditary possibility down more specifically? A Scandinavian research group from Linköping University (Sweden) demonstrated that chickens can actually inherit behavioral modifications induced by stress in their parents. The group raised chickens, some under stressful conditions, others in a normal environment to investigate whether there was any genetic basis for the results. The expression levels of approximately nine thousand genes in the brain of the chickens were studied: those exposed to stress showed a number of genes where the expression was either increased or decreased, and the same

---

15   Ibid., 34–36. Referring to Eric Bapteste, evolutionary biologist at the Pierre and Marie Curie University, Paris, France.

16   *The Guardian*, Jan 21, 2009: http://www.guardian.co.uk/science/2009/jan/21/charles-darwin-evolution-species-tree-life. Furthermore, "Last year [2008], scientists at the University of Texas at Arlington found a strange chunk of DNA in the genetic make-up of eight animals, including the mouse, rat and the African clawed frog. The same chunk is missing from chickens, elephants and humans, suggesting it must have become wedged into the genomes of some animals by crossbreeding."

4. Creation and The Fall IV: The Human Condition before God

genes were similarly affected in their offspring. The results therefore demonstrated that both the changes in gene function and the behavioral changes caused by stress were transferred to the offspring. In addition the results were evident in domesticated chickens, not in the ancestor, the Red Junglefowl (*Gallus gallus*).[17]

v. Graceless Stress in a Hostile World

If controlled environmental stress in chickens changes their behavior, which in turn is encoded in their DNA and passed on to their offspring and descendants, then what did the full exposure, after the *fall*, of our graceless experience of this world, the violence of this reality, do to create an inherited predilection for the proud Godless self-interest that now defines original sin? Given that the proto-humans, Adam and Eve, were "expelled" from paradise, "Eden," then found themselves alone, apart, separated, from the now invisible presence of God, fighting for survival adrift in a hostile world, it is no small wonder that the stress of survival would have had a detrimental effect on their genomes, and thus, in effect, encoded the results of original sin in them and their descendants, leading to the selfish, proud, behavior that is characteristic of original sin to be passed on to their offspring and descendants. So Lewis is right; and the "Liberal" Anglican neo-Pelagian wrong. Lewis commented, long before the discovery of DNA, especially HGT:

> This condition was transmitted by heredity to all later generations, for it was not simply what biologists call an acquired variation; it was the emergence of a new kind of man—*a new species, never made by God, had sinned itself into existence.* The change which man had undergone was not parallel to the development of a new habit; it was a radical alteration of his constitution, a disturbance of the relation between his component parts, and an internal perversion of one of them.[18]

A new species had sinned itself into existence? Does this not sound like a case of HGT? So where does this leave original sin? After the *fall* the human is governed, to a large degree, by genetic heritage, by impulse and instinct, even if it tries to believe it has rationalized and decided on a course of action for itself, from its own free will. Our decisions, after the fall, are too often subject to, rather than masters of, lower physical impulses, base instincts; but even when they contradict our genetically driven survival instincts they are for self-interest and contradict the will and law of God. It is not so simple as to say that Eve, and Adam's, willful decision was immediately encoded in the DNA and thereby transmitted to their descendants' brains, these changes happen gradually, synaptic pathways in the brain are reinforced bit by bit, bombarded over a few generations by HGT? Original sin is transmitted by nature and nurture: once alone, outside of grace, in the wilds of nature, humanity was forced to *fall* back on its

---

17   Lindqvist, *et al.*, "Transmission of stress-induced learning impairment and associated brain gene expression from parents to offspring in chickens." For full details of the nuts-and-bolts mechanistic science involved see, online (open access): http://www.plosone.org/article/info%3Adoi%2F10.1371%2Fjournal.pone.0000364. Accessed Feb 2012.
18   Lewis, *Problem of Pain*, 79.

own innate survival instincts. Nurturing their offspring to repeat their own willful mistakes as the *selfish* brain patterns became more and more dominant, humanity took this egocentric and willful behavior as a God-given norm, putting the individual above God, considering itself more important than God. Decision-making becomes as instinctive as circling in grass to make a bed (even when the domestic feline has never been out of doors, and has had no example to copy from its mother). The cure for original sin lies in the grace of the Holy Spirit which will press on and re-orientate the mind, the person, the heart, *if s/he will allow it to*; a grace that issues from the defeat of sin and death in the crucifixion, the sacred Hebrew blood of the Christ, spilt for our salvation, poured out into the promised land of the chosen people of God. There will still be today graceful children and adults who seem to rise above the nature and nurture of original sin, for whom the instinctive genetically driven behavior (generated in many ways by spiritual concupiscence, but also the hereditary element encoded into their human nature) is less dominant than in others, whose upbringing, whose nurturing, seems to raise them above the debased selfishly sinful and egotistical wallowing's of the rest of humanity. These are graceful individuals who subconsciously have opened their heart and mind, preveniently, to the Holy Spirit even if they, through geographic and cognitive isolation, have never heard of Jesus Christ or come to realize how they can make a decision for Christ; but such people are rare.

3. THE INDEPENDENCE/INTERDEPENDENCE OF DECISIONS

Therefore, the fall into original sin is not about the capacity within the human brain to make decisions. The biological history of the human (evolution? development?) has fitted the human brain with a phenomenal capacity to make decisions, to survive, though this ability has been changed, altered, and now issues from the effects of original sin, because the fall is about making *wrong* and *bad* decisions in the light of God's will for us; the *fall* is not about making decisions, *per se*, as some critics will assert in an attempt to dismiss Genesis 3 as a fiction. The precedent to make these wrong decisions that contradict the will of God we can name original sin; this behavior was transmitted through nature and nurture to the extent that humanity arrived at a point where there was no way out, where even if they thought they were doing the right, it was simply for selfish reasons. When we try to do the good of our own intentions we fail, indeed our very act of trying condemns us further. We noted earlier the apostle Paul's comments that "I do not do what I want, but I do the very thing I hate. . . . I can will what is right, but I cannot do it. For I do not do the good I want, but the evil I do not want is what I do."[19] Through nature and nurture, humanity is true to type (a commonly asserted theological phrase) and is trapped in this situation when it should not be, when it brought about this condition itself. Yet, God turns to humanity to save it from this perilous situation: through the grace of the Holy Spirit the human can turn and do the good, but by itself it cannot. The fall is not about decision making, it is about the nature of those decisions, it is about selfish decisions, it is about self-

---

19   Rom 7:15 and 19.

glorification, self-aggrandizement, self-gain, then defining the bad as the good. In so doing humanity convinces itself that what it has decided is for the best. Religious people are not immune from this; at times the churches have acted out of self-interest, defining such egotistical power and oppression as being the will of God (do we blame Jesus for the sins of the churches?).

> Evolution's gift is a complex brain that endows humanity with free will, enabling personal moral responsibilities towards our neighbor and towards God. We are not puppets. God's gift at Christmas is forgiveness and new life through Christ for those who realize how far we've fallen from using that free will responsibly.[20]

So, original sin is defined by the capacity to make bad decisions, wrong judgements; try as hard as we can, we cannot make good judgements. If we are no more than the product of evolution, of nature, and everything about our brain and our being is physically determined by nature, which is itself defined by evolution, then good and bad decisions do not exist—only the ability to make a decision, where according to a *theory* of evolution through natural selection, the only criteria as to whether a decision is good or bad is survival. So then morality ceases to exist. But the mind is independent, to a degree, from the brain. The mind, and its decisions, do not issue from or are not wholly conditioned by nature. Therefore there are good and bad decisions, judgements; nature has quite rightly, and through evolution (even if one accepts the theory of evolution through natural selection as the be-all-and-end-all of life, the universe, and everything) we have been fitted with a complex brain that enables us to make free will judgements, *but* the moral probity of these decisions does not issue from nature. It is defined and measured in relation to God, the LORD. This need to discriminate to make reasoned judgements is gifted to us by God so that we may decide, discriminate, and judge what is best, we must follow what is the good and see how to live for God, for in the LORD is our ultimate well-being and happiness. But because of the fall we get it wrong. Western humanity used to discriminate and make these decisions—getting them occasionally nearly right but most often wrong. Postmodernism in some of its cruder forms eschews the need to discriminate, it claims we must not judge or decide something is wrong, yet the very act of deciding not to discriminate is a decision, a judgment. So humanity ends up drifting around from lifestyle to lifestyle, from belief system to belief system, where the moral probity of a decision is defined by self-interest, which is the history of *postlapsarian* humanity. Therefore, our *postlapsarian* thoughts and decisions are no longer free creative acts of the will, in keeping with the law of God and what we were created for. We are buffeted about, at the influence of the tyranny of physical impulses, needs, and desires over reason. The key to understanding reality and the human condition is therefore in a doctrine of original sin, the fall: Satan put the idea into the minds of our ancestors that we could be like "gods," that we could set up on our own, define our own happiness, our own morality, *according to our own criteria*. This idea and our assent, and thereby the conditions we lived under outside of Eden has changed us (graceless stress in a hostile world, bombarded by HGT). This

---

20   Alexander, "We are not descended from Adam and Eve," 37.

attempt was hopeless and led merely to human history. A history characterized by, for Lewis, money and poverty, war and ambition, prostitution and sexual degradation, the class struggle, empires and slavery. Lewis takes this further. Original sin is the key to history: civilizations and cultures grow up, often founded on sound principles, good laws are formulated, but something always goes wrong: "some fatal flaw always brings the selfish and cruel people to the top and it all slides back into misery and ruin."[21] For years Marxism was the ultimate neo-Pelagian pseudo-religion, which would solve all of humanity's problems; in recent times, in Britain, both "Thatcherism" and "New Labour" have been defined by apparent universal good, the ultimate political system and blessing for all humanity, only to be exposed as selfishness, greed, and death. This is the human condition before God; this is the crisis of human existence.

4. *ERITIS SICUT DEUS*: "THE IDEA"

In the previous chapter we examined examples of the story of the fall rewritten, retold; however, in numerous ways countless writers have for centuries implicitly borne witness to the fall by simply presenting humanity turned in on itself: *homo incurvatus in se*. In many instances they have done so simply by presenting stories of human folly and selfishness, depravity and wickedness, however, certain writers, have done this with the aim of bearing witness implicitly to the reality of the human condition defined as it is by the fall. Lewis shares with Dostoevsky a profound understanding of the delusional independence and individuality, superiority, in a word pride, that the *fall* generates. This is the human, so often an individual, who through self-confessed atheistic beliefs comes to realize that s/he is free to invent morality according to personal ambition and desire, furthermore that there are special individuals who transcend normal rules and regulations, laws and statutes, and can break the law to redefine it. Indeed that there are super-individuals who have taken the freedom to transcend law and redefine law because they know what is right (and wrong).

i. *The Fall: The Freedom Taken to Redefine*

Lewis voices this in *The Chronicles of Narnia: The Magician's Nephew*. Uncle Andrew talks to Digory, his nephew, about right and wrong, about honoring commitments, but how the rules of society—laws and statutes for that matter—don't apply to him. He speaks of a serious commitment he made to someone, which he chose not to honor:

> ". . . that promise I did not keep."
> "Well, then, it was jolly rotten of you," said Digory.
> "Rotten?" said Uncle Andrew with a puzzled look. "Oh, I see. You mean that little boys ought to keep their promises. Very true: most right and proper, I'm sure, and I'm very glad you have been taught to do it. But of course you must understand that rules of that sort, however excellent they may be for little boys—and servants—and women—and even people in general, can't possibly be expected to apply to profound students and great thinkers and sages. No, Digory.

---

21 Lewis, *Broadcast Talks*, 49.

4. Creation and The Fall IV: The Human Condition before God

Men like me, who possess hidden wisdom, are freed from common rules just as we are cut off from common pleasures. Ours, my boy, is a high and lonely destiny."[22]

This is, of course, original sin writ large: taking control of the knowledge of right and wrong, good and evil (Gen 3); Uncle Andrew will decide for himself what is acceptable behavior, according to his personal needs, because he possesses hidden wisdom and knowledge that raises him above the common herd. Having been beguiled by possibility, he cannot resist temptation. He knows he is contradicting an external rule, but his self-interest, turned in as he is on himself, is too strong and he will happily acquiesce—all he has to do is redefine the rules and how they apply to him and other people. In eating the fruit of the knowledge of good and evil, he does indeed become like the gods. Later in the book, having tricked Digory and his friend Polly into going into another world through the use of magic rings, the children encounter a powerful witch—Jadis (the White Witch of *The Lion, the Witch and the Wardrobe*)—who has become personified evil. In her lust for supremacy and status, authority and control, and in a power-struggle with her sister, she destroys every living thing in Charn (her world). There had been a solemn binding agreement, a promise as such, between the two sides in the "world war" not to use magic, certainly not the so-called "deplorable word." But Jadis's pride and self-interest allowed her to transcend normal rules and agreements:

"Then I spoke the Deplorable Word. A moment later I was the only living thing beneath the sun."
"But the people?" gasped Digory.
"What people, boy?" asked the Queen.
"All the ordinary people," said Polly, "who'd never done you any harm. And the women, and the children, and the animals."
"Don't you understand?" said the Queen (still speaking to Digory). "I was the Queen. They were all my people. What else were they there for but to do my will?"
"It was rather hard luck on them, all the same," said he.
"I had forgotten that you are only a common boy. How should you understand reasons of State? You must learn, child, that what would be wrong for you or for any of the common people is not wrong in a great Queen such as I. The weight of the world is on our shoulders. We must be freed from all rules. Ours is a high and lonely destiny."
Digory suddenly remembered that Uncle Andrew had used exactly the same words. But they sounded much grander when Queen Jadis said them; perhaps because Uncle Andrew was not seven feet tall and dazzlingly beautiful.[23]

Jadis's status as queen gives her, endorses for her, the superiority and immunity according to *natural law*, and thereby the self-generated authority to, in effect, do as she pleases. The danger is to place these amoral people in a category on their own and

---

22 Lewis, *The Magician's Nephew*, 23.
23 Ibid., 60–61. There is, of course, something of an analogy between the "deplorable word" and nuclear weapons, given the power of utter destruction that could be a nuclear holocaust.

not see how the beliefs and actions of Jadis and Uncle Andrew can apply to ordinary people on a daily basis who will lie for protection, cheat and steal—because they deserve it, or because they can get away with it.

ii. "I deduced from all of this the utter necessity of faith in Christ."

The Russian prophet and writer Dostoevsky identified the same trait in humanity, a deep-seated and willful justification for redefining the good in one's own image—original sin—which he called "The Idea." And like Lewis he wrote theological stories weaving into them an observation of the human condition. In *Crime and Punishment*, Dostoevsky presents the character Raskolnikov rejecting belief in God, and as a result behaving *as if* he were God. The idea of Raskolnikov parading himself as God is paradoxical: he claims at times not to believe in God—but as a result he ends up behaving as if he were God (*eritis sicut Deus*) because if there is no God then there are no limits on human behavior, no morals, no ethics. Humanity, therefore, claims the right to define what is right and wrong, having eaten of the fruit of the tree of the knowledge of good and evil—the *fall*. Or more pertinently certain individuals claim the right to transcend traditional morals and ethics and thereby redefine—hence Raskolnikov's so-called Napoleonic delusions! When Raskolnikov confesses his crime of murdering the elderly pawnbroker to Sonya (not for money, but just because he becomes fascinated with the idea of killing her) he raves about how marvelously Napoleon redefined the good by killing many, abandoning thousands, razing whole cities—"and thus everything is permitted."[24] This is, in Dostoevsky's work, "The Idea"; that is, the idea that if there is no God then there are no limits on human behavior, human depravity—*everything* is permitted, provided an elite is allowed to redefine law. Or as C. S. Lewis's character of Uncle Andrew comments, rules and laws can't apply to profound students and great thinkers and sages, whilst Jadis asserts that such must be freed from all rules. What Dostoevsky was saying was that this man, this murderer and intellectual, is prepared to "sacrifice fellow human beings on the altar of theoretical premises and his own satanic pretensions to moral freedom";[25] furthermore, that this is "startlingly modern and by now distressingly familiar"[26] and is in many ways representative of the history of Western civilization in the twentieth-century, and as such represents the schism brought about by the fall of humanity away from God through original sin. Dostoevsky goes to great pains to paint word pictures of some of the most sinful of humans—who through radical socio-cultural political beliefs, are prepared to kill, steal, maim and destroy, claiming it is for the betterment (such is the delusion generated by the fall) of humanity—where betterment, the good, is defined by, effectively, looking in the mirror! Dostoevsky has often been criticized for focusing too much on the utter nihilistic depravity of these characters. Why does he present such deplorably fallen and depraved characters? Does he revel in it? Is it for effect?

---

24   Comments voiced by Raskolnikov expounding his theory to Sonya, in Dostoevsky, Crime and Punishment, 274–76, specifically 274.
25   William J. Leatherbarrow, "Introduction" in Dostoevsky, *Crime and Punishment*, xxvi.
26   Ibid.

4. Creation and The Fall IV: The Human Condition before God

Dostoevsky did so, "[because] I deduced from all this, the utter necessity of faith in Christ."[27] Christ's sacrifice and resurrection is the only way out; humanity cannot of itself solve the problem created by the fall, if it tries to it only makes matters worse. This is a principle we have discovered already in Lewis's works.

"The Idea" is existential because it is centered on human decisions and actions. Initially there is the decision to disbelieve in God or to reject God for one's own agenda; or people may define God and truth in their own image. This results in the paradox of consciously or unconsciously asserting one's own ego as God—to be, therefore, as if one were God (*eritis sicut Deus*), to act *as if* ("you will be like God, knowing good and evil." Gen 3:5). The next stage is to decide to redefine human morality and ethics according to one's own principles (for example, Raskolnikov's Napoleonic agenda in *Crime and Punishment*[28]); then to storm heaven, that is the attempt to redefine human morality/ethics, thereby to realize that without God there are as a result no limits or constraints on human behavior. This results in rebellion: to rebel, even in the face of God-and-immortality. This leaves only one option: suicide. Suicide is the ultimate statement, the ultimate rebellion. As archetypes of humanity some of these characters do pull back from the brink: Raskolnikov (*Crime and Punishment*) does; Uncle Andrew (*The Magician's Nephew*) does. But while Ivan Karamazov (*The Brothers Karamazov*) disappears into nihilistic insanity, Jadis (*The Magician's Nephew* and *The Lion, the Witch and the Wardrobe*) becomes more and more evil, subsisting as evil, even after "death." There is therefore another agent involved in "The Idea"—humanity is not self-contained, making these decisions for itself. Satan, personified evil, either directly or through a host of demonic forces presses on the human mind, influences the thoughts of the individual. But the Holy Spirit presses on the human mind also. We are at the center of a supernatural battle, and our thoughts may not necessarily be our own. These characters may be fiction, but they tell us about the truth of original sin, the theological truth of humanity.

5. REASON AND NATURAL LAW

Throughout his apologetics Lewis speculates, philosophically, as to the existence of God, as the basis of presenting gospel truth to a skeptical readership. Such a speculative religious view tells us that this God is more like a mind than a life force. This personal God is "good," a God who can forgive: for only a person can forgive, not necessarily a life force, that is, a some*one*, not a some*thing*.[29] Lewis is speculating, philosophically, as to the existence of God, but ever moving towards the idea of the Christ through ethical grounds, through natural law. This leads to the need for a redeemer, a forgiver, which must be grounded in the proposition that the universe is governed by absolute goodness. If this absolute goodness did not exist, "then all our efforts are in the long run hopeless. But if it is, then we are making ourselves enemies to that goodness every

---

27 Dostoevsky writing to his brother, April 5, 1864, in Coulson, *Dostoevsky: A Self-Portrait*, 124.
28 Dostoevsky, *Crime and Punishment*, 274.
29 Lewis, *Broadcast Talks*, 12.

day, and aren't in the least likely to do any better tomorrow, and so our case is hopeless again. . . . God is the only comfort, he is also the supreme terror: the thing we most need and the thing we most want to keep out of the way of. He is our only possible ally, and we have made ourselves his enemies."[30] Lewis is quite apposite here: people need to recognize that they have gone wrong and need forgiveness; if they don't then the gospel has nothing to say to them. Acknowledging the existence of, and then perceiving the authority and power behind, the moral law, the realization is arrived at that we are in the wrong relationship with this moral law and therefore the righteous Lord that sits in judgment. God is triune and personal, and we can never meet the demands of the moral law but "God himself becomes a man to save man from the disapproval of God."[31] Underlying this is the *fall*—an orthodox-traditional doctrine of original sin.

In the last year of his life Lewis returns, amidst the welter of relativity in the West, to the human moral crisis by again re-asserting the reality of natural law. Here human morality, defined by *reason*, meets the rebellion of original sin. Published posthumously, "We have no 'Right to Happiness,'"[32] dealt with humanity's craving for happiness, for earthly pleasure and worldly satisfaction to the extent that the universality of the *God-given* moral order was compromised. Lewis reasserts the truth of natural law in the face of the growing moral relativity of the West in the decades after World War II. Humanity claims a right to happiness, yet a right is a freedom guaranteed by law, and if natural law is an eternal truth given by God, then how do we frame such happiness? Without a natural, God-given, law, the statutes of the nation state become a tyranny; whatever the state decrees becomes an absolute. Without natural, God-given, law, the statutes passed by a parliament are considered higher than morality. Lewis commented that "Without it [Natural Law], the actual laws of the state become an absolute, as in Hegel. They cannot be criticized because there is no norm against which they should be judged."[33] So often people—and law makers—do not consider the issues from this perspective; so often they are talking, Lewis asserts, about sexual happiness (hence Lewis uses the divorce laws for the context of his criticism) with no thought for the implications within the family, within the community, or, more pertinently, before God. Is there no longer such a thing as a morality that is higher than humanity's laws? Where is the will and judgment of Christ in this? To talk of the moral ought is to speak of Christlikeness; our ultimate happiness lies with being in and for Christ. The danger is, and again grounded in the rebellion that is the fall, whatever humanity invents in terms of law and morality will seem perfectly *reasonable* to the law makers and to those who seek their happiness in this world: *reasoning* contradicts *revelation*. Repenting over uncontrollable sins is one thing; *reasoning* out and codifying into law justification for immoral behavior is quite another and will smother over any pangs of conscience that are *revelations* from God. This is what we have witnessed in Lewis and Dostoevsky's all-too-real characters of Uncle Andrew, Jadis, Raskolnikov, the

30 Ibid., 31.
31 Ibid., 32.
32 Lewis, "We Have No 'Right to Happiness,'" 265 and 269.
33 Ibid., 266.

4. Creation and The Fall IV: The Human Condition before God

Karamazovs, etc.: *eritis sicut Deus*—by denying God in the public sphere there are as a result no limits on human behavior, though a pretense is needed to give the impression of permanence and respectability to what is defined as the norm.

We are fast approaching the point where the principle is accepted without question that laws passed by a democratically elected government, which has defined morality in its own image, must be absolute, whereby there is, as Lewis wrote, "no higher authority" *if* God is to be rejected, that is the God of revelation. Contemporaneous with Lewis's comments in "We have no 'Right to Happiness,'" and likewise swimming against the tide of modern atheistic liberalism, was the Russian writer Aleksandr Isaevich Solzhenitsyn who understood this only too well from his experience of a dictatorial totalitarian Marxist regime:

> At the present time it is widely accepted among lawyers that law is higher than morality—law is something which is shaped and developed, whereas morality is something inchoate and amorphous. This is not the case. The opposite is true: morality is higher than the law! Law is our human attempt to embody in rules a part of the moral sphere which is above us. We try to understand this morality, bring it down to earth and present it in the form of law. Sometimes we are more successful, sometimes less. Sometimes we have a mere caricature of morality, but morality is always higher than law.[34]

Writing on these issues, Canon Andrew Pearson notes, quoting Solzhenitsyn:

> For the logical outcome of such a position is that there is no higher legal and moral authority than the State. Whatever the State decides must be right, for the State is all. And that, of course, is totalitarianism. Under such a system all truth is relative. What the State decides today it can undecide tomorrow. How like communism which, as Solzhenitsyn wrote out of bitter experience, "has never concealed the fact that it rejects all absolute concepts of morality. Depending upon circumstances, any act, including mass slaughter, may be good or bad, it all depends upon the State's ideology, as defined by a handful of people at any given time."[35]

Morality must be considered above the law, because the law can often be immoral; morality can claim to be atheistic, but all good and right morality issues from God because morality, ethics, and the will of God are intimately intertwined: this is why we *fell* in the first place, this is why we are contaminated by original sin! The fall affects our ability to reason and to know, and to understand with any cogency and accuracy. Humanity will be utterly convinced of the rightness of any *particular* course of action, or a belief, once it feels comfortable with a given action or belief—in this humanity so often is convinced its morals and ethics are untainted and infallible.

---

34   Solzhenitsyn, *Warning to the West*, 45–46.
35   A. Parsons, "On the Judges & the Christian Conscience," 6, quoting from, Solzhenitsyn, *Warning to the West*, 57–58.

6. CREATED FREEDOM AND CUSTODIANSHIP: THE HUMAN CONDITION

i. Lewis on the Hell of the Self: Condemnation and Destruction

We have seen enough to establish, certainly for Lewis, that it is the self that is the problem, that is, selfishness, self-love, egotism, self-centeredness, self-admiration, self-deception: in a word, pride. How does Lewis's understanding of the self relate to his doctrine of the fall and original sin? We examined the relationship between selfishness and sin earlier, so what does Lewis understand about the ontology of self-awareness, and the pride that is at the heart of original sin?

It is important, notes Lewis, for us to accept that it is regarding the self as the center of our existence that is the sin that underpins all other sins: "An essentially dependent being whose principle of existence lies not in itself but in another, tries to set up on its own, to exist for itself.* Such a sin requires no complex social conditions, no extended experience, no great intellectual development. From the moment a creature becomes aware of God as God and of itself as self, the terrible alternative of choosing God or self for the center is opened to it."[36] In denying the self we are not repudiating what God has given us; in other religions, notes Lewis, the self dissolves into a greater something, but only in Christianity does the self become involved into the life of God yet remain distinct, being more than it was when it was alone in its own kingdom.[37] This self exists only to be denied, but that denial is not a negation, for in denying the supremacy of our ego, paradoxically we become more truly our self.[38] If we do not deny the self it only becomes worse—locked into itself, which is the beginning of hell,[39] therefore the self must be denied, for Lewis this is what is involved in taking up our cross.[40] This is the daily struggle, to deny the self, "the gravitation away from God" will destroy us; the homeward journey must be a daily denial.[41] However difficult, we must hand over our whole self to Christ. It is the opposite of the fall; the fall was the turning from God to self; Christ's atoning sacrifice opens up the way whereby we can turn from self to God,[42] but all the time we fear to do this simple act, turning from our self-interest to God. The incarnation is both the contradiction and the fulfillment of this. Lewis comments:

> The result of this was that you now had one man who really was what all men were intended to be: one man in whom the created life, derived from *his* mother, allowed itself to be completely and perfectly tuned into the begotten life. The natural human creature in *him* was taken up fully into the divine Son. Thus in one instance humanity had, so to speak, arrived: had passed into the life of

---

36 Lewis, *Problem of Pain*, 57. * Lewis is referring to Augustine *The City of God*, Bk. XIV, Ch. xiii.
37 Lewis, *Beyond Personality*, 15.
38 Lewis, *Problem of Pain*, 127–28. (See also, Lewis, *Beyond Personality*, 57f.)
39 Ibid., 127–28.
40 Lewis, *Mere Christianity*, 162.
41 Lewis, *Problem of Pain*, 58–59.
42 Ibid., 69.

4. Creation and The Fall IV: The Human Condition before God

Christ. And because the whole difficulty for us is that the natural life has to be, in a sense "killed," *he* chose an earthly career which involved the killing of *his* human desires at every turn—poverty, misunderstanding from *his* own family, betrayal by one of *his* intimate friends, being jeered at and manhandled by the Police, and execution by torture. And then, after being thus killed—killed every day, in a sense—the human creature in *him*, because it was united to the divine Son, came to life again.[43]

So much to do with the self is toxic and therefore deadly: vanity, self-regard, self-praise, and self-promotion.[44] Eventually too much self-preoccupation leads to hell, for Lewis, even if we begin with altruistic good intentions, too often the self rears its ugly head.[45] Good intentions may initially drive us, but the problem is a sort of humanitarian sentimental kindness: "A man easily comes to console himself for all his other vices by a conviction that 'his heart's in the right place' and 'he wouldn't hurt a fly,' though in fact he has never made the slightest sacrifice for a fellow creature."[46] This relates to self-justification—we want our actions to be good, so we simply define them as good, but this so often is merely "need love."[47] Such self-justification often grows out of feeling hurt—or a victim mentality. Self-centeredness is *now* fundamental to our nature, because we have changed human nature, *after the fall*: "The natural life in each of us is something self-centered, something that wants to be petted and admired, to take advantage of other lives, to exploit the whole universe. And specially it wants to be left to itself[;] . . . it's afraid of the light and air of the spiritual world . . . and in a sense it's quite right. It knows that if the spiritual life gets hold of it, all its self-centeredness and self-will are going to be killed and it's ready to fight tooth and nail to avoid that."[48] This is the sin of Satan: to put self first, not simply in the place of others, but in disobedience to the will of God: "The moment you have a self at all, there is a possibility of putting yourself first—wanting to be the center—wanting to be God, . . . that was the sin of Satan: and that was the sin he taught the human race."[49] This is nothing to do with sex, though disordered sex follows on from the *fall*. Rather, "What Satan put into the heads of our remote ancestors was the idea that they could 'be like gods,' could set up on their own as if they had created themselves—be their own masters—invent some sort of happiness for themselves outside God, apart from God."[50]

Dostoevsky, as we saw earlier, cited Napoleon as an extreme example of original sin: the delusion generated by self-interest, whereby millions are slaughtered, society upturned, only to end up with the protagonist being hero-worshiped. Lewis would have concurred with Dostoevsky (though I doubt he read his works), he presents Napoleon *post mortem* in hell. In *The Great Divorce* we find Napoleon having *imagined*

---

43   Lewis, *Beyond Personality*, 29–30.
44   Lewis, *Screwtape Letters*, and "Screwtape Proposes a Toast."
45   Lewis, *Problem of Pain*, 57f.
46   Ibid., 41.
47   Lewis, *Four Loves*, 2f.
48   Lewis, *Beyond Personality*, 29–30.
49   Lewis, *What Christians Believe*, 68.
50   Ibid., 68–69.

for himself a marvelous palace to live in, indeed all the residents of this upper level of hell can merely think what they would like and it materializes. But this leads to arguments, squabbling, fights, and eventually degradation: "All get what they want; they do not always like it."[51] The condemned live a life outside of God living entirely in a world of their own selfish making. Napoleon is seen walking from window to window in his giant palace, lights blazing from every room, in full dress uniform wanting the world to see him, admire him, but there is no-one else around, he is alone—he courts attention, adulation, from others but no-one is there, his is utterly alone locked into his own selfish and self-generated world. Two people in these upper reaches of hell make the "fifteen thousand year" journey, "nothing else near it for millions of miles" to see him in his isolation.[52]

> "But they got there?"
> "That's right. He'd built himself a huge house all in the Empire style—rows of windows flaming with light, though it only shows as a pin prick from where I live."
> "Did they see Napoleon?"
> "That's right. They went up and looked through one of the windows. Napoleon was there all right."
> "What was he doing?"
> "Walking up and down—up and down all the time—left-right, left-right—never stopping for a moment. The two chaps watched him for about a year and he never rested. And muttering to himself all the time. 'It was Soult's fault. It was Ney's fault. It was Josephine's fault. It was the fault of the Russians. It was the fault of the English.' Like that all the time. Never stopped for a moment. A little, fat man and he looked kind of tired. But he didn't seem able to stop it."[53]

Serving self merely locks a person into his or her own little world, the obsessive and compulsive manner in which this little world is created and maintained ensures the condemnation of the person: it is the beginning of hell. This self-centeredness generated by the fall leads to a diminished existence. We will deal with Lewis's doctrine of hell in the final part of this volume, however, it is pertinent to note how the residents of hell, in *The Great Divorce*, feel intense pain when walking on grass, when some "visit" the plains of heaven is utterly painful, like walking on glass shards, grass does not bend or crush under these "ghost" of hell.[54] As the saints of heaven walk to meet these visitors from hell, the grass bends and crushes under their feet, under their weight, releasing a sweet perfume: "The earth shook under their tread as their strong feet sank into the wet turf. A tiny haze and a sweet smell went up where they had crushed the grass and scattered the dew."[55] By contrast for the visitors from hell, "Walking proved difficult. The grass, hard as diamonds to my unsubstantial feet, made me feel as if I

---

51   Lewis, *The Magician's Nephew*, 162.
52   Lewis, *The Great Divorce*, 10.
53   Ibid., 10–11.
54   Ibid., 15f.
55   Ibid., 18.

were walking on wrinkled rock, and I suffered pains . . ."[56] Lewis's genius is shown in *The Great Divorce*, where the spiritual resurrected people who populate heaven are more *real*, more *physical, corporeal*, in their spiritual resurrection, than the near-to-nothingness, the vague, ethereal-ghostlike apparitions, of those condemned to hell. The ontological structure of hell-purgatory-heaven, in *The Great Divorce*, reflects a temporal paradox: hell exists, but it is so close to nothingness that it barely exists in time and space and the redeemed cannot enter hell because they are too substantial, the condemned may draw close to the fringes of heaven, but this is too painful for their nihilistic insubstantial pseudo-corporeality, teetering as they are on the abyss of nothingness.[57] There are numerous examples of *the turn inward* to redefine the good in a self-image throughout Lewis's analogical narratives (for example, *The Chronicles of Narnia*, and, *The Great Divorce*), which may not be as dramatic as Jadis and Uncle Andrew, or Raskolnikov Ivan Karamazov, but the result is the same—a lost soul.

ii. What If?—Ontological Custodianship

Why, asks Lewis, does God not do more to control, restrict, and limit humanity? We might add, save it from its own self-willed destructive stupidity! Lewis notes that the human is characterized by the gift of free will, and as such, if God cured though miraculous intervention the results of each and every individual sin issuing from the fall, we would cease to be what we are:

> We can, perhaps, conceive of a world in which God corrected the results of this abuse of free will by his creatures at every moment: so that a wooden beam became soft as grass when it was used as a weapon, and the air refused to obey me if I attempted to set up in it the sound-waves that carry lies or insults. . . . That God can and does, on occasions, modify the behavior of matter and produce what we call miracles, is part of Christian faith; but the very conception of a common, and therefore stable, world, demands that these occasions should be extremely rare.[58]

Furthermore, this is not just about custodianship in the way a parent limits the freedom of an infant once it starts to crawl and walk, this is also about a doctrine of creation—it is about the very exact ontological nature of humanity, the human as conceived and created by God:

> It would, no doubt, have been possible for God to remove by miracle the results of the first sin ever committed by a human being; but this would not have been much good unless he was prepared to remove the results of the second sin, and of the third, and so on forever. . . . [A] world thus continually underpropped and corrected by Divine interference, would have been a world in which nothing important ever depended on human choice[;] . . . the chess player's freedom to play chess depends on the rigidity of the squares and the moves.[59]

---

56   Ibid., 18, see also 20–25, 30, 41–48, 75–76, 121 and 124.
57   Ibid., 103–4.
58   Lewis, *Problem of Pain*, 19–20.
59   Ibid., 53–54.

Given Lewis's love of theological stories, analogical narrative, and in particular how science-fiction can carry God's truth, we can examine the implications of what we could call ontological custodianship—the severe restriction upon the activities and therefore the very nature of being of humanity—and how this was explored by the science fiction writer and president of the American Humanist Association, Isaac Asimov (1920–92) in his collection of short stories, *I, Robot*. The 2004 film *I, Robot* was based on Asimov's short stories, but wove them into a new plot. As such, and without the intention of the writers and producers, this became a profound theological statement about the nature of humanity, original sin, and the free will of humanity in relation to what, for the purposes of this study, we may term ontological custodianship. The story is set in the year 2035, where humanity is utterly reliant upon robots and their artificial intelligence, which is controlled by "the three laws" that prevent the robots harming humans and also require the robots to protect humans from harm. However, a new generation of robots starts to imprison people and enacting a strict curfew: the authorities, the military, the police, even ordinary people on the street can do nothing, because their lives are serviced and controlled by the robots. The computer controlling the robots explains that if it, through the robots, is charged with guarding, protecting, humanity, then it must control, shepherd, and restrict. This robotic revolution has caused suffering and severely curtailed humanity's freedom; however, this is a small cost in terms of lives lost and a loss of human rights compared to the destructive ways of humanity. The computer comments that humanity has charged it with humanity's safekeeping, yet despite our best efforts we wage wars, pollute, and toxify the earth and are bent on a path of self-destruction, so much so that we cannot be trusted with our own survival; therefore some humans must be sacrificed, freedoms curtailed, so as to ensure the survival of humanity. The computer likens humanity to children who must be saved from themselves. The computer's messianic pretensions in order to fulfill its custodian commission are reminiscent of the fall: it has taken control of the knowledge of good and evil and tyrannously restricts humanity. This complaint is similar to the criticism of skeptics and atheistic who expect God to prevent humanity from hurting itself, messing itself up, wrecking the environment, destroying each other. But where would such interference stop, is Lewis's question.

This raises profound questions about the creation of humanity, that which now characterizes *postlapsarian* humanity, how God cares for humanity, and issues of intervention and divine providence. Should God have intervened to save humanity from original sin? Have matters now gone so far that humanity should be reined in (even culled) by God? Perhaps the answer is scriptural: however far from God humanity goes, we are no longer irredeemable because of Christ's sacrifice. In addition, the promise at the end of the story of Noah stands: "Never again will I curse the ground because of man, even though every inclination of his heart is evil from childhood. And never again will I destroy all living creatures, as I have done. As long as the earth endures, seedtime and harvest, cold and heat, summer and winter, day and night will never cease" (Gen 8:21b–22). So, does this mean the *eschaton* will never happen, the world will never end? The world will end, humanity will eventually perish, but not

4. Creation and The Fall IV: The Human Condition before God

at God's hands and not as punishment for the *fall*. In all probability because of the *fall* into original sin, and in keeping with humanity's ability to take all decisions on to itself, then *we* will end the world! There are enough weapons of mass destruction stock-piled to do this. In addition, if climate change and global warming is a reality, and given humanity's inability to make the right decisions (Rom 7), then the end is already in place: within a couple of hundred years, planet earth with be too hostile to live on through climate change and environmental degradation. We have taken the power to ourselves to make all decisions in our own image and this we have done: we will end the world and humanity.[60]

And God in Christ will judge us as we come before the throne. Not necessarily because of the fall, but we will be judged on how we have responded to Christ's forgiveness, Jesus's atoning sacrifice, God having shared our humanity through the incarnation; the Holy Spirit has been there, the helper, but how will we fare, how will we stand before *him*? Christ *will* judge us. Lewis never ceased to stress the reality of the coming *eschaton*.

---

60   Religion (i.e. Christianity) may have identified the corruption of the human through the *fall*, and offered the solution in *the Christ*, but it is the technological and scientific abilities issuing from the Enlightenment that have—in humanity's rebellion against God—enabled humanity to achieve this destruction. Religion *per se* could never have ended the world (though it has often predicted it), a scientific technological Enlightenment *has*.

Part Two

Christ Revealed Through Analogical and Symbolic Narrative

"Behind my own stories there are no facts at all,
tho' I hope there are truths.
That is, they may be regarded as imaginative hypotheses
illustrating what I believe to be theological truths."

Lewis writing to Tony Pollock, May 3, 1954

"The Whole Narnian Story is about Christ."

Lewis writing to Anne Jenkins, Mar 5, 1961.

5

Analogical and Symbolic Narratives I: Narrative Theology, Supposition and Genre, Mythopoeic Theorizing—Imagining The Christ

SYNOPSIS:
We now move from creation to sub-creation, from Lewis's doctrine of creation to his (and other Inklings) belief in and practice of *sub-creation* as part of God's creation.

Postmodern or postliberal theologians cannot escape writing and preaching, proclaiming and teaching, in the social context in which they work. Lewis wrote long and hard against "Modernism" and "Liberalism." But he is not a postliberal: Lewis is in many ways akin to a pre-Kantian theologian, a pre-Enlightenment philosopher, ultimately Platonic. Lewis appealed to a biblical and patristic core, innately mistrusting, until proved otherwise, anything "Modern" and "Liberal." This notwithstanding, his mission and work (as a pre-modern orthodox traditionalist) is a precursor in many ways to postliberal theology. The exponents of postliberal theology and narrative theology ground the revelation of God and all our theological enterprises in Scripture: the narrative. The revelatory value of narrative, parable, and metaphor is biblical. The precedent is scriptural: Emmaus (Luke 24:25–27). Narrative and parable are a proclamation, and, like the kingdom of God, point beyond themselves: theological language is parabolic.

Tolkien and Lewis advocated sub-creation: that nature brought forth, but so did humanity. Both wrote theological stories to advance understanding of God's salvation. This is sub-creation. Lewis's analogical and symbolic narratives—*The Space Trilogy* (1938–45), *The Screwtape Letters* (1942), *The Great Divorce* (1945), *The Chronicles of Narnia* (1950–56), and *Till We Have Faces* (1956)—are, in many ways, parables; metaphors of the kingdom of God. As such they are deeply scriptural; and in form and structure they are influenced by Lewis's doctrine of Christological prefigurement. Lewis's narratives and stories are implicitly theological and draw people into an understanding of God's salvific purposes—a religious economy. Genre and source: what are these narratives of Lewis—fantasy, allegory? Lewis specifically denied any one-to-one correspondence; also, that there is no allegorical or hidden meaning; furthermore, they are not fantasy because of their theological content. They are "supposals"; that is, analogy and metaphor—what if? The Narniad is a form of mythopoeic theorizing: what would happen if Christ were incarnated into another reality, died, and were resurrected for the salvation of the "people" there? Lewis commented that, "The Whole Narnian Story is about Christ." Therefore in the genre of analogical-symbolic narratives the events and characters symbolize, but not necessarily the detail. Lewis elucidated further in his correspondence with children, readers of Narnia, but also by analyzing Charles Williams's novels—where the probable and the marvelous combine. Though often categorized today by critics as fantasy, we can demonstrate that these narratives of Lewis's are not fantasies.

ON THE CHRIST OF A RELIGIOUS ECONOMY. I. CREATION AND SUB-CREATION

1. INTRODUCTION

Lewis wrote theological stories. They are not about facts, but they do contain profound truths. These stories we may call analogical narratives—because by analogy he is telling us about God's truth. They are symbolic, they are representative, emblematic, they should remind us: they represent God's truth and God's kingdom. Lewis's stories—like biblical parables—actually tell us more about humanity's *postlapsarian* rebellion against God than many theological treatises. Lewis presented his understanding of the relationship between revelation and reason, and the teleological move towards Christlikeness, through story and parable in his mature work. This is an example of Tolkien and Lewis's concept of sub-creation. The greater methodological emphasis in the 1950s is on the full development of his analogical and symbolic narratives, his pictures, images, and stories that will—by analogy—inform us, and reveal to us: they tell us about revelation, and at the heart of revelation is *the Christ*. So what value is there to these narratives? Indeed what context is there to them? Lewis was in many ways working against the grain of some mid-twentieth-century Anglican theology, but not necessarily against the flow in some theological quarters of continental Europe, or in parts of the church and academy in America.

2. THEOLOGY AFTER "MODERNISM" AND "LIBERALISM"

Lewis's writings are set against the background of liberal culture and society in Britain specifically, and the United States and Europe generally. In contrast to the theological "Liberalism" that claimed freedom from traditional dogmas, creeds, and Scripture, Lewis was skeptical of the Age of Reason and the Enlightenment. Furthermore, Lewis is like a pre-Kantian, a pre-Enlightenment philosopher, ultimately Platonic, which filters into his understanding of theology. He is in effect a pre-liberal and a pre-modern, whereas today many philosophers and theologians who share Lewis's skepticism towards the Enlightenment would invoke the term postliberal or postmodern.

Postliberal theology is a late-twentieth-century development initially centered on Yale Divinity School[1] and Duke Divinity School, both in the United States, and focusing on the work of Thomas Aquinas, Karl Barth, and Henri de Lubac; in philosophical terms postliberal theology was grounded in the philosophy of Ludwig Wittgenstein and Alasdair MacIntyre, specifically Wittgenstein's analysis of language. Postliberal theologians define themselves as being in opposition to the individualism, the apparent rationalism, and the Western Romanticism of theological liberalism, which they saw had dominated theological debates from the mid-nineteenth century until the later twentieth century. The openness to other denominations and the challenge to a "Modern"/"Liberal" orthodoxy by the Second Vatican Council is also considered contributory to the development of a postliberal theological perspective. One aspect of postliberal theology is that it mirrors, to a degree, the fragmentation

---

1 This is seen essentially in the work of George Lindbeck, Hans Wilhelm Frei, and Stanley Hauerwas. See, for example: Wright, P*ostliberal Theology and the Church Catholic*; Pecknold, *Transforming Postliberal Theology*; Lindbeck, *The Nature of Doctrine*; Campbell, *Preaching Jesus.*

5. Analogical and Symbolic Narratives I: Narrative Theology, Supposition and Genre

of postmodernism. Exponents regard Liberal Theology as a dominant movement, something to react against; Lewis did not, he simply saw theological liberalism as a fashionable aberration, a backwater, a blind alley, an impasse. Lewis, by declaring "Mere Christianity," appealed to the unity of the patristic heritage. Postliberal is only one of many late-twentieth-century theologies after liberalism.[2]

Is Lewis, then, a precursor of postmodernism, or of the postliberal? Is he a harbinger of these late-twentieth-century movements? Ironically, although there are considerable similarities, the answer is no, for Lewis did not seek to invent a new theological and philosophical position. However, his mission and work is a *precursor* in many ways to postliberal theology. Lewis is, in effect, a pre-modern orthodox traditionalist. He referred to himself as a dinosaur to a younger generation—that they should listen to him before his species disappeared altogether.[3] Lewis appealed to a patristic core: truth was given in the gospel, the early church and established in doctrinal and creedal detail in the patristic era; in addition he appealed to a "mere" core (borrowing the term from the pre-Enlightenment Puritan, Richard Baxter): the veracity of what the church proclaimed did not change; but the quality of its witness became diluted and changed due to denominational schisms, and attacks from secularism.[4] Postliberalism may appeal in limited degrees to such a scriptural and patristic core, but it may be seen as also seeking new forms of theology absorbing some of the principles of "Modernism" and postmodernists. There are strong similarities between Lewis, operating in the mid-twentieth century, and postliberals operating in the later twentieth and early twenty-first centuries: how do the two compare? Both are orthodox and accept the biblical witness of God's revelation and salvation history—the religious economy. By contrast with many postliberals, Lewis was not a professional theologian, employed by the academy, which gave him a degree of freedom; he was not compromised by the philosophical methods of "Modernism"/"Liberalism." Lewis thrived on an apologetic defense of the gospel; by contrast postliberal theologians generally eschew apologetics, concentrating on systematic theology.

A self-absorption with linguistic philosophy, issuing to a degree from Wittgenstein, which Lewis eschewed, has led postliberal theologians to spend an inordinate amount of time analyzing the method of how they do theology. It can be argued with some veracity that there have been more studies produced since 1960 on theological method than in the preceding two millennia of the church's history. However, this absorption with how we do theology started, it may be argued, with Aquinas, and although the preoccupation with language itself has been characteristic of Western theology in the second half of the twentieth-century, it must be remembered that theological method can never be but self-conscious after the Enlightenment: "Philosophy, often theology's arch-rival, seemed to have entered a process of self-dissolution,"[5] contemporary

---

2   For example, neo-liberal theology, neo-orthodoxy, radical orthodoxy, nouvelle théologie, paleo-orthodoxy, postmodern Christianity, emerging church movement.
3   Lewis, "*De Descriptione Temporum*," 9–25.
4   This is dealt with in depth in the first book in this series: *C. S. Lewis—Revelation, Conversion, and Apologetics*, Pt. 2, Chs. 6–7, 103–32.
5   Vidu, *Postliberal Theological Method: A Critical Study*, xiii.

theology likewise has often seemed to be preoccupied (at least in the university, the academy—but not in the Catholic and Evangelical churches) with an introspection that has led to a fragmentation akin to this self-dissolution. In contrast to theological liberalism and its marginalization of scriptural narrative, "Postliberals firmly place knowledge of God and of the world in the context of Scripture. Deciding about matters of faith becomes a matter of revealing the Scriptural grammar."[6] However, because of its context in the academies, the universities, it can be questioned whether postliberal theologians fully realize the apparent contradiction between the academy's philosophical assumptions and the requirements of the Christian faith, particularly in terms of God's prevenience.

3. NARRATIVE THEOLOGY

Postliberal theology is considered to be the ground for such movements as Radical Orthodoxy and Scriptural Reasoning, but also postliberal interpretations of Roman Catholicism, and recent theological developments in the Evangelical churches. Narrative is important to all; Scripture is important as the collective memory, the church's story of salvation on which theology must be built. If Lewis gave a value and authority to Scripture, which many of the theological Liberals in the Church of England of his day repudiated, then there is a strong connection between Lewis's apologetics and such narrative theology, that is, the primacy of Scripture. Scripture is narrative, the *Word* of God become a *word* of God,[7] witness to the religious economy of salvation history. Narrative Theology is therefore a form of postliberal theology that emphasizes the scriptural narrative, and the nature of the "story."[8]

Narrative theology, like many postmodern terms, is broad in its use and meanings. Specifically it is a method, an approach, which focuses on story, narrative, because here we will find revelation and meaning. Story may therefore tell us a greater level of truth than philosophical propositions. Scripture is pre-eminent for narrative theologians. Scripture will teach us about salvation history, the economic Trinity and the religious economy. The precedent for this (commonly cited by many postliberal and narrative theologians) is in Jesus's encounter on the Emmaus road and the resulting conversation, biblical exegesis: "He said to them, 'How foolish you are, and how slow to believe all that the prophets have spoken! Did not the Messiah have to suffer these things and then enter his glory?' And beginning with Moses and all the Prophets, he explained to them what was said in all the Scriptures concerning himself" (Luke 24:25–27). The true context for real theology is therefore eucharistic. So what value is there to starting with narratives? R. A. McLaughlin comments, "When we recognize truth in narratives, we call our recognitions 'theology.' When we formulate our recognitions into logical relationships, we are doing 'systematic theology.' When we formulate our recognitions

---

6   Ibid., 244.
7   For the distinction between the Word of God (the Christ) and a word of God (Scripture) see the second book in this series, *C. S. Lewis—The Work of Christ Revealed*, Pt. 1, Ch. 2.
8   See, specifically, Hauerwas, *Revelations and Story*. See also, Stroup, *The Promise of Narrative Theology*; Loughlin, *Telling God's Story*; and, Donahue, *The Gospel in Parable*.

5. Analogical and Symbolic Narratives I: Narrative Theology, Supposition and Genre

along historical lines, we are doing 'biblical theology.' . . . Narrative theology is not all good or all bad (just like systematic theology and biblical theology). When used rightly, it provides helpful insights and true understanding. Used wrongly, it causes as many problems as any other misused approach to theology."[9]

So what is a good use of narrative theology and how does this relate to Lewis? The answer is scriptural because the focus on narrative and metaphor is found in the Gospels. For example, John Donahue in *The Gospel in Parable: Metaphor, Narrative and Theology in the Synoptic Gospels* asserts that Jesus's parables give us a narrative within a narrative that mirrors in many ways the gospel, and gives direction and shape, added meaning to the gospels. The parables are therefore the gospel in parabolic form.[10] Like Lewis's analogical and symbolic narratives, the parables, for Donahue, transcend the ordinary:

> As metaphors, the parables of Jesus point to an order of reality other than that described in the parable. Often it is an element of the parable itself, such as the extraordinary harvest (Mark 4:8), or the order of payment (Matt 20:8), where the ordinary has gone askew and thereby shocks us into realizing that the parables lead into another way of thinking about life. Jesus thus spoke a language of the familiar and concrete which touched people in their everyday lives but which pointed beyond itself and summoned people to see everyday life as the carrier of self-transcendence. . . . The new age has begun and God has entered history in a new way. In effect the message of the kingdom is that the world points beyond itself. The use of parable with the native power of metaphor to point beyond itself means that in effect the medium is the message. . . . Thus theological language is radically parabolic.[11]

How does this apply to Lewis? Lewis's analogical and symbolic narratives are, in many ways, parables, they are metaphors of the kingdom of God: Screwtape as a portrait and warning of the beguiling and corrupting influence of evil; *The Great Divorce* as a parable of how humanity gets what it deserves, what it wants, and how it locks out the Christ; but above all, the Narniad as a parable of salvation, in a different reality. However, for Narnia generally, for Aslan specifically, this is not necessarily, or primarily, based on Scripture, but on the reality of the Christ who is the *Word* of God, and from whom issues the word of God. Narrative may be the means but the reality, as we will see, for Lewis, is the Word of God, the second person of the Trinity: the Christ. Lewis is not trying to mimic the scriptural narrative, or be allegorical, but he is pointing to the reality of Christ and postulating. Lewis's analogical and symbolic narratives point beyond themselves, beyond the written word, the narrative, to a God given reality.

---

9   Third Millennium Ministries. Online:
http://thirdmill.org/answers/answer.asp/file/99702.qna/category/th/page/questions/site/iiim.
10   See Donahue, *The Gospel in Parable*, 20–24, and, 194–216
11   Donahue, *The Gospel in Parable*, 10–11.

4. LEWIS: ANALOGICAL-SYMBOLIC NARRATIVES

i. A Veiled Understanding Outside the Church

An important element of Lewis's theology was his doctrine of Christological prefigurement. Lewis identified an apparent prefiguring of elements of the incarnation-cross-resurrection narrative in non-Christian religious myths. Such a doctrine is summarized in two propositions: first: the actuality of the historical event of the incarnation-cross-resurrection was previsioned in Pagan religion and myth (i.e., in non-Judaic-Christian religious stories and myths); second, the gospel account, the incarnation-cross-resurrection narrative, acts on us, whether spoken or read, both as fact and myth. From his teenage years on, Lewis the apostate atheist held the North European pagan myths in very high regard, but also Middle Eastern and Asiatic-Indian-Oceanic myths—in particular ancient Hindu. With his conversion he sought to understand how they related to the Christ event—an event that was an actuality, an event that he had come to realize was central to human history. Lewis came to regard these prefigurements as the work of the Holy Spirit—intimations of God's salvific action in Christ. These pagan myths speak of the appearing and reviving from death of pagan gods, avatars, and spirits, but none speak of an actual incarnation, or an actual resurrection, the evidence internal to these myths led Lewis after his conversion to analyze why and how these religious myths/stories related to the actual Christ-event. His cautious respect for these intimations of prefigurement were as a mode of revelation rooted in Augustine's doctrine of illumination and the proposition that there is no un-aided *true* knowledge of God, knowledge and understanding given through prevenient grace and imbued through the faculty of the imagination. Lewis eventually saw how stories and myths, whether religious or otherwise, were to be seen teleologically in relation to the Christ-event. Reinterpreting what Plato wrote about the suffering, just person in the light of the Christ-event is entirely admissible, likewise the ramifications of Balder's death (a Norse, Christlike, character) and his failed resuscitation is meant to reverberate with the true story of Jesus's death and the actual resurrection when the two are seen together because of the cosmic implications of the one true myth—the Christ-event: Christological prefigurements work towards God's loving purposes which are the potential transformation and salvation of all humanity.[12]

ii. Genre and Source

Lewis went beyond an academic study characterized by Christological theorizing about the evidence or otherwise of intimations, echoes or refractions, of the gospel narrative in the world's religions and mythologies: he wrote his own Christian myths—*The Space Trilogy* and *The Chronicles of Narnia*, stories that echoed the Christ event. In terms of genre as English literature they were relatively unique, at the time. They

---

12   Lewis's doctrine of Christological prefigurement is dealt with in depth in the second book in this series: *C. S. Lewis—The Work of Christ Revealed*, Pt. 3, Chs. 9–10, 191–264.

5. Analogical and Symbolic Narratives I: Narrative Theology, Supposition and Genre

are not fantasy novels, which is as they are so often categorized. They are not fantasy because of their theological content. But neither are they allegory, Lewis specifically denied any one-to-one correspondence, and there is no allegorical, hidden, meaning. (*The Pilgrim's Regress* was allegorical, the correspondence and layers of allegory is quite complex—Lewis realized after the book's publication that the dense allegory was lost on many readers.[13]) In *The Space Trilogy* and *The Chronicles of Narnia* the stories and the characters are not the same *dramatis personæ*, the same setting, as the gospel, and the stories were not meant to be the same as the gospel story, they were not the incarnation-Resurrection narrative hidden behind heavy constructed allegory. The genre we will designate them as is analogical-symbolic narratives. There is an intended relationship between the events, characters, and the stories, in *The Space Trilogy* and *The Chronicles of Narnia*, but this is by analogy—that is, there is a comparison between one and another made for the purpose of explanation or clarification. Therefore, the characters and events in *The Lion, the Witch and the Wardrobe* are similar, related, by comparison, intentionally, for the purposes of explanation, clarification, elucidation—they are analogous but also symbolic.[14] A mark or character, a symbol, is used as a representation of something else, it is a thing that represents or stands for *something other* than itself. Therefore, in the genre of analogical-symbolic narratives the events and characters symbolize, but not necessarily the detail. Aslan's death on the stone table, stabbed through the heart by the White Witch is not an allegory of the Crucifixion, but everything about the story and the characters leads us to *compare* Aslan's death with Jesus' crucifixion, and therefore Aslan with the Christ.[15] This was intentional, it is not accidental. But there is no one-to-one correspondence in analogical-symbolic narratives. Lewis's analogical-symbolic narratives draw on and are related to the genres of science fiction and children's literature, though anyone who believes that the Narnia stories are only read by children is severely mistaken, likewise those who believe that *The Space Trilogy* are aimed only at science fiction aficionados. These two series reflect Lewis's interest in and reading of such literature as a child and as a young atheistic adult: first, like most of his generation, he developed a deep love for the genre of what is often termed "Boy's Own" adventure stories—in this instance the stories of H. Rider

---

13 Lewis, *The Pilgrim's Regress* (1st ed.), 1933. An excellent guide to the allegory, mythology and allusion used by Lewis in *The Pilgrim's Regress* can be found at:
http://www.lewisiana.nl/regressquotes/index.htm

14 The word analogy was derived from the Latin *analogia*—proportion—from the Greek (ἀναλογία/ἀνάλογος, *analogia/analogos*—proportionate), therefore a thing regarded as analogous to another, or the process of making such a comparison, is a thing subject to a measure of judgement or evaluation: the reader identifies with the intended aim of Lewis in writing something comparable to the gospel story. The word symbol was derived from Middle English where it denoted the creed, from the Latin *symbolum*—symbol—the creed was considered to be the mark of a Christian; the word was derived from Greek σύμβολον, *symbolon*, "a sign or token by which one infers a thing," in ecclesial Greek it was used for "the distinctive sign of a Christian, a confession of faith," from σύν + βάλλειν. OED, and Liddell, *An Intermediate Greek-English Lexicon*.

15 For an analysis of what is implied in identifying second or subsequent meanings to these narratives, and the consequences, see the second volume in this series: *C. S. Lewis—The Work of Christ Revealed*, Pt. 3, Ch. 10, "i. Intention and Validity," 218–19, and, "ii. Plato and the Christ," specifically, 219–21.

Haggard (Lewis cites *King Solomon's Mines* as one such example);[16] as a young man Lewis's atheism resonated proximately with that of H. G. Wells, a writer whose science fiction works Lewis valued. As a child and teenager Lewis was an avid reader, much of which he forgot and dismissed as he matured, however, he does cite Haggard and Wells as being of primary importance to him—"the work of Rider Haggard, and also the 'scientifiction' of H. G. Wells. The idea of other planets exercised upon me then a peculiar, heady attraction, which was quite different from any other of my literary interests."[17] But H. G. Wells was a self-confessed atheist, something of a firebrand anti-Christian, and this fed Lewis's teenage rebellion that led to apostasy. He admits to having seen the writing of *The Space Trilogy* as something of an exorcism.[18] He took Wells's scientific atheism and naturalism and turned it on its head—we might add very successfully—"I may perhaps add that my own planetary romances have been not so much gratification of this fierce curiosity as its exorcism. The exorcism worked by reconciling it with, or subjecting it to, the other, the more elusive, and genuinely imaginative, impulse."[19] If Wells gave Lewis a fascination for the possibility of other sentient species, other planets, other worlds, this only gave him a naturalist view of the universe, a nihilistic atheistic driving of nature to survive: Lewis had to refute this evolutionary picture of blind matter striving to survive though unexplainable consciousness.[20] In addition, Lewis became puzzled by H. G. Wells's strong moral consciousness, his insistence on ethics, which contradicted with his naturalism. Speaking of Wells and his fellow naturalists Lewis commented: "A moment after they have admitted that good and evil are illusions, you will find them exhorting us to work for posterity, to educate, revolutionize, liquidate, live and die for the good of the human race. A Naturalist like Mr. H. G. Wells spent a long life doing so with passionate eloquence and zeal."[21] So what gave Lewis the inspiration to combine intimations of the supernatural, that creation is God-given, with this proto-"scientifiction"? Lewis comments in a letter from 1944 to Charles A. Brady, listing the influences on the development of his Christocentric space trilogy, though specifically, the work of David Lindsay:

> Space-and-time fiction. . . . The real father of my planet books is David Lindsay's Voyage to Arcturus, which you also will revel in if you don't know it. I had grown up on Well's stories of that kind: it was Lindsay who first gave me the idea that the "scientifiction" appeal could be combined with the "supernatural" appeal—suggested the "Cross" (in biological sense). His own spiritual outlook is detestable, almost diabolist I think, and his style crude: but he showed me what a bang you could get from mixing these two elements. [And there is] my whole Norse complex—Old Icelandic, Wagner's Ring and (again) Morris. The Wagner

---

16 See, Lewis, "The Mythopoeic Gift of Rider Haggard," 128 and 130.
17 Lewis, *Surprised by Joy*, 26.
18 See, Downing, "Rehabilitating H. G. Wells: C. S. Lewis's *Out of the Silent Planet*."
19 Lewis, *Surprised by Joy*, 26–27.
20 See: Lewis, "The Funeral of a Great Myth," 82–83.
21 Lewis, *Miracles* (2nd ed.), 64. See also, 65 and 88.

is important: you will see, if you look, how operatic the whole building up of the climax is in *Perelandra*.[22]

It is fair therefore to cite these authors as an influence, something of a foundational influence on Lewis's analogical and symbolic narratives, certainly in terms of storytelling and the value of a distant, other, world, but the *primary* influence must be the Bible, both in the context of salvation history, and the genre of parable and metaphor. Apart from the fact that the Bible has a form of analogical narrative—parable—the aim of Lewis's Narniad was to explore what would happen if the second person of the Trinity was incarnated in another reality.

Lewis's main two analogical-symbolic narrative series are deeply and profoundly theological, and are also intentionally didactic; they were to teach something about the faith without the formality of church which Lewis believed put many children—and adults—off. In the case of the Narnia stories, they are not without logic or reason, and a systematic theological framework can be read from them as much as from Lewis's apologetic works from the 1940s.

5. NARNIA: LEWIS'S "SUPPOSAL"

i. Mythopoeic Theorizing

In his later years Lewis reflected about the method of his analogical narratives. In a short article written for *The New York Times*, Lewis describes the relationship between the creative process and his faith.[23] He explains how ideas seem to "bubble up" in his mind but the impulse to write, to compose, will only happen if the idea of a form offers itself—poem or narrative, play or short story. If this impulse is a desire, then aspiration and longing will see the idea take form. Therefore, *The Chronicles of Narnia* started with an image coming into Lewis's mind—"a faun carrying an umbrella, a queen on a sledge, a magnificent lion. At first there wasn't even anything Christian about them; that element pushed itself in of its own accord."[24] The form was dictated by the content, Christian analogy (rather than allegory). The aim was given by Lewis's realization that as a child he had been paralyzed by religion, failing to feel as he was expected to feel about God, or the sufferings of Christ, such an obligation stifled any true religion in him.[25] Therefore, Lewis wanted to bypass any remainder of the formality of Victorian and Edwardian respectful religion that in effect stifled, near killed, the spirit of the gospel, for Lewis. Lewis believed he did this by transposing the Christ event into an imaginary world. But these became more than children's stories—for Lewis the form

---

22 Lewis to Charles A. Brady, Oct 29, 1944. *Collected Letters, Vol. II*, 630. David Lindsay's *Voyage to Arcturus*, was first published in 1920. It is a synthesis of philosophy and scientifiction, and explores the nature of good and evil.

23 Lewis, "Sometimes Fairy Stories may say best what's to be said," 35-38. See also: Lewis, "On Three Ways of Writing for Children," 22-34, a paper given to the Library Association Conference, Apr 29 to May 2, 1952.

24 Lewis, "Sometimes Fairy Stories," 36.

25 Ibid.," 37.

is "the fantastic or mythical."[26] The gestation of the Narnia books was over several decades. The initial picture in his mind of a faun carrying an umbrella and walking through a snowy wood had been in his mind since he was sixteen years of age.[27] The decision to put the idea into a form came when he was around forty years of age, before the Second World War, but it would be another twelve years before the first book would appear.

By contrast with analogy, Lewis defines allegory as "a composition (whether pictorial or literary) in which immaterial realities are represented by feigned physical objects, e.g., a pictured Cupid allegorically represents erotic love (which in reality is an experience, not an object occupying a given area of space) or, in Bunyan, a giant represents despair."[28] The Narniad and *The Space Trilogy* are not feigned objects. There is no one-to-one correspondence. The characters are meant to seem real, in the context of the world invented for them. In addition they are supposed to be different, but tantalizingly like, they are meant to resonate with humanity, the earth, and the human condition as defined by the *fall*. They are speculative, but based upon the human condition defined by and in relation to God. They are a supposition: a belief, guess, a theoretical idea. They are a hypothesis, a deductive possibility. Lewis therefore invents the term, "supposal."[29] There are pointers to this method in *The Screwtape Letters* and *The Great Divorce*,[30] but it is in the Narniad that Lewis's ultimate use of the method and genre of symbolic or analogical narrative is exhibited (going beyond his doctrine of Christological prefigurement, which had focused on the intimations, echoes or refractions of the gospel narrative in the world's religions and mythologies). The pinnacle of Lewis's analogical and symbolic narratives was a series of books—his own Christian myth—in effect aimed at children, yet read and theologically reflected on by adults: *The Chronicles of Narnia*.[31] Lewis's aim was to present the love, light, and truth of God's turn towards creation, as represented in the gospel. He did this because he believed it had been buried, almost extinguished to a degree, by Victorian and Edwardian Pietism, by obligation and moralizing, and by adult superiority towards children. Lewis wrote:

26   Ibid.," 38.
27   Ibid.," 36.
28   Lewis to Mrs Hook Dec. 29, 1958. *Collected Letters, Vol. III*, 1004–5.
29   The verb "to suppose" is to think or assume that something is true or probable, but without proof (OED). In terms of Lewis's aim he assumes that something is the case as a precondition. Narnia is therefore "supposable." Though speculative, the Narniad should enable us to have a better appreciation of the Christ event.
30   Lewis, *Screwtape Letters* (1942), followed by, Lewis, *The Great Divorce* (1945).
31   Lewis, *The Chronicles of Narnia*:
The Lion the Witch and The Wardrobe, 1950.
Prince Caspian, 1951.
The Voyage of the Dawn Treader, 1952.
The Silver Chair, 1953.
The Horse and His Boy, 1954.
The Magician's Nephew, 1955.
The Last Battle, 1956.

5. Analogical and Symbolic Narratives I: Narrative Theology, Supposition and Genre

> I thought I saw how stories of this kind could steal past a certain inhibition which had paralyzed much of my own religion in childhood. Why did one find it so hard to feel as one was told one ought to feel about God or about the sufferings of Christ? I thought the chief reason was that one was told one ought to. An obligation to feel can freeze feelings. And reverence itself did harm. The whole subject was associated with lowered voices; almost as if it were something medical. But supposing that by casting all these things into an imaginary world, stripping them of their stained-glass and Sunday School associations, one could make them for the first time appear in their real potency? Could one not thus steal past those watchful dragons? I thought one could.[32]

Lewis's initial inspiration was with images: "All my seven Narnia books, and my three science-fiction books, began with seeing pictures in my head. At first they were not a story, just pictures. *The Lion* began with a picture of a faun carrying an umbrella and parcels in a snowy wood . . . then suddenly Aslan came bounding into it."[33]

ii. "The Whole Narnian Story is about Christ"

Lewis's asserted that God gave images to the Pagans, as compared to the law and revelation given to the Hebrews; that is, he poses a dialectic—neither is independent of the other—in that God gave the *Shepherds* (the Hebrew people) ideas and rules and set their feet on the road but that he gave pictures, images (myths, stories), to the *pagan* peoples.[34] However, there are multifarious dangers in how revelation is perceived, internalized and used by both groups. The danger Lewis talks about is manifold; speaking of the pagan peoples he commented that, "They had pictures for their eyes instead of roads for their feet, and that is why most of them could do nothing but desire and then, through starved desire, become corrupt in their imaginations."[35] It is the Shepherds (Israel) who have the road for their feet to travel, but this was not without its pitfalls: the Shepherds, for Lewis, rejected the Christ and became over protective about the Hebrew religious tradition and law. The point of the journey is to arrive, whether one is a Shepherd or a pagan, the journey should lead to what the church represents: the Hebrew law and the pagan previsions were not to be seen as ends in themselves: "It is a starting point from which one road leads home and a thousand lead into the wilderness . . . the truth is that a Shepherd is only half a man, and a pagan is only half a man, so that neither people was well without the other, nor could either be healed until the Landlord's Son [Christ] came into the country."[36] One of the aims of analogical symbolic narratives was then to take on the role of pagan myths that prefigured the incarnation, death and resurrection of the Christ. Therefore, Lewis's more formal aim was to explore what he termed a "supposal": *what if* Christ became incarnate in the flesh, the physical reality of another world, as part of another

---

32   Lewis, "Sometimes Fairy Stories May Say Best What's to be Said," 36.
33   Lewis, "It All Began with a Picture. . ."
34   Lewis, *The Pilgrim's Regress*, (3rd ed.), 189–94. Also, see the second book in this series: *C. S. Lewis—The Work of Christ Revealed*, Pt. 3, Chs. 9–10, 248–51.
35   Lewis, *The Pilgrim's Regress*, (3rd ed.), 193.
36   Ibid., 193–94.

sentient life? Not another planet or world within our universe but an entirely different universe, another reality. Lewis decried the label allegory, concentrating on this term "supposal"—a what if supposition.[37] In writing to a parent in 1958 Lewis asserted,

> If Aslan represented the immaterial Deity he would be an allegorical figure. In reality however he is an invention giving an imaginary answer to the question, "What might Christ become like if there really were a world like Narnia and He chose to be incarnate and die and rise again in that world as He actually has done in ours?" This is not allegory at all. . . . The Incarnation of Christ in another world is mere supposal: but granted the supposition, he would really have been a physical object in that world as he was in Palestine and his death on the stone table would have been a physical event no less than his death on Calvary.[38]

In reply to a letter from an eleven-year-old child, Anne Jenkins, who is puzzled by Aslan's comment at the end of *The Silver Chair*, about having died and come to life again, Lewis actually outlined, in summary, the Christology of the Narniad. He states explicitly that he whole story of Narnia is about Christ: the incarnation—*sacrifice*—resurrection, the revelation of Christ, the judgment and conversion of individuals, the care for the creation through a religious economy, and so forth:

> What Aslan meant when he said he had died is, in one sense, plain enough. Read the earlier book in the series called *The Lion the Witch and the Wardrobe*, and you will find the full story of how he was killed by the White Witch and came to life again. When you have read that, I think you will probably see that there is deeper meaning behind it.
>
> The whole Narnian story is about Christ. That is to say, I asked myself "Supposing there really were a world like Narnia, and supposing it had (like our world) gone wrong, and supposing Christ wanted to go into that world and save it (as *he* did ours) what might have happened?"
>
> The stories are my answer. Since Narnia is a world of Talking Beasts, I thought he would become a Talking Beast there, as *he* became a Man here. I pictured *him* becoming a lion there because (a) The lion is supposed to be the King of beasts; (b) Christ is called "The Lion of Judah" in the Bible* . . .[39]

Lewis continues by outlining the progression of salvation history in the Narniad: the creation and then corruption of Narnia by evil, the sacrifice and resurrection, the calling and conversion of the heathens, the restoration of true religion, the spiritual life, the continuing war against evil and the powers of darkness, and finally the coming of the anti-Christ prefacing the end-of-the-world and the last judgment.[40] (See figure 3.)

Unlike the prefigurement myths which were in effect created and heard outside of cognitive knowledge about, or awareness of the incarnation-resurrection, Aslan

---

37   Walter Hooper has collated the material gleaned from various letters, essays where Lewis explains his aims, and what he meant by "supposal": Hooper, *C. S. Lewis: A Companion and Guide*, 423–26
38   Lewis to Mrs Hook Dec. 29, 1958., *Collected Letters, Vol. III*, 1004–5.
39   Lewis to Anne Jenkins, Mar. 5, 1961. *Collected Letters, Vol. III*, 1244–45. *: Rev 5:5.
40   Ibid.

5. Analogical and Symbolic Narratives I: Narrative Theology, Supposition and Genre

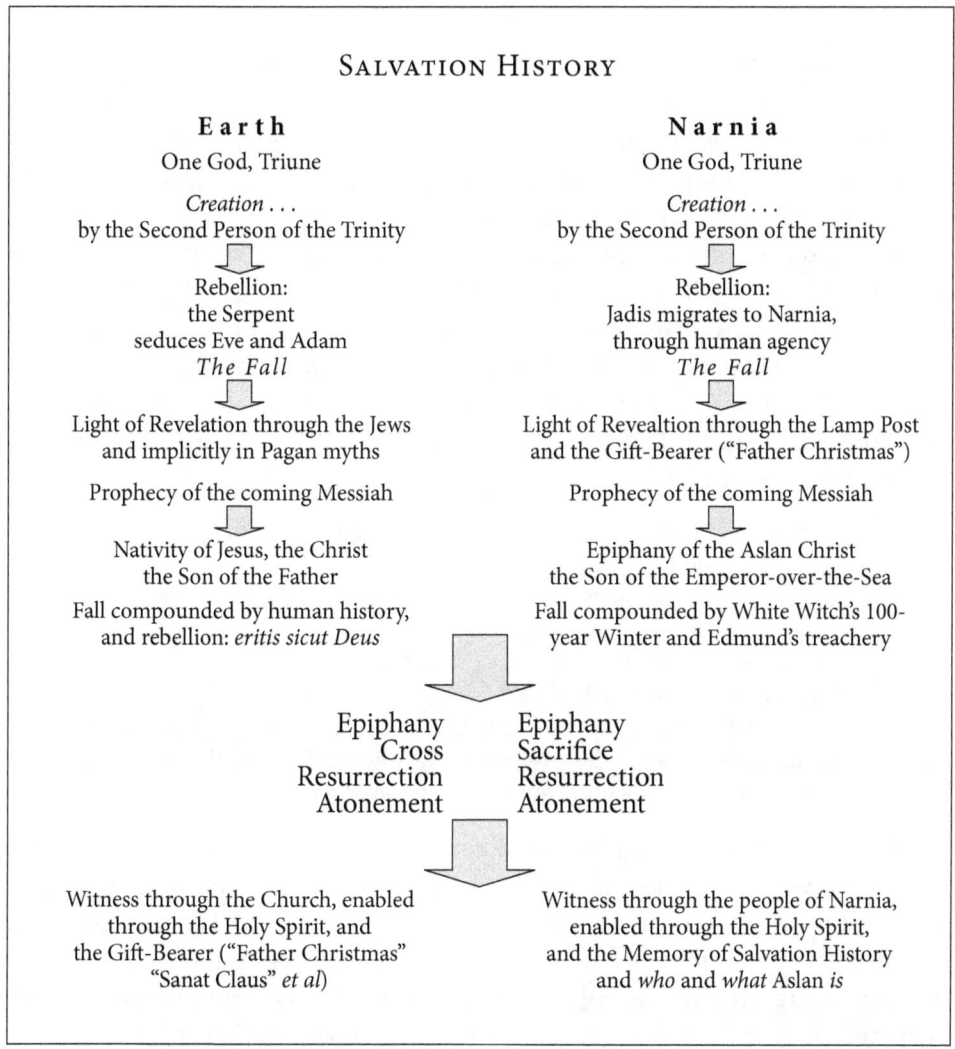

Figure 3 Salvation History and a Christocentric Religious Economy in the Narniad

is a conscious attempt at Christian education within and for a society and tradition that knew about Christ Jesus' atoning sacrifice, but for Lewis had lost the plot due to Pietism and moralizing. However, with over 100 million copies sold (which gives a readership of upwards of half a billion) since their original publication in the early 1950s, having been translated into most of the world's main languages and because of the nature of a post-Christian society in Britain it is now a fair assumption to say that most of the readers of *The Chronicles of Narnia* in the early twenty-first century may not have heard of the gospel reality—the same sort of target audience that received and heard the prefigurement myths we have been considering.

iii. Aslan . . . or Christ?

Lewis's "supposal" is therefore something of a fanciful conjecture, a "what if . . ."; he is postulating the possibility of theophanic appearances or incarnations in other worlds or universes. However, Aslan is not meant to be a separate incarnation from Jesus Christ. They are not separate or distinct "gods," neither are they independent of the Father. The two would not vie for precedence in the *eschaton*—they are one and the same. They differ only in form, the form taken in a corporeal reality: the form of a man or the form of a lion, in either case a form appropriate to each created reality. Understanding Lewis's Platonism here is crucial, but this does not make them pagan or gnostic "gods." The manifestation is unique and local, the form taken in a hypothetical Narnia, and the form taken in our world. This is why Aslan says to Lucy that he has a different name in our world, and the very reason she came into Narnia was so as to get to know *him* in our world:

> "You are too old, children," said Aslan, "and you must begin to come close to your own world now."
> "It isn't Narnia, you know," sobbed Lucy. "It's you. We shan't meet you there. And how can we live, never meeting you?"
> "But you shall meet me, dear one," said Aslan.
> "Are—are you there too, Sir?" said Edmund.
> "I am," said Aslan. "But there I have another name. You must learn to know me by that name. This was the very reason why you were brought to Narnia, that by knowing me here for a little, you may know me better there."[41]

Here Lewis is actually stating the explicit aim of the stories within the narrative! It is like an actor in an ancient play or in Shakespeare talking to the audience. These are broadly speaking, matters beyond our present concern. The Narnian stories are like the pagan myths for Lewis, they do not exist in their own right to point to their own internal reality and logic (though it is essential that as part of the supposition, conjecture, deductive hypothesis, that there is a clear internal logic to the stories): they exist to point to the single historic event in our reality.

There is a Platonic principle here, which reflects the action of the Holy Spirit: that whatever diversity there is within our world of God's actions—the evidence in and through a religious economy—there is unity in eternity, in the *immanent* Trinity. This inherent and essential nature of God is reflected, but transposed, diluted, for our reception.

iv. "The Probable and the Marvelous"

Lewis commented further, in more depth, on this "supposal" genre in a BBC broadcast in 1949 in the context of the novels of his friend and colleague Charles Williams.[42] For Lewis, Charles Williams combined "the realistic and the fantastic," however, "I would

---

41 Lewis, *The Voyage of the Dawn Treader*, 269–70.
42 Lewis, "The Novels of Charles Williams," Broadcast on BBC radio, the Third Programme, Feb. 11, 1949. Part of this broadcast is still extant and can be heard online: http://www.cslewisandthechrist.net/links.html.

5. Analogical and Symbolic Narratives I: Narrative Theology, Supposition and Genre

rather fall back on an older terminology and say that they mix the probable and the marvelous."[43] The probable is the ordinary suburban world that is a commonplace understanding, but then there is intimation of the *marvelous*, and a breaking in of another reality, an eternal and supernatural reality, a *marvelous* reality: "[Williams] is writing that sort of book in which we begin by saying, 'Let us *suppose* that this everyday world were, at some point, invaded by the marvelous. Let us, in fact, suppose a violation of frontier.' The formula is no novelty."[44] Critics would argue that this is a fantasy, but, although Lewis does not systematize his explanation, the violation he speaks of, the breaking-in within our reality, is incarnational, and reflects and echoes the breaking-in of eternity in the form of the incarnation, the Word made flesh. The violation of frontier, as Lewis puts it, is prefaced by the incarnation and made possible by the incarnation: therefore it is perfectly valid to "suppose," as Lewis does. Lewis argues firmly that this combination, of the probable and the marvelous, works, despite "Modern"/"Liberal" skepticism:

> On the contrary, it keeps its own level throughout: that level on which we suppose that a violation of frontier has occurred in the actual world. Now some people doubt whether the kind is permissible. Of what value, it may be asked, are such supposals? And one answer to that question I myself would rule out at once. They are not allegories. . . . The starting point is a supposal. "Suppose I found a country inhabited by dwarves. Suppose two men could exchange bodies." Nothing less, but equally nothing more, is demanded.
>
> Every supposal is an ideal experiment: an experiment done with ideas because you can't do it any other way. And the function of an experiment is to teach us more about the things we experiment on.[45]

Furthermore, asserts Lewis, it is not possible to turn such a story into an allegory without doing it injustice, twisting and altering the reality and the meaning. They key is not simply to postulate an alternate reality, such a story would be wide open to allegorical interpretation; no, the key is commerce between the two realities. For a violation of one reality by another to take place the supposition must be intelligible and it must cohere to a degree, but not totally, with our reality. So, for example, Narnia is not self-contained and there is commerce between our reality and Narnia, this breaking-in occurs from its creation: there is human migration to Narnia. Lewis writes that we put these two worlds together and watch how they react, and then consider and feel, imagine and think, more attentively to our reality and what God has done for us in a religious economy. However, an important element to both the Narniad and Williams novels is that although they may be underpinned by an "explicitly Christian conception",[46] this is not always obvious and it is not a form of Christian preaching. Many may read and gain sustenance without believing (critics of the Narniad see this as underhand, sneaky, and a form of indoctrination).

---

43 Ibid., 46.
44 Lewis, "The Novels of Charles Williams," 47.
45 Ibid., 47–49.
46 Ibid., 51f.

Is there theological justification for this, more pertinently, Christological reasoning and validation? Yes; by contrast it is science-fiction that is the mundane and probable. Science fiction stories, dramas, and films postulate aliens that are supposed to be utterly different, yet they are always framed in a manner that is perceivable to us (most are humanoid—a projection of humanity's power lust and destructive capabilities, neuroses and obsessions, and, yes, sins!). If these aliens were truly alien they would be utterly different, and we could barely, if at all, conceive of them. Often in science-fiction stories, if someone or some group of people disappear it is because they have been drawn in an instant by an alien force to the other side of the galaxy and are thereby out of sight and out of communication. This is not much different to a nine-month long sea voyage from England to Australia in the eighteenth century! Science-fiction does not allow for the supernatural, the beyond, the truly other, but merely postulates the different, the intelligible within a naturalistic framework. Lewis's supposal method for analogical and symbolic narratives asserts the completely other, detached from our reality, a truly other world, and above all eternity, and a God that breaks into, cares for, and redeems the creature, that authorizes the commerce and traffic between realities, and *haunts* these creations through the Holy Spirit.

6. HOW SUCCESSFUL IS LEWIS'S SUPPOSITION?

In addressing questions of doctrine, and also the nature of *prelapsarian* humanity, Lewis appeals to his stories, such as, the science fiction trilogy. He comments:

> Behind my own stories there are no facts at all, tho' I hope there are truths. That is, they may be regarded as imaginative hypotheses illustrating what I believe to be theological truths. *Silent Planet* is in part an answer to the popular objection: "In the light of modern astronomy how can you go on believing God was incarnate on one petty little planet of a minor star?" Answer: perhaps it was the only one that needed redemption, that one lost sheep whom he went seeking, leaving the ninety-nine.
>
> *Perelandra* answers the view "By a Fall, don't you really mean only the inevitable finiteness and incompletion of man?" Answer: no, I don't. I believe it resulted from a free act of sin and could have been avoided. If God created any other rational animal in some other part of the universe, perhaps they did not Fall. One may imagine..."[47]

So there may be other sentient creatures elsewhere in the universe who maintained a state of grace by not disobeying God, by not *falling*. However, this leaves open the question of multiple incarnations: if another rational animal, a sentient species, in another part of the universe *had fallen*, what then? Does Christ's atonement for the humans on earth apply universally to them; are they part of the same creation?

If aims and objectives are to be acknowledged then Lewis and Tolkien's stories are not fantasy but as we have established, analogical and symbolic narrative. For example, both *The Lord of the Rings* and *The Chronicles of Narnia* (and for that matter *The Space Trilogy, The Screwtape Letters* and *The Great Divorce*) were written to reflect a deeper

---

47   Lewis to Tony Pollock, May 3, 1954. Lewis, *Collected Letters Vol. III*, 466.

5. Analogical and Symbolic Narratives I: Narrative Theology, Supposition and Genre

Platonic truth about reality. Tolkien's Middle Earth echoed humanity's existential crisis whereby, through its own fault, humanity is haunted by an evil that is a very real reality. For Lewis analogical and symbolic narrative in the form of Narnia was this supposition. Therefore, these are intimations of analogical supposition, Platonically bequeathed and Christologically grounded (not allegory as so many mistake Narnia for).

How successful is Lewis? Because the Narniad is a supposition we cannot tell how much it aligns with God's religious economy in other worlds, other creations, other realities, because we do not know those realities, though you would have to look hard and long to find someone—believer or atheist—who does not acknowledge the possibility of other intelligent life either in our universe or beyond. However, according to the internal logic of supposal, the question is, to what extent does the Narniad make sense *as compared to* the revelation of God in our reality, and the sacrifice of the second person of the Trinity for humanity and for the care and maintenance of the creation.

How are Lewis and Tolkien's analogical and symbolic narratives received? Children and adults value them greatly, including many who are not Christian, and are tacitly receiving something of a Christian education. How successful was Lewis primarily in writing for children but also in sneaking past the Sunday School teacher to instill some sort of understanding of the Christ of a religious economy? In general terms Richard Dawkins has consistently criticized monotheistic religions (Judaism, Christianity and Islam) as opposed to, presumably, religions with relativistic personal "god." However, in specific terms, the newspaper columnist, and self-confessed liberal atheist Polly Toynbee reviewing the film of *The Lion, the Witch and the Wardrobe* upon its release (December 2005), castigated it stating, "Narnia represents everything that is most hateful about religion."[48] Toynbee quotes Pullman's infamous comment that Narnia is one of the most poisonous things he has ever read, she then continues by advising unbelievers to take a sick-bucket with them if they go to see the movie. Edmund who betrays his siblings and Narnia, this boy is singled out for praise by Toynbee as though the rebel is a saint. However, if this invokes praise, like Pullman, for the *fall*, the cross as the answer to original sin is roundly rejected by her: "Of all the elements of Christianity, the most repugnant is the notion of the Christ who took our sins upon himself and sacrificed his body in agony to save our souls. Did we ask him to?"[49] Toynbee's criticism was in effect a back-handed compliment to Lewis.

---

48 Toynbee, "Narnia represents everything that is most hateful about religion." Film review in The Guardian. Online:
http://www.guardian.co.uk/books/2005/dec/05/cslewis.booksforchildrenandteenagers
49 Ibid.

6

Analogical and Symbolic Narratives II: Christology and Christlikeness— Hiddenness and Multiple Incarnations

SYNOPSIS:
What understanding of the Christ does Lewis present in his analogical and symbolic narratives— specifically, but not exclusively, in *The Space Trilogy*? Lewis's narratives were written to help people understand what had happened two thousand years ago, and how this relates to the human predicament and the truth of the gospel, where the method is analogical rather than allegorical. *The Space Trilogy* and *The Chronicles of Narnia* are primary here, but where is Christ in *The Screwtape Letters* and *The Great Divorce*, also, *Till We Have Faces*? Is Christ absent from *The Great Divorce* ? Is this a Pelagian picture of humanity trying to work out salvation for itself, or one of prevenient grace? What images/word pictures does Lewis paint of Christ in Aslan, Ransom, Psyche, etc., and how do the characters in these stories relate to the Christ event? What is the place of beauty in the revelation that is Aslan the lion? What does Lewis understand and present of Christlikeness? Christ is often veiled, hidden, in these narratives.

The question of multiple incarnations is raised by Lewis's speculative suppositions. Is the incarnation, and therefore the cross and resurrection, unique? Can the Christ be incarnated human more than once in our reality, or perhaps somewhere else in our universe, in a distant galaxy, or another reality outside our universe? Lewis goes to the heart of the problem: "If there are species, and rational species, other than man, are any or all of them, like us, *fallen*?" Any explanation relates to how we define the limits, of the atonement for humanity. Reason will take us thus far; after which pneumatologically inspired imagination will take over: reason and logic will be superseded by analogical narrative. Alice Meynell's poem *Christ in the Universe* was a profound influence on the young atheistic Lewis. After his conversion, it gave him an explanation for what critics called Christian parochialism; also it provided a framework for *The Space Trilogy* and for the Narniad.

We may, therefore, analyze Lewis on the question of multiple incarnations, and in conclusion some contemporary philosophers of religion and theologians (Karl Rahner, with Christopher L. Fisher and David Fergusson; Sjoerd L. Bonting and William B. Drees; E.L. Mascall and Brian Hebblethwaite; Oliver Crisp and Keith Ward): Can Lewis resolve the argument? Could alien species have witnessed wholly different acts, equally unique, costly to God, and necessary to the process of salvation?

ON THE CHRIST OF A RELIGIOUS ECONOMY. I. CREATION AND SUB-CREATION

1. INTRODUCTION

We may now examine Lewis's analogical and symbolic narratives—what they tell us about the Christ. What understanding did Lewis weave into *The Space Trilogy*, and other stories? Though veiled, these writings are doctrinal statements: the doctrine is presented analogically, where doctrine is an analogy of the reality of the Christ event (this is a principle that also underpins much postliberal and narrative theology). Then there is the question of Christlikeness. Whatever understanding of the Christ Lewis imbued into these writings, it is part of a doctrine of God—which itself must reflect the triune nature of God. The Christ may be the visible manifestation, the corporeal knowability, of God, but we cannot separate the second person of the Trinity from the other distinct persons ever in loving communion that form the God-head. In practical terms we will be looking at *The Space Trilogy*, *Till We Have Faces*, *The Great Divorce*, and *The Screwtape Letters*; examining *The Chronicles of Narnia* will be in the following chapters.

2. CHRIST, TRANSLATED AND TRANSPOSED

At the heart of Lewis's analogical and symbolic narratives is Christlikeness, sometimes explicit, sometimes veiled, often triune in that it is the *effect* of the presence of God in an encounter that is presented, which is most often the Holy Spirit, drawing the individual into Christ's redemption and the glory of the Father. The Spirit then re-orientates the creature, redeeming it in the process, a redemption wrought by Christ on the cross and actualized in the resurrection, through the power of the Father, gifted through the Holy Spirit.

i. The imago Christi and the imitatio Christi

Lewis noted that, "The whole Narnian story is about Christ."[1] In the Narniad, as with his other analogical narratives, Lewis is demonstrating the *imago Christi* (the image of Christ) and the *imitatio Christi* (the imitation of Christ). This is rooted in Lewis's patristic reading: the divinization of those who turn to Christ—those who are raised up to be "sons of God."[2] Therefore, it is Christ who is the proof of God, not a reasoned philosophically cogent string of words forming a proposition. This represents change, or more pertinently a development, that occurs throughout Lewis's Christian life. Throughout his life Lewis is moving towards death, he is therefore moving towards Christlikeness—the thinking and speculation ends with death. This move towards Christlikeness is paradoxical: it exposes the flaws in humanity and postulates the only possible good, which is Christ. But this is not a simple task of copying, or trying to ape, the character and person of Jesus Christ. It is through the indwelling of the Holy

---

1   Lewis writing to Anne Jenkins, Mar 5, 1961. In *Collected Letters, Vol. III*, 1244–45.
2   Ideas essentially drawn from Athanasius (c. 296–373); see, Lewis, "Introduction," in, *St. Athanasius: The Incarnation of the Word.*, 5–12. See also, Lewis, *Beyond Personality*, Ch. I, 11–13; Ch. IV, 27–28; Ch. V, 28f.; Ch. XI, 59. These ideas were further expanded in *Mere Christianity*, Bk. 4, Chs. 1, 4, 5 and 11, also, *Miracles* (2nd ed. 1960).

6 Analogical and Symbolic Narratives II: . . . Hiddenness and Multiple Incarnations

Spirit (prevenient grace) that we are raised up from what we are, the human condition we subsist in, to be resurrected with Christ. It is this theme of Christlikeness that takes over from the philosophical speculations that Lewis excelled in, and which, it may be argued, is less dominant in his mature work. His spiritual autobiography, *Surprised by Joy*, focuses this concern with Christlikeness—the person before and in Christ, and how the Holy Spirit will change and mould, break and rebuild the person on an individual and communal level.[3] This process may take time. Lewis had already commented, in the 1940s, in the *Broadcast Talks*, how the whole point of the church was to make people into little Christs.[4] In effect this is the drawing out of the *imago Christi* within people. However, more pertinently, this is the *recovery* of this *image of Christ*, tarnished and buried deep, but not lost. The *imago Christi* is not an affectation we project for the benefit of others, it does not issue from our vanity, it is the essential nature and character that is deep within us, it is the ground from which everything that constituters us emerges. It is at the heart of our creation. This recovery of Christlikeness issues from the incarnation. Incarnation is defined by the apparent self-emptying of God, that is, kenosis (Phil 2:7). Jesus, the Christ, is characterized by beauty of character, graceful humility; he exudes self-denying love, he gives joy, light, and he is compassionate. His words and actions are characterized by messianic authority. In suffering he takes on death voluntarily, for the sake of others—"for love my savior now is dying." Clearly there are certain characteristics that are unique to the Christ, to his absolute nature as the second person of the Trinity—only Christ as the one perfect human can offer the perfect sacrifice for sin, only he can atone. However, people can in a haltingly limited way, through being in Christ, begin to be drawn into Christlikeness: beauty of character, graceful compassion, self-denying altruistic love, joyous yet suffering, humble but self-effacing, they may radiate an inner Christlikeness despite manifold difficulties and oppression. People who begin to exhibit this Christlikeness are therefore at odds with the world as they are changed by Christ's Holy Spirit, through the will of the Father.[5] The *imago Christi* relates closely to the *imitatio Christi* though the two must not be seen as equal, indeed often the *imitatio Christi* issues from the *imago Christi*, however any imitation of Christ must be unself-conscious, or it is likely to be a feign, a pretense, issuing from our ego. Imitation if it is conscious can only, perhaps, be Christlike when it involves self-denial, and leads us to do something (self-sacrifice) which every fiber of our being rebels against, but we still go ahead with it. If we submit gracefully this will often be the work of the Holy Spirit in us rather than our innately fallen and selfish will.

---

3   Lewis, *Surprised by Joy*. This is dealt with in depth in the first book in this series, *C. S. Lewis—Revelation, Conversion and Apologetics*, see Pt. 1, Chs. 1-5.
4   Lewis, *Beyond Personality*, 28.
5   The question of Christlikeness in Lewis's later works is dealt with in depth in the first book in this series, *C. S. Lewis—Revelation, Conversion and Apologetics*, see Pt. 3, Ch. 12

ii. Christlike—and the Christ

There are allusions to the development of the human towards Christlikeness in *The Pilgrim's Regress*, however, this work is early and is heavily allegorical. The genesis of this concern with Christlikeness is with the character of Elwin Ransom in *Out of the Silent Planet* (1938). This is extended in *Perelandra* (1943) with again the character of Ransom but also the development of Weston as the anti-Christ; further early development in Lewis's work is in the "good", or redeemed, people in *The Great Divorce* (1945). Lewis sees this Christlikeness evident in pagan North European and Middle Eastern myths, and in Greek mythology (Balder, Adonis, Osiris, Plato's suffering servant[6]), but Christ is clearly more than all of these. Lewis asserted in the war-time broadcasts how we are changed into Christ-like people;[7] likewise he clearly asserts in his apologetics the reality of original sin and the *fall* in forming our present state. In his mature works he states this doctrinal reality through Christlike people building on what was established. As a storyteller and myth maker Lewis recasts, he re-presents doctrinal truth in his analogical and symbolic narratives. In effect he interprets Christ into ordinary mortals. The most prominent example of this developing absorption with Christlikeness is, in many ways, the character and person of Aslan. Aslan is not simply a creature imitating Christ, or a Christlike figure. He *is* the Christ. Steven P. Mueller uses the term "translates" for when Lewis presents Christlike figures in his stories, drawing on Lewis's own aims and objectives in writing these stories and noting Lewis's comment that if "real" theologians had undertaken this task of translation in the nineteenth century (when they began to lose touch with ordinary Christians) there would have been no work for him to undertake.[8] Lewis, as Mueller notes, does more than merely dress-up characters in an appearance of Jesus: something of the reality of Christ is recast in the form of ordinary people (therefore confirming the *imago Christi*).

iii. Christlikeness—Ransom and Psyche

Elwin Ransom (*Out of the Silent Planet*), whose calm sufferance is reminiscent of Christlikeness, translates something of Christ to us, likewise the character of Psyche in *Till We Have Faces* (1956). Psyche is widely acknowledged as Christlike. But this is not easy: as a child and as an adult she loves altruistically, always helping others, putting others first; her beauty is deep within her person, not just her appearance; she heals people, taking their diseases away, often to her own loss; she willingly allows herself to be sacrificed for the good of others; she is doomed, dying on a tree, her sacrifice

---

6   The extent to which Christlike figures are present in other religions (the question of Christological Prefigurement) is a large and complex subject, which was dealt with in the second book in this series: *C. S. Lewis—The Work of Christ Revealed*, Pt. 3, Chs, 9–11.

7   Lewis, *Beyond Personality*, 28.

8   Mueller, "Christology in the Writings of C. S. Lewis", 280-81, 283, 286, 293, 296-97, and 299. Mueller is referring to Lewis's comments in Lewis, "Rejoinder to Dr Pittenger," 1361-69; Lewis was responding to Pittenger, "Apologist versus Apologist: a Critique of C. S. Lewis as 'Defender of the Faith,'" 1104-7.

6 Analogical and Symbolic Narratives II: . . . Hiddenness and Multiple Incarnations

leads to her being named blessèd. Both Ransom and Psyche's lives are characterized by a movement, a pilgrimage into Christ (an unselfconscious journey): this does not exclude danger and suffering. Psyche dies; Ransom is permanently injured. But this pilgrimage is the gradual process of sanctification, the rebirth of the old person into the new: into the drawing-out of *imago Christi*. In terms of story and myth, this concern with Christlikeness is completed with *Reflections on the Psalms* (1958) and in the posthumously published *Letters to Malcolm: Chiefly on Prayer* (1964).

3. THE HIDDEN CHRIST I: BY ANALOGY

In two short books published during the Second World War Lewis paints pictures— word pictures—he uses narrative, analogy, even humor, to reveal some frightening truths about the human predicament issuing from the *fall*, from original sin, in relation to the immensity of God's justice in Christ: *The Screwtape Letters* and *The Great Divorce*.[9] There are no doctrinal statements relating to Christ or a systematic analysis of revelation and the Christ event, however, both works are imbued with a sound Christology and understanding of revelation—presented analogically. Christ is present throughout both works, though in many ways obliquely, hidden, yet *he* is a colossal and substantial presence that presses on both people and demons and influences them if they will allow this awesome and terrible holy presence to change them. We can imagine Christ just behind the shoulder of Screwtape, the senior devil, threatening his demonic plans and machinations; Christ fills him with loathing, for without Christ he would never have existed, and now without God he would cease to be or have anything to focus on or hate. Is Christ absent from *The Great Divorce*: is this a Pelagian picture of humanity trying to work out salvation for itself, or one of prevenient grace? The hidden Christ is also the "bleeding" charity that stands ever open to forgive people in *The Great Divorce*, if only they will have the courage, if only they would have the will, the audacity, and the faith, to step forth out of the hell they have created and believe. The initial decision to turn to Christ will be the most difficult and often painful thing they have ever done, particularly when they were alive, but it is grace that generates this turn—unless they hold out against Christ in their willfulness. Because of our kingdom of religion, Christ is often hidden—he is the threatening Lord that intimidates and daunts Screwtape's machinations, yet he is the "bloody charity" that stands ever open to forgive people their stupid arrogant sins in *The Great Divorce*.[10]

Christ is revealed in conversations between the redeemed from heaven coming to meet the damned from hell in *The Great Divorce*. Hell is the greatest compliment God can pay to humanity. God has waited all through a person's life for the rebellious individual to utter in prayer, "Thy will be done," therefore in the final reckoning—*post mortem*—God says to the rebellious, "Your will be done."[11] The damned can travel

---

9   See: Lewis, *Screwtape Letters* (1942), and, Lewis, *The Great Divorce* (1945).
10   The Christological issues in *Screwtape Letters* and *The Great Divorce* are dealt with in the first book in this series *C. S. Lewis—Revelation, Conversion, and Apologetics*, Ch. 10, 177–204, specifically, 191f.
11   Lewis, *The Great Divorce*, 58.

to the fringes of heaven, if they so desire, to converse with the redeemed who have travelled as far as it is possible towards the damned and their hell. In the resulting conversations the damned have the opportunity to change, to move into heaven, move deeper and deeper into Christ. Behind these conversations is the love that Screwtape is incapable of understanding—the disinterested, altruistic love, a love that ever gives, and in giving denies itself, yet through the denial it lives the greater life. And that love is the sacrifice of Christ on the Cross: Lewis refers to this explicitly as the "bleeding charity."[12] The reality of Christ may be unknown to the damned—either they did not know of Christ or had the wrong idea about Christ, or the wrong relationship with him—but the greatest stumbling block appears to be their inability to go beyond themselves, to begin to love, truly to love, after the example of Christ. By contrast one character—visiting her damned husband on the fringes of hell where he can perceive the joy of heaven that could be his—refuses to be blackmailed or bullied by her dead husband's emotional self-centeredness. She is truly "in love"—that is, *in Christ*, for Lewis "in love *himself*"—and refuses to abandon the Lord of Love to the twisted demands of the damned.[13] As the redeemed leave the damned to their self-generated hell they sing praises to "the Lord," to the "Love that redeems," as they subsist in "the happy Trinity..."[14]

4. THE HIDDEN CHRIST II: *THE SPACE TRILOGY*

i. Christ's Servants

Published between 1938 and 1945, *The Space Trilogy*[15] is a series of novels, but is also an implicit work of Christian apologetics. The framework is science fiction, grounded initially in Lewis's fascination for the possibility of other sentient species, other planets, other worlds, an interest from his atheistic days influenced by the novels of H. G. Wells. *The Space Trilogy* is a series of interconnected stories, which are implicitly biblical though more pertinently existential given that they focus on the crisis caused, for humanity, by existence and the God-given relationship, a bond, liaison and indelible association, between creator and creature. But, we are talking here about a multiplicity of creatures. Fundamental to *The Space Trilogy* and to the Narniad, is the supposition that there are a multiplicity of creations, a multiplicity of creatures, sentient creatures with the ability to know God, and to make *decisions*, as to what is right and wrong *in relation* to the creator. These conscious sentient creatures, whether human or otherwise, are dependent upon God; not just for their existence,

---

12   Ibid., 21.
13   Ibid., Chs. 12–13, specifically, 95.
14   Ibid., Ch. 13, specifically, 100–101.
15   Sometimes referred to as *The Cosmic Trilogy*: Lewis, *Out of the Silent Planet* (1938); Lewis, *Perelandra* (1943); and Lewis, *That Hideous Strength* (1945). A fragment of another work (which would have been between *Out of the Silent Planet* and *Perelandra*, was published as *The Dark Tower* in 1977. See Lewis, "The Dark Tower," written c. 1938–40, published, in *The Dark Tower and Other Stories* (1977) 3–88.

6 Analogical and Symbolic Narratives II: . . . Hiddenness and Multiple Incarnations

but for their character, and the constraints upon their created nature. They have the freedom to choose, but if they choose wrongly they will suffer and cause others to suffer, and risk damnation. This dependent relationship should be before them all the time, in their lives and in the decisions they make. It is so for many of the sentient alien creatures Lewis creates. But not so for the human, who has taken this ability to decide right and wrong, good and evil, onto itself (*eritis sicut Deus*) and has thus sealed itself into a cocoon: the *fall*, once again.

The first book in the series, *Out of the Silent Planet*, illustrates the gospel; it is set on another planet and compares fallen humanity with non-fallen intelligent creatures. Therefore early on (1938) Lewis went straight to myth and symbolic narrative as a form with which to communicate gospel truth: *Out of the Silent Planet* is about the doctrine of original sin, naturalism and the human propensity to corrupt. Lewis was in effect apologizing and saying that this component of orthodox Christian doctrine was sound, true, whatever scientists and astronomers might decide to the contrary. Lewis is asserting that the Bible story in Genesis 3, however mythopoeically phrased, reflects a deeper truth about humanity: that we brought the perilous situation we find ourselves in onto ourselves, that we are lost. Whatever a reader knew or did not know about Lewis's beliefs, if they had been to Sunday school as a child and had never been near a church since, they could not mistake the underlying Christian framework behind *Out of the Silent Planet*. The book was published around twelve months after Lewis had read, and then translated from the Latin, Augustine's massive tome *The City of God*,[16] which laid out the orthodox doctrine of the fall that has influenced the church for fifteen-hundred years. Elwin Ransom is an ordinary human, educated, responsible, who ends up being kidnapped by Weston and taken to Mars (Earth is the "Silent Planet"—as other sentient alien species see it). Ransom's character is deliberately Christlike, but inevitably human and flawed. He struggles to do the good in the face of manifold evil, but in his struggle he essentially succeeds, overcoming evil. In *Perelandra* (the second book in the series), when faced with Weston's attempt to corrupt and despoil the creation from its genesis (i.e., tempt the Green Lady to *fall*) Ransom wonders why God was not doing more to help the Green Lady to prevent her succumbing to temptation, but then he realizes his mission is from God—to stop Weston corrupting her. God's hands, eyes, and ears are now, in this context, Ransom. Further, the Green Lady must come to a decision herself, which will prove her obedience and her independence in a way that humanity, through Eve, and then Adam, failed to.

ii. The Anti-Christ

Anyone who seriously works against Christ, or the will of God in Christ, or even in the absence of knowledge about the Christ consistently develops their character, person, and will *against* Christlikeness, is in effect the anti-Christ. This is clearly so with manifestly evil persons, but the risk is there also with the faithful: "Peter took him

---

16 See, Lewis writing to Dom Bede Griffiths, April 24, 1936; and, Lewis writing to Dom Bede Griffiths, May 23 1936. Lewis, *Collected Letters Vol. II*, 187–90 and 191–95.

aside and began to rebuke him. 'Never, Lord!' he said. 'This shall never happen to you!' Jesus turned and said to Peter, 'Get behind me, Satan! You are a stumbling block to me; you do not have in mind the concerns of God, but merely human concerns'" (Matt 16:22–23). Edmund in *The Lion, the Witch and the Wardrobe*, prior to his repentance and conversion, is the anti-Christ;[17] likewise even Lucy when she perceives Aslan but fails to follow him, as is Peter the High King for trying to go it alone and belittling Lucy's perception:[18] so even Christ's disciples can mistake their own willfulness for the will of God. The Fox is a character in *Till We Have Faces*, who plays out this role. The Fox is an example of how beguiling heresies may be, but he is wrong. The Fox is a Greek slave in the King of Glome's court; he is a philosophical naturalist who will believe and argue and conduct his life according to nature, pouring scorn on anything religious or superstitious. He rejects the idea of the supernatural, the "gods," or God, the universe, nature is all there is. The irony is that he is right to reject the pagan "gods", but wrong not to see beyond these irrational and credulous religious customs: for the Fox it is chance and serendipity that rule reality, not divine intervention and providence. The character and mission of the Fox is a sub-plot in *Till We Have Faces*, however, he represents the corrosive effect such naturalistic rationalists have had on Western thinking over the last two hundred and fifty or so years: "By employing rhetorical techniques and well-reasoned arguments, the Fox eventually manages to turn Glome upside down . . . he even succeeds in uprooting the country's religion."[19] Despite his rejection of the "gods" and the religious customs of Glome, "The Fox" is obsessed with religion, in disproving and overturning everything that might relate to the transcendent, to holiness, therefore he is probably among the most religious of people in Glome; he simply wants everyone to conform to his personal atheistic religion. As such the Fox is, in effect, an evangelical atheist. He was right to belittle and reject Glome's religion, but not to reject *all* religion, and not to drag all Glome's citizens into his amoral atheism. Evil, the anti-Christ, is so often present in leadership, in powerful rulers, and in governments, high places; a Christlike struggle is against the rulers, against the corrupt authorities, against dark powers, against the agencies of this world, evil spiritual forces: "For we wrestle not against flesh and blood, but against principalities, against powers, against the rulers of the darkness of this world, against spiritual wickedness in high places" (Eph 6:12 KJV). This is taken to its limit in the final book in *The Space Trilogy*, *That Hideous Strength* (1945), which exposes the corruption of humanity and the manifold obsession with evil and self-justification. Speaking of the anti-Christ (though he does not use that term) in *The Space Trilogy*, David C. Downing comments,

> [The villains] are not hard to find; they do not, as St. Paul warned, cloak themselves as angels of light. Lewis's bad characters range from the merely pompous to the outright demonic, but they share a few common traits: they set

---

17   Lewis, *The Lion, the Witch and the Wardrobe*, Ch. 4, 35f.
18   Lewis, *Prince Caspian*, Ch. 9, 101f.
19   Balsbaugh, "The Pagan and the Post-Christian: Lewis's Understanding of Diversity Outside the Faith," 201

6 Analogical and Symbolic Narratives II: . . . Hiddenness and Multiple Incarnations

aside ordinary morality in favor of utility or in favor of some lofty, abstract goals for humanity; they disregard the sanctity of life, whether human or animal; they are "progressive" and find little value in history, tradition, or the classics; they prefer the scientific, artificial, and industrial over the simple and natural; they use language to conceal and distort reality, rather than to reveal it.[20]

The central characters in *That Hideous Strength*, Jane and Mark Studdock, are rootless "Modern" and "Liberal" academics, who gradually begin to find God's truth through an awkward and painful pilgrimage, set against the sheer devilry at NICE (the National Institute of Co-ordinated Experiments), as representative of naturalism, scientism, and scientific pragmatism: "Like her husband, Jane Studdock will also be 'shaken out of the modest little outfit of contemporary ideas which had hitherto made her portion of wisdom' (p. 150). Mark discovers the Straight by the *via negativa*, by almost losing himself to the crooked, the perverse, and the bent. Jane moves in the opposite direction as she is drawn closer to Ransom's community at St. Anne's."[21] These are opposite pilgrimages, but they are slowly drawn into redemption and Christlikeness.

Judith Wolfe notes how for Rowan Williams, the community around Ransom at St Anne's is in effect the church in *That Hideous Strength*.[22] Christlikeness presented by Lewis in his analogical and symbolic narratives is in our reality in the form of the invisible church.[23]

The commission of custodianship is given to humanity *before* the fall: humanity bears a responsibility for the creation. Original sin therefore corrupts this commission and the results are self-evident. Edward Weston, in *Out of the Silent Planet* and *Perelandra*, is the anti-Christ. Weston believes that his discernment of creation is loftier, more insightful, than all others, thus he rules over all creation—if he can. Weston acts *as though he were* God. He displays a proud racial superiority over all creation, over all other sentient creatures, and over lesser humans as he sees them, such as Ransom. He destroys for his own ends. Weston eventually comes to some sort of belief in spiritual matters, but mistakenly believes that God and the devil are one, and invites possession of himself by this dual pseudo-deity (in effect, the devil). Weston ceases to exist but endures as a corpse animated by personified evil. Ransom eventually destroys what remains of Weston, thus preventing the *fall* of the Green

---

20   Downing, "That Hideous Strength: Spiritual Wickedness in High Places" 54.

21   Ibid., 62–63. The *via negativa* is invoked in this instance—Mark Studdock—because he arrives at God's truth through wandering through the opposite, by exhausting himself in the beliefs and activities of NICE. The *via negativa* is essentially apophatic theology, from Greek ἀπόφασις, *apophasis*, from, ἀπόφημι *apophemi*, "to deny, I deny." and attempts to account for God not through the positive attributes, but by citing what God *is not*.

22   Wolfe, "C. S. Lewis and the Eschatological Church," 115.

23   *That Hideous Strength* is a novel—analogical narrative. Using the parable genre Lewis criticizes; the same criticism of scientism, naturalism, and modern liberalism, is carried through in terms of philosophical theology in *The Abolition of Man* (1943) and is essentially a defence of natural law and therefore objectivity in judgements. *The Abolition of Man* was based on a series of lectures, the Riddell Memorial Lectures (Feb 24–26, 1943), delivered at King's College, Newcastle. See, Walsh, *C. S. Lewis Apostle to the Skeptics*, Ch. 16 "Science and Satan", specifically, 128-33. See, also, Aeschliman, *The Restitution of Man. C. S. Lewis and the Case against Scientism*.

Lady, but is injured in the process: the cost of Christlikeness. Weston subsists in a hell of his own making: "The forces which had begun, perhaps years ago, to eat away his humanity had now completed their work. The intoxicated will which had been slowly poisoning the intelligence and the affections had now at last poisoned itself and the whole psychic organism had fallen to pieces. Only a ghost was left—in an everlasting unrest, a crumbling, a ruin, an odor of decay."[24]

5. THE QUESTION OF MULTIPLE INCARNATIONS

i. The Limits of Atonement?

A question that applies to *The Space Trilogy* and *The Chronicles of Narnia* is, are multiple incarnations possible? Is the incarnation, and therefore the cross and resurrection, unique? Does it happen only once? Can the Christ be incarnated more than once in our reality, or perhaps somewhere else in our universe, in a distant galaxy? Or even in another reality, a parallel universe? Why should the incarnation be seen as unique, a one-off?

Baptism (and confirmation, years later, in the case of infant baptism) is considered unique. You cannot be baptized twice; you may decide to re-dedicate your baptismal vows, but baptism is a one-off. Why? Because once you have been committed to Christ there is no going back, and on a deeper level, there is the question of ownership: you belong to Christ and not to Satan. The Holy Spirit will change you, re-orientate you, you are born again. You can only be born once, from your mother's womb; you can only be baptized once, and likewise, the incarnation-cross-resurrection only happens once: there is no going back. Narnia is not in our universe; Lewis is not saying that Narnia is in the same reality as our world; crucially it is outside of the salvation history of the world we live in. The Aslan-Christ dies, sacrificed, and is resurrected, in another reality. Human atonement is physically, geographically, contained. The question applies really to our universe. Lewis is not necessary asserting and exploring the possibility of multiple incarnations, though he did not completely eliminate the possibility. Lewis will argue that this leaves open the possibility of incarnations and theophanies to other life forms in other worlds or universes. In addition his understanding of multiple incarnations is derived from Aquinas, and then presented in his science–fiction writings. At the heart of the question of multiple incarnations is the fall, original sin. If the purpose and function of the incarnation is the cross and resurrection, if the cross and resurrection is to save humanity from its *fall* into original sin, then how far in physical space, in the reality we live in, do the effects of the *fall* permeate, and likewise how far in our reality does the *cure* effect: i.e., what are the *limits* of atonement? Humanity can reject the atonement. Humanity can, as individuals, accept the atonement, internally and be saved, turn to Christ. But then humanity can still sin, become evil, but such individuals, *post-baptism* still belong to

---

24 Lewis, *Perelandra*, 130.

Christ and must face Christ *post mortem*. The question of salvation outside of baptism does not really relate to this question.

ii. Aquinas Poses the Question

Thomas Aquinas wonders, in the context of an exploration of the mode of union in the incarnation, whether it is befitting for God to assume human form, whether it is appropriate to the divine nature, how the nature abstracted from the personality can be assumed, whether one divine person can assume without another, and how fitting it was for the Son of God to assume human nature. In essence Aquinas deals with the question of multiple incarnations through the question, "Whether one Divine Person can assume two human natures?"

Aquinas wrote, "Now the power of a Divine Person is infinite, nor can it be limited by any created thing. Hence it may not be said that a Divine Person so assumed a human nature as to be unable to assume another. For it would seem to follow from this that the personality of the divine nature was so comprehended by one human nature as to be unable to assume another to its personality; and this is impossible, for the uncreated cannot be comprehended by any creature."[25] If God is infinite, and if God's infinity can manifest itself in the finite as a proof of God's infinity (to say that God cannot be finite—incarnated—would be to place limits on God's infinitude) then creation cannot limit God. Therefore, Aquinas is asserting that (according to the creature's supposition) to restrict God to one and only one incarnation is to place human limitations on God. Humanity cannot say that the divine nature of the second person of the Trinity was so "comprehended" by incarnation as to render such an incarnation elsewhere in creation impossible. To say so is for the creature to comprehend the creator on its own terms, its own *fallen* and limited terms. Aquinas therefore sets out the basics of the problem. How does Lewis deal with the question? How have other theologians and philosophers dealt with this question?

6. LEWIS ON MULTIPLE INCARNATIONS

Lewis postulated on this question early on. The novel *Perelandra* has no incarnation, no theophanic appearance, but Ransom comes to realize that although he feared God was not doing anything to help the Green Lady in her struggle against Weston's temptation, God was inspiring and empowering Ransom, as God does others, though the Holy Spirit to battle with Weston, as with other forms of evil: we must not underestimate that independent of an incarnation, or especially because of *the* incarnation, God through the Holy Spirit, is active in creation.

---

25   Aquinas, *Summa Theologiae*. See: 'QUESTION 3: OF THE MODE OF UNION ON THE PART OF THE PERSON ASSUMING', P(3)-Q(3)-A(7), 'Whether One Divine Person Can Assume Two Human Natures?'. See, in a related field, also, 'QUESTION 47: OF THE DISTINCTION OF THINGS IN GENERAL', P(1)-Q(47)-A(1).

i. The Doctrine of Universal Redemption

Lewis held cautiously to a doctrine of universal redemption—*in potential*. Such a doctrine has implications for the question of multiple incarnations. Lewis approaches this from the perspective of philosophical theology rather than analogical narrative.[26] Lewis argues that if God has "entered" nature it is not possible to leave nature unchanged, likewise, the glorification of the human creature cannot be realized without the glorification of the rest of nature: "the union between God and nature admits no divorce."[27] The glorification of the rest of nature is not a by-product from human redemption, the incarnation flows into nature: "Where a God who is totally purposive and totally foreseeing acts upon a nature which is totally interlocked, there can be no accidents or loose ends."[28] Nothing in nature, for Lewis, is higher or lower, first or last. The influence of incarnation is not subject to modern concepts of specificity, equality, the effect is not arbitrary.

Lewis's position is therefore that multiple incarnations are irrelevant. If the incarnation of the Christ has universal implications, and is diffuse in its effect throughout nature then strange as it may seem the corrective to original sin in humanity will have ontological implications throughout the cosmos—or does it? This raises questions about the boundaries of the incarnation, and the precise character of whatever was necessary for the redemption of other far-flung sentient species:

> If other natural creatures than man have sinned we must believe that they are redeemed: but God's incarnation as man will be one unique act in the drama of total redemption and other species will have witnessed wholly different acts, each equally unique, equally necessary and differently necessary to the whole process, and each (from a certain point of view) justifiably regarded as "the great scene" of the play.[29]

ii. Quarantine, Cosmic Implications and Atonement: Wither Humanity?

What does Lewis have to say on these matters? Although he touched on related ideas in "The World's Last Night,"[30] the apologetics in "Religion and Rocketry"[31] (written late in life) focus on these issues to a much greater extent. In "Religion and Rocketry" he uses orthodox biblical theology to address worries and concerns caused by the space age and the space race: apprehensions that space exploration (the first man in orbit—Apr. 12, 1961—occurred just months after the final edition of Lewis's paper) would mean the death of God. Lewis was familiar with *The Time Machine* by H. G. Wells and had valued it as an atheistic apostate; as a Christian he saw no problem or challenge

---

26   Lewis, *Miracles* (1st ed). Ch. XIV "The Grand Miracle," 149–50.
27   Ibid., 149.
28   Ibid., 149–50.
29   Ibid., 150.
30   Lewis, "The World's Last Night," 93–113.
31   Lewis, "Religion and Rocketry." The ideas for this were initially sketched out in 1958 and first published as, Lewis, "Will We Lose God in Outer Space" (1958). This was then expanded and published as a pamphlet, Lewis, *Shall We Lose God in Outer Space* (1959), and finally as, Lewis, "Religion and Rocketry," in 1960, 83–92.

raised by science fiction, astronomy or cosmology: none could irrefutably deny the gospel or God's revelation, but puzzling questions could be raised. The fundamental issue in the question of cosmology and the space race was not, for Lewis, the doctrine of a hypothetical or impersonal "god." The fundamental question related to the *fall* and original sin: why the incarnation. The orthodox answer was because of the *fall*. This is the question at the heart of objections to the gospel in the light of cosmology and space travel. For example, Lewis commented:

> If there are species, and rational species, other than man, are any or all of them, like us, fallen? This is the point non-Christians always seem to forget. They seem to think that the incarnation implies some particular merit or excellence in humanity. But of course it implies just the reverse: a particular demerit and depravity. No creature that deserved redemption would need to be redeemed. They that are whole need not the physician. Christ died for men precisely because men are not worth dying for; to make them worth it. Notice what waves of utterly unwarranted hypothesis these critics of Christianity want us to swim through. We are now supposing the fall of hypothetically rational creatures whose mere existence is hypothetical![32]

There is a problem, readily identified, posed by the question of multiple incarnations, however, this potential problem revolves around how you define the limits, the boundaries, of the scope and effect of the atonement for humanity. We may perceive stars and galaxies and claim they are part of our universe (in other words cosmologists and scientists place humanity at the center of the universe—something they criticized Christians for doing) but where are other galaxies, for example, in terms of the scope and effect, in terms of the limit and boundary of Christ's atonement: Christ died for humanity; did he die for other sentient species billions of light years away? Aslan is a theophanic appearance and atonement for creatures within the reality Lewis named Narnia; this place is clearly not part of our universe. In *The Space Trilogy* there is no second atonement, but there are Christ-like people (but they are "connected" to our reality and humans have travelled there and corrupted). On the potential of other rational species within the universe Lewis commented:

> If all of them (and surely all is a long shot) or any of them have fallen have they been denied redemption by the incarnation and passion of Christ? For of course it is no very new idea that the eternal Son may, for all we know, have been incarnate in other worlds than earth and so saved other races than ours. As Alice Meynell wrote in *Christ in the Universe*:
>
> > . . . in the eternities
> > Doubtless we shall compare together, hear
> > A million alien Gospels, in what guise
> > He trod the Pleiades, the Lyre, the Bear.[33]

---

32   Ibid., 86.
33   Ibid., 86. Quoting from *Christ in the Universe*, verse 6, by Alice Christiana Gertrude Thompson Meynell (1847–1922), writer, editor, critic, and poet. Published in *The Oxford Book of English Mystical Verse*, 1917 edition, 463–4. Meynell's poem can be read online: http://www.poetry-archive.com/m/christ_in_the_universe.html

Meynell's poem, published in 1917, and readily available for Lewis to peruse, faces head on a problem for Lewis: as an apostate atheist he abhorred the parochialism of the Christian story as if the universe rotated around the needs of humanity, and a little planet, with all its idiosyncrasies and distinctiveness statistically unlikely to occur elsewhere in the universe. Meynell questions "With this ambiguous earth, *his* dealings have been told us," the virginal conception, the atonement, through "the young man crucified," but this is not knowledge to all the stars, the celestial heavens—or is it?

> Of his earth-visiting feet
> None knows the secret, cherished, perilous,
> The terrible, shame fast, frightened, whispered, sweet,
> Heart-shattering secret of his way with us.
>
> No planet knows that this
> Our wayside planet, carrying land and wave,
> Love and life multiplied, and pain and bliss,
> Bears, as chief treasure, one forsaken grave.[34]

For we know not what the Christ's dealings were/are with other worlds far flung beyond our reach and comprehension: "May *his* devices with the heavens be guessed, his pilgrimage to thread the Milky Way."[35] We must be prepared, wrote Meynell, to comprehend the inconceivable, myriad, forms of love that God has bestowed through the Christ "as the stars unroll."[36] After Lewis's conversation the basic principle of the multiplicity of action by the Christ across unimaginable worlds across the vastness of space puts the parochial objections into perspective. It is this plurality of distinction: similar religious economies across vastly different times and spaces that underpin *The Space Trilogy*, and the canvas of space and time that is the Narniad (especially in *The Magician's Nephew*, with the death of the world/planet of Charn, and the creation of Narnia). Lewis also refers to Meynell's perceptions in the chapter on the doctrine of universal redemption we examined above:

> For this reason I do not think it at all likely that there have been (as Alice Meynell suggested in an interesting poem) many incarnations to redeem many different kinds of creature. One's sense of style—of the divine idiom—rejects it. The suggestion of mass-production and of waiting queues comes from a level of thought which is here hopelessly inadequate.[37]

Therefore, as we noted above, if other sentient creations, other than the human, have fallen then in all probability they are redeemed, but in ways such redemption may be different to the incarnation but may equally have been as costly to God. The (our) incarnation may be unique.

---

34   Meynell, *Christ in the Universe*, verses 3 and 4, 463–4.
Online: http://www.poetry-archive.com/m/christ_in_the_universe.html.
35   Ibid., verse 5.
36   Ibid.
37   Lewis, *Miracles* (1st ed.), 150.

6 Analogical and Symbolic Narratives II: ... Hiddenness and Multiple Incarnations

Does humanity have a cosmic meaning that transcends the plant earth and the solar system? Lewis does comment that there is a pointer to the possibility of this in Paul's letter to the Romans where he writes of the creation waiting in eager anticipation, groaning for renewal, waiting to be liberated from the bondage of decay (Rom 8:19-23): "It may be that Redemption, starting with us, is to work from us and through us. . . . This would no doubt give man a pivotal position. But such a position need not imply any superiority in us or any favoritism in God."[38]

On a related question, if there are dangers involved in inter-stellar contact, the danger is of humanity having contact with alien species. Human history demonstrates how humanity will overcome, overwhelm and dominate a weaker more innocent society and culture once it makes contact with it.[39] Lewis comments how we know what humanity does to strangers, how humanity destroys and enslaves all it can: "Civilized man murders, enslaves, cheats, and corrupts savage man. Even inanimate nature he turns into dust bowls and slag-heaps. There are individuals who don't. But they are not the sort who are likely to be our pioneers in space."[40] It will be the greedy and arrogant, the powerful and dominant, who discover alien species, and their history bodes not well: the weaker will be corrupted and perish, and Lewis notes how the stronger will righteously destroy these arrogant space travelers. Humanity, if it is possible to cross the vast distances of space, will take its *fallenness* with it. "It is interesting to wonder how things would go if they met an unfallen race. At first, to be sure, they'd have a grand time jeering at, duping, and exploiting its innocence; but I doubt if our half-animal cunning would long be a match for godlike wisdom, selfless valor, and perfect unanimity. I therefore fear the practical, not the theoretical, problems which will arise if ever we meet rational creatures which are not human."[41]

The question therefore arises of quarantine: is humanity sealed off from other sentient species? This raises again the question of boundaries: how far does the atonement reach? Does it affect other potentially fallen species? Or is humanity isolated in the way TB patients were shut away in isolation hospitals to prevent the disease infecting the healthy? Lewis notes how the vast unimaginable inter-stellar distances may be a God-given quarantine, isolating humanity from other created species:

> I have wondered before now whether the vast astronomical distances may not be God's quarantine precautions. They prevent the spiritual infection of a fallen species from spreading. And of course we are also very far from the supposed theological problem which contact with other rational species might raise. Such species may not exist. There is not at present a shred of empirical evidence that they do. There is nothing but what the logicians would call arguments from *"apriori* probability"—arguments that begin "It is only natural to suppose," or "All analogy suggests," or "Is it not the height of arrogance to rule out?" They

---

38 Lewis, "Religion and Rocketry," 88–89.
39 Ibid., 89.
40 Ibid. See also, Lewis, "The Seeing Eye," 173, for similar comments.
41 Ibid., 89–90. Also, "The Seeing Eye," 174–75.

> make very good reading. But who except a born gambler ever risks five dollars on such grounds in ordinary life? [42]

So we have the question of fallenness again: are these other species fallen? Perhaps the cosmic implications are that it is only humanity that has gone wrong (a proposition Lewis used successfully, as we have seen, in *Perelandra*), therefore although Christ's death and atonement is unique and cosmic/universal in its implications, it is only humanity that benefits: are we alone/isolated in the universe amongst millions, billions, of potential intelligent species and is it us alone/isolated who are contaminated by original sin?.

> And, as we have seen, the mere existence of these creatures would not raise a problem. After that, we still need to know that they are fallen; then, that they have not been, or will not be, redeemed in the mode we know; and then, that no other mode is possible. I think a Christian is sitting pretty if his faith never encounters more formidable difficulties than these conjectural phantoms.[43]

Lewis is here redeveloping, or restating, ideas he wrote initially in 1943, around the time of the publication of *Perelandra*, and gets to the heart of the question: that is the doctrine of the incarnation. Why should God be incarnated into a tiny obscure part of the creation going to such trouble to save an obscure and rebellious creature obsessed by a death-wish? Does the doctrine of the incarnation conflict with cosmology?—

> The doctrine of the Incarnation would conflict with what we know of this vast universe only if we knew also that there were other rational species in it who had, like us, fallen, and who needed redemption in the same mode, and that they had not been vouchsafed it. But we know none of these things. It may be full of life that needs no redemption. It may be full of life that has been redeemed. It may be full of things quite other than life which satisfy the Divine Wisdom in fashions one cannot conceive. We are in no position to draw up maps of God's psychology, and prescribe limits to *his* interests. We would not do so even for a man whom we knew to be greater than ourselves. The doctrines that God is Love and that *he* delights in men, are positive doctrines, not limiting doctrines. *He* is not less than this. What more *he* may be, we do not know; we know only that *he* must be more than we can conceive. It is to be expected that his creation should be, in the main, unintelligible to us.[44]

Irenaeus postulated that Christ would have come even if we had not fallen; therefore perhaps Christ has visited, in incarnate form—or some other mode of existence—other intelligent life in the universe? Does this absolve the problem of multiple incarnations? Is the validity of an argument against multiple incarnations only operative if other intelligent life is *fallen*?

---

42   Ibid., 91.
43   Lewis, "Dogma and the Universe," 21. Originally published in *The Guardian* (the Anglo-Catholic newspaper) across two weeks, Mar. 19, 1943, 16, and, Mar. 26, 1943, 104 and 107. Quotations here are from the single edition revised paper, published posthumously in 1971.
44   Ibid..

6 Analogical and Symbolic Narratives II: . . . Hiddenness and Multiple Incarnations

> If I remember rightly, St. Augustine raised a question about the theological position of satyrs, monopods, and other semi-human creatures. He decided it could wait till we knew there were any. So can this. . . . What we believe always remains intellectually possible; it never becomes intellectually compulsive.[45]

The question of multiple incarnations does not come up if, as with the Narniad, this occurs in a reality utterly different and outside of our universe. Within our universe, then we need to consider what the limits are, where the boundaries are, for the *effect* of the atonement wrought by Christ for humanity. Looking at simple geography (that a planet orbiting a star millions of light years away from us) does not work, for it takes no account of the nature of the *fall* other species might or might not undergo, or even any similarity/links between humanity and another hypothetical species. And crucially, any contact with other *fallen* species: in Narnia it is humanity that infects this new world with sin, though the Narnians are quite happy to follow humanity's lead.[46]

iii. Created Diversity

The question of the invalidity of multiple incarnations, within our universe, may simply be erroneous because of the utter diversity of created species. Elfland was a popular subject of myths. Elfs were neither good nor bad, neither innocent nor fallen. They were simply *different* from humanity, and as created by God. The ancient medieval ballad, *Thomas the Rhymer*, postulates the travels of its composer through an eternity of different creations and worlds, where species are intelligible but so different.[47] Time and space are different—years roll by, in the story, yet on Thomas's return only days have passed (a temporal paradox of the sort used by Lewis in the commerce/travel of humans between earth and Narnia). Elfland, if anything like it exists, is clearly outside of the range of human atonement, and is simply so different, diverse and dissimilar, and will be managed in a religious economy by God in ways *we cannot conceive of*:

> O see not ye yon narrow road,
> So thick beset wi' thorns and briers?
> That is the path of righteousness,
> Tho after it but few enquires.
>
> And see not ye that braid braid road,
> That lies across yon lillie leven?
> That is the path of wickedness,
> Tho some call it the road to heaven.

---

45   Lewis, "Religion and Rocketry," 91.
46   Lewis, *The Magician's Nephew*, 88; see, also, 99–100.
47   Thomas Learmonth (c. 1220–98), known as Thomas the Rhymer or True Thomas, a thirteenth-century Scottish laird is the protagonist and probable author of the ballad *Thomas the Rhymer* (Child no 37) and the writing down of the (Anglo-Saxon) legend of *Tam Lin* (Child no. 39). Both ballads entered the folk tradition, eventually being recorded by Francis James Child, along with scores of others, in the nineteenth century.

> And see not ye that bonny road,
> Which winds about the fernie brae?
> That is the road to fair Elfland,
> Whe[re] you and I this night maun gae.[48]

In postulating the existence of realities that are neither good nor evil, heaven nor hell, are we saying there are realities outside of the authority of God? No. It is the *fall* that forces everything in our reality into light or dark, good or evil, heaven or hell. The Queen of Elfland offers Thomas a precious gift: "It will give the tongue that can never lie."[49] But he declines, such is the power of original sin—how could he return to live among people without the ability to lie, or to veil or twist the truth! Ancient English literature, an oral and folk tradition, points to the reality of the *fall*. Lewis and Tolkien knew these works (particularly those rooted in Anglo-Saxon and Celtic cultures) and the postulation of a created reality beyond good and evil (in the context of the *fall*). In *Perelandra* Lewis cites a reality before, outside of, different, from the conditions of original sin. It just may be that such realities exist as God created them. And is our universe large enough for them to exist independent of our world, our reality and its *fallen* condition, and the atonement wrought though the incarnation? This is a theory that Lewis is pointing towards.

7. THE ARGUMENT EXTENDED

i. Rahner and Fisher and Fergusson on Multiple Incarnations

Karl Rahner has considered the probability of sentient alien life, extra-terrestrial intelligence, the possibility that cosmic evolution has developed intelligent life capable of perceiving God's revealedness. Rahner was aware of the difficult ethical and theological questions such a proposition raises. Rahner was therefore aware of the question of multiple incarnations and the difficulties surrounding a repetition of Christ's unique incarnation, but did not explore the issues in any depth.[50] Christopher L. Fisher and David Fergusson assess Rahner's position in the light of astronomical and scientific research in the later twentieth century after Rahner's death. They note that as the theoretical potential of extra-terrestrial intelligence has become a central topic of scientific investigation (and popular conjecture), this has generated questions of ethical and theological significance; Rahner was, they acknowledge, open to the potential inherent in the process of cosmic evolution for sentient life in other galaxies, he did not subscribe to theological parochialism. This does raise questions about multiple incarnations but he left the answer open: "with its Christological intensity, his theology seems to militate against any repetition of the incarnation."[51]

---

48   *Thomas the Rhymer*: 37A.Verses, 12–14.
Online: http://www.sacred-texts.com/neu/eng/child/ch037.htm.
49   *Thomas the Rhymer*: 37C.Verses, 17–18.
50   Rahner concentrates on the theological and philosophical ramifications of the possibility of extra-terrestrial intelligent life, only considering the basic question of multiple incarnations in passing.
51   Fisher and Fergusson, "Karl Rahner and the Extra-Terrestrial Intelligence Question," 275.

6 Analogical and Symbolic Narratives II: ... Hiddenness and Multiple Incarnations

ii. Bonting, Drees, and Mascall on Multiple Incarnations

Thomas Campanella, writing in 1661, quoted by William B. Drees,[52] argued that extra-terrestrial beings may not be in need of salvation: "they do not descend from Adam and thus are not tainted by his sin."[53] Simple and concise though this is, it is pertinent and to the point. Campanella's concern does indicate that the speculation as to the possible existence of extra-terrestrials really arrives post-Reformation, though much earlier Augustine had declared that speculation about salvation applied to satyrs, monopods, and other mythological creatures was irrelevant until the existence of such was proved.[54] The question of extra-terrestrial life and multiple incarnations is considered seriously post-Copernicus. (The principle of human-centered parochialism that placed the earth at the center of the solar system and the universe was seriously questioned following Copernicus, likewise the idea of extra-terrestrial life was considered and speculated on).[55] Sjoerd L. Bonting explores the question of extra-terrestrial life in other galaxies and the religious implications of this, but rejects a doctrine of original sin, regarding it as scientifically unprovable.[56] Despite the probability, according to scientific speculation, Bonting notes how scripture and church tradition remain silent on sentient and conscious extra-terrestrial life, with few theologians confronting the subject. For Bonting the key question is whether and how such alien creatures would develop a religious and moral life—would they be characterized ontologically by free will, and "would [they] be prone to sin and in need of salvation?" Bonting argues that though free from the taint of *original sin* (but still sinners) such alien creatures would have evolved in a similar way to humanity and would therefore be subject to the same ontological conditions as humanity: such creatures would have a similar way of thinking to humanity, they would have been given free will and therefore the opportunity of disobedience—"Thus there seems to be good reason to expect extra-terrestrials to be sinners just as much in need of salvation as we are."[57] But this is for Bonting generalized sinning and not a doctrine of original sin issuing from the *fall*. Bonting's approach to the possibility of multiple incarnations is to adopt a cosmic universalist position: "this would not require multiple incarnations, since Jesus is the cosmic Christ."[58] Such extra-terrestrials would receive their salvation at the point of the second coming: all creation (i.e., the universe) would be healed. Bonting assumes the universe is a single system, invoking William Temple's concept of the *sacramental universe* to show how a second or subsequent incarnation would be irrelevant (the universe itself therefore poses the boundary of atonement).[59] In this context Bonting

---

52   Drees, "Theologie over Buitenaardse Personen," 259–76.
53   Thomas Campanella, Italian philosopher and theologian, astrologer and poet; For Campanella's work, see: http://www.gutenberg.org/browse/authors/c#a1040.
54   Referred to by Lewis, "Religion and Rocketry," 91.
55   See Crowe, "A History of the Extra-Terrestrial Life Debate," 147–62.
56   Bonting, "Theological Implications of Possible Extra-terrestrial Life," 587–602
57   Ibid., 598.
58   Ibid.
59   Ibid., 599, referring to Temple, *Nature Man and God*, 473–95.

quotes E. L. Mascall's contribution to the debate,[60] he demonstrates how Mascall has discussed the question in a deeper theological manner by initially rejecting an extreme kenotic view whereby Christ's incarnation "scaled down" his divinity to the limits of humanity therefore a duplicate incarnation would not be possible.[61] To Mascall, a second incarnation is irrelevant because Christ had already been taken up in glory, drawing humanity with him, and the rest of creation. Bonting and Mascall note "the orthodox view [is] that the incarnation is not the conversion of Godhead into human flesh but rather the taking up of humanhood into Godhead" (a point of confluence with Lewis who also asserted the divinization of the human as God descended to reascend[62]), so, Bonting asserts, there is no reason why another finite rational nature of inhabitants of another planet could not also be taken up in this way. Bonting concludes that,

> On the basis of my earlier argumentation that extra-terrestrials, if they exist, will strongly resemble us in body and mind, I suggest that they also will participate in the reconciliation brought about by Christ's incarnation, death, and resurrection two thousand years ago in Palestine, without necessarily requiring a repetition of these events on their planet. And as God has made the message of Christ's saving work heard in all times and in all corners of our planet, so he will also bring it in an appropriate way to any of his creatures on another planet: God's communicative Spirit fills the entire world. They will then also be offered the opportunity to participate in the New Creation that we expect to be part of.[63]

iii. Hebblethwaite on Multiple Incarnations

The Anglican philosopher of religion Brian Hebblethwaite has examined the idea of multiple incarnations, citing the Thomist belief that although multiple incarnations are theoretically possible, there has never been more than one incarnation of the Word of God to rational humanity.[64] What is more he challenges the assumption of theoretical possibility: "I argue that multiple incarnations, in the sense of incarnation outlined by Ward, are logically impossible."[65] Hebblethwaite is referring to Keith Ward who argued that God could take many finite forms if God so willed, further there is nothing to preclude an infinite God from assuming any number of finite forms.[66] So what is Hebblethwaite's position? Hebblethwaite argues against the Thomist position: "God could indeed—and does—reveal himself and act in many ways throughout the history

---

60 Mascall, *Christian Theology and Natural Science*, 40–45.
61 Ibid.
62 Lewis's descent-reascend proposition for Christ's saving of humanity, drawn very much from the writings of Athanasius, along with other patristic theologians, is dealt with in the second book in this series. See: *C. S. Lewis—The Work of Christ Revealed*, Pt. 3, Ch. 11, §6.ii. "The Death-Descent/Rebirth-Reascent Paradigm," 260f.
63 Bonting, "Theological Implications of Possible Extra-terrestrial Life," 599–600.
64 See Hebblethwaite, "Impossibility of Multiple Incarnations," 323–34. See also, Kevern, "Limping Principles," 342–47. In a related field of see: Fisher and Fergusson, "Karl Rahner and the Extra-Terrestrial Intelligence Question," 275–90.
65 Ibid., 323.
66 Ibid., 323, quoting from Ward, *God, Faith and the New Millennium*, 162–64.

of religions; he could not become more than one of us in the full sense of incarnation. For, if God the Son is one divine subject, only one human subject can actually be the incarnate, human, form of that one divine life. Otherwise, one would be attributing a split personality to the divine Son."[67] From a human perspective Hebblethwaite analyses in detail why this is so—for the human. God the Son incarnate is not in sympathy with the human but incarnate, at one with, one of, and suffers: God subjects himself to the suffering and death as the Son. Therefore, there would be "unacceptable eschatological implications of the idea of multiple implications."[68] (Lewis noted in a similar vein, "The suggestion of mass-production and of waiting queues comes from a level of thought which is here hopelessly inadequate."[69]) Resurrection is intimately intertwined with incarnation: one cannot be seen without the other. Hebblethwaite notes how many who object to the idea of the incarnation argue that God has done insufficient for the human race, they are expecting multiple—human—incarnations. As such, this moral objection is met by claiming that multiple incarnations are a logical impossibility.[70] (This leads some to claim universalism.) The question then moves to extra-terrestrial life. Again Hebblethwaite rejects the possibility: "there could only be one incarnation of the divine Son in a finite *personal* form, it would make more sense to suppose that humanity is the sole instantiation of finite *personal* life in the universe."[71] However, is there a sufficient distinction between manifestation and incarnation? Also, all questions have to be based on, or issue from, a high Christology (Jesus is not ontologically distinct in existence from God,[72] he is God in human form). A low Christology (Jesus is regarded by us *as if* he were "god") will allow for any number of apparent incarnations, or even just a divine possession of a human form. Hebblethwaite notes Aquinas's argument that since the power of the divine is infinite, we should not state that God assumes a human nature in such a way as to be powerless to take up another: the divine nature has precedence.[73] Hebblethwaite digresses into a brief examination of patristic heresies and how this affects his argument—precisely what is the human nature thus assumed by God and thus states, "Sadly, it is this generic, adjectival, talk of human nature being assumed that permits Thomas to envisage the possibility of multiple incarnations. Even he does not take seriously enough the fact that a series of divine incarnations would have to be the same person, human as well as divine. And there lies incoherence—an incoherence brought out only too clearly by the eschatological implications of the simultaneous existence of a number of risen

---

67 Ibid., 323–34.
68 Ibid 324.
69 Lewis, *Miracles* (1st ed.), 150. See also, on the question of multiple human incarnations, Lewis, *Beyond Personality*, VI "Two Notes," 32–33: "But when you are talking about God—i.e., about the rock bottom, irreducible fact on which all other facts depend—it is nonsensical to ask if it could have been otherwise. It is what it is, and there's an end of the matter. But quite apart from this, I find a difficulty about the very idea of the Father begetting many sons from all eternity. In order to be many they would have to be somehow different from one another."
70 Hebblethwaite, "Impossibility of multiple incarnations," 324–26.
71 Ibid., 325.
72 Ibid., quoting Ward, *God, Faith and the New Millennium*.
73 Ibid., 326; quoting, Aquinas, *Summa Theologiae* IIIa, Q. 3. 7.

ON THE CHRIST OF A RELIGIOUS ECONOMY. I. CREATION AND SUB-CREATION

humans each alleged to be the incarnate Son of God."[74] But then Hebblethwaite will assert that we have "no business to be imposing arbitrary limitations on infinite divine power..."[75]

So far Hebblethwaite is quite correct: the incarnation of the second person of the Trinity—the assumption of specifically *human* form—could only happen once; more than once would lead to confusion. Also, "For as in Adam all die, so in Christ all will be made alive" (1 Cor 15:22). Furthermore, the *purpose* of the incarnation-cross-resurrection is to cure humanity of original sin. This is a once-and-for-all act because once the incarnation-cross-resurrection has happened as a single event the way is open to the righteous who through faith are saved (though again this raises questions about the boundaries of atonement). Humanity is cured *in potential* through this single act and this is the reason for the incarnation. (Hebblethwaite as a philosopher of religion perhaps underestimates the theological issues—redemption, salvation, atonement, *et al.*).

But leaving the question aside of a second or further incarnation of the Christ as a human here on earth as not just a logical impossibility but simply unnecessary, there is then the question of other worlds, a question Lewis excelled in! By "other worlds" we need to distinguish between other planets and sentient intelligent creatures *within our universe* and the possibility of such creatures *totally outside of what we take to be the universe*, as Lewis postulated. Scripture and revelation assert that we will be judged by Christ Jesus, resurrected and ascended, in the Last Judgment, after the end of all things (from our perspective). We will have no knowledge of how other sentient species from within or without of what we take to be reality, the universe, have behaved, whether they are in a state of grace or corruption, and if they are in need of salvation and therefore what God has done to prepare them for judgment, as God has prepared us for judgment through the incarnation-cross-resurrection.

Hebblethwaite does helpfully distinguish between Hindu avatars and an actual incarnation: avatars relate to spiritual occupation and possession, such gods "do not suffer the limitations of having a real human nature."[76] Successive incarnations in the human would have the potential of being reincarnations.[77] Hebblethwaite verges into the anthropomorphic—projecting human concerns onto totally alien species (hypothetically in our universe or without)—by arguing that if multiple incarnations in the human nature are not intelligible and are a logical impossibility then they are also unintelligible and a logical impossibility in other rational natures.

Christian soteriology, writes Hebblethwaite, has always raised difficulties for the hypothetical existence of other rational creatures, and has asserted the uniqueness of incarnation and atonement,

---

74 Ibid. Hebblethwaite may not like the idea of human nature being "assumed" but it is scriptural (Phil 2:7).
75 Ibid.
76 Ibid., 329; quoting Ward, *God, Faith and the New Millennium*, 164.
77 Ibid.

6 Analogical and Symbolic Narratives II: . . . Hiddenness and Multiple Incarnations

> In itself the notion of extra-terrestrial intelligent life is perfectly coherent. . . . But it may be the case that, while the stuff of the universe certainly has it in it to evolve intelligent life, it is highly unlikely actually to do so without some providential direction. The many extraordinary coincidences, from those factors in the early stages of cosmic evolution that have given rise to talk of an anthropic principle, through the many factors that have to coincide for there to be a stable, life-supporting environment, to the many factors that have to coincide if the higher organisms are to appear, may only be accountable for in terms of divine providence, and may well have only have been realized once, if there are valid theological reasons for this.[78]

So we may be alone in the universe. Just so—but this ignores the question projected by Lewis of intelligent sentient life/creatures *beyond our reality*. Again we are talking about the as yet unanswerable question relating to the boundaries of atonement within our universe but also without. What we take to be the incarnation of the second person of the Trinity is almost certainly unique *in relation to humanity and original sin*.[79]

iv. Crisp on Multiple Incarnations

From the perspective of systematic philosophical theology Oliver Crisp does establish the parameters of the incarnation, and examines the question of multiple incarnations.[80] Crisp starts from an orthodox perspective. He outlines how the incarnation is *the* event whereby the second person of the Trinity *assumes* a human nature *in addition* to his divine nature. This is an important event for human redemption; but, is it unique?

> Can one divine person assume two (or more) human natures? . . . I argue that multiple incarnations are metaphysically possible, contrary to the objections raised in the recent literature by the Anglican theologian Brian Hebblethwaite. However, although such a divine act is metaphysically possible—there is no metaphysical obstacle to God becoming incarnate on more than one occasion—there is good reason to think that the incarnation is in fact a unique event in the divine life. . . . God could have become incarnate more than once, but *he* has not done so.[81]

To explicate, Crisp comments on the metaphysics of the incarnation, discusses the root of Hebblethwaite's objection, and in so doing analyses what it is that constitutes the human—will and/or personhood—and how this effects what institutes, ontologically, the incarnation. This leads into an account of the human in the work of Anselm and Descartes, therefore Crisp considers the possibility, but not *actuality*, of multiple incarnations. If we work from the premise that the incarnation is "a consequentially necessary account . . . that the primary motivation for the incarnation is the

---

78   Ibid., 331; see also Barrow and Tipler, *The Anthropic Cosmological Principle*.
79   Ibid., 332. Hebblethwaite does digress at this point to explore the potential philosophical proposition that theoretically the Father or the Holy Spirit might be subject to incarnation.
80   Crisp, "Multiple Incarnations," 155–75.
81   Ibid., 155; referring to Hebblethwaite, "Impossibility of Multiple Incarnations."

reconciliation of some number of humanity,"[82] if we had not *fallen* the incarnation would not have been necessary, then the incarnation is a one-time and unrepeatable event (Crisp notes that this is the dominant theme/account in many Catholic and Protestant theologies): the sacrifice offered by the Christ is *sufficient* for the purpose of reconciliation. Such a motive renders multiple incarnations superfluous.

However, this still leaves open the question of incarnation, or what we take to be incarnation, in and for other sentient beings elsewhere within what we take to be the universe. Crisp acknowledges that despite human speculation the chances of "the emergence of corporeal intelligent life elsewhere in the cosmos is slim,"[83] but it has not stopped theologians speculating that if such alien life exists and they need salvation God would have provided for them. If this is so, then there are, for Crisp, four possible propositions:

- **First**: God does not save such beings and the work of Christ does not apply to them.
- **Second**: no additional incarnation is required, the scope of Christ's salvation extends to them.
- **Third**: the work of Christ might apply to them (it is cosmic in its scope) but God has not deigned to save any of these creatures.
- **Fourth**: the work of Christ does not apply to them, but God has stooped to provide some means of salvation for these creatures.[84]

The fourth option allows for the possibility of multiple incarnations. Though this is purely speculative Crisp does acknowledge that it would seem strange for God not to provide some means of salvation for such a "benighted race of extra-terrestrials. . . . For the Christian God is gracious and merciful, a matter attested to by Scripture."[85] We can of course add to this list Lewis's speculation in *Perelandra*, that there may well be alien species that simply did not *fall* and thus were in no need of redemption: humanity failed the test (original sin); the Green Lady (Eve) on Perelandra did not fail, did not rebel and cross the boundary, all that was withheld was then granted to her and her progeny.

Crisp does conclude that "Thus, on balance, I think that although Hebblethwaite is mistaken in thinking there is a logical or even metaphysical impediment to the possibility of multiple incarnations, there are good biblical and theological reasons for thinking that in actuality there is only one incarnation of the Son of God."[86]

---

82   Ibid., 156.
83   Ibid., 174.
84   Ibid.
85   Ibid., 174–75.
86   Ibid., 175.

6 Analogical and Symbolic Narratives II: . . . Hiddenness and Multiple Incarnations

v. Ward on Multiple Incarnations

Keith Ward, who was quoted above by Hebblethwaite, briefly considers the possibility of multiple incarnations: "God could in theory take many minds and bodies to be finite forms of the divine nature. There is nothing to prevent the infinite God from taking any number of finite forms. But two main factors are necessary if a human person is to be a finite form of God. That person must be wholly obedient to God, and there must be an historical and cultural context which makes the expression of the divine nature in that person intelligible. The number of people who are wholly obedient to God must be very small indeed."[87] The possibility of a human nature, a person, being, in effect, good enough, holy enough, perfect enough, for subsequent incarnation is to be extremely rare. Ward notes the profound difficulties and unpredictability of this. "A human life that shows perfect knowledge and love of God, and which is selflessly devoted to the service of God, is so rare that its appearance is almost, if not quite, a miracle. It becomes truly a miracle if that human soul is such that it could not fall away from God, but is indissolubly united to the divine will."[88] Ward then recounts the orthodox, patristic, view that in Jesus God so united a human personality to the divine enabling Jesus to have an overwhelming sense of the presence of *his* Father in heaven. Jesus's unreserved openness to God's love is unique and unpredictable, and, yes, unrepeatable: "We can then say that his human existence was not distinct from the reality of God. In him, human and divine found a profound unity."[89] Jesus, as Ward notes, is a unique human being. Also, the historical and cultural context is important: i.e. salvation history, the cure for original sin. Once enacted this does not need to be repeated. Therefore, the necessity for further incarnations is not present.

8. THE ARGUMENT RESOLVED?

Crisp notes how Christopher L. Fisher and David Fergusson[90] begin to point towards the possibility of forms of salvation for extra-terrestrial aliens, sentient creatures who can know God, in ways that we cannot begin to *imagine*; Crisp then draws close to Lewis's position by offering that multiple incarnations might not compromise the salvific work of Christ, *if* God's saving action towards humanity is *restricted* to humanity.[91] But this falls far short of the imaginative theologoumena Lewis is postulating in the limitless creativity of the triune God. Lewis noted, "other species will have witnessed wholly *different* acts, each equally *unique*, equally *necessary* and differently necessary to the whole process"[92] of salvation. Lewis echoes the thought of Meynell where we cannot begin to imagine the ends and means God has gone to, the costly and severe sacrifice God has gone to, to redeem alien creatures. Reason will

---

87   Ward, *God, Faith and the New Millennium*, 162.
88   Ibid., 162–63.
89   Ibid., 163.
90   Fisher and Fergusson, "Karl Rahner and the Extra-Terrestrial Intelligence Question," 275–90.
91   Crisp, "Multiple Incarnations," 174.
92   Lewis, *Miracles* (1st ed.), 150. My emphasis.

take us thus far; after which pneumatologically inspired imagination will take over: reason and logic will be superseded by analogical narrative, God will give those with a baptized imagination parables to hint at, to point to, the possibility not of multiple incarnations but a *multiplicity of redemptions*. Such salvation may not be defined by incarnation (the mode) but always by the cost—the sufferance of salvation—and will issue from the triune God.

7

Analogical and Symbolic Narratives III: Christology and Christlikeness— Trinitarian Considerations

SYNOPSIS:
If the Christian perception is correct, that God is a Trinity, that this is an axiomatic truth about God, if Lewis's analogical narratives are orthodox, then they should not only reflect a triune understanding of God, but, the readers should recognize that God is love, and perceive that such love dictates that God is triune: within the *immanent* Trinity the three persons each ever focus on the other. What understanding of the Trinity and of the God that is love does Lewis present in his analogical and symbolic narratives—specifically, but not exclusively, in *The Chronicles of Narnia*? What is the manifestation and the relationship between the Father, the Son, and the Holy Spirit in Lewis's narratives? Is the God Lewis portrays in the Narniad Trinitarian? In *The Space Trilogy* there is a doctrine of the Trinity held by alien species, there is evidence for the Trinity in the beliefs of the *hnau* (*Out of the Silent Planet*), and we also see the Holy Spirit working through alien creatures.

Is there a triune salvation history in the Narniad? The religious and salvation history of Narnia should resemble that of our world, to a degree. To this end there should be the framework of a systematic theology in the Narniad: creation, freedom, sin, fall, rebellion, redemption, *eschaton*, and completion. If God is universally triune then over all of the world of Narnia there should be the evidence of a religious economy reflecting the action of the triune God, even though, according to Lewis's stated aim, this may be an implicit religious economy. Scholars have identified Christian concepts from creation, through sacrifice and redemption to the end times and judgment, in *The Chronicles of Narnia*. Lewis's construct is orthodox, therefore it is implicitly Trinitarian. We need, therefore, to examine, initially, Lewis's doctrine of the Trinity, then to identify a Narnian Trinity, and the three-fold actions of God in the "supposal" world that is Narnia. Why is there no nativity for Aslan, but theophanic appearances instead? How "real" is Aslan within the confines of the supposal? Is Aslan Docetic? Or is *he* reminiscent of an avatar, possessing, or occupying, safely from heaven? These are pertinent questions if we are to consider the Narniad orthodox.

What does the Narniad tells us about the Holy Spirit's mysterious actions within a religious economy—veiled, hidden, but very active? Lewis paints a picture of a world where what is intelligible and imaginative in our reality is real in Narnia. A triune statement of self-revelation: Lewis pulls all the disparate Trinitarian references in the Narniad together in two examples that we can examine from *The Voyage of the Dawn Treader* and *The Horse and his Boy*. There is forgiving judgement in this presence—there is a unity yet diversity of person in God. In conclusion, what can we observe of a Narnian doctrine of God, defined by creativity and love, by joy and forgiving judgement?

ON THE CHRIST OF A RELIGIOUS ECONOMY. I. CREATION AND SUB-CREATION

1. A DOCTRINE OF GOD

i. God is Triune

Most people if pressed would acknowledge belief in God, or some sort of "god," subscribing to a vaguely defined monotheism. The truth about God revealed is that God is Trinitarian: the Father is God, the Son is God, and the Holy Spirit is God—but there is only one God. This is the teaching of the church; it is the core of Christian doctrine. Three-in-one requires distinctness yet simultaneity. Humanity could not have invented such a concept as the Trinity for itself. The innate religious impulse in humanity is to conceive of a "god" as a single unity, a pure oneness, unknowable, distinct from creation. The idea that such a "god" could be three "persons" in "one God," become incarnate, be simultaneously born into creation while remaining God distinct and outside of creation, is often beyond comprehension. Immediately, theological talk about the Trinity raises questions about incarnation, redemption, the invisible power and influence of the Holy Spirit, and so forth. The realization that God was "Three-in-One" dawned slowly in the early church. There was evidence in the Old Testament, there was evidence in the sayings of Jesus, and the emerging documents we now call the Gospels and the New Testament. This realization, or understanding, became the bedrock of Christian doctrine and was summarized in the earliest of the creeds— the Apostles' Creed. The Trinity is one God in three persons, not three separate gods, and not one God expressed in three different ways or modes. Therefore, the perennial danger with theological talk is two-fold: Modalism (God appears, is active towards humanity, in three different, often *subsequent*, modes: God is Father, then God becomes the Son, then God becomes the Holy Spirit, but not simultaneously-yet-distinctly One); and/or Polytheism (too much individuality creates three separate "gods").

ii. Immanence and Economic Action

Lewis's writings generally, his Christology specifically is orthodox and Trinitarian. Central to Lewis's Christology and his perception of the workings of God is an understanding of the *economic* Trinity, as distinct from the *immanent* Trinity. The economic Trinity is our understanding of the presence and action of God in our reality, the world of human affairs.[1] By contrast, the immanent Trinity is God's "life," "existence," within God's triune self, the three persons of the holy and indivisible Trinity that subsist and persist in love.[2] The opening of John's Gospel is about the Trinity: it sets out the immanent—"In the beginning was the Word, and the Word was with God, and the Word was God. He was in the beginning with God" (John 1:1–2). This then proceeds into the economic—"And the Word became flesh and dwelt among

---

1   *Economic*: management of resources, interaction—supervision, administration, and controlling—of persons within a social context; origin: fifteenth century, from French *économie*, via Latin from Greek οἰκονομία, *oikonomia*—"household management," often, "the rule or law of the house."

2   *Immanent*: existing or operating within God, from sixteenth century Latin *immanent-*, *immanere*, "remain within."

us, and we have seen his glory, the glory as of the only Son of the Father, full of grace and truth." (John 1:14). Also, "For God so loved the world that he gave his one and only Son, that whoever believes in him shall not perish but have eternal life" (John 3:16). Trinitarian immanence is also witnessed to by the apostle Paul: "For the Spirit searches everything, even the depths of God" (1 Cor 2:10b). The Christ event is about the economic Trinity, how God interacts with the world, to redeem humanity and raise us up in our fallenness. A classic example is in the baptism of Jesus: the Father declares: "This is my beloved Son with whom I am well pleased," as the Holy Spirit descends upon Jesus (Matt 3:13–17; Mark 1:9–11; Luke 3:21–23). Many modern theologians will argue that the distinction between immanence and economic is invalid: one is the other. Lewis's Platonism argues for a distinction. For Lewis this distinction is at its greatest in *kenosis* (Phil 2:1–11): God descends to reascend with humanity, where triunity defines the reality of God.[3]

iii. God is Love

But God is love: if God is three-in-one what does this tell us about God being love, and where is the God of love in Lewis's analogical narratives or is the God of Narnia an adventurous demi-"god," a child-like divine for the readers to grow out of?

Deus caritas est—ὁ θεὸς ἀγάπη ἐστίν—*God is Love*

Paradoxically, love is defined in the New Testament in the negative: to love truly may cost you your life! This is a scriptural principle, the astonishing negativity and nihilism of the crucifixion, with the resultant atonement and life for humanity is of course an obvious example. But: *Deus caritas est*, ὁ θεὸς ἀγάπη ἐστίν: "God is Love." The New Testament informs us that God is ἀγάπη (*agapē*, altruistic love, as distinct from friendship, sexual attraction and family love). The apostle Paul's understanding of the self-giving and sacrificial ἀγάπη of the Trinitarian God, is of a form of love oblivious to self, ever focusing on the other, such love denies self and is prepared to self-sacrifice for others. We can never initiate such ἀγάπη; we can only respond in faith thereby enabling the ἀγάπη that is the triune persons of God in the immanent Trinity, the eternally loving subject, to work through us by faith. God as love also represents the Christian life. Paul's hymn to ἀγάπη—1 Corinthians 13—is phrased in the negative (love is not, it does not, if I have not love I am nothing) rather than the positive to emphasize the difference between our human expectations of love and the ἀγάπη that is God.

The Eschatological Direction of the Love of God

Traditionally Christians and theologians, ministers and priests, have represented the fulfillment of the commandment to love God and to love our neighbor by placing the human as the subject at the center of the action of loving. The human then directs love

---

3 See, Lewis, *Beyond Personality*, Ch. I, 11–13; Ch. IV, 27–28; Ch. V, 28f.; Ch. XI, 59. These ideas were further expanded in *Mere Christianity*, Bk. 4, Chs. 1, 4, 5 and 11, also, *Miracles* (2nd ed.).

to God and simultaneously love to his/her neighbor. This traditional understanding is that we direct our love, human love that belongs to us, that is generated by us, to God and to our neighbor (or whoever we choose to be our neighbor): this is the human-centered direction of the love of God. This is essentially egocentric. The true nature of this love is eschatological. The eschatological direction is Trinitarian: it is not from us but from God. Why eschatological? Because humanity is so corrupt we can achieve no pure or real love for ourselves, we are pulled down by our biological and genetic make-up all the time (because of the *fall* we are now subject to the vagaries and vicissitudes of this reality, including being ruled by the genetic imperative unless we allow God's ἀγάπη to give us the grace to exercise restraint). Only the love of God acting on us, flowing through us, can achieve anything resembling true ἀγάπη. This is eschatological because it comes from Christ's final judgment, the final reckoning where we will all be measured against Christ (Matt 25), though because of Christ's resurrection it can flow to us now through the actions of the Holy Spirit: this ἀγάπη that is God in Christ flows to us, it judges, and in judging begins to re-orient us and to sanctify us as we focus on this triune God in prayer and action. Therefore, the Trinitarian ἀγάπη that is God flows to us and through us to our neighbor, and from our neighbor to us, and is reflected back to God in a loving response. This is the work of the Holy Spirit, which in so doing begins to conform us to the image of Christ Jesus in the beauty and majesty of the Father. God is the eternal subject, the human and his/her neighbor must always be the object. We are the object of God's ἀγάπη, whether it flows directly to us and to our neighbor or to us from our neighbor. The individual through the indwelling Trinitarian Spirit of Christ merely allows the Father to love through the Spirit in the form of the eternal Son, Christ Jesus. Through conversion, being born again in the Spirit, through the *faith* (πίστις) that indwells in us we will to a greater of lesser degree—repentance and sanctification are essential—conform to Christ as the model of humanity, and thereby ἀγάπη will flow through us from the Trinitarian dialogue of persons that is God, that is ἀγάπη.

Ever-Focusing on the Other

This is dependent upon and reflects the mutual indwelling of the persons within the triune God; this ontology of love is the communion of being within the godhead, it is perichoretic.[4] All three persons of the triune God mutually inhere in one another, draw "life" from one another; ontologically they are what they are by relation to one another, and that relation is of love-ἀγάπη. This love-ἀγάπη is personhood and is intimate, pure, and unadulterated with no loss of identity or confusion. Therefore ἀγάπη is God and this God is the coinherence of the triune persons in the divine essence and in each other; that these three persons are ἀγάπη implies ontologically that within

---

4   Περιχώρησις, from patristic Greek (περί: around and χώρησις: going, proceeding, a progression), the triune God is to be seen as a mutually interdependent, interpenetration, of three persons each preserving its identity. For example, John Damascene (c.645–749), also, earlier, Gregory of Nazianzus (329–389/90), used περιχώρησις to indicate the mutual and dynamic reciprocity of the divine persons that affirms mutuality and individuality.

7. Analogical and Symbolic Narratives III: . . . Trinitarian Considerations

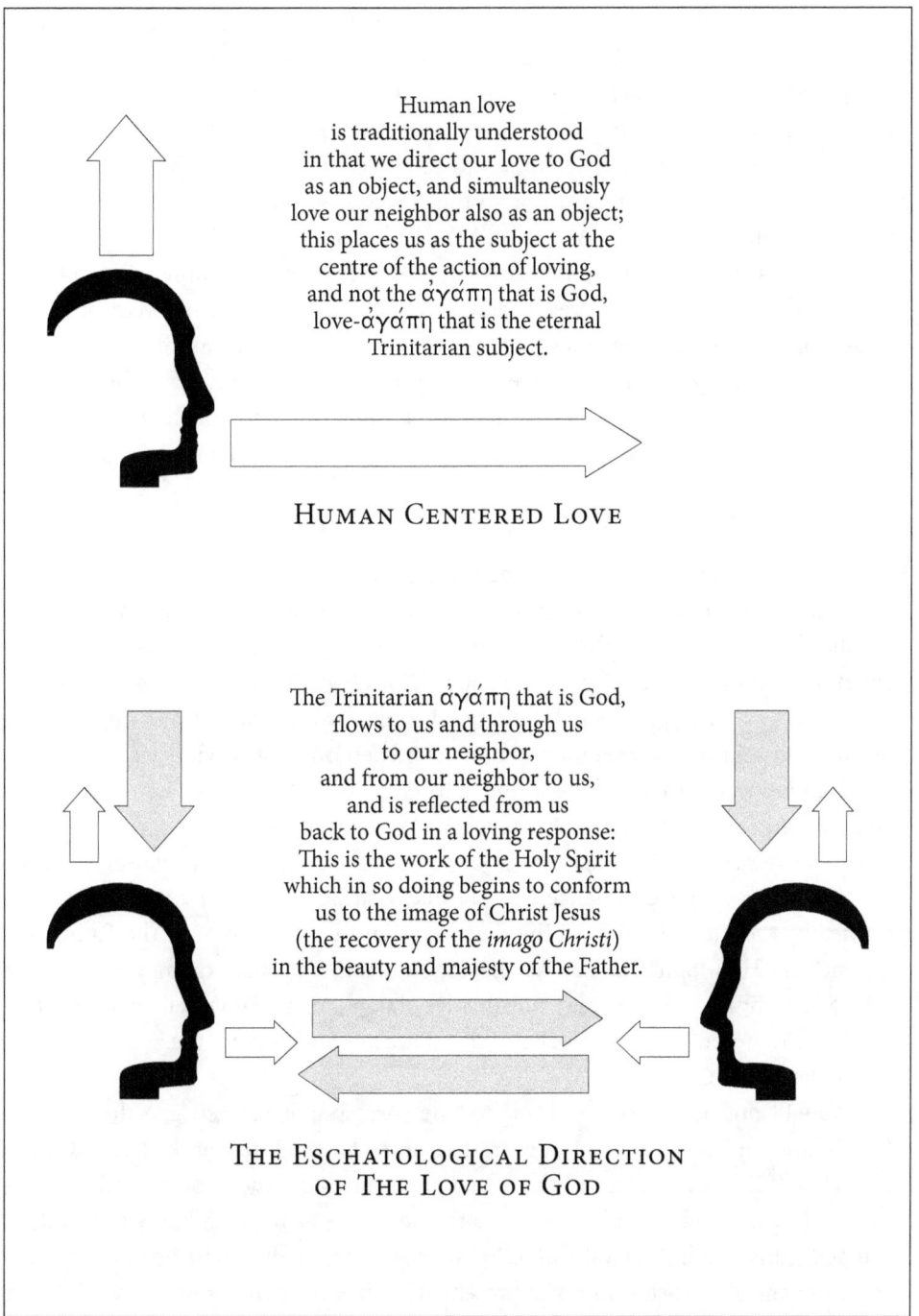

Figure 4 Ἀγάπη: the Love of God

the *immanent* Trinity the three persons each ever focus on the other and never on itself. Therefore, God cannot be a monist entity, a singularity, for then would not God be dependent upon another onto which to focus in love/ἀγάπη? This ever-focusing on the other within the *immanent* Trinity is an essence of love/ἀγάπη that indwells us, flows through us. This is a dynamic and active relationship with the believer in the Holy Spirit drawing him or her through the Son to the Father: "this *Spirit* of Love is, from all eternity, a love going on between the Father and the Son."[5]

If Lewis's analogical narratives are orthodox they should not only reflect a triune understanding of God, but, even though *The Chronicles of Narnia* were primarily written for children, the readers should recognize something of this love that is God, and, perhaps, perceive that such love dictates that God is triune. Also, the center of the economic Trinity in, say, Narnia, should be this love-action of the Holy Spirit in converting people and re-orientating such creatures—human or alien—to God's love.

2. A CHRISTIAN ANALOGY?

In Lewis's analogical narratives what do the creatures make of the God of love who is triune? In terms of Lewis's analogical narratives, Screwtape is acutely aware of God, but shields his mind from the truth about God's very nature as three-in-one.[6] The condemned, in their own self-generated hell in *The Great Divorce*, knew of God's triune nature, but by-and-large rejected it along with their salvation, and find approaching the truth too painful to contemplate. Human and demonic (in varying degrees, as they hide from God) ignorance of the triune nature of God characterizes Lewis's portraits of hell. Where is God in *The Space Trilogy*? And what of Narnia? Given its over-arching place in Lewis's *corpus* the crucial question to consider is, are *The Chronicles of Narnia* Trinitarian? Do we have evidence from Lewis's writing of the *immanent* Trinity, and pertinently, the manifestation of the *economic* Trinity—the action of the Father, the Son and the Holy Spirit in Lewis's theologoumena? This may or may not involve an incarnation; this may or may not involve theophanies.[7] However, there must be something represented in the stories of the character and person, the actions and the love, of the triune God.

We will not necessarily find one-to-one correspondence between the doctrine of the Trinity in Lewis's analogical narratives and what we know of the triune God in our reality. If Lewis is correct, aliens, reasoning species in other worlds, will not have exactly the same understanding of God's triune nature as us: such knowledge will be local and transposed. But God *will be* Trinitarian. There will also be no allegory—the characters and the stories do not represent what has happened in our world. We've established Lewis's stated ground of "supposition" as being at the heart of his method of analogical narrative. The understanding of the *immanent* Trinity in Narnia should be the same as in our reality (the common source in the God-head); but the *economic*

---

5   Lewis, *Mere Christianity*, 176.
6   Lewis, *Screwtape Letters*, 81–82.
7   Theophany—a visible manifestation to humankind of God or a god (OED).

7. Analogical and Symbolic Narratives III: ... Trinitarian Considerations

activity should be different—leastwise, not identical to the action of the *economic* Trinity and salvation history in our reality. This examination will form the next three chapters:

- Chapter 7. Trinitarian Considerations in Lewis's Analogical Narratives, specifically in the Narniad
- Chapter 8. Encounters: The Work of the Aslan-Christ in Narnia
- Chapter 9. Salvation and Atonement in Narnia

Lewis's "Supposal," is a mythopoeic sub-creation, and as such it issues from a baptized imagination. What do these analogical-symbolic narratives tell us by *analogy* about the *economic* Trinity, a religious economy, and therefore Christology and salvation in our reality (does this supposal generate a "religious" understanding in its target audience—children?). This was Lewis's stated primary aim, but, following on from what we have established about God's salvific actions towards other, hypothetical, sentient species throughout the universe or beyond the universe, what does the Narniad intimate to us about the economic Trinity and salvation history in other realities?

3. THE TRINITY IN THE SPACE TRILOGY

In *Out of the Silent Planet*, the evidence for the Trinity is amongst the beliefs of the *hnau* (meaning "reasoning species", a sentient race, on the planet Malacandra who are very different to humans in form, but their reasoning sentience makes them comparable with humanity). In existential terms the Triune evidence is of the Holy Spirit working through various species, but also working amongst good humans where the effects of the cross of Christ gives them the freedom to be Christlike, preveniently supported by the Holy Spirit. Lewis's doctrine of God in *The Space Trilogy*, amongst such alien peoples, is complicated but Trinitarian. The *eldila* are super-human aliens, extra-terrestrials who have an intimate relationship with the *Oyarsa*—angelic beings—on the planet Malacandra (a relationship reminiscent of prelapsarian humanity?). Throughout *The Space Trilogy* is the same doctrine of God: above all these supernatural beings is Maleldil: God. But this is the triune God, though perception and naming is different to humanity's theology: it is meant to be the same divine reality. The "Old one" the initiator is God the Father; "Maleldil the Young" is the Christ, the second person of the Trinity; "the Third One"[8] is un-named but very present and very active (*eldila* are spirit beings that are difficult to perceive but their presence is felt even though they cannot be seen or heard, what is more they guide those open to holiness to truth, which makes them comparable in purpose, if not in form, with the Holy Spirit). Lewis elaborates through a conversation between Ransom, the human, and the alien creatures on Malacandra in *Out of the Silent Planet*:

> [Hnohra asked] "Did people in Thulcandra not know that Maleldil the Young had made and still ruled the world? Even a child knew that."

---

8   The Holy Spirit is so named as "The Third One" initially in *Perelandra*, 208, and is also thus cited in *That Hideous Strength*.

> "Where did Maleldil live," Ransom asked.
> "With the Old One."
> "And who was the Old One?" Ransom did not understand the answer. He tried again. "Where was the Old One?"
> "He is not that sort," said Hnohra, "that he has to live anywhere," and proceeded to a good deal which Ransom did not follow. But he followed enough to feel once more a certain irritation. Ever since he had discovered the rationality of the hrossa he had been haunted by a conscientious scruple as to whether it might not be his duty to undertake their religious instruction; now, as a result of his tentative efforts, he found himself being treated as if he were the savage and being given a first sketch of civilized religion—a sort of hrossian equivalent of the shorter catechism. It became plain that Maleldil was a spirit without body, parts or passions.[9]

In structure and ontology this is an orthodox doctrine of the Trinity, but by comparison, it is exotic, seemingly strange, and different: other alien species can recognize and know something of the triune nature through their God-given reasoning. And Lucifer, the "bent one," the corrupt one, is present. Analogically this is an orthodox doctrine of God and the Trinity translated into other worlds by Lewis with the intention of persuading skeptics of the veracity and relevance of the Trinity to humanity, and of challenging, as we saw in the last chapter, Christian parochialism.

4. A TRIUNE SALVATION HISTORY?

The religious and salvation history of Narnia should *resemble* that of our world, to a degree, partly because of the nature of sin but also because of the corrosive effect on the creature and on creation, any creation, of evil. Also, this is specifically so because Lewis placed human immigrants in Narnia—from its creation, and in considerable numbers. To this end there should be the framework of a systematic theology in the Narniad: creation, freedom, sin, fall, rebellion, divine sacrifice, resurrection, redemption, *eschaton*, new creation, and completion. If God is universally triune then over all of the world of Narnia there should be the evidence of a religious economy reflecting the action of *the* triune God.

The creation of Narnia is by the second person of the Trinity, *ex nihilo*. Evil is introduced by an external agency (humanity, and the White Witch). Protection is given (the tree of silver apples) but the creation goes its own way and evil gathers pace. There are religious attempts to correct and punish (the stone table), but matters slowly, progressively, worsen. Evil gains control (the White Witch's one hundred year winter). The interim solution (the four Pevensie children) given by God, generates a crisis of evil: Edmund's treachery is the final trigger which would have caused the utter destruction of Narnia—consumed in fire and water. Only the appearance, the theophany, of the second person of the Trinity—Aslan—can restore: he offers himself freely as sacrifice. Post-resurrection and with the defeat of the White Witch, and after

---

9   Lewis, *Out of the Silent Planet*, 83. See also, 91–93, 106, 129, 129, 152–53, 156–57, 168, 172, and, 177–79.

the four Pevensie children leave, there is an underlying spiritual battle: this conflict is characterized by an often invisible "religious" economy generated by the Holy Spirit, defined by gains and losses. The Spirit provides and enables individuals to maintain the consciousness of Aslan's sacrifice and cause, but matters never again reach the demonic crisis they had under the White Witch: there are still sinners, but the crisis of the utter destruction of Narnia through fire and water due to the accumulation of sin and treachery, is avoided—because of the unique sacrifice in Narnia of Aslan. God the Father (The Emperor-beyond-the-Sea) watches over and prepares a place for the righteous besides *his* Son (Aslan) in eternity, and initiates through the agency of the Holy Spirit (the Spirit of the Emperor-beyond-the-Sea, and of Aslan) the invisible "church" in Narnia, while the Spirit instills sanctification, preveniently, to those who turn to Aslan and to God's truth. All the time, during the life of Narnia, people (whether human or other creaturely forms) turn to Aslan, or turn away, are influenced by the Holy Spirit, or not. Sentient creatures, persons, make decisions that move them closer to God . . . or further away.

Eventually time is up: the anti-Christ ushers in the destruction of Narnia (Shift the Ape's sin and treachery is greater than even that of the White Witch and Edmund). This annihilation triggers the *eschaton*: the end of all things. And Narnia is fulfilled, supplanted, by death, judgment, heaven, and hell. The redeemed live a resurrected life in the new creation, a fuller life in the new heaven and the new earth, born out of the old, the shadowlands, drawing ever closer into the Aslan-Christ whose form changes as they draw deeper into God's eternity. The unredeemed, through Aslan's judgment, condemn themselves to hell, subsisting in the utter darkness of their own self-generated willfulness.

5. TRINITARIAN CONSIDERATIONS

i. Christian Concepts

Martha C. Sammons has collated an account of the Christian concepts in the Narniad. These concepts, or more pertinently events in the narrative, reflect a religious economy where the Aslan-Christ is the visible manifestation of God; the Son *is* the visibility and the knowability of God. Sammons identifies the concepts that are implicitly and explicitly representative *by analogy* of the Christ of a religious economy. Sammons notes how for generations of readers Aslan "reminds" (analogical) them of Jesus Christ, yet the two persons are not the same (allegorical).[10] This confirms Lewis's stated aim of supposition: "Although biblical principles are very much present in the Narnia series, they are certainly not allegory—characters and events in Narnia do not 'represent' anything. If one tries to find such correspondences—for example, a comparison of Aslan's sacrifice with Christ's crucifixion—he will be disappointed. Instead, Lewis believed that a writer, as 'creator' in a sense, 'rearranges' elements God has already

---

10 Sammons, *A Guide Through Narnia*, 116.

provided in *his* world and which already contain *his* meanings."[11] In terms of the theology—specifically Trinitarian theology—the images are symbolic, analogous; they are biblical, they are not isomorphic, there is no one-to-one correspondence with biblical concepts and actualities.

ii. Creation

Our world was created by Christ, God's Word; Aslan *sings* Narnia into existence.[12] The fabric of Narnia is created, then the creatures. Sammons notes how "God's 'Let there be's' are echoed by Aslan's 'Be walking trees. Be talking beasts. Be divine waters.'"[13] But the human is not the ruler of all—Aslan chooses two of each beast and anoints them, they are changed, they become talking sentient and rational beasts displaying personhood: "With Aslan's breath comes a flash-like-fire upon the chosen animals. This images seems to be used throughout the Narnia tales as a signal of the Holy Spirit."[14] But they have a warning: disobey and they will return to their beast-like state, they will lose sentience: a warning of the *fall* and the responsibilities they have been given, and the consequences of consciousness. Digory's temptation to know is a repeat of the fall of Eve and Adam's in our reality,[15] it is meant to strike a chord with Lewis's readers. As the serpent introduces original sin into our world the White Witch does so into Narnia, ably helped by the human children: "When Digory succumbs to the temptation to know, he awakens the Witch."[16] Aslan confesses that much evil will come but he will take the worst of it onto himself.[17] However, as with our world, Narnia is good, declared good, by God.

iii. The Tree and the Garden

The tree and the garden are central images charged with biblical meaning in the Narniad, and relate to God's dealings with the creation. Sammons notes "the Tree of the Knowledge of Good and Evil" and "the Tree of Life" were both planted in the Garden of Eden. The former led to our downfall (Gen 3) but we will be restored to partake in the latter (Rev 22:2); the restoration will be "because of Christ's sacrifice on a tree on a hill"[18] (Matt 26:47–27:66; Mark 14:32—15:47; Luke 22:47–23:56; John 18:2—19:42). Lewis interweaves these arboreal symbols into the Narniad—by analogy, not isomorphic one-to-one correspondence. Sammons notes how Digory, because he has brought personified evil into Narnia at its creation, goes into the Western Wilds to retrieve—at Aslan's request—a silver apple from a *tree* in a *garden* atop a hill, to plant

---

11   Ibid., 117.
12   Lewis, The *Magician's Nephew*, 110f.
13   Sammons, *A Guide through Narnia*, 119.
14   Ibid., 119–20.
15   Lewis, *The Magician's Nephew*, 42f.
16   Sammons, *A Guide through Narnia*, 120.
17   Rahner, *The Trinity*, Pt. II, 49–79, specifically "The Trinity as Absolute Mystery," 50f., and, "The Meaning and Limits of the Employed Concepts," 51–57.
18   Sammons, *A Guide through Narnia*, 121.

7. Analogical and Symbolic Narratives III: ... Trinitarian Considerations

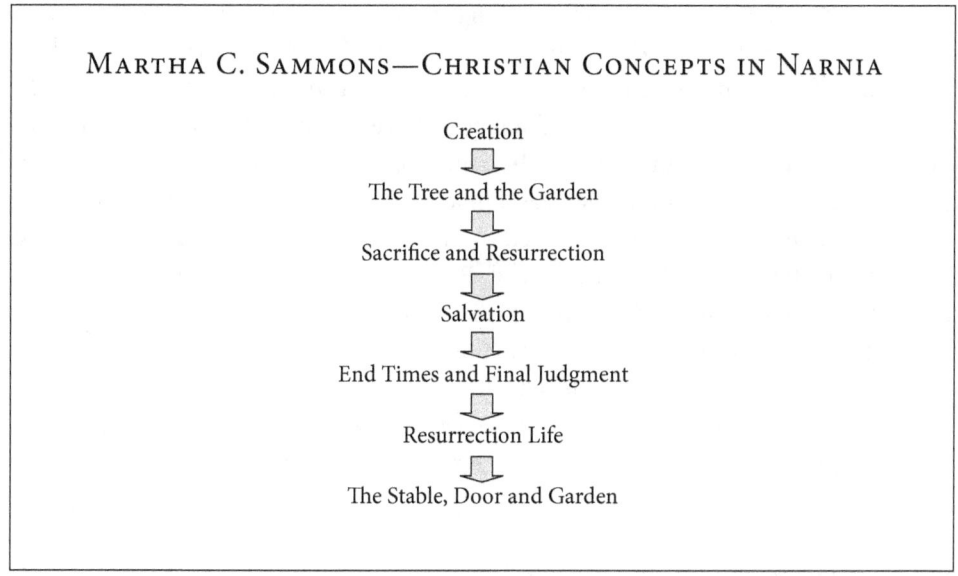

Figure 5 Sammons' identification of Christian Concepts in the Narniad

its seed to form a tree of protection.[19] Like the metaphorical fruit from the Eden tree that carries the knowledge of good and evil, this fruit also carries a prohibition with it—it can only be used with the permission of the Aslan-Christ: "it is called the 'Apple of Life' for Digory's mother because it is eaten in the right way and time, but gives an endless life of misery to the Witch because she plucked the apple in her own way, for herself."[20] The symbol of the tree and its relationship with salvation also occurs in the final book, *The Last Battle*.

iv. Sacrifice and Resurrection

Central to the Christian concepts in the Narniad is Aslan's sacrifice and resurrection, but they "in no way parallel the account in the Bible."[21] The deep magic that demands sacrifice is comparable in many ways with the Mosaic Law (c.f. Rom 8:2; 1 Cor 15:16). Sammons notes how the law is written, engraved, on the stone table, and on the Emperor's (God the Father) scepter. The shedding of blood is important, and is biblical: this is, "similar to God's Old Testament Law which is written on the stone tablets, requiring death and the shedding of blood as the penalty for sin."[22] Sammons sees the deeper magic from before the dawn of time as comparable with the New Testament law of love—when an innocent victim is sacrificed, death will work backwards: "This Law

---

19   Lewis, *The Magician's Nephew*, 11–14.
20   Sammons, *A Guide through Narnia*, 122.
21   Ibid.
22   Sammons, *A Guide through Narnia*, 122. This was dealt with in depth in the first book in this series, *C. S. Lewis—Revelation, Conversion, and Apologetics*, Ch. 11, §. 4, iii.

[the deeper magic] states that when a willing victim who has committed no treachery is killed in the traitor's stead, the stone table will crack and death will start working backwards. What a marvelously succinct expression of the New Testament message! According to New Testament 'Law,' the Law of Love, when Christ is sacrificed as the perfect substitute for man, the Old Testament Law is 'cracked'—God's demand is met, paid for, and death no longer has a hold on us."[23] But we have our part to play. Sammons notes how Aslan expects Peter to be at the forefront of the (spiritual and temporal) battle against the forces of evil. Prior to his sacrifice, Aslan, accompanied by the two Pevensie girls, is troubled, as Christ was in Gethsemane. We then have the scenes of humiliation and torture prior to the execution, all at the hands of personified evil. Susan and Lucy stay, and in the morning are faced with the puzzle of resurrection, which they cannot understand. They do not witness the actual moment of resurrection, they meet, like the broken stone table, the result of *resurrection*: Aslan raised up to confront them.[24]

v. Salvation

Aslan's sacrifice analogically reflects the need and basis for atonement rooted in the sacrifice of the innocent one, whose spilled blood is the mechanism for change. This leads to salvation: Narnia and its creatures are not as they should be, but they will be changed. Edmund's treachery in *The Lion, the Witch, and the Wardrobe* is the final trigger—the pinnacle of an accumulation of sin and treachery. Sammons sees Eustace's un-dragoning in *The Voyage of the Dawn Treader* as an example of personal salvation.[25] Central to this is the command Aslan issues to the proud and mean-spirited, the cruel and vindictive, Eustace: "Follow me." Eustace has been turned into a dragon by his selfish greed. He tries to un-dragon himself but fails. Only Aslan can dig into and remove the hard scales that have built-up.

> This episode is a perfect illustration of what happens when Christ gets hold of a sinner and makes him a new creature. We ourselves are unable to peel away our layers of sin and selfishness; in fact, we find that such ugliness has penetrated to the very roots, the center of our lives. The experience of letting Christ do it for us may hurt, but he bathes us in the water of new life, and re-clothes us as new creations.
>
> In another vivid example, Lewis uses the same biblical symbol of water to show the regenerating power of salvation.... In *The Silver Chair*, Jill is thirsty but afraid to approach a stream because a great Lion is standing on the other side: "I daren't come and drink," said Jill. "Then you will die of thirst," said the Lion. "Oh dear! said Jill, coming up another step nearer. "I suppose I must go and look for another stream then." "There is no other stream," said the Lion. So Jill kneels and drinks the coldest and most refreshing water she has ever had and it quenches her thirst at once.[26]

---

23   Ibid., 122–23.
24   Lewis, *The Lion, the Witch, and the Wardrobe*, Ch. 15.
25   Lewis, *The Voyage of the Dawn Treader*, 84–87.
26   Sammons, *A Guide through Narnia*, 127. Referring to Lewis, *The Silver Chair*, 23–25. Note, c.f. Rev 22:1–2, and, John 7:37–39.

7. Analogical and Symbolic Narratives III: . . . Trinitarian Considerations

Aslan is the great bridge builder; it is the Aslan-Christ who initiates sanctification. Lewis therefore uses very real corporeal images to symbolize this. For example, "Aslan's Table" near the end of the world—freely given generosity for those who are in need.[27] All this issues from the sacrifice and resurrection of the Aslan-Christ, and the sanctification offered by the Holy Spirit.

vi. End Times and Final Judgment

The Last Battle has Lewis presenting a biblically inspired word picture of the end times with the, according to Sammons, "ridiculous anti-Christ figure." False rumors, and rumors of rumors, abound, as war engulfs Narnia, and the faithful are led astray. For the actual end of Narnia Lewis borrows quite explicitly from Matthew 24:29–31, and Acts 2:19–20: as the sun and moon darken, and chaos reigns, a mighty horn blast summons all to Aslan's judgment.[28]

vii. Resurrection Life

For glimpses of the resurrection life Lewis returns to analogy. We have two examples, endorsed by Sammons: Caspian's resurrection given at the end of *The Silver Chair* with the emphasis on the thorn and the power of Christ's blood to redeem and to raise-up.[29] The second is in the train crash that kills the remaining Pevensie children, coinciding with the end of all things in Narnia, where the humans and the Narnians find themselves in a very real corporeal new heaven and a new earth—the new creation.[30] The old can run like the young, they are exhilarated in this eternal new creation; they are full of life, never exhausted (Isa 40:28–31). Lewis simply takes the biblical prophecy and fleshes it out, by analogy.[31] However, this is only a precursor to the real heaven, this is the outer fringes—the oft-repeated line in these final pages of the Narniad is "Come further up and further in."[32]

viii. The Stable, Door, and Garden

Three key biblical images are invoked by Lewis throughout the Narniad: the stable, the door, and the garden. The stable comes from the Nativity of Jesus, though it is used initially, in *The Last Battle*, in the context of housing the anti-Christ! However, despite its use it becomes the door/gateway to eternity for the redeemed but also the door/gateway to hell for the damned as—with the eschatological destruction of Narnia—the stable mutates into a "doorway" for all of Narnia to pass through to face Aslan's judgment.

---

27 Lewis, *The Voyage of the Dawn Treader*, 151–55.
28 Lewis, *The Last Battle*, 141–51.
29 Sammons, *A Guide through Narnia*, 129. Referring to, Lewis, *The Silver Chair*, 180f.
30 Lewis, *The Last Battle*, Ch. 12, 126–28, and 132f.
31 Sammons, *A Guide through Narnia*, 129–30. Referring to, Lewis, *The Last Battle*, 162f.
32 Referring to, Lewis, *The Last Battle*, 185, 189, 192, 198, 201–3, and 207.

> Lewis uses the door, not only here, but in several of his other writings, as a symbol for the reality we have always longed for and for which Lewis, as we have seen, longed all his life. We long to be inside of some door which we have always seen from the outside... to be at last summoned inside would be both glory and honor beyond all our merits and also the healing of that old ache. Someday... pass in through Nature, beyond her, into that splendor which she fitfully reflects. And in there, in beyond Nature, we shall eat of the tree of life.[33]

In *The Last Battle*—in response to puzzlement by her peers commenting on how the stable seems bigger inside than outside, and how the stable as a gateway appears different when seen from inside than when contemplated from outside—Lucy notes, with reference to the nativity of the Christ, "In our world too, a stable once had something inside it that was bigger than our whole world."[34]

Such a door/gateway—often merely three timbers (two posts and a cross-beam)—initiated by Aslan, forms the means of access between the worlds. In *The Silver Chair* Jill and Eustace pass through an ordinary door in a garden wall and find themselves in Aslan's country.[35] It is used for the return of the Pevensie children from Narnia back to England (*Prince Caspian*).[36] In *The Magician's Nephew*, Digory and Polly secretly and inadvertently enter Uncle Andrew's study and laboratory, and therefore into danger and other worlds, through a disused attic door.[37] In *The Lion, the Witch, and the Wardrobe*, Lucy initially enters Narnia through the wardrobe door.[38] Sammons notes how Lewis's imagery is biblically grounded: "I am the gate; whoever enters through me will be saved. They will come in and go out, and find pasture" (John 10:9). In *The Last Battle*, when the redeemed pass through the eschatological door/gateway that was formerly the stable they do find themselves in rich pastures, being beckoned to come further up and further in.[39] As they do, Lewis uses the garden motif, reminiscent of the Garden of Eden (Gen. 1–3) for the rich verdant land. The garden image is used often in the Narniad—in *The Magician's Nephew*, the tree from which Digory takes a silver apple,[40] and in places of rest amidst a challenging journey in *The Voyage of the Dawn Treader*,[41] also, in *The Horse and his Boy*, as staging posts on a perilous escape from Calormen.[42] The door/gateway is a profound symbol, evoking a passing through, a change of state, an enabling of redemption. It also exemplifies a holding-out, the human propensity to keep God at bay. Jesus seeks entry, he knocks on the door, but we can refuse to open-up: "Here I am! I stand at the door and knock. If anyone hears my voice and opens the door, I will come in and eat with that person, and they with

---

33   Sammons, *A Guide Through Narnia*, 131.
34   Lewis, *The Last Battle*, 132.
35   Lewis, *The Silver Chair*, 15.
36   Lewis, *Prince Caspian*, 175f.
37   Lewis, *The Magician's Nephew*, 9–10.
38   Lewis. *The Lion, the Witch, and the Wardrobe*, 6.
39   Lewis, *The Last Battle*, 162f.
40   Lewis, *The Magician's Nephew*, Chs. 11–14.
41   Lewis, *The Voyage of the Dawn Treader*, 101–5.
42   For example, the residence of the Hermit of the Southern March. See, Lewis, *The Horse and his Boy*, 115f.

me" (Rev. 3:20). This verse formed the basis of William Holman Hunt's (1827–1910) famous painting, "The Light of the World,"[43] of Jesus standing in an overgrown garden, knocking on the door, seeking entry. Hunt wrote, "I painted the picture with what I thought, unworthy though I was, to be by divine command, and not simply as a good subject. The door in the painting has no handle, and can therefore be opened only from the inside, representing 'the obstinately shut mind.'"[44] Jesus, the eternal Christ, holds in his hand a lantern giving the only light to the world.[45] Millions of reproductions graced the homes of Lewis's parents' generation as the original hung in Keble College Chapel, in Lewis's Oxford (with painted copies in St Paul's Cathedral and numerous galleries and museums).

6. A DOCTRINE OF THE TRINITY

First, what is Lewis's general understanding of the Trinity? This is presented in the fourth series of the broadcast talks (Feb 22 to Apr 4, 1944) entitled *Beyond Personality: The Christian Idea of God*. For the revised and complete edition of the broadcast talks published as *Mere Christianity* in 1952 the sub-title was changed to *Beyond Personality: or First Steps in the Doctrine of the Trinity*.[46] Ironically the words Trinity, triune, and Trinitarian are not cited once in the main text of *Mere Christianity*, and yet this fourth part (consisting of the radio talks originally delivered in 1944) is imbued with a sound orthodox and traditional doctrine of the Trinity, and an understanding of the three persons of God in one unity. This is characteristic of Lewis's apologetics: many readers familiar with the term "Trinity" would have turned-off at the mention of the word, so he approaches the veracity and reality of the Trinity in a subversive manner—persuading people first, then showing them that this is the doctrine of the Trinity. The same is true with the Narniad—being narrative, effectively parable, it would be inappropriate to outline doctrine. Lewis does, in *Mere Christianity*, use the term, "three-personal God." For example, "You may ask, 'if we cannot imagine a three-personal being, what is the good of talking about *him*?' Well, there isn't any good talking about *him*. The thing that matters is being actually drawn into that three-personal life, and that may begin any time—tonight, if you like."[47] Likewise, "The whole threefold life of the three-personal being is actually going on in that ordinary little bedroom where an ordinary man is saying his prayers."[48] The doctrine of the Trinity issues from the scriptural record, developing into early Church theology:

> And that is how Theology started. People already knew about God in a vague way. Then came a man who claimed to be God; and yet *he* was not the sort of man

---

43   William Holman Hunt, "The Light of the World" (1853–54), oil on canvas; location: Chapel, Keble College, Oxford.
44   W. H., Hunt, *Pre-Raphaelitism and the Pre-Raphaelite Brotherhood*, Vol. 1, 350.
45   See also, Patrick, "Letting In and Shutting Out: Themes in the Thought of C. S. Lewis," issues which will be dealt with in the final chapters of this series, on the *eschaton*, heaven and hell.
46   Lewis, *Mere Christianity*, Pt. 4, 125–87.
47   Ibid., 135.
48   Ibid.

you could dismiss as a lunatic. *He* made them believe *him*. They met *him* again after they had seen *him* killed. And then, after they had been formed into a little society or community, they found God somehow inside them as well: directing them, making them able to do things they could not do before. And when they worked it all out they found they had arrived at the Christian definition of the three-personal God.[49]

The Trinity is the pattern of self-surrender that we must conform to: for Lewis God, through the Trinitarian relationship, does all that is needed; we merely submit to it being done to us.[50] The doctrine of the Trinity demonstrates to us that God is three-personal and yet more, persons and more, beyond personality.[51] Analogy is fundamental to Lewis in trying to understand Trinitarian thinking: analogy and models.[52] The value to Trinitarian doctrine is that it describes the positive structure of what is truly real: such doctrinal assertions are—"statements about spiritual reality, not specimens of primitive physical science."[53] Imagery may, or more pertinently may not, help. Lewis notes that anthropomorphic mental pictures do not assist in understanding how the triune Godhead may be; "When they say that Christ is the 'Son' of 'the Father' they may have a picture of two human forms, the one looking rather older than the other. But we now know that the mere presence of these mental pictures does not, of itself, tell us anything about the reasonableness or absurdity of the thoughts they accompany."[54] To this end we must remember that in the early church the Trinity was not defined philosophically; speculation about God's being came later, added to the basic doctrine.[55] Lewis stressed the basic premise from the BBC radio talks, and from *Mere Christianity*, that the Trinity is three-personal but God is revealed as super-personal: "For I suppose we, by affirming three Persons, especially, say that God is not a Person. Would it be fair to say that *he* is revealed to us as super-personal, which is very different from being impersonal?"[56] Lewis uses Screwtape to articulate some of the dangers in speculation about God: speaking inadvertently about God Screwtape comments, "Thus *he* is not content, even *himself*, to be a sheer arithmetical unity; *he* claims to be three as well as one, in order that this nonsense about Love may find a foothold in *his* own nature. At the other end of the scale, *he* introduces into matter that obscene invention the organism . . ."[57] This exposes the ever present danger when trying to write narrative to teach about the Trinity, the danger being of tri-theism, three gods: "even adult and educated Christians in trying to think about the blessed Trinity have to guard constantly against falling into the heresy of tritheism . . . and 'another of whom *he* was not quite sure' is perhaps no bad beginning for a knowledge

49   Ibid., 136.
50   Ibid., 160; see also Lewis, *Problem of Pain*, Ch. 6.
51   Lewis, "Must Our Image of God Go," 149–50.
52   Lewis, *Mere Christianity*, 141–43.
53   Lewis, *Miracles*, 124.
54   Ibid., 116.
55   Ibid., 75–76.
56   Lewis writing to Dom Bede Griffiths, Aug. 4, 1962. *Collected Letters Vol III*, 1362.
57   Lewis, *Screwtape Letters*, 81–82.

7. Analogical and Symbolic Narratives III: ... Trinitarian Considerations

about the Holy Ghost."[58] Then there is the danger of subjectivism (God becomes less, as *he* progresses down the Trinity).[59] Lewis does draw out the importance of the statement in the Athanasian Creed where Jesus is "'equal' to his Father as touching *his* Godhead.'"[60]

As Jesus is the visible manifestation of God, it is of no surprise that there should be such an emphasis on the second person of the Trinity.[61] It is vital that we see Jesus as both God and man.[62] Lewis does invoke mathematical analogies, of limited use, but analogically they can help—

> At this point we must remind ourselves that Christian theology does not believe God to be a person. It believes *him* to be such that in *him* a trinity of persons is consistent with a unity of Deity. In that sense it believes *him* to be something very different from a person, just as a cube, in which six squares are consistent with unity of the body, is different from a square. (Flatlanders, attempting to imagine a cube, would either imagine the six squares coinciding, and thus destroy their distinctiveness, or else imagine them set out side by side, and thus destroy the unity. Our difficulties about the Trinity are much of the same kind).[63]

At the heart of the Trinity is divine love, which forms something of a society.[64] Whatever analogies we use the image generated will fall short of the reality of God's tri-unity.

7. A NARNIAN TRINITY

i. *The Triune God: Father, Son, and Holy Spirit*

The God underpinning and referred to explicitly by Lewis in the Narniad is Trinitarian: the Emperor-beyond-the-Sea (the Father)—invisible, distant, primordial—simply and *sheerly is*; Aslan (the Son)—corporeal, knowable, actual—is in the creation but is not totally of it; and the un-named manifestations, spiritual apparitions, conscience-stirring-hauntings, a reassurance, a comforting in mind and soul, proceeding from the Emperor-beyond-the-Sea and from Aslan, haunts the world, but is impossible to pin down and again *sheerly is* (the Holy Ghost, the Holy Spirit). Lewis is at pains to be Trinitarian in the Narniad; he is likewise aware of the need to avoid Panentheism whereby God would be tied into creation to an irrevocable degree. The name of God is not mentioned, which is something of an acknowledgment of the tradition among the ancient Hebrews, of not mentioning the name. The way that there are un-named divine visitations in the Old Testament, the same is true in Narnia; also that some

---

58 Lewis writing to 'An American Lady,' Apr. 17, 1953. *Letters to An American Lady*, 14.
59 Lewis writing to Dom Bede Griffiths, Dec 21, 1941. *Collected Letters Vol II*, 500–503.
60 Ibid.
61 Lewis, *Beyond Personality*, 26f. Ideas developed in *Mere Christianity*, 143f.
62 Lewis writing to "a former pupil," Jan. 4, 1941, in *Letters of C. S. Lewis*. 357; Lewis writing to Sr. Penelope, Jul. 29, 1942. *Collected Letters Vol II*, 525f.
63 Lewis, "The Poison of Subjectivism," 79–80.
64 Lewis, *Problem of Pain*, 16f.

creatures/persons are simply not ready for the nature of God to be revealed to them.[65] Overall is a triune understanding of the un-named God in the Narniad, some begin to perceive the truth, others do not. But what sort of balance do we find. The name "Emperor-beyond-the-Sea" is only cited a handful of times: six references through the whole Narniad; the name "Aslan" and "*the* Lion" over one thousand times. The un-named Holy Spirit, often referred to obliquely by its *effect* more than in *person*, the third person of the Trinity, is mentioned much more than "the Emperor" but less than Aslan.

ii. The Father: The Emperor-beyond-the-Sea

"The Emperor-beyond-the-Sea," sometimes, "Aslan's great Father," and, "The Emperor-over-the-sea,"[66] lives beyond the eastern edge of the Narnian world, in "Aslan's Country." He is God, Lord and ruler of all worlds, including Narnia. The Emperor-beyond-the-Sea created the deep magic (engraved upon the Emperor's scepter, and clearly available for some of the creatures to know about) from the point of Narnia's creation—the dawn of time—but also, crucially the deeper magic (unknown to the creation and the creatures) from before the dawn of time. Both forms of "magic" are comparable to the Mosaic Law and operate in Aslan's sacrifice and Jesus's crucifixion. The Father (the Emperor-beyond-the-Sea) and the Son (Aslan) work in harmony and unison, but each have a particular character role and duty, and person, hence Aslan's obedience to the "great Father."

The "Emperor-beyond-the-Sea" is cited by the Beavers in *The Lion, the Witch, and the Wardrobe*, only this is in a Trinitarian statement of relationship: "'Aslan a man!' said Mr. Beaver sternly. 'Certainly not. I tell you he is the King of the wood and the Son of the great Emperor-beyond-the-Sea. Don't you know who is the King of Beasts? Aslan is a lion—the Lion, the great Lion.'"[67] This is revelation—certainly to the Pevensie children—which fails to remind them of the doctrine of the Trinity they should have come across at church back in England. The other reference in *The Lion, the Witch and the Wardrobe*[68] is quoted by the White Witch of all people. In the context of Aslan's discussion with her about Edmund's treason, and Aslan's pleading for him—his offence was not against the Witch—he feigns ignorance of the deep magic that asserts that traitors must die; the witch taunts him—

> "Tell you?" said the Witch, her voice growing suddenly shriller. "Tell you what is written on that very Table of Stone which stands beside us? Tell you what is written in letters deep as a spear is long on the fire-stones on the Secret Hill? Tell you what is engraved on the scepter of the Emperor-beyond-the-Sea? You at least know the Magic which the Emperor put into Narnia at the very beginning.

---

65 Lewis, *The Voyage of the Dawn Treader*, 124–25.
66 Note Lewis does on occasion refer to the Emperor being "over" and not "beyond" the sea. This may have been an inadvertent mistake but it does not invalidate the doctrinal assertion.
67 Lewis, *The Lion, the Witch and the Wardrobe*, 79.
68 Ibid., 141–42.

7. Analogical and Symbolic Narratives III: ... Trinitarian Considerations

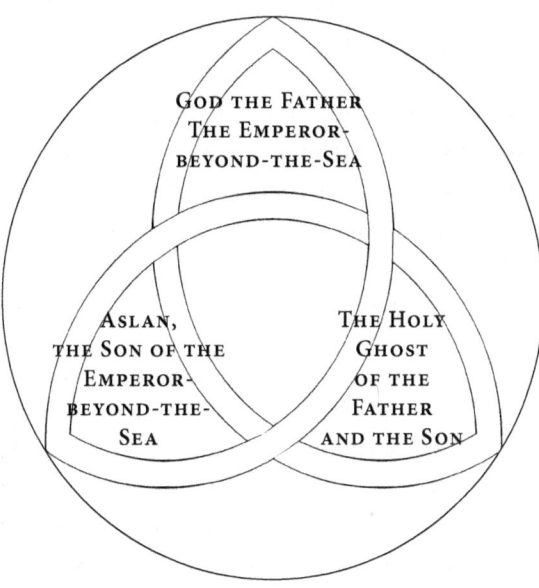

Christian Triquetra
A *triquetra* (from the Latin for triangle) is a three-cornered shape, often formed of three *vesicae piscis*. Since the nineteenth century it has come to symbolize the Trinity: it is three shapes formed of *one continuous line*.

Although similar patterns/shapes occur in modern and ancient Paganism, the Christian triquetra has its roots in three-leafed shamrock which was taken by Saint Patrick as a symbol of the Trinity. As a symbol of the Trinity the triquetra is three distinct identical shapes/patterns, interlaced with each other, which form the whole; take one away the whole ceases to be.

Three-in-one; one in three.

John Donne Circle
To John Donne (1572–1631, English poet, lawyer and Church of England priest, the circle was a perfect symbol of God: it is endless, perfect, and complete, it is a single infinite line. "Whom God loves, he loves to the end: and not only to their own end, to their death, but to his end, and his end is, that he might love them still." JOHN DONNE, SERMON II

Figure 6 A Narnian Trinity

You know that every traitor belongs to me as my lawful prey and that for every treachery I have a right to a kill."[69]

The beavers try to argue with the Witch accusing her of being the Emperor-beyond-the-Sea's executioner, the bull offers force/violence as a defense, but the Witch reminds them all that it is the law: unless she has her right all Narnia will be destroyed:

He [Aslan] knows the Deep Magic better than that. He knows that unless I have blood as the Law says all Narnia will be overturned and perish in fire and water."
"It is very true," said Aslan, "I do not deny it."
"Oh, Aslan!" whispered Susan in the Lion's ear, "can't we— I mean, you won't, will you? Can't we do something about the Deep Magic? Isn't there something you can work against it?"
"Work against the Emperor's Magic?" said Aslan, turning to her with something like a frown on his face. And nobody ever made that suggestion to him again.[70]

---

69   Ibid., 141.
70   Ibid., 142.

In Trinitarian terms the Father cannot really be considered in the same breath without the Son: there is often, as here, a tri-unity to Lewis's implicit doctrine of the Trinity in the Narniad. The two *persons* are distinct, yet unified. The distinction is expressed in separation between Aslan and the Emperor-beyond-the-Sea, yet there is a unity of purpose. Aslan is obedient to the Father's wishes, even unto death. The Son talks with, listens to the creatures, but knows the framework of creation *he* must work within. In *The Horse and His Boy*, Lewis as narrator, comments that Shasta "knew none of the true stories about Aslan, the great Lion, the son of the Emperor-over-the-sea, the King above all High Kings in Narnia."[71] The relation of Father and Son is again stated explicitly, invoking a doctrine of the Trinity. In *Prince Caspian*, Aslan is referred to on one occasion as "the Son of the great Emperor-over-the-Sea,"[72] likewise Edmund, in *The Voyage of the Dawn Treader*, in explaining to Eustace, comments, "He is the great Lion, the son of the Emperor-beyond-the-Sea, who saved me and saved Narnia. We've all seen him. Lucy sees him most often."[73] When faced by the demon-"god" Tash, Peter (inspired by the Holy Spirit), asserts—as in the name of Jesus—"Begone, monster, and take your lawful prey to your own place: in the name of Aslan and Aslan's great Father the Emperor-over-the-Sea."[74] The triune relationship is established, but Lewis offers little to develop the Trinitarian doctrine. In true triune nature the Emperor-beyond-the-Sea is never seen, or beheld or touched, or known—apart from obliquely in reasoned statements.

iii. The Son: Aslan—An Epiphanic Enfleshed Theophany

There is no incarnation in the Narniad. Aslan "arrives," he "appears." He is fully flesh, fully beast (as Christ is fully human in our reality). In the absence of an incarnation, what are the options? Is Aslan merely, inadvertently, an avatar? Avatars in Hinduism represent the descent of a "god" to earth in incarnate form.[75] This is often an incarnation or embodiment, or a manifestation (but not *the* incarnation). For example, Krishna was the eighth avatar of Vishnu, incarnated to help the five brothers regain their kingdom. Sometimes these "gods" *appear* in human form. Avatar was usually to counteract some evil in this world. In many stories an avatar is a possession by a spirit, presumably disembodied, of a corporeal fleshly body here on earth. This possession is not permanent (through possession by evil spirits can appear permanent). However, "possession," "descending," "appearing," or "abiding" is not ontologically synonymous with the risks inherent in a *real* incarnation. That is, an avatar is not of the nature of existence, the same sort of being, as with the nature of incarnate being in Jesus of Nazareth. There are similarities but the two are not synonymous: being made flesh,

---

71   Lewis, *The Horse and His Boy*, 130.
72   Lewis, *Prince Caspian*, 97.
73   Lewis, *The Voyage of the Dawn Treader*, 117–18.
74   Lewis, *The Last Battle*, 151.
75   Avatar, from Sanskrit for "descent," and chiefly found in Hinduism. Avatars are "gods" in incarnate form, the term is therefore used for a manifestation of a deity or released soul in bodily form on earth, the term also applies to an incarnation or embodiment of a person or idea. (OED)

7. Analogical and Symbolic Narratives III: . . . Trinitarian Considerations

with all that is implied in being human, is a different concept of ontology altogether. Being made flesh carries with it mortality and risk. Aslan is no avatar. The second person of the Trinity does not "possess" the body of a beast. He *is*, the beast, the lion, with the risk of pain and suffering, and is sacrificed on the stone table.

Is Aslan merely a Docetic appearance? The Docetists believed Jesus was not really human, his humanity was only an appearance—hence the title, Docetism (from the Greek verb δοκέω, *dokeō*, which meant to appear or to seem to be). The Docetists believed that Jesus's human body of flesh was a *chimera*, and so in the crucifixion he only seemed to suffer and die, that he was really incorporeal, a pure spirit, and hence could not physically die. Is this so with Aslan? Some animals in Narnia believe that Aslan is not really a lion but only lion-like—strong fearless, powerful and superior, given his messianic and divine nature they cannot believe that he can be a flesh and blood, breathing, animal like them, he must be spirit. In *The Horse and His Boy*, Bree—a massive stallion and a war horse—comments that Aslan is not really a lion, only lion-like, he is no beast; to be a beast would be too demeaning for him. This Docetic heresy is immediately countered by Aslan coming up behind Bree, inviting (as Jesus did to doubting Thomas) to sense his breath, feel him to see how real he is.[76] Lewis goes to great pains to present a real corporeal beast that lives and breathes and is subject to the same pain and suffering, limitations, as all the other creatures, including the humans in Narnia.

Is Aslan a theophany of the second person of the Trinity? If a theophany is a visible manifestation of God to humankind what is implied by the word "manifestation"? What stops a theophany being an Avatar, or even Docetic? The difference is in God being enfleshed, corporeal, and in submitting God's-self to the conditions of being enfleshed: the risk factor. As such Aslan is an enfleshed manifestation of the Christ to the creation; with this epiphany comes *revelation*. There are epiphanic/theophanic appearances of the Christ in the Old Testament. For example, the fourth figure in the fiery furnace (Dan 3:25), or the three visitors to Abraham at the Oaks of Mamre (Gen 18:1–15). Aslan, as presented by Lewis, is in effect, in the absence of an incarnation, an epiphanic enfleshed theophany.[77]

iv. The Son: Aslan—an Enfleshed Logos—Corporeal and Creaturely

Incarnation or Theophany

There is no incarnation in Narnia; there is no nativity, no crib, no shepherds and visiting magi. These are all presumably unique to our reality. But this raises a serious question: if there is no nativity, is there no incarnation: how come Aslan to be enfleshed? Aslan is real, we've established that, *he* is no Docetic or Gnostic spiritual appearance, he is no avatar, no spirit "god" safely possessing and controlling a lion, safely from heaven

---

76   Lewis, *The Horse and His Boy*, 156–57.
77   For the presence of *the Christ* to the ancient Hebrews see also Paul's comments: 1 Cor 10:1–13

with the ability to leave at a moment's notice. Aslan is clearly at one with the beasts of Narnia, he is fully "beastly" (as Jesus is fully human).

There is no incarnation in the Narniad. Did Lewis do this intentionally—note the problems he identified relating to multiple incarnations, how writing in the first edition of *Miracles*, published only a few years before *The Lion, the Witch and the Wardrobe*, Lewis considers the possibility of multiple incarnations but comments that however possible, however much it should be within the realm of an infinite God, it is too difficult to conceive. Lewis cautiously discards the idea of "many incarnations to redeem many different kinds of creature . . . the divine idiom rejects it." Lewis comments that the image of "mass-production and of waiting queues" comes to mind in an *eschaton* populated by different creatures with their different incarnations of God.[78] If there is no incarnation in Narnia, how did Aslan get there, how did he become enfleshed?

Perhaps it was this concern regarding the questionability of multiple incarnations that led Lewis to avoid an actual incarnation in Narnia. Furthermore how would he have represented the creation scene in the first book (*The Magician's Nephew*) if Christ was to be incarnated as a lion cub in the next book—and what of his brothers and sisters in the lioness's litter. Lewis expressed doubts that we examined in the previous chapter regarding multiple incarnations and the problem of them all coming together in the *eschaton*. Aslan is truly enfleshed but the problem is avoided, to a degree. Like God in the Garden of Eden walking with the proto-humans, Aslan is with, and is known to, the first creatures. Sin causes his disappearance. His reappearance to die on the stone table involved a form of enfleshment utterly and totally different—we might say alien—to humanity. Hence Lewis's comment that, "other species will have witnessed wholly *different* acts, each equally *unique*, equally *necessary* and differently *necessary* to the whole process"[79] of salvation. Lewis echoes the thoughts of Alice Meynell, we considered in the previous chapter, where we cannot begin to imagine the ends and means God has gone to, the costly and severe sacrifice God has gone to, to redeem alien creatures.

λόγος ἄσαρκος/λόγος ἔνσαρκος

According to the text Aslan simply appears; he is uncreated. Is this orthodox?—the second person of the Trinity is eternally begotten, uncreated. Just so. But this very uncreated appearing raises its own set of problems, if we assume he is complete in *his* appearances in Narnia. It is like an actor who lives day and night in the costume, adopting the language and life of a character in a play. The lack of a nativity story within Narnia raises questions yet to be explored by Lewis scholars. A crucial biblical proposition regarding Jesus and the nativity story is that God, the second person of the Trinity, *took on human form*. Aslan does not appear to take on a lionized form. If only the divine nature is uncreated this could be taken to apply only to the Father; asserting that the incarnate Son is uncreated appears to mingle the two natures—a

---

78 Lewis, *Miracles* (1st ed.), 150.
79 Ibid., 150. My emphasis.

7. Analogical and Symbolic Narratives III: . . . Trinitarian Considerations

concept that led to thousands of words being exchanged by theologians in the fourth to fifth centuries, a debate that was resolved through the Chalcedonian declaration—to a degree. However, if the Christ is perpetually enfleshed, clothed in human form, this raises questions about the λόγος ἄσαρκος/λόγος ἔνσαρκος (the *logos asarkos/ logos ensarkos*; from the Greek for flesh—σάρξ, *sarx*). And it raises similar problems to the difficulties posed by the question of multiple incarnations, if the second person of the Trinity is perpetually enfleshed in human flesh. Christ is the second person of the Trinity, is the Word of God—the λόγος (the *logos*, John 1). In becoming incarnate he goes from being unfleshed (ἄσαρκος—*asarkos*, i.e., without flesh) to being enfleshed (ἔνσαρκος—*ensarkos*, i.e., with flesh). Why is this relevant? Because an aspect of Lewis' Christology is that the Aslan-Christ (the feline, lionized, creator in *The Magician's Nephew*) is perpetually enfleshed, the Aslan-Christ does not appear to have had a time when he was the λόγος ἄσαρκος (*logos asarkos*).[80] Nothing is written by chance or ignorance in Lewis's theology and perhaps Lewis could see that this issue was to do with Platonic forms, temporality—or more pertinently a temporal paradox in the form of the relationship between eternity and our reality of time-space—and "the lamb that was slaughtered from the foundation of the world" (Rev 13:8).

If Jesus was just an ordinary human, super-religious, holy man—and there have been many of them—who had an unusually high understanding of God so that he called God his father, if Jesus was in fact—ontologically—no different to any other human being, if his followers considered him *as if* he were God to them, then there is no problem in all of this. The problem arises if we realize and accept that Jesus was more than human yet also *fully* human, if he was God incarnate and on an equal plane in terms of his nature of being as us, yet being *fully* God, then these problems are pertinent: was he always enfleshed? Could God be incarnated more than once? What are the boundaries of the salvation he wrought for us? And so forth. Lewis tackles these problems not using the direct form and language of theology but in his analogical and symbolic narratives, i.e., Aslan in the Narnia books.

"He no longer looked to them like a lion."

So is the second person of the Trinity according to Lewis's theologoumenon in the Narniad perpetually enfleshed? If multiple incarnations raised problems of precedence and multiplicity in the *eschaton* does not the *logos ensarkos* do the same? Perhaps Lewis, using, as ever, narrative, creative narrative, solves the problem. At the end of *The Last Battle*, the Narnian end of all things and the *eschaton*. All the persons (human or otherwise of Narnia) come face-to-face with Aslan—he is still the enfleshed lionized beast—but as the redeemed move deeper and further into heaven and eternity ("in my Father's house are many mansions" John 14:2, KJV) things change. Aslan no longer looks like a lion. So the deeper into the Platonic source of everything, a purity of nature and appearance one reaches, the closer one comes to the God-head. At the

---

80   For those unfamiliar with the λόγος ἄσαρκος/λόγος ἔνσαρκος debate see, Gunton, *The Barth Lecture*, Ch. 11, 2. "The Act of God in Time/The 'Economy,'" §. ii. 167–70, which examines the issues involved and how Barth wanted to justify the λόγος ἔνσαρκος but found too many difficulties.

very end of *The Last Battle*, as the Pevensie children, *post mortem*, draw "further in and further up" in and of what they take for reality, what they perceive, changes. Not a sudden shift, but a gradual Platonic transposition, translation, and alteration: "And as *he* spoke *he* no longer looked to them like a lion; but the things that began to happen after that were so great and beautiful that I cannot write them."[81] So the form of an incarnation or theophany or appearance changes the deeper into God's reality we draw. This is a profound statement that could not have been stated so effectively using the language and traditions of theological discourse. Lewis's method and model of analogical narrative allows the creative freedom for such a proposition. (Just as Jesus's use of parable allows for a much deeper and more profound assertion of God's truth, and the ethical dilemma we live in, than ordinary preaching.)

v. The Holy Spirit: The Spirit of the Emperor-beyond-the-Sea and of Aslan

If Lewis's construction is Trinitarian, if the God that rules over Narnia, creates and sustain, then saves it, and cares for its creatures, eventually judging and redeeming those who love this God, as must be so, then we must ask, where is the Holy Spirit in Narnia? An oft-considered criticism is that the Narniad presents a binary God (Father-Son) not a triune God. This criticism are superficial and come from a cursory reading of the text, these denunciations ignore the Western Trinitarian tradition that Lewis subscribed to. What is Lewis's understanding of the Holy Spirit/Ghost? In terms of Christian discipleship, sanctification, in the context of a religious economy, Lewis comments:

> What grows out of the joint life of the Father and Son is a real person, is in fact the third of the three persons who are God. This third Person is called, in technical language, the Holy Ghost or the "spirit" of God. Do not be worried or surprised if you find it (or *him*) rather vaguer or more shadowy in your mind than the other two. I think there is a reason why that must be so. In the Christian life you are not usually looking at *him*. *He* is always acting through you. If you think of the Father as something "out there," in front of you, and of the Son as someone standing at your side, helping you to pray, trying to turn you into another son, then you have to think of the third Person as something inside you, or behind you. Perhaps some people might find it easier to begin with the third person and work backwards. God is love, and that love works through men— especially through the whole community of Christians. But this spirit of love is, from all eternity, a love going on between the Father and the Son.[82]

This is what Lewis does in the Narniad. The Holy Spirit—if it is manifest in working through people, pressing on their minds, influencing them—accounts for a far greater presence in the text than the second person of the Trinity (Aslan). However, what is the evidence for the Holy Spirit in Narnia? Lewis gives no name for the third *person* of the Trinity in the Narniad; the first *person* is clearly "The Emperor-over-the-Sea," the second *person* is "Aslan," but the third *person* is nameless. The word God does

---

81   Lewis, *The Last Battle*, 210.
82   Lewis, *Mere Christianity*, 176.

7. Analogical and Symbolic Narratives III: ... Trinitarian Considerations

not appear in the Narniad, though there is good Old Testament precedent for not naming God and thus reducing him to a mere object to study; also, if Lewis's stated aim was to creep past the severe Sunday School teachers and present the gospel fresh and vibrant to a young generation, then this is indeed subversive. In *The Space Trilogy* God is Maleldil: The "Old One" is the initiator, God the Father; "Maleldil the Young" is the Christ, the second person of the Trinity; "the Third One" is the Holy Spirit. In the Narniad we only have the Father and the Son named. But this does not mean that the third person is absent.

The Holy Spirit is nameless but very present in the Narniad; it is behind people, it works through people and profoundly affects the religious economy, however implicitly that economy is in Narnia. Lewis was obviously inspired in his writing by *the* Holy Spirit, but, also, he wove the Holy Spirit's presence *into* the Narniad as he did the other two persons of the Trinity. Lewis uses the word spirit only twenty-six times in the seven books, but these are ancillary. The word is used to refer to alcoholic drink (whisky, brandy);[83] it defines human confidence—being brave and bold, courageous and plucky;[84] spirit refer to the essence of an activity (the spirit of adventure);[85] spirit is the human soul/heart, the immortal in the human;[86] and it is used for enchanted nature—the spirits of walking trees, and so forth;[87] and, for the supernatural.[88]

In addition there is a nameless use, referring to the Holy Spirit, a divine force governing over people and events in Narnia, the divine action within a religious economy.

8. PNEUMA THE HOLY ONE:
I. A DISQUIETING PRESENCE

Pneuma (πνῦμα—pronounced *p-new-ma*) is the Greek word for *breath* and *wind*; in Greek translations of the Hebrew Bible and in the Greek New Testament it is used predominantly for *spirit*: "Jesus answered, 'I tell you the truth, no-one can enter the kingdom of God unless he is born of water and the *Spirit*. Flesh gives birth to flesh, but the *Spirit* gives birth to *spirit*. You should not be surprised at my saying, you must be born again. The *wind* blows wherever it pleases. You hear its sound, but you cannot tell where it comes from or where it is going. So it is with everyone born of the *Spirit*'" (John 3:5–8). For the sake of this study we will name the presence and action—the *person*— of the Holy Spirit in Narnia as "Pneuma the Holy One", drawing on Lewis's precedent in *The Space Trilogy* ("the Third One").

---

83 For example, Lewis, *The Magician's Nephew*, 102.
84 Ibid., 116 and 119; Lewis, *The Horse and his Boy*, 53; Lewis, *The Silver Chair*, 52f.
85 For example, Lewis, *Prince Caspian*, 18.
86 For example, Lewis, *The Horse and his Boy*, 110; Lewis, *Prince Caspian*, 114 and 122; Lewis, *The Voyage of the Dawn Treader*, 21 and 162; Lewis, *The Silver Chair*, 57, 59, 62, 63, 84, 100, 106, 120, 167, and 173.
87 For example, Lewis, *The Lion, the Witch, and the Wardrobe*, 96, 136 and 152; Lewis, *Prince Caspian*, 80.
88 Lewis, *The Last Battle*, 51.

i. A Haunting

Pneumatology is the study or doctrine of the Holy Spirit. What we are looking at here is the doctrine, as such, of the Holy Spirit in Lewis's supposal of Narnia. Joy Davidman, C. S. Lewis's wife, drew an analogy between a cat stalking, and the manner in which the Holy Spirit surreptitiously crept up on people unawares, pressing on them to convert them. Davidman notes with poignancy that, as Francis Thompson symbolized God as the Hound of Heaven pursuing on relentless feet, in her case God was acting more like a cat in that he had been stalking her for many years. Christ, through the Holy Spirit, had been courting her, patiently judging the time was right to reveal his Lordship: "He crept nearer so silently that I never knew he was there. Then, all at once, he sprang."[89] Lewis draws an analogy with children at home playing at burglars, who then hear a creak and a footfall and wonder if a real burglar has sneaked in. This, for Lewis, is like people playing at religion and then finding God has crept into the game and taken over: "There comes a moment when people who have been dabbling in religion ('Man's search for God!') suddenly draw back. Supposing we really found him? We never meant it to come to that! Worse still, supposing he had found us?"[90] For this reason Lewis often in his apologetics and philosophical theology used the phrase *Holy Ghost*, from the King James Version of the Bible, rather than the more modern and fashionable *Holy Spirit*: we are *haunted* by God, the third person of the Trinity, ghost-like, whether we know it or not, whether we want *his* interest or not, God haunts us for our own best interest. From the mid-nineteenth century on, in Christian Native North American art, pictorial representations of the Trinity show, conventionally enough, three persons, the Father as a wise old chief, the Son young and compassionate, then, not a tiny delicate dove for the Holy Spirit, but a massive, powerful and soaring eagle. This surreptitious, secretive, some might say underhand, behavior, of the Holy Spirit is reflected in the Narniad. If Jesus knocks on the door of our willful stubbornness waiting for our response, "Pneuma the Holy One" infiltrates and converts, claims ownership and Lordship for the Christ—justifiably—over the self-obsessed and wayward creatures, human or otherwise, in Narnia.

ii. "Who Proceeds from the Father and the Son"

Lewis doctrine of God is, we might say, Western Orthodox—i.e., it is in keeping with the ecumenical councils, the Latin and Catholic tradition issuing from Augustine, and the Protestant tradition issuing from the sixteenth-century Reformers. To this end he subscribes to the *filioque* clause: that the Holy Spirit proceeds from the Father and from the Son.[91] Creation cannot receive the Holy Spirit (John 14:17), though

---

89   Davidman, "The Longest Way Round," 22.
90   Lewis, *Miracles* (1st ed.), 113
91   The *filioque*, or *filioque* clause, is Latin for "and from the Son," and is a phrase found in the Nicene Creed in use in most Western denominations and churches. The Eastern Orthodox argue that the Holy Spirit proceeds from the Father. The Western tradition is "from the Father *and from the Son*": "And I believe in the Holy Ghost, The Lord and giver of life, Who proceedeth from the Father *and the Son*, Who with the Father and the Son together is worshipped and glorified, Who spake by the Prophets," Nicene Creed.

it proceeds *from* the Father (John 15:26), proceeds by Christ from the Father (John 15:26, 16:7) indeed is sent in the *name* of the Christ (John 14:26), the Holy Spirit is given through Christ's intercession (John 14:16). Therefore, s/he imparts hope (Rom 15:13; Gal 5:5) thereby communicating joy to saints (Rom 14:17; Gal 5:22; 1 Thess 1:6), which is the love of God (Rom 5:3–5). S/he dwells with and teaches the church, the saints of God (John 14:16–17; 14:26), enlightens, comforts and corrects the church (Acts 9:31) thereby testifying to the Christ (John 15:26).

So what is the presence for the Holy Spirit/Ghost in Narnia. "Pneuma the Holy One" is elusive and unquantifiable, though known by its effect, *a posteriori* (after the event) often in relation to Aslan. The Holy Spirit is not absent from the Narniad, it is veiled, hidden, but very active? Some critics may raise concerns that there is a syncretism between the second and third persons of the Trinity, however Lewis goes to great effort to show the actual, personable, activity of the Holy Spirit within Narnia; although he paints a picture of a world where what is intelligible and imaginative in our reality is real in Narnia, this presence is subtle, veiled, *apophatic*, often working through the tangible, through the intelligible made real. If "Pneuma the Holy One" is inherently invisible and unknowable but touches and moves, disturbs and shakes, one might say influences un-noticeably like radiation, it is not surprising that in terms of the corporeal and tangible it is associated with "Aslan the Son," but carries with it the creative initiation and authority of "The Father, the Emperor-over-the-Sea." So, what constitutes the presence and action of the third person of the Trinity in Narnia?

9. PNEUMA THE HOLY ONE: II. ACTION AND EVENT

i. *The Breath of Aslan*

"Pneuma the Holy One" may be elusive, unquantifiable, invisible and difficult to define but it is still a person: the third person of the Trinity. The presence of God is corporeal—i.e., Aslan. But this corporeality can hide the Trinitarian nature within Narnia. The Father is distant, unknowable, except by name (the Emperor-beyond-the-Sea), and the name is given by Aslan, the name is revealed to the inhabitants of Narnia. If the Holy Spirit is corporeal, then it issues, *proceeds*, *processes*, from the Son (Aslan)—i.e., *his* breath. Is the Holy Spirit a separate person from the Son and from the Father, yes, they are distinct persons and ever focus on each other in a communion of love, but they are also one God: distinct yet part of. This is the triune nature. There may appear an element of syncretism between the second and third persons, but this is inadvertent and existential: are these manifestations from Aslan, that is, the spirit of Aslan, or does the Spirit proceed from the Father as well? For Lewis, one of the most common examples of the work of the Holy Spirit is in the symbol of Aslan's breath: "Breathe on me breath of God, Fill me with life anew."[92] In the *The Lion, the Witch,*

---

92   From the mid-nineteenth century hymn, "Breathe on me Breath of God" (Edwin Hatch, 1835–89), No. 671, in, *Hymns Ancient and Modern*, 2nd ed. 1875 [1861].

and the Wardrobe, the White Witch has turned many of Aslan's allies into stone, Aslan moves slowly through the witch's palace (after his resurrection, prior to the battle) to regenerate those imprisoned in stone in her courtyard—calcified, petrified—breathing new life into them: he literally breathes on to them.[93] This is the power of resurrection; the resurrecting power of the Holy Spirit (c.f. Ezek 37:1-14, the valley of dry bones). Eustace Scrubb and Jill Pole, at the opening of *The Silver Chair* find themselves in Aslan's Country (the fringes of heaven?) where they meet Aslan. Eustace falls from a great height, but the breath of Aslan glides him to safety (along with Jill).[94] Spirit equates with breath: "Pneuma the Holy One". Consider Susan Pevensie's meeting with Aslan, "Then, after an awful pause, the deep voice said, 'Susan.' Susan made no answer but the others thought she was crying. 'You have listened to fears, child,' said Aslan. 'Come, let me breathe on you. Forget them. Are you brave again?'"[95] Also: "between them a figure they could not recognize, nor indeed would the other boys at Edmund's school have recognized him if they could have seen him at that moment. For Aslan had breathed on him at their meeting and a kind of greatness hung about him."[96] Also: "Aslan [was] bending toward him and touching the man's nose with his own. As soon as the Lion's breath came about him, a new look came into the man's eyes."[97] When Shasta is making his way over the mountains into Narnia he gradually becomes aware of a powerful presence by his side, in the fog-bound-night-air: "What he could hear was breathing. His invisible companion seemed to breathe on a very large scale, and Shasta got the impression that it was a very large creature. And he had come to notice this breathing so gradually that he had really no idea how long it had been there."[98] This is Aslan. He wonders if it is a ghost—then he hears a sigh and feels the hot breath on his cold hand: corporeal yet Spirit. "Once more he felt the warm breath of the thing on his hand and face. 'There,' it said, 'that is not the breath of a ghost. Tell me your sorrows.' Shasta was a little reassured by the breath..."[99] "Pneuma the Holy One" is with Aslan, denies it is a ghost, yet is the most powerful of Holy Spirit, it restores people from God's-self personhood. In *The Magician's Nephew*, Aslan sings creation into being. Then, he gathers together many of the animals and anoints them: he touches them on the nose with his nose—beastlike. The large creatures grew smaller; the small larger:

> "The Lion opened his mouth, but no sound came from it; he was breathing out, a long, warm breath; it seemed to sway all the beasts as the wind sways a line of trees. Far overhead from beyond the veil of blue sky which hid them the stars sang again; a pure, cold, difficult music. Then there came a swift flash like fire (but it burnt nobody) either from the sky or from the Lion itself, and every drop of blood tingled in the children's bodies, and the deepest, wildest voice they had

---

93   Lewis, *The Lion, the Witch, and the Wardrobe*, 152–53.
94   Lewis, *The Silver Chair*, 16.
95   Lewis, *Prince Caspian*, 153–54.
96   Ibid., 178–79.
97   Ibid., 219.
98   Lewis, *The Horse and his Boy*, 128–31.
99   Ibid., 128–31.

7. Analogical and Symbolic Narratives III: . . . Trinitarian Considerations

ever heard was saying: 'Narnia, Narnia, Narnia, awake. Love. Think. Speak. Be walking trees. Be talking beasts. Be divine waters.'"[100]

The select animals become conscious sentient reasoning animals through the power of the Holy Spirit—"Pneuma the Holy One". In commissioning Digory to gather the silver apple Aslan blesses him with the Holy Spirit: "The Lion drew a deep breath, stooped its head even lower and gave him a Lion's kiss. And at once Digory felt that new strength and courage had gone into him."[101] With Uncle Andrew, the cause of all the trouble, who has closed himself into his own hellish mental state, Aslan still offers compassion: "'If I spoke to him, he would hear only growlings and roarings. Oh Adam's sons, how cleverly you defend yourselves against all that might do you good! But I will give him the only gift he is still able to receive.' He bowed his great head rather sadly, and breathed into the Magician's terrified face. 'Sleep,' he said."[102] The Holy Spirit breath of the second person of the Trinity is the action of God. It will blow away worlds, and return God's servants to their rightful place: "'Yes. I have come to bring you Home,' said Aslan. Then he opened his mouth and blew. But this time they had no sense of flying through the air: instead, it seemed that they remained still, and the wild breath of Aslan blew away the ship and the dead King and the castle and the snow and the winter sky. For all these things floated off into the air like wreaths of smoke, and suddenly they were standing in a great brightness of mid-summer sunshine, on smooth turf, among mighty trees, and beside a fair, fresh stream. . . . Aslan turned to Jill and Eustace and breathed upon them and touched their foreheads with his tongue."[103] Emeth, a good Calormen warrior, is restored by "Pneuma the Holy One", through Aslan's breath, *post mortem*: "Then he breathed upon me and took away the trembling from my limbs and caused me to stand upon my feet."[104]

ii. The Comforter

The Holy Spirit is the comforter. As comforter the Holy Spirit is known by Christians (John 14:17). Aslan's followers are comforted, lifted-up, empowered to pursue the establishment of his kingdom. The examples of "Pneuma the Holy One" as comforter and enabler are too numerous to mention in total. Whenever the Pevensie children or the other humans loyal to Aslan, or creatures who have the ability to know and understand God's purposes, are in trouble, puzzled, lost, the Holy Spirit proceeding from the Emperor-beyond-the-Sea and Aslan will comfort and enable, build up and strengthen. For example, Lucy when imprisoned to be sold as a slave,[105] Tumnus the Faun imprisoned by the White Witch,[106] Eustace and Jill when facing battle.[107] When

---

100 Lewis, *The Magician's Nephew*, 106–8.
101 Ibid., 152–53.
102 Ibid., 183.
103 Lewis, *The Silver Chair*, 186 and 189–90.
104 Lewis, *The Last Battle*, 189.
105 Lewis, *The Voyage of the Dawn Treader*, 63f.
106 Lewis, *The Lion, the Witch, and the Wardrobe*, Ch. 9 "In the Witch's House."
107 Lewis, *The Last Battle*, 107, 129, 135f., and 143–48.

creatures face manifold evil "Pneuma the Holy One" will comfort, bring relief, and enable. When creatures rebel and attempt to go-it-alone, the comforter is absent: Nikabrik the Dwarf, the creatures who have gone over to the side of the White Witch.[108] Some readers of *The Lion, the Witch and the Wardrobe* see the character of Father Christmas as representing the Holy Spirit, in this instance imparting gifts to combat evil with, remembering that ideas in our reality become corporeal and real in Narnia.[109]

iii. The Enabler

Not long after being back in Narnia the four Pevensie children feel older, stronger, more confident: this is the work of the Holy Spirit (Isa 40:28–31). These changes in humans and Narnian creatures are caused, preveniently generated, by the Holy Spirit, who has no name in Narnia. The work of the Holy Spirit is manifest, corporeal, in the creatures, yet it is invisible, as in our reality? Creatures are "raised up" to know the Aslan-Christ. For example, the creation of the talking animals in *The Magician's Nephew*—an anointing characterized by breath and fire (as on day of Pentecost).[110] The new life "in the Spirit" post-*eschaton* in *The Last Battle* in the new heaven and the new earth, the faithful are enabled, they run and never get tired (Isa 40:28–31).[111] When they return to Narnia the Pevensie children find they have a strength that they never had in our world, they appear older, taller, and more mature.[112] King Tirian, the last king of Narnia, when he is captured and tied up to a tree and left alone pleads in prayer to Aslan: "And still there was no change in the night or the wood, but there began to be a kind of change inside Tirian. Without knowing why, he began to feel a faint hope. And he felt somehow stronger."[113] Tirian is rescued by Jill and Eustace: "He was surprised at the strength of both children: in fact they both seemed to be already much stronger and bigger and more grown-up than they had been when he first met them a few hours ago."[114]

iv. The Chastiser and the Moral Guide

"Pneuma the Holy One" chastises and corrects the faithful—out of love and concern, to correct and ensure they follow the way of the Lord. Near the end of their long voyage as they draw close to the end of the world on the Dawn Treader, King Caspian insists with anger that he will abdicate and go with the humans to cross over into Aslan's country. All on board know this is the wrong course of action but Caspian in a fit of temper storms away into his cabin. He emerges after a while chastened having

---

108   Lewis, *Prince Caspian*, 66–71, 76–77, 82, 88, 90, 94, 96–98, 163–70, 172–73, 203.
109   See, Ford, *Companion to Narnia. A Complete Guide to the Magical World of C. S. Lewis's The Chronicles of Narnia*, 92–94, 208. See, also, Hinten, *The Keys to the Chronicles: Unlocking the Symbols of C. S. Lewis's Narnia*, 15–16; and, Timothy Dunharn, "The Lion, the Witch and the Wardrobe: Summary."
110   Lewis, *The Magician's Nephew*, 106–8.
111   Lewis, *The Last Battle*, 50.
112   Lewis, *The Lion, the Witch, and the Wardrobe*, 131–32, 183; *Prince Caspian*, 105–6, 143.
113   Lewis, *The Last Battle*, 50.
114   Ibid., 67.

seen a vision of Aslan that has corrected his willful rebellion. This is the work of the Holy Spirit but the Spirit has to use temporal, corporeal means to communicate:

> But when the others rejoined him a little later they found him changed; he was white and there were tears in his eyes. "It's no good," he said. "I might as well have behaved decently for all the good I did with my temper and swagger. Aslan has spoken to me. No—I don't mean he was actually here. He wouldn't fit into the cabin, for one thing. But that gold lion's head on the wall came to life and spoke to me. It was terrible—his eyes. Not that he was at all rough with me—only a bit stern at first. But it was terrible all the same.[115]

A related chastisement happened earlier in the story when they discover a pool of water that turns everything to solid gold, Caspian and Edmund start a bitter argument about who will own the pool and the island—greed has consumed them. Then they see a vision of Aslan on the hillside, very large, and staring at them. They relent. But it is not just the men who are subject to such correction. Lucy, always envious of her elder sister's good looks, rebels and decides she will say a spell from the book in the magician's house that will make her so beautiful that men will die for sight of her. She contemplates the spell but is shocked by the results. Aslan seems to appear:

> There in the middle of the writing, where she felt quite sure there had been no picture before, she found the great face of a lion, of The Lion, Aslan himself, staring into hers. It was painted such a bright gold that it seemed to be coming towards her out of the page; and indeed she never was quite sure afterwards that it hadn't really moved a little. At any rate she knew the expression on his face quite well. He was growling and you could see most of his teeth. She became horribly afraid and turned over the page at once.[116]

Following the analogical construct of the story, Aslan did not appear in the flesh. "Pneuma the Holy One" focused Lucy's mind, convincing her, through using the temporal, the corporeal, that for a moment the veil between eternity and the created thinned for the understanding to be communicated. Something similar happens to Jill Pole who has blithely ignored and forgotten the signs for her mission. The Holy Spirit, in Narnia, feeds her dreams with sufficient clues and vision so that when she wakes and looks out of the window at the rocky winter landscape *she remembers*. And she now knows what to do and where to go.[117] The important element given the wealth of pictures and ideas that occur to the human when dreaming is that she remembered the dream and that it tied in with the landscape and view from the window when she woke—it related to the real world. Those closest to Aslan are often the most troubled: Lucy is the "dear one" to Aslan, therefore she experiences a troubled conscience the most.[118] If the creature will allow it then the Holy Spirit will correct and keep the person close to Christ through the action and influence of "Pneuma the Holy One": it is therefore the sin against the Holy Spirit that is unforgiveable? Those who did not

---

115 Lewis, *The Voyage of the Dawn Treader*, 262.
116 Ibid., 165.
117 Lewis, *The Silver Chair*, 96–98.
118 For example, Lewis, *The Voyage of the Dawn Treader*, 24 and 182.

"meet" or "know" of Aslan in Narnia may still be forgiven in the *eschaton* because they had not *denied* the Holy Spirit

v. The Guide and a Symbol of Hope

The eagle is often a symbol of hope in the Narniad, and may be interpreted as not just sent by the Holy Spirit but is a manifestation of "Pneuma the Holy One". Farsight the Eagle in *The Last Battle* brings news of the Calormen invasion and the fall of Cair Paravel, the capital of Narnia. King Tirian with Jill and Eustace know the moment that they see a tiny dot in the sky and wonder if, by its movement, it is Farsight, but already it is too late for them to hide from the eagle—they regard it with trepidation and caution—for he can see persons and creatures long before they are aware; *he* knows them.[119] The Dawn Treader and her crew are saved from a demonic dark cloud that has the power to drive them insane when, in answer to a prayer of Lucy's, a beam of light appears and an albatross with divine attributes guides them.[120] Father Christmas, if sent by "Pneuma the Holy One", is also a symbol of hope—he brings courage, and a belief in the future amidst dark evil times, which is why his absence is so acute to the creatures.

10. A TRIUNE STATEMENT OF SELF-REVELATION

i. Trinitarian Language

If, as outlined by the Roman Catholic theologian Karl Rahner, the second person of the Trinity—the Word—is the immanent self-expression of God, this creative divinity is expressed to us, in our reality, in human form. The Father is essentially invisible and unoriginated: the Son is the visibility and the knowability of God. This concurs with the Swiss Reformed theologian Karl Barth—who was only too familiar with the dangers of subordinationism (the belief that the Son and the Holy Spirit are subordinate to God the Father in nature and being; that the Son is obedient to the Father is not a form of subordinationism, a common mistake) and modalism (that God appears in three modes, first the Father, then the Son, then the Spirit).[121] The second person of the Trinity is the self-communication of God, and the self-possession of God. The danger with Trinitarian thinking is always the separation, the compartmentalism of God into separate "gods" (tritheism), and of progression (modalism): one follows the other. Is there a danger of subordinationism in Narnia? We never see the Emperor-beyond-the-Sea, but we cannot see the Father; the Son, the Aslan-Christ is the knowability of God but is simultaneously the Father and the Spirit. The Emperor-beyond-the-Sea does not cease being the Father to become the Son and then the Spirit. Modalism is sometimes an accusation raised against the Narniad: God appears or progresses in three different modes, but this is simply not so, at any given point the action of the economic Trinity

---

119 Lewis, *The Last Battle*, 101–2.
120 Lewis, *The Voyage of the Dawn Treader*, 200–201.
121 Karl Barth, *Dogmatics in Outline*, Chs. 6, 10, 11–13, and specifically, Ch. 21.

7. Analogical and Symbolic Narratives III: . . . Trinitarian Considerations

in Narnia may be from the Emperor-beyond-the-Sea or from Aslan, or from the Spirit of Aslan—"Pneuma the Holy One"—or the Spirit may appear to issue from the Father. The American Lutheran theologian and minister Robert Jenson articulates the rejection of a modalistic subordinationism well, a denial that applies well to the triune framework of the Narniad.[122] Subordinationism is dismissed in orthodox theology as it is in the Narniad; God simply is Father, Son, and Holy Spirit.

The theophanic appearances and the Trinitarian roles may not be obvious but they are there in Lewis's supposition. The inner relations of the triune God have been revealed by the prayers of the Aslan-Christ for the people of Narnia to the Emperor-beyond-the-Sea, and by the gifting of the Holy Spirit into the mind and soul of the faithful Narnians. We can consider in relative depth two examples that constitute a triune statement of self-revelation from the Narniad.

ii. A Trinitarian Revelation: Courage and Hope

We noted briefly above how the Dawn Treader and her crew are saved from a demonic dark cloud that has the power to drive them insane. The cloud and the island it hides have the power to make dreams come true—nightmares—and the crew start to hallucinate and are being overwhelmed by fear. Lucy, "the dear one" appears to be the only one in this dire situation to pray: her prayer is to and through Aslan the second person of the Trinity: "Lucy leant her head on the edge of the fighting top and whispered, 'Aslan, Aslan, if ever you loved us at all, send us help now.' The darkness did not grow any less, but she began to feel a little—a very, very little—better. 'After all, nothing has really happened to us yet,' she thought." In an apparent answer a beam of light appears:

> Lucy looked along the beam and presently saw something in it. At first it looked like a *cross*, then it looked like an airplane, then it looked like a kite, and at last with a whirring of wings it was right overhead and was an albatross. It circled **three times** round the mast and then perched for an instant on the crest of the gilded dragon at the prow. It called out in a strong sweet voice what seemed to be words though no one understood them. After that it spread its wings, rose, and began to fly slowly ahead, bearing a little to starboard. Drinian steered after it not doubting that it offered good guidance. But no one except Lucy knew that as it circled the mast it had whispered to her, "Courage, dear heart," and the voice, she felt sure, was Aslan's, and with the voice a delicious smell breathed in her face.[123] [My emphasis.]

Lewis places intentional clues here as to his meaning. The crew are in deadly peril and suffering, at first Lucy perceive the image of a cross—the means of crucifixion in our world—then it circles three times, a triune statement—it is the triune God. This is a visitation from God, the God who is the Lord of all love crucified, the God of suffering for the creation. Is the albatross real?—or meant to be a vision from "Pneuma the Holy One" using temporal and corporeal means to communicate to the crew and then to

---

122   Jenson, *Systematic Theology*, Vol. 1, Ch. 5 "The Persons of God's Identity."
123   Lewis, *The Voyage of the Dawn Treader*, 200–201.

save them? Aslan as the visible and aural manifestation of the Trinity speaks to Lucy, the "dear one," (comparable with John the beloved disciple), leastwise she hears what she takes for his voice. This is not the same sort of corporeal fleshly manifestation as we find with the second person of the Trinity, when the Aslan-Christ is actually real, as real as any other beast or creature. The albatross is a triune manifestation of the third person of the Trinity: a haunting by the Holy Spirit that can pierce through an evil darkness and save the faithful. There is no conflation or syncretism between the second and third persons here, both are distinct yet part of one divine *person*; there is no modalism here, one does not proceed as the other form ceases. The Father oversees all, the Spirit guides and imparts hope, the second person communicates and reassures.

iii. A Trinitarian Revelation: "I am that I am"

Lewis pulls all the disparate Trinitarian references in the Narniad together in a portrait in *The Horse and His Boy*. This is both a statement of the persons of the Trinity and the reality of their co-existence. There is a judgment in this presence; there is a unity yet diversity of person in this God. In a deliberate invocation of the revelation of God in the book of Exodus Lewis allows the three persons to announce themselves in their own distinct yet unified way, but—crucially—in response to the creature, thus we have the movement from the *immanent* Trinity to the *economic* Trinity. Shasta, a boy of around twelve years of age, has escaped from Calormen, however now exhausted from the adventure he is alone and lost, hungry and near the end of his strength, and making his way over a mountain range. The situation overwhelms him and he starts to cry, feeling sorry for himself. He is shaken out of this reverie by the realization that amidst the fog-bound path, in the darkest of nights, through the mountain, there is someone or somebody else next to him.

> The Thing (or Person) was going so quietly that he could hardly hear any footfalls. What he could hear was breathing. His invisible companion seemed to breathe on a very large scale, and Shasta got the impression that it was a very large creature. And he had come to notice this breathing so gradually that he had really no idea how long it had been there . . .
> The thing (unless it was a Person) went on beside him so very quietly that Shasta began to hope he had only imagined it. But just as he was becoming quite sure of it, there suddenly came a deep, rich sigh out of the darkness beside him. That couldn't be imagination! Anyway, he had felt the hot breath of that sigh on his chilly left hand . . .
> "Who are you?" he said, scarcely above a whisper.
> "One who has waited long for you to speak," said the Thing.
> Its voice was not loud, but very large and deep. . . . Once more he felt the warm breath of the thing on his hand and face.
> "There," it said, "that is not the breath of a ghost. Tell me your sorrows."[124]

---

124   Lewis, *The Horse and His Boy*, 128–29.

Shasta opens up and pours out his life story and his problems: enslaved from a young age in Calormen, escaping across the desert, and all the unfortunate difficulties that ensnared them. The presence reassures him that he was in control all the time and that the difficulties actually helped them escape. But Shasta is still puzzled:

> "Who are you?" asked Shasta.
> "Myself," said the Voice, very deep and low so that the earth shook: and again "Myself," loud and clear and gay: and then the third time "Myself," whispered so softly you could hardly hear it, and yet it seemed to come from all round you as if the leaves rustled with it.
> Shasta was no longer afraid that the Voice belonged to something that would eat him, nor that it was the voice of a ghost. But a new and different sort of trembling came over him. Yet he felt glad too.
> . . . He turned and saw, pacing beside him, taller than the horse, a Lion. The horse did not seem to be afraid of it or else could not see it. It was from the Lion that the light came. No one ever saw anything more terrible or beautiful.[125]

"I am that I am" (Exod 3:14, often "I will be what I will be") becomes simply, in Lewis's portrait, "myself." For Lewis this triune unity is shown in personal distinctness: the power and authority of the Father, the clear joy of the Son, and the ghost-like presence of the Holy Spirit. There is no localized presence but "it seemed to come from all round," therefore the revelation is in time, yet distinct from the temporality of time and space. God is not tied to creation, yet loves the creation; he meets it, but is distinctive, divergent, and discreet, in God's triune persons and separate and dissimilar from the creation (i.e., not Panentheistic). Therefore, this is no impersonal force, no pantheistic life force, but personable, and revealed as three persons. This is no gnostic appearance, no spiritual presence: the breath is real and warm, it is fleshy and corporeal. It is the Son yet it is all three. There is no risk of a modalistic procession here; Lewis is very, very careful in his construction to complement—analogically—an orthodox doctrine of the Trinity. The three statements of "myself" indicate a three-in-one God. However, in keeping with something of a Western tradition, there is procession: the Father utters first, then the Son, then the Holy Spirit. But this is not a modalistic procession because the Father is not replaced by the Son, who then morphs into some sort of manifestation of the Spirit. The three are distinct, co-eternal, and equal, but within the confines of the temporality of a creation one must speak first, and one must speak last. Perhaps this procession relates to the limitations of the creation: the Father initiates, the Son creates, the Holy Spirit upholds and haunts the creation. The perception is tied in with the encounter, which is the revelation: The deity, Aslan, meets with a human individual and reveals God's self through God. This echoes with scripture: it is the Son who reveals the Father, and sends the advocate: "Jesus spoke to his disciples: 'When the Advocate comes, whom I will send to you from the Father, the Spirit of truth who comes from the Father, he will testify on my behalf.'" (John 15:26).

---

125   Ibid., 130 and 131.

11. CONCLUSION: A NARNIAN DOCTRINE OF GOD?

It is easy to forget amidst the theorizing about the *nature* of God as Trinity that God is love, and therefore the triune God Lewis sketches out *is* love. God is love, and such love (ἀγάπη) works *through* people; that is why the Narnian creatures, not merely the humans, are characterized by personhood. The love that is God works through the community of Christians and therefore Lewis will postulate the love of God will work through the sentient creatures in Narnia that are *in*-Aslan, as the redeemed are *in*-Christ in our world. Aslan may be the visible corporeal manifestation—*person*—of God but it is the Holy Spirit, this spirit of love, from all eternity to all eternity that binds and reveals, a love going on between the Father and the Son and the Holy Spirit eternally.

The signature of this love is in us and is heaven.[126] And this love is unpossessive: God loves in freeedom, we respond in freedom and are drawn into heaven, into the triune life of the *immanent* Trinity:

> The golden apple of selfhood, thrown among the false gods, became an apple of discord because they scrambled for it. They did not know the first rule of the holy game, which is that every player must by all means touch the ball and then immediately pass it on. To be found with it in your hands is a fault: to cling to it, death. But when it flies to and fro among the players too swift for eye to follow, and the great master *himself* leads the revelry, giving *himself* eternally to his creatures in the generation, and back to *himself* in the sacrifice, of the Word, then indeed the eternal dance "makes heaven drowsy with the harmony"[127]

Ever loving, ever focusing on the other, heaven is defined by the God of love who is Trinity. The triune God Lewis draws in the Narniad is defined by God's actions in a religious economy—by creativity and love, by forgiveness and grace, by joy. When sinful creatures meet Aslan they repent, are forgiven by the justifying judgment, and dance with joy! Aslan sings creation into being. The Trinity is for Lewis a dance, a drama. The whole dance, or drama, or pattern of this three-Personal life is to be played out in each one of us: or (putting it the other way round) each one of us has got to enter that pattern, take his place in that dance. There is no other way to the happiness for which we were made.[128]

---

126   Lewis, *Problem of Pain*, 121.
127   Ibid., 127.
128   Lewis, *Mere Christianity*, 176–77. See also, Ross, "C. S. Lewis, Augustine, and the Rhythm of the Trinity," 322.

8

Analogical and Symbolic Narratives IV: Salvation, Encounters, and Judgment— the Work of the Aslan-Christ

SYNOPSIS:
If, according to Lewis's supposition, Aslan could be the form taken by the second person of the Trinity in another totally different and separate reality, and if the salvation histories in different disparate created realities converge the closer each gets to the issues at the heart of atonement and salvation, then we may examine what encounters Lewis wrote between God in Christ (Aslan) in Narnia and individual sentient creatures (human or otherwise)—both general and specific—and how these compare analogically with the salvation history and religious economy for humanity in our world. Lewis's Aslan is written in the knowledge of the gospel narrative and is constructed to parallel our economy of God's salvation. We can see how these existential meetings between Aslan and individuals, or even communities, are eschatological. They are often characterized by crisis: reminiscent of Nicodemus's encounter with Jesus (John 3). It is in specific encounters, meetings, that we can extrapolate the nature of salvation. For example, Shasta (*The Horse and his Boy*— Lewis described this book as being about the conversion of a heathen) whose encounter, based in religious ignorance of who and what the Aslan-Christ is, is characterized by repentance and openness in the human, by beauty and forgiveness in God, and is a revelation of the *immanent* Trinity through the corporeal. Likewise Emeth (*The Last Battle*), whose religio-political allegiances appear to condemn him, is saved, which illustrates the loving purposes of God.

Eschatology: what is the nature of the last judgment in Narnia? What does this tell us about our fate? There is a clear assertion of God's authority, but there is sometimes paradox. For example, the characters of Shift the Ape and Puzzle the Donkey, also what we may term, the neo-Kantian, Feuerbachian dwarves (*The Last Battle*). Was Lewis a closeted relativist? Was he subjective? Was he mistaken? If he is right, if he was *inspired* in what he wrote, then what does this tell us about salvation for those who know Christ? But also what does this tell us about salvation for the pagan and heathen, outside of the knowledge of Christ, as an exegesis of Matthew 25?

1. INTRODUCTION

According to Lewis's supposition, the second person of the Trinity could take the form of a lion in another reality, a world outside of our universe but totally different and separate, though in this case related to our reality by human presence. This form— Aslan—is present in Narnia from its foundation. It is the work of the Christ to create.

However, in addition to *his* presence, Aslan is essential for salvation history in this hypothetical reality. If the salvation history between numerous and multifarious, disparate and created realities is marked by distinction, and is defined by localized needs, there will be greater and greater similarities the closer each gets to the issues and needs at the heart of atonement and salvation. Such a convergence is seen in Jesus's agony in the Garden of Gethsemane, and his suffering and humiliation on the cross, as compared to Aslan's agonized and somber walk (the *Via Dolorosa*—"the Way of Grief" or "the Way of Suffering"), to the stone table, his humiliation and execution.[1] This being so we may examine what encounters Lewis wrote between the second person of the Trinity (the Aslan-Christ) and individual sentient creatures (human or otherwise) in Narnia—both general and specific. Lewis's sub-creation—Aslan—is written in the knowledge of the gospel narrative. As such it is constructed to elucidate, to parallel didactically though not ontologically, our economy of God's salvation.

2. THE ASLAN-CHRIST I: LEWIS'S MYTHOPOEIC SUB-CREATION

i. Aslan

So how does Aslan re-present Jesus Christ, as the second person of the Trinity, as God incarnate? The important question is not necessarily about multiple incarnations but do we come to a much deeper, more profound understanding of the incarnation-cross-resurrection through Lewis's Christological portrait. How similar to the form taken by the second person of the Trinity in our reality is this lionized Christ?:

> Well, I think in his religious books you tend to get a rather hard view of God. Now the conception of Aslan, which you have in the children's stories seems to me quite different and seems to me to come from a far deeper level in Lewis's character. Aslan is the deity; it is an extraordinarily original achievement. He has, Aslan has, divine qualities of awe, power and authority, yet he exudes love and is himself somehow intensely lovable, so lovable that it is possible for children to want to embrace him, to put their arms about his neck and kiss him. I think that this is perhaps Lewis's, yes, highest religious achievement.[2]

Aslan is clearly lionized, he is not dressed up to appear. However, there are pertinent question which must be addressed: he appears at will (like the resurrected Christ) yet has no incarnation. What does this imply? Does the form vary?—is this a biblical principle?

---

[1] John 18–19. Lewis, *The Lion, the Witch and the Wardrobe*, 132–41.

[2] Comments from *Beyond Personality—A Memoir of C. S. Lewis*, a documentary broadcast on BBC Radio 4, Sunday Dec. 18, 1988, compiled by Ann Bonsor. Quotation transcribed from a personal recording made from the broadcast in 1988.

8. Analogical and Symbolic Narratives IV: Salvation, Encounters and Judgement

ii. Perception: A Human Model

If humanity ceased to exist all temporal human knowledge of the Christ would go. But that is not the end of the Christ: the incarnation happened, the sacrifice and resurrection, the parables and teaching all happened and were real, but the human mental model—knowledge and understanding—of Jesus, the Christ, would be lost, if all humanity were to cease. But a greater reality would exist, still, because Christ exists from eternity to eternity. Individuals today will have different understandings of Jesus. Some valid, others invalid: with subtle variations between people's perception and mental model. And their perception and model of Jesus will change as they grow and mature, move deeper into faith, or out of faith as apostates and atheists. This is true with the Narniad as an analogy of human perception of the Christ. Individuals in the stories have preconceived ideas of Aslan, who he is and what he does. Some valid; others hold strange ideas. What do these persons know about Aslan, what models of the Aslan-Christ do they hold to?

Dread and Wrath, Terror and Amazement

Lewis writes that Aslan will present himself to individuals when the time is right. Too soon and they will not understand who and what he is. For example, when Coriakin asks Aslan if he will finally present himself to the Dufflepuds, Aslan answers that it is too soon, "'Nay,' said the Lion, with a little half-growl that meant (Lucy thought) the same as a laugh. 'I should frighten them out of their senses.'"[3] Lewis is saying that it is clearly too early in the development of some people for the full revelation of the Christ. One only has to think of the long nurturing God undertook with the ancient Hebrews to prepare them, and then for the early church—indeed the history of the church—in preaching the good news to people. But even then, people may shut out any true understanding and try to explain away providence as serendipity. For example, The Green Witch tries to convince Jill, Eustace, and Puddleglum that what they knew was only an illusion, a projection:

> The Witch shook her head. "I see," she said, "that we should do no better with your lion, as you call it, than we did with your sun. You have seen lamps, and so you imagined a bigger and better lamp and called it the sun. You've seen cats, and now you want a bigger and better cat, and it's to be called a lion. Well, 'tis a pretty make-believe, though, to say truth, it would suit you all better if you were younger. And look how you can put nothing into your make-believe without copying it from the real world, this world of mine, which is the only world . . .[4]

There is, therefore, no Aslan; the witch's skepticism is beguiling but ultimately fails. Skepticism is rife. Trumpkin the dwarf should know better, but cynicism has possessed him and he scorns any mention of Aslan.[5] Like Thomas in John's Gospel, Trumpkin has to face Aslan and his sin. When he learns of Aslan's arrival he fears seeing him, but when he does and by facing the truth about himself he can then accept forgiveness

---

3   Lewis, *The Voyage of the Dawn Treader*, 124–25.
4   Lewis, *The Silver Chair*, 143–44.
5   Lewis, *Prince Caspian*, 111–12.

and redemption.⁶ Nikabrik the dwarf goes further and says he will believe in anything and everything (including personified evil) that will rid him of his enemies.⁷ Nikabrik is lost to evil. Many simply cannot perceive what and who Aslan is (as is true in our reality). Uncle Andrew only hears roars and growls when Aslan speaks.⁸ What should be beauteous to him is only wrath: "He thinks great folly . . . he has made himself unable to hear my voice. If I spoke to him, he would hear only growlings and roarings. Oh Adam's sons, how cleverly you defend yourselves against all that might do you good!"⁹ But even the beloved can through their own sinful defense cause a barrier between themselves and the Christ. Lewis illustrates this in the growing distance and coldness caused by Susan's "growing-up"—her fascination with the superficial glamour and glitter, the lure of vanity and appearances, adult "relationships." Peter and Susan, the oldest of the Pevensie children, on their return to Narnia, cannot see Aslan, when Lucy clearly can, and has just woken up her brothers and sister to go meet *him*. Susan argues that there is nothing to see, Lucy is imagining *him*.¹⁰ Edmund—who on their first visit had been the traitor—cannot see Aslan either but out of faith will trust Lucy as she always was the one to first see and know Aslan and argues they should follow her. After being persuaded, they do set out. Gradually, imperceptibly at first, Peter then Susan begin to get glimpses of Aslan. First his shadow, then moments of perception:

> "Lucy," said Susan in a very small voice.
> "Yes?" said Lucy. "I see him now. I'm sorry."
> "That's all right."
> "But I've been far worse than you know. I really believed it was him—he, I mean—yesterday. When he warned us not to go down to the fir wood. And I really believed it was him tonight, when you woke us up. I mean, deep down inside. Or I could have, if I'd let myself. But I just wanted to get out of the woods and—and—oh, I don't know. And whatever am I to say to him?"¹¹

When they meet Aslan Susan hangs back: "After an awful pause, the deep voice said, 'Susan.' Susan made no answer but the others thought she was crying. 'You have listened to fears, child,' said Aslan. 'Come, let me breathe on you. Forget them. Are you brave again?' 'A little, Aslan,' said Susan."¹² Even the faithful in church can fall away, set-up barriers around their religious ego to protect themselves, inadvertently sometimes, from God in Christ. Lewis knew this, observed it amongst his fellows at Oxford as well as amongst ordinary people at his parish church in Headington. As Lewis noted, all get what they want but may not like what they get.¹³ Susan is an analogy of the lapsed, the apostate, who live happily without the Christ, but may not always understand the consequences of their actions that issue from going it alone (which is the *fall*, again):

6   Ibid., 132–34.
7   Ibid., 70.
8   Lewis, *The Magician's Nephew*, 116–17.
9   Ibid., 158.
10 Lewis, *Prince Caspian*, 128.
11 Ibid., 132.
12 Ibid., 133.
13 Lewis, *The Magician's Nephew*, 162.

8. Analogical and Symbolic Narratives IV: Salvation, Encounters and Judgement

"My sister Susan," answered Peter shortly and gravely, "is no longer a friend of Narnia." "Yes," said Eustace, "and whenever you've tried to get her to come and talk about Narnia or do anything about Narnia, she says, 'What wonderful memories you have! Fancy your still thinking about all those funny games we used to play when we were children.'" "Oh Susan!" said Jill. "She's interested in nothing nowadays except nylons and lipstick and invitations. She always was a jolly sight too keen on being grown-up." "Grown-up, indeed," said the Lady Polly. "I wish she would grow up. She wasted all her school time wanting to be the age she is now, and she'll waste all the rest of her life trying to stay that age. Her whole idea is to race on to the silliest time of one's life as quick as she can and then stop there as long as she can."[14]

There is symbolism in the four Pevensie children: one is a traitor to Christ, but repents (Edmund—who becomes wise and just); another understands the importance of authority as bequeathed by God (the high king Peter); Lucy is the holy innocent, the fool for God even when others doubt her; and Susan—like the Parable of the Seed and the Sower—takes the Word (the Aslan-Christ) with joy and pride, but *falls* away, is lost. Does the symbolism mirror the church, the people who constitute the church? Can we see subtle varying degrees of these four in churchgoers, and how they perceive the Christ? Is Lewis giving us a template, a model?

Distance can so easily turn to setting up our own empire which excludes God. This is what the fall was about. Given authority, power, and status, will people classify good as evil, effectively a holy inversion. Rabadash, the first-born son of the Tisroc (effectively the king of Calormen) is not blind to Aslan but condemns him: "'Demon! Demon! Demon!' shrieked the Prince. 'I know you. You are the foul fiend of Narnia. You are the enemy of the gods. Learn who I am, horrible phantasm.'"[15] This is, of course, true; Christ is the enemy, so to speak, of all the *false* "gods" that draw people away from the one true God. Rabadash is convinced he, like Roman Emperors, is divine, and despite Aslan's will that he should accept the forgiveness, in repentance, from those he has sorely wronged, Rabadash insists on condemning Aslan. In this he condemns himself (an example of Lewis's Arminianism we will encounter in depth later): reject the truth of God's revelation and we invent truth in our own image; reject the love of God and we will experience God's forgiveness as wrath, and in that wrath be condemned, which then reflects God's will and judgment on us

Inevitably this leads to the perception of the love and goodness of God in Christ as fear and wrath, which in turn leads to hatred, and back to self-justification. This is probably best symbolized, analogically, by Lewis in the scene leading up to Aslan's sacrifice on the stone table. The venomous hatred, the teasing and belittling, the taunts and jibes, the humiliation and cruelty, the pain and suffering, the depths of affliction all focused onto the Aslan-Christ for what? Simply because *he* is who *he* is. They have a right perception, a right judgment, in basis, but it leads them to condemn the Aslan-Christ: simply because what he represents and who *he* is. Aslan is shorn, muzzled, tied

---

14   Lewis, *The Last Battle*, 127–28.
15   Lewis, *The Horse and his Boy*, 170.

with bitterly painful ropes, he submits when he could so easily have defeated all his assailants, finally Aslan is pierced to the heart by the White Witch wielding a stone knife.[16] Their perception of the ferocity and wrath of God is then, post-resurrection, turned on them: Aslan confronts the White Witch and annihilates her in an instant: she is reduced to nothingness, but a consciousness that persists and subsists. In the moment of her end, the White Witch cannot believe what is happening as she is faced by the resurrected Aslan, in a moment she knows and faces all she has been and done, believed and denied: "With a roar that shook all Narnia from the western lamp-post to the shores of the eastern sea the great beast flung himself upon the White Witch. Lucy saw her face lifted toward him for one second with an expression of terror and amazement."[17]

A Troubling Presence, An Enfleshed Form

Though fully enfleshed within the confines of an alternate reality, Aslan appears to take different forms. These is a resemblance here to the resurrection appearances. At first Mary did not recognize the resurrected Jesus; neither did the disciples on the Emmaus road. Lewis is not postulating a syncretistic relativism. Each theophany, each incarnate appearance, is in accordance with what the individual is able to *perceive*, and what s/he is able to comprehend and take. This relates to *expectations*, preconceptions. The Narnian horse Bree, when challenged about the precise nature of Aslan comments that of course he is not really a beast, he is referred to as a lion because he is lion-like. Bree, who has never consciously met Aslan, projects what is essentially a Docetic Christology—he does not expect him to be enfleshed; Aslan is too important and too divine to be a mere beast.[18] When Lucy successfully makes the Dufflepuds visible, along with everything else in Coriakin's house, Aslan also appears commenting that he had been there all the time. When Lucy queries this, that through her will and a magic spell she could make him visible or invisible, Aslan comments that, "Do you think I wouldn't obey my own rules?"[19] This is the creator in creation; not an avatar, or an apparition, not a fleshless Docetic form.[20] This is real; as the incarnation is real. As an incarnate God, Aslan obeys the rules of the creation he has created. Lucy notes on several occasions that Aslan seems bigger. His response is that *he* has not changed, but she has, and as she grows, matures, her perception of him will change.[21] Again, is this subjective relativism on Lewis's part? Or does it concur with the resurrection appearances in the Gospels? Does it also concur with how our understanding of the reality of Jesus of Nazareth changes with our maturity, and with our relationship with the risen and ascended Christ? But it is not simply expectations which govern

16   Lewis, *The Lion, the Witch and the Wardrobe*, 138–41.
17   Ibid., 160–61.
18   Lewis, *The Horse and his Boy*, 156–57.
19   Lewis, *The Voyage of the Dawn Treader*, 123.
20   The relationship between the actual incarnation on the one hand, and prefigurements on the other, which were often avatars, myths, or super-powerful Docetic "gods," is examined in depth in the second book in this series. See, *C. S. Lewis—The Work of Christ Revealed*, Pt. 3, Ch. 9.
21   Lewis, *Prince Caspian*, 124.

8. Analogical and Symbolic Narratives IV: Salvation, Encounters and Judgement

our perception of the Christ. Given the enchanted nature of Narnia Aslan is always more real than perhaps we expect. And so God takes form to meet people (humans, talking animals, creatures) according to what the conditions allow, but this still relates to perception. For example, when the Dawn Treader is lost in a massive dark cloud, an enveloping darkness, from which it cannot escape, and is trapped in a manifold evil, Lucy prays to Aslan to save them. After a while a shaft of light breaks through the cloud, and she sees an albatross. The albatross guides them out, however, "no one except Lucy knew that as it circled the mast it had whispered to her, 'Courage, dear heart,' and the voice, she felt sure, was Aslan's, and with the voice a delicious smell breathed in her face."[22] The form is a result of practical needs: a dense impenetrable dark evil cloud in the middle of the ocean is no place for a lion! This albatross, as we noted earlier, is a triune manifestation of the third person of the Trinity that speaks through Aslan's voice: a haunting by the Holy Spirit, which can pierce through an evil darkness and save the faithful. Later in *The Voyage of the Dawn Treader*, at their final meeting, Lucy and Edmund see a lamb appear that then transfigures into the lion they know so well.[23] The form of the lamb is to remind Lucy and Edmund that Aslan is in their reality—Christ, the sacrificial lamb (Rev 13:8). In *The Horse and his Boy*, Shasta is forced to shelter amongst some ancient tombs outside the Calormen city of Tashbaan. He is befriended in the night by a small cat. This is not the right time for Aslan to reveal himself to the boy; however, he is in mortal danger. Shasta wakes and becomes aware of a lion near the far edge of the tombs frightening-off some jackals or hyenas, which have picked up his Shasta's scent. The lion then turns and comes for him. But as it approaches he realizes that it is only a cat, the cat that had befriended him. The cat looked at him knowingly, clearly understanding what Shasta said to it.[24] This cat is later revealed to have been Aslan.[25]

Fear and Trembling, Hidden and Apophatic

In *The Great Divorce* Lewis presents a hidden apophatic Christ, known but not seen, not tangible, haunting the unredeemed like a memory they want to escape from. In *The Screwtape Letters* this is even worse: Christ, this apophatic hidden Christ, despite his absence from hell, is a threatening presence to the evil machinations of Screwtape. *The Screwtape Letters* and *The Great Divorce*,[26] reveal some truths, analogically, about the human predicament in relation to the immensity of God's justice These two works are imbued with a sound Christology and understanding of revelation. Christ is present, obliquely, throughout both works; Christ is hidden, *he* is a colossal and substantial presence that presses on the inhabitants of hell and "purgatory." The perception of Christ is veiled and sublimated; there is an awesome and terrible holy presence that threatens. We can place Christ behind Screwtape, the senior devil, threatening his

---

22   Lewis, *The Voyage of the Dawn Treader*, 142–45.
23   Ibid., 186–88.
24   Lewis, *The Horse and his Boy*, 70–75.
25   Ibid., 130.
26   See: Lewis, *Screwtape Letters*, and, Lewis, *The Great Divorce*.

demonic plans and machinations; Christ fills him with loathing, for without Christ he would never have existed, and now without God he would cease to be or have anything to focus on or hate. This apophatic hidden Christ is also the "bleeding" charity that stands ever open to forgive people their stupid arrogant sins in *The Great Divorce*, if only they will have the courage—*post mortem*, for all this happens after death in a state of "purgation"—if only they would have the will, the audacity, the faith, but above all the courage, to step forth out of the hell they have created, to step beyond their tiny little republics where they believe they reign supreme and journey the pilgrimage, however painful it will be at first, towards and into the Christ. It is the sins, the unrepented evil, or these dead people, postulates Lewis, that cause their perception of the Christ to be a threatening presence; this is part of the inversion that is *the fall*.

The apophatic Christ that underpins, threatens, in *The Screwtape Letters* and *The Great Divorce*, is threatening those in hell and a state of purgation. For Lewis hell is a state of mind more than a physical geographic reality (but still issues from the judgment of God), and all turned in on themselves are in hell; heaven by comparison is not a state of mind. Heaven is real; it is a fully real reality: therefore, for Lewis, there is still choice after death. It is not important whether we name this a state of purgation or identify something of a reality (the medieval purgatory), partial and incomplete by comparison with heaven. What is important is the state of loss and regret that possesses the near to nothing existence that these damned souls must endure and who languish outside of Christ. By comparison the redeemed are those in whom flows an "abundance of life in Christ from the Father." [27] For Christ is the King of Justice and their High Priest.[28]

The perception of Aslan by the four Pevensie children—the sons of Adam and the daughters of Eve, even though they have never heard of him before their arrival in Narnia, is indicative of humanity's perception of the Christ: some intuitively love him, others loathe him. This initial response (Peter, Susan and Lucy's, then Edmund's) at the mention of Aslan by Mr. Beaver sets the plot and story as it unfolds: Edmund's loathes the name and betrays his siblings to the White Witch; the others love the sound of his name:

> "They say Aslan is on the move—perhaps has already landed." And now a very curious thing happened. None of the children knew who Aslan was any more than you do; but the moment the Beaver had spoken these words everyone felt quite different. Perhaps it has sometimes happened to you in a dream that someone says something which you don't understand but in the dream it feels as if it had some enormous meaning—either a terrifying one which turns the whole dream into a nightmare or else a lovely meaning too lovely to put into words, which makes the dream so beautiful that you remember it all your life and are always wishing you could get into that dream again. It was like that now. At the name of Aslan each one of the children felt something jump in its inside. Edmund felt a sensation of mysterious horror. Peter felt suddenly brave and adventurous. Susan felt as if some delicious smell or some delightful strain

---

27 Lewis, *The Great Divorce*, 91.
28 Ibid., 87.

8. Analogical and Symbolic Narratives IV: Salvation, Encounters and Judgement

of music had just floated by her. And Lucy got the feeling you have when you wake up in the morning and realize that it is the beginning of the holidays or the beginning of summer.[29]

Later, in conversation, after the shock revelation that Aslan is not a man but a beast, "the Son of the great Emperor-beyond-the-Sea,"[30] the King of Beasts, the great lion, any comforting religious stereotypes they might have are denied: "'Safe?' said Mr. Beaver . . . 'Course he isn't safe. But he's good. He's the King, I tell you."[31] What is more he is "not a tame lion,"[32] he is not a pet idol or god to be safely controlled and contained. Lucy may be called beloved and dear one by Aslan but she reaches the limits of human understanding and at times simply does not know Aslan. Aslan may be revealing of himself to her, but all revelation is both an unveiling and a veiling, only post-*eschaton* will we know how we should know;[33] we can never fully know and understand another person. When Lucy finally "sees" Aslan and goes to him in *Prince Caspian*, she is taken aback at the low almost imperceptible growl, which she did not expect, even though she tells herself she knows his moods.[34] By comparison Peter's response is more formal and worshipful.

Beauty and Love, Grief and Intensity

Aslan is not simply a word picture of Christ, or a Christ-like figure. He *is* the Christ, as Macbeth is a character that mirrors, in a limited way, someone in the real world. Language allows a description—an analogy—that generates in our mind a valid understanding of the Christ, inspired, illumined, gifted pneumatologically. Lewis lays great stress in his apologetics and philosophical theology on the raising up of the human into the divine life; Christ's descent to reascend carrying with him the *fallen human*.[35] This being so, as an individual in Christ is drawn more and more into the Christlike divine life, s/he will become less and less comprehensible to the powers and principalities of this world. By resituating this dilemma in *Till We Have Faces*,[36] Psyche's sister Orual, perceives her own spiritual ugliness but regards Psyche's deep beauty of person as puzzling and paradoxical, to a degree. Psyche is sacrificed to the pagan god of the mountain for the benefit of the people. Orual, only for a moment, recognizes the castle—the paradise—in which her sister lives; but she regards this perception as a momentary illusion. The beauty and love of Christ and the redeemed will ever be a paradox to the people enslaved to this world and to Satan the tempter;

---

29   Lewis, *The Lion, the Witch and the Wardrobe*, 65.
30   Ibid., 75.
31   Ibid.
32   See: Ibid., 166; *The Voyage of the Dawn Treader*, 125. Also, *The Last Battle*, 20–21, 24, 29, 32, and, 72–73.
33   1 Cor 13:9–10.
34   Lewis, *Prince Caspian*, 124–27.
35   Lewis, "Introduction". In, *St. Athanasius, The Incarnation of the Word*, 5–12. See, This is dealt with in the first two books in this series: *C. S. Lewis—Revelation, Conversion, and Apologetics*, Ch. 10, §.2.vii; also, *C. S. Lewis—The Work of Christ Revealed*, Pt. 3 Ch. 11, §.i–ii.
36   Lewis, *Till We Have Faces*, Pt. 1, Chs. 9 and 10, specifically 75f.

Christlike spiritual beauty will so often, mistakenly, be confused with fleshly vanity, or something of no consequence.

Lewis invokes the language of beauty and mystery, color and creativity, and the intensity of love, but also the depth of grief, unspoken hidden grief, when writing of the ultimate path of Christlikeness. This is Lewis's method expressed through the genre of analogical and symbolic narrative, at its most complete and unreserved. For example, when Digory confesses his fear for his dying mother, he is surprised to see how much Aslan empathizes with him:

> "But please, please—won't you—can't you give me something that will cure Mother?"
>
> Up till then he had been looking at the Lion's great feet and the huge claws on them; now, in his despair, he looked up at its face. What he saw surprised him as much as anything in his whole life. For the tawny face was bent down near his own and (wonder of wonders) great shining tears stood in the Lion's eyes. They were such big, bright tears compared with Digory's own that for a moment he felt as if the Lion must really be sorrier about his Mother than he was himself.
>
> "My son, my son," said Aslan. "I know. Grief is great. Only you and I in this land know that yet."[37]

As the crucifixion is the center of our reality, and of Christlikeness, so at the center of the Narniad is Aslan's sacrifice. Susan and Lucy accompany Aslan on his way to sacrifice, though they have no idea why he is so sad, so preoccupied, or where and what he is going to: "His great, royal head drooped so that his nose nearly touched the grass. Presently he stumbled and gave a low moan. . . . And so the girls did what they would never have dared to do without his permission, but what they had longed to do ever since they first saw him—buried their cold hands in the beautiful sea of fur and stroked it and, so doing, walked with him."[38] Shasta's Damascus Road meeting generates an encounter beyond words where he perceives of Aslan in the beauty and magnificence of God. The form of a lion, unique to Narnia for the second person of the Trinity, becomes changed—post-*eschaton*—as Aslan and the redeemed approach deeper into heaven and eternity, indicating the common source between Jesus, for Lewis, and Aslan.[39]

3. THE ASLAN-CHRIST II: ENCOUNTERS

i. *The Nature of the Encounters*

Lewis's Aslan is written in the knowledge of the gospel narrative and is constructed to elucidate, to parallel didactically though not ontologically, the economy of God's salvation. Written into this are existential meetings between Aslan and individuals

---

37 Lewis, *The Magician's Nephew*, 131.
38 Lewis, *The Lion, the Witch and the Wardrobe*, 135–36.
39 Lewis, *The Last Battle*, 171.

8. Analogical and Symbolic Narratives IV: Salvation, Encounters and Judgement

or even communities. These meetings are eschatological, they are often characterized by crisis, and matters coming to a head for the individual involved: they must decide and go one way or the other—for and to Aslan, or against him. In these encounters are a judgment by Aslan on the person's sins and life. These meetings are reminiscent of Nicodemus' encounter with Jesus in John's gospel. These people-creatures can turn one way or the other: they can turn to Aslan, or away. There are many encounters with Narnians who believe in Aslan. However, there are other encounters between people-creatures who have not heard of Aslan, or hold diametric religious beliefs, or are explicitly hostile to Aslan having been given a false picture of him. These encounters illustrate to a degree Lewis's belief about the intimations given to the pagans that we have been considering, and how God's salvific actions through Christ relate to, in this instance, the North European pagan tribes. We can consider two examples—Shasta and Emeth.

ii. Encounters: An Awesome Meeting

Creaturely perception of the Aslan-Christ is one thing; encountering is another. Lewis's conversion was about an encounter, being confronted by the risen and ascended Christ, at the most opportune moment in Lewis's life—and his reluctance to give in:

> You must picture me alone in that room in Magdalen, night after night, feeling, whenever my mind lifted even for a second from my work, the steady unrelenting approach of Him whom I so earnestly desired not to meet. That which I greatly feared had at last come upon me. In the Trinity Term of 1929 I gave in, and admitted that God was God, and knelt and prayed: perhaps that night, the most dejected and reluctant convert in all of England.[40]

The Narniad is full of encounters. These are based on Lewis's experience; but also drawn from other people's experience of the Christ, and from pagan myths where Christ is veiled, hidden. Crucially, all sentient creatures must come before Aslan in the Last Judgment, as we must before Christ, for by no other name are we judged and saved, *in potential*. However, as in our reality, Christ may confront people before death, to give them a chance of acceptance or rejection. This is so with the Narniad and these encounters are supposed to reflect, to a degree, the religious economy of our reality. But this is presented with the sort of differences that cohere with the imagined reality of Narnia, such is the internal logic of Lewis's supposal. For example, at their first meeting (we know not of what encounters may have transpired in Charn in the past[41]) during the creation of Narnia, Jadis, the White Witch, tries to kill Aslan, such is the threat he poses to her evil plans; but she fails.[42] At their second encounter she demands her rights: the handing over of the traitor Edmund.[43] At their third encounter

---

40   Lewis, *Surprised by Joy*, 221. For a detailed analysis of Lewis's protracted conversion(s), see the first book in this series: C. S. Lewis—Revelation, Conversion and Apologetics.
41   Lewis, *The Magician's Nephew*, 53f.
42   Ibid., 99–100.
43   Lewis, *The Lion, the Witch and the Wardrobe*, 126–31.

she tortures and humiliates, then sacrifices Aslan in Edmund's place.[44] So far Aslan *allows* her to set the agenda, call the shots, however, as we noted earlier, at the fourth meeting she is annihilated by the resurrected Aslan because of what she had done to him and to his creation—she gets her just rewards.[45]

Edmund's first encounter with Aslan—days after his brother and sisters—epitomizes traditional orthodox Christian soteriology. In repentance Aslan judges him—a justifying forgiving judgment. Edmund is rescued from the White Witch. He comes alone before Aslan. No one else is near. Despite the fact that treason, Edmund's treason, is a very public sin, he faces Aslan in solitude with no one listening in. He must confess, look on Aslan face-to-face, and repent. He does; in perceiving the ferocity, the magnanimity of Aslan, he is forgiven: a justifying and loving, a forgiving judgment, because he has faced the full depravity of his sin, and accepted Aslan's judgment on him—which is not pleasant—and in that judgment is forgiveness.[46] This is the soteriological model throughout the Narniad. If created persons face this they are redeemed and live; if they shy away from it they are unforgiven and face death. This is also the model in Lewis's apologetics and philosophical theology which we will examine in the final chapters of this work.

In a deliberate invocation of the iconography of sacrifice in the Old Testament, the *agnus Dei*, and the resurrection appearances (the miraculous catch of fish in John's Gospel), Lewis has Lucy, Edmund, and Eustace at the end of *The Voyage of the Dawn Treader* meet Aslan—as a lamb.

> "Come and have breakfast," said the Lamb in its sweet, milky voice. Then they noticed for the first time that there was a fire lit on the grass and fish roasting on it. They sat down and ate the fish, hungry now for the first time for many days. And it was the most delicious food they had ever tasted.
>
> "Please, Lamb," said Lucy, "is this the way to Aslan's country?"
>
> "Not for you," said the Lamb. "For you the door into Aslan's country is from your own world."
>
> "What!" said Edmund. "Is there a way into Aslan's country from our world too?"
>
> "There is a way into my country from all the worlds," said the Lamb, but as he spoke, his snowy white flushed into tawny gold and his size changed and he was Aslan himself, towering above them and scattering light from his mane.
>
> "Oh, Aslan," said Lucy. "Will you tell us how to get into your country from our world?"
>
> "I shall be telling you all the time," said Aslan. "But I will not tell you how long or short the way will be; only that it lies across a river. But do not fear that, for I am the great Bridge Builder. And now come; I will open the door in the sky and send you to your own land."[47]

---

44 Ibid., 132–41.
45 Ibid., 160–61.
46 Ibid., 126. See, for example, Terry, *The Justifying Judgement of God*.
47 Lewis, *The Voyage of the Dawn Treader*, 186–88.

8. Analogical and Symbolic Narratives IV: Salvation, Encounters and Judgement

Upon learning that they are not to return to Narnia again, Lucy and Edmund plead with Aslan: "'It isn't Narnia, you know,' sobbed Lucy. 'It's you. We shan't meet you there. And how can we live, never meeting you?' 'But you shall meet me, dear one,' said Aslan. 'Are—are you there too, Sir?' said Edmund. "I am," said Aslan. 'But there I have another name. You must learn to know me by that name.'"[48]

Lewis is deliberately making the connection in the minds of his readers (children) between Aslan and Christ, the internal logic of supposal. There is also the fluidity of form: what is an idea in our reality (the *agnus Dei*) is real in another reality (the lamb that greets them), and however much the incarnate presence is real, fleshly and vulnerable, it is so because of the will of God, and is in the power and control of God always: the temptation in the wilderness—turn rocks into bread (Matt 4:3–4); the garden of Gethsemane—invoke a legion of angels to smite oppressors (Matt 26:53); come down from the cross and save yourself (Mark 15:30; Matt 27:40 and 42). There was always the potential to exercise the omnipotence of God in Jesus, but, a kenotic incarnation is characterized by humility and submission, powerlessness and service to others.

4. THE ASLAN-CHRIST III: PAGAN ENCOUNTERS

Specific examples of these encounters can be read from *The Horse and His Boy*, which recounts a time in Narnia under the rule of the four Pevensie children, a time happening just after *The Lion, the Witch and the Wardrobe*. The plot concerns the travels to Narnia, the escape, from a neighboring country named Calormen, of two young people, around twelve to thirteen years of age. One is a high-born princess who seeks to escape an arranged marriage to an old man; the other is a peasant boy who having been adopted by a fisherman seeks to escape being sold into slavery. During their travels and adventures, both, separately and individually meet with the Aslan-Christ at the most opportune moment in their lives.

i. Encounters: Shasta and Aravis, Bree and Hwin

Shasta—The Conversion of a Pagan?

We mentioned earlier a character named Shasta, in the context of a Trinitarian statement by Lewis. We can examine what Lewis has to say here further, and what it tells us about how the triune God the Father courts and redeems individuals, through the Holy Spirit (Pneuma the Holy One), in the presence of Christ (Aslan). Shasta is a boy who runs away from his adoptive father (a fisherman in Calormen who found him adrift in a boat—Shasta is really the first born son of the King of Archenland, but this is not known till near the end of the story) who is persuaded to trade him as a slave.[49] Shasta is raised in ignorance and treated as an unpaid servant by his adoptive father. He

---

48 Ibid., 88.
49 Lewis, *The Horse and His Boy*

flees to Narnia with the aid of a Narnian talking horse, Bree, in the company of Aravis, a Calormen high-born princess. Shasta's religious education is in whatever names and ideas he has picked up in conversation with the rural peasants and fishermen he lives amongst. None of this religious knowledge has any effect on him, yet, despite the cruel upbringing he is a kind, forgiving and generous boy. After many heroic adventures, and crossing, alone, the fog-bound mountains into Narnia he becomes aware of a presence by his side. This is for Shasta, a Damascus Road encounter. At first he wonders if it is a ghost, a ghoul, or some monstrous creature. As time passes it does not attack him, and he is more and more concerned, he can hear it moving alongside him; he can sense it sigh and can feel the warm breath on his arm. He eventually plucks up the courage to speak to it, to enquire who or what the thing is: "'Who are you?' he said, scarcely above a whisper. 'One who has waited long for you to speak,' said the Thing. Its voice was not loud, but very large and deep. . . . Once more he felt the warm breath of the Thing on his hand and face. 'There,' it said, 'that is not the breath of a ghost. Tell me your sorrows.'"[50] Shasta shares his woes and troubles from a cruel and bitter childhood—the thing comforts him and explains that it was he all along who has guided Shasta and Aravis in their escape, and protected him on many occasions. When he presses the thing to explain why he treated the others differently, even harshly, the voice explains:

> "I was the lion who forced you to join with Aravis. I was the cat who comforted you among the houses of the dead. I was the lion who drove the jackals from you while you slept. I was the lion who gave the horses the new strength of fear for the last mile so that you should reach King Lune in time. And I was the lion you do not remember who pushed the boat in which you lay, a child near death, so that it came to shore where a man sat, wakeful at midnight, to receive you." "Then it was you who wounded Aravis?" "It was I." "But what for?" "Child," said the voice, "I am telling you your story, not hers. I tell no one any story but his own."[51]

Despite his religious ignorance of who or what Aslan is, Shasta trusts this *being* implicitly. He slips his feet from the stirrups, dismounts and falls in worship before Aslan. In seeing Aslan—face to face—he was silent. He could not say anything, neither did he want to say anything: the face he perceived was both terrible and beautiful. In answer to his thought more than a question—Who are you? Lewis then gives us the tripartite *I am* statement that we noted earlier: the three declarations of *I am* that reflect the Father, the Son, and the Holy Spirit (The Emperor-beyond-the-Sea; Aslan, and, Pneuma the Holy One). So far this encounter has merely established a relationship between the second person of the Trinity, and Shasta: between creator and created. Once the relationship is established, the encounter becomes a deeply mystical experience:

> The mist was turning from black to grey and from grey to white . . . the whiteness around him became a shining whiteness; his eyes began to blink. He could see

---

50   Ibid., 129.
51   Ibid., 130.

8. Analogical and Symbolic Narratives IV: Salvation, Encounters and Judgement

> the mane and ears and head of his horse quite easily now. A golden light fell on them from the left. He thought it was the sun.
>
> It was from the Lion that the light came. No one ever saw anything more terrible or beautiful . . . after one glance at the Lion's face he slipped out of the saddle and fell at its feet. He couldn't say anything but then he didn't want to say anything, and he knew he needn't say anything.
>
> The High King above all kings stooped towards him. Its mane, and some strange and solemn perfume that hung about the mane, was all round him. It touched his forehead with its tongue. He lifted his face and their eyes met. Then instantly the pale brightness of the mist and the fiery brightness of the Lion rolled themselves together into a swirling glory and gathered themselves up and disappeared. He was alone with the horse on a grassy hillside under a blue sky. And there were birds singing.[52]

This is a picture of a truly incarnate God, not because of the mysticism Lewis invokes, but precisely because "the swirling glory," of "fiery brightness" are an incarnational manifestation: God and the world, not fused into one, but co-operating, co-inhabiting, flesh and reality intermingled; the individual entity of each is not lost, not annihilated. This evokes what incarnation is about: God linked to the world, to the creation, but not dependent or trapped, not possessed by the world. To be otherwise would be Panentheistic; God is in the world at God's choice, God loves the world in freedom. What we have here is a hint, a glimmer, of how the human is drawn up into the triune communion that is the three persons of God in the immanent Trinity. Love that denies itself by focusing ever on the other and in that *agape* returns to the lover in a communion of wonder and beauty and glory. Response is part of God's revelation; that is, our relationship with this God colors our understanding. There is awe and trembling, rightly so, but in Shasta's case there is no guilt over unrepented sins. If he has done wrong, he knows it, and repents of it before the Aslan-Christ: "Shasta was no longer afraid. . . . But a new and different sort of trembling came over him. Yet he felt glad too."[53] The encounter is redemptive and triune. But this is no modalistic diversity or sequence of revelation (i.e., three separate gods, each announcing itself one after the other). This is a triune unity even though it has revealed itself as three. It is three in one: beauty and love characterize this Trinitarian statement. But that is not how all perceive God in Narnia. Others will know of the wrathful judgment of God. But how unrepentant sinners perceive of God is not a correct judgment, a right reflection of the true nature of God. But this is the true perception, and it is possible in a created individual who is not weighed down by un-repented sins and guilt. The key to the revelation of God is in *The Christ*.

So a pagan unbeliever—who from ignorance and geographical isolation knows nothing ("he knew none of the true stories about Aslan, the great Lion, the son of the Emperor-over-the-sea, the King above all High Kings in Narnia."[54])—meets with Aslan, at the right moment in his life (cf. John 3) and is born again. Everything that

---

52 Ibid., 130–31
53 Ibid.
54 Ibid., 131.

Shasta has done and believed, all he is responsible for, is contained in that moment. In that moment what guilt there is from sins is washed away (this would not be so if his sins were great and if he had become corrupted and possessed by evil), he is lost for words, yet in the look of love that passes between them, no words are required (unlike the apostle Peter's embarrassed response to the transfiguration, worriedly suggesting they should built a shelter, rearrange the furniture[55]). Shasta has clearly been influenced by Aslan's Spirit in the past—more pertinently, by the Holy Spirit—so that what good there is in him is preveniently generated (Pneuma the Holy One) and so it is God who has brought him to God, and it is God who has forgiven him because of God's sacrifice, and it is God who breathes new life in him. Shasta could have resisted in his willfulness this prevenient action (Pneuma the Holy One), but he had not.

Lewis described *The Horse and His Boy* as being about "the calling and conversion of a heathen."[56] Shasta's religious education has corrupted him from a true understanding of Aslan, yet when he eventually meets Aslan, religious concepts and words become irrelevant: he senses and perceives the beauty and love of God incarnate, the fiery brightness and swirling glory, and knows that all he must do is respond in love and gratitude, obedience and commitment. Is Lewis asserting that many pagans will not only have led lives under the grace, protection and influence of Christ but also, preveniently speaking (the subtle and secretive influence of Pneuma the Holy One), had become people who were ready and able to respond to Christ should he choose to reveal himself to them? This encounter is in many ways a narrative we have from Lewis that forms an answer to questions raised by the pagan myths that were so prominent in his doctrine of Christological prefiguration: the pagans would have encountered God in the form of the Holy Spirit, breathing Christ's new life into them; in addition, the pagan myths recounted such encounters, the hearing of which (remembering that this was an oral tradition) might have generated a prevenient baptism by the Holy Spirit in the hearer.

Aravis—The Conversion of a Religious?[57]

How does Shasta's encounter compare with Aravis's? Aravis accompanies Shasta on his escape. Leastwise, first, the horse Bree, reveals to Shasta that he is a Narnian talking beast and together they can escape to Narnia (captured as a foal, he has hidden his true nature; now, as a war horse for a rich and powerful Tarkaan, he can defend and sustain such a journey with Shasta as his rider). One night Bree and Shasta meet Aravis and Hwin. Aravis is royalty, but does not want to be forced into marrying an elderly powerful politician. Hwin, like Bree, a Narnian talking horse, captured in youth, can also see the opportunity to escape to Narnia. She persuades Aravis not to commit suicide but escape with her. The four meet one night trying to flee from lions alongside a river

---

55   Matt 17:1–9; Mark 9:2–8; Luke 9:28–36. See also 2 Pet 1:16–18.
56   Lewis to Anne Jenkins, Mar 5, 1961. *Collected Letters, Vol. III*, 1245.
57   The intention here in referring to Aravis as "a religious" is explicitly to compare her with a man or woman under monastic vows. Her religious behaviour defines her life even though she is a typical teenage girl in some ways.

8. Analogical and Symbolic Narratives IV: Salvation, Encounters and Judgement

estuary. Together they travel, having many adventures. Aravis's religious education in Calormen has been in the cult of Tash—reminiscent of the religions characteristic of the mighty nations that surrounded and preyed on the Ancient Hebrews. This is something of an established religion at the heart of the body politic in Calormen. In the Temple in Tashbaan the golden statue of Tash is in the form of a giant bird of prey with multiple arms/limbs, people are sacrificed to Tash, this "god" Tash feeds on human blood. Aravis is dutiful and respectful to the Tash religion; in addition, she has been taught that Narnia is a land of evil magic ruled by a sorcerer in the "malevolent form of a lion" (Aslan). Aravis's religious life is dominated by the Tash religion, which castigates Aslan as a demon and his followers in Narnia as primitive, superstitious heathens. Aravis displays haughtiness and superiority, arrogance and pride towards lesser people (especially slaves and peasants). In planning her escape she drugs her servant so she oversleeps, allowing Aravis to escape. The servant is then subjected to a beating, whipped across her back for over-sleeping.[58]

Aravis's relationship with Aslan, more pertinently the Holy Spirit (it is crucial to remember that all sentient creatures are created to know and love God, and this relationship is triune), is hidden. It is also compromised and confused in with her relationship with other spiritual forces relating to the religion of Tash, many are dark and demonic, for example, her "secret sacrifices to Zardeenah, Lady of the Night."[59] Aslan's influence on her is there. For example, the "lion" frightens her horse into changing direction alongside the estuary so as to meet and join up with Bree and Shasta. Her meeting with Tarkheena Lasaraleen was no coincidence, given the crucial information she learns when inadvertently overhearing the conversation between the Tisroc and Rabadash and their plans for an invasion of Archenland and Narnia. The Spirit of Aslan and the Emperor-over-the-Sea, presses on Aravis and influences her, but many of her actions are contrary to the will of God, yet she is "steered," preveniently (by Pneuma the Holy One), prior to her own thoughts and decisions. However, all does not go well when she eventually comes face-to-face with Aslan: her own Damascus Road encounter. Bree and Shasta, Hwin and Aravis, make it across the desert into Archenland (Narnia's neighbor) but they need to get to the Hermit of the Southern March before Rabadash's army has crossed the desert. They are attacked by a lion. This is Aslan, driving them forward so as to get to the hermit in time (they have been idling along having thought themselves safe). But the driving-on goes beyond a push. The lion attacks Aravis. Shasta orders Bree to stop, to go to their aid. Bree feigns deafness. Shasta slips the saddle and runs back to Hwin and Aravis:

> One of the most terrible noises in the world, a horse's scream, broke from Hwin's lips. Aravis was stooping low over Hwin's neck and seemed to be trying to draw her sword. And now all three—Aravis, Hwin, and the lion—were almost on top of Shasta. Before they reached him, the lion rose on its hind legs, larger than you would have believed a lion could be, and jabbed at Aravis with its right paw. Shasta could see all the terrible claws extended. Aravis screamed and reeled in

---

58   Lewis, *The Horse and His Boy*, 41.
59   Ibid., 38.

> the saddle. The lion was tearing her shoulders. Shasta, half mad with horror, managed to lurch toward the brute. He had no weapon, not even a stick or a stone. He shouted out, idiotically, at the lion as one would at a dog. "Go home! Go home!" For a fraction of a second he was staring right into its wide-opened, raging mouth. Then, to his utter astonishment, the lion, still on its hind legs, checked itself suddenly, turned head over heels, picked itself up, and rushed away.[60]

Aravis's back has been torn, not deeply, but bloody, with many cuts, skin-deep. Later, when she has recovered, Aslan visits them in the compound of the hermit; this time Aravis realizes and recognizes who the lion is.

> Draw near, Aravis my daughter. See! My paws are velveted. You will not be torn this time."
> "This time, sir?" said Aravis.
> "It was I who wounded you," said Aslan. "I am the only lion you met in all your journeyings. Do you know why I tore you?"
> "No, sir."
> "The scratches on your back, tear for tear, throb for throb, blood for blood, were equal to the stripes laid on the back of your stepmother's slave because of the drugged sleep you cast upon her. You needed to know what it felt like."
> "Yes, sir. Please—"
> "Ask on, my dear," said Aslan.
> "Will any more harm come to her by what I did?"
> "Child," said the Lion, "I am telling you your story, not hers. No one is told any story but their own."[61]

Aslan has ordained that Shasta returns to Archenland for he is really the first-born son of King Lune, and he is to marry Aravis—in years to come! Aravis has followed inadvertently, the will of the Aslan-Christ, but has needed correction and re-orienting. Fortunately she accepts what has befallen her, changed her way of thinking, and discarded the false religious ideas she had grown up with (even though some of these pagan religious concepts and practices have partially and inadvertently, even unconsciously, assisted her in fulfilling the will of God, expressed through the Aslan-Christ; as was the case, argues Lewis, in the North European pagan myths in our reality): if there is any value now to her religion it is existential—it is defined and validated in the immediate relationship with the Aslan-Christ, whether explicit or hidden.

Bree and Hwin—The Conversion of Sentient Beings?

Unknown to them Shasta and Aravis have a God-given purpose in restoring the line of monarchy in Archenland: Shasta as the long-lost heir apparent, Aravis one day to be his wife and Queen (though both are blissfully ignorant of this knowledge!). Weeks spent travelling through the vast land of Calormen would not have been possible without the two Narnian horses: conscious sentient rational creatures with the ability to talk,

---

60   Ibid., 114–15.
61   Ibid., 158.

8. Analogical and Symbolic Narratives IV: Salvation, Encounters and Judgement

to converse. Both are petrified out of their wits by Aslan when they are frightened together at the estuary, and in the race for the safety of the hermit's compound, driven by Aslan as a powerful roaring lion threatening to tear them apart. Days later when Aslan, as we saw, visits Aravis and reveals *himself* to her, *he* likewise confronts Bree and Hwin at this the most opportune moment in their lives (John 3).

Aslan has brought the two horses together, but each has a different response to him at the hermit's: in both cases their expectations are refuted, though for each there was tiny inklings of truth in some of their ideas and expectations. Aravis, Bree, and Hwin are together when Aslan appears over the wall. Bree is theologizing about Aslan not being an actual beast (a proposition we touched on earlier), explaining how, when Narnians speak of *the lion* he is not really a flesh and blood creature, which would be a dishonor to *him*. Aravis states that all the accounts of Aslan in Calormen affirm he is a real creature: "'No doubt,' continued Bree, 'when they speak of him as a Lion they only mean he's as strong as a lion or (to our enemies, of course) as fierce as a lion. Or something of that kind. Even a little girl like you, Aravis, must see that it would be quite absurd to suppose he is a real lion. Indeed it would be disrespectful. If he was a lion he'd have to be a beast just like the rest of us . . . if he was a lion he'd have four paws, and a tail, and whiskers!'"[62] Aslan announces himself; Hwin's immediate response is to trot over to him, and submit herself to him:

> "Dearest daughter," said Aslan, planting a lion's kiss on her twitching, velvet nose, "I knew you would not be long in coming to me. Joy shall be yours."
>
> Then he lifted his head and spoke in a louder voice.
>
> "Now, Bree," he said, "you poor, proud, frightened horse, draw near. Nearer still, my son. Do not dare not to dare. Touch me. Smell me. Here are my paws, here is my tail, these are my whiskers. I am a true beast."
>
> "Aslan," said Bree in a shaken voice, "I'm afraid I must be rather a fool."
>
> "Happy the horse who knows that while he is still young. Or the human either."[63]

These four encounters—two talking animals and two humans (descended from the original immigrant couple who came into Narnia on the day of its creation) represent analogically how Christ encounters humans in our reality. Each encounter was defined, to a degree, by the condition of the creature as it met the Aslan-Christ: pride or humility, repentance or sin, valid or invalid religious beliefs, and so forth. Hwin (female) and Shasta (male) are more open to the Aslan-Christ than Aravis (female) and Bree (male). Aslan will "cure" all of their wrong beliefs and their wrong attitudes, reforming them and making them acceptable to the Father—if they are open to be changed by the Holy Spirit. Lewis's own protracted conversion was probably closer to that of Aravis and Bree, than to Shasta and Hwin.

---

62 Ibid., 156–57.
63 Ibid., 158.

ii. Encounters: Emeth

Whether these persons are human or animal is of little consequence. Whether they follow the Narnia religion, acknowledging Aslan, or the Calormen religion worshipping Tash, is only of minor consequence: there are bad Narnians condemned by Aslan's judgment; there are good Calormenes who are acceptable to Aslan's judgment. We can elucidate by examining Emeth from *The Last Battle*.[64] Set in Lewis's apocalyptic, eschatologically charged end-of-time, Emeth (Hebrew for faithful, true) is a Calormen warrior who along with an army has invaded Narnia. After death—his death and the destruction of the entire world that was Narnia and the surrounding lands/countries (including Calormen)—Emeth comes face-to-face with Aslan. What strikes Emeth is the size, power and awesomeness of Aslan, but equally his beauty, glory and truth. Emeth fears the encounter with Aslan because he considers himself to be a servant of Tash, however, Aslan bends down to greet him, touching his forehead: "'Son, thou art welcome.' But I said, 'Alas, Lord, I am no son of thine but the servant of Tash.' He answered, 'Child, all the service thou hast done to Tash, I account as service done to me.'"[65] Why does Lewis assert this? What is he saying? Are all religions equal, and equally valid before Christ? This seems rather puzzling. Lewis extrapolates. Emeth asks,

> "Lord, is it then true . . . that thou and Tash are one?" The Lion growled so that the earth shook (but his wrath was not against me) and said, "It is false. Not because he and I are one, but because we are opposites, I take to me the services which thou hast done to him. For I and he are of such different kinds that no service which is vile can be done to me, and none which is not vile can be done to him. Therefore if any man swear by Tash and keep his oath for the oath's sake, it is by me that he has truly sworn, though he know it not, and it is I who reward him. And if any man do a cruelty in my name, then, though he says the name Aslan, it is Tash whom he serves and by Tash his deed is accepted."[66]

What is Lewis saying here? Is he saying that people outside the Christian religion may be acceptable to God? Well, yes. We have seen something of this already. But does this not contradict the gospel assertion that by no other name we are saved? That Christ is the only way to salvation: "Jesus answered, 'I am the way and the truth and the life. No one comes to the Father except through me'" (John 14:6). Lewis does not deny this. To say that the people of the United States of America are governed by the President is a truism. Americans may not believe in the President but they are still *ruled, in temporal terms, by no other name*. We may say that in temporal terms British citizens are judged *by no other name* than Queen Elizabeth II, because the judiciary is in her name and in her authority. Christ is God, the second person of the Trinity; Christ has all power and authority to judge whether people are acceptable or not. Perhaps this contradicts our religious categories. Lewis continues:

---

64 Lewis, *The Last Battle*, Ch. 15.
65 Ibid., 154.
66 Ibid., 154–55.

8. Analogical and Symbolic Narratives IV: Salvation, Encounters and Judgement

> [Emeth] But I said also (for the truth constrained me), "Yet I have been seeking Tash all my days."
>
> "Beloved," said the Glorious One, "Unless thy desire had been for me thou wouldst not have sought so long and so truly. For all find what they truly seek."[67]

Are we not saved by faith in Jesus Christ? Are we now talking about works, about earning our salvation through good works? Actually, yes; for faith is a work: faith as a verb—to believe. Grace initiates; works respond. The grace of God initiates, our only acceptable response is *to believe*: though *faith* we will be drawn into Christ, our beliefs and actions will change, and we will—re-oriented—become acceptable to Christ's all-powerful, absolutely superior, judgment. The key is in the phrase, "Unless thy desire had been for me thou wouldst not have sought so long and so truly."[68] Belief is expressed in desire? Is Lewis right here? Well, yes. We cannot deny an element of the will or emotions in our religious beliefs and, more pertinently, in what we seek. Lewis's Platonism will help us here: if we truly desire and seek the good, as distinct from the evil, then even if we know not the name of Jesus, we *may* be deemed acceptable to *him*: a person's service (religious beliefs and actions) may be done in another "god's" name, but if they are good, rather than evil, then Christ's absolute authority may deem them acceptable. This raises questions about true and false disciples. Christ Jesus will judge on this matter, not humans, even if some humans claim the authority of God on these matters:

> Do not judge, or you too will be judged. For in the same way you judge others, you will be judged, and with the measure you use, it will be measured to you.
>
> Matt 7:1-2

> Not everyone who says to me, "Lord, Lord," will enter the kingdom of heaven, but only the one who does the will of my Father who is in heaven. Many will say to me on that day, "Lord, Lord, did we not prophesy in your name and in your name drive out demons and in your name perform many miracles?" Then I will tell them plainly, "I never knew you. Away from me, you evildoers!"
>
> Matt 7:21-23

There is a chilling eschatology here: we may consider our service acceptable to Christ, but then we must not forget the sins of the churches. Emeth, who sought long and hard for the good, for the righteous, even having been raised in a false religion where he had no opportunity to come across true and acceptable religion, is deemed comparable with an acceptable Aslanian (i.e., Christian!).

If we are reading Lewis correctly and what he is saying about salvation in Narnia, which by default is an analogy of how salvation works out under Christ for us, then the person of Emeth illustrates four propositions:

---

67   Ibid., 155. Emeth's words, indeed the phraseology Lewis uses, are very similar to that used by Augustine in the crucial passages relating to his conversion in *Confessions*: Bk. X, "Memory," 179–221. For the specific wording see Bk. 1, para. i(1 and 2), 3.

68   Lewis, *The Last Battle*, 155.

- **First**, it represents the absolute authority of God to judge and decide in these matters even if we are confused or the decisions appear to contradict our religious convictions (prejudices?).

- **Second**, that in the absence of true knowledge about God's salvific actions towards humanity, individuals may still be acceptable to God if what they believed in and sought reflected the truth and goodness of the second person of the Trinity.

- **Third**, because of the fall (and all humans in Narnia come after the fall—they are "Sons and daughters of Adam and Eve"[69]) no human can any longer elect through free will to do the good of their own volition; any good we seek or do is preveniently engendered in us by the Holy Spirit.

- **Fourth**, Christ is Lord of all; and by no other name (i.e., authority) is the human saved. The decision is Christ's and Christ's alone and is made in the light of the actions that issue from a person's *faith* (faith itself being an act, often of the will).

Is there a biblical basis for what Lewis is asserting about Emeth's salvation, his acceptability before God? The key is perhaps in the phrase, "my name." This occurs twenty times in the Gospels,[70] some citations are a warning, others relate to the type of salvation and standing before God that we find in Lewis's analogical portrait of Emeth. For example, "Whoever welcomes a little child like this in my name welcomes me" (Matt 18:5; c.f. Mark 9:37, 39). Such a welcoming is presumably independent of religious knowledge about "the name"—where the name represents the authority of God?—such a welcoming is a seeking after the good when the good is to seek after Jesus Christ. Consider this as a portrait of Emeth: "'Do not stop him,' Jesus said. 'No-one who does a miracle in my name can in the next moment say anything bad about me, for whoever is not against us is for us'" (Mark 9:39-40; cf. Luke 9:49–50). Emeth is considered as being for Aslan because he seeks after what is righteous and good, noble and honest, decent and altruistic, when such attributes align him with the Aslan-Christ. However, from a human perspective, there are dangers in "the name": false prophets, evil spirits masquerading, pretending (Matt 24:5; Mark 13:6; c.f. 2 Cor 11:14). The validity in the name comes from the judgment of God—in Emeth's case, the righteous justifying judgment of the Aslan-Christ.

Emeth may have denied the Aslan-Christ, but Jesus warns that it is the sin/blasphemy against the Holy Spirit that is unforgivable and seals our damnation, not necessarily denying the Son, the second person of the Trinity (for what we may be denying is, in some instances, only a religious mental model in our minds): "Truly I

---

69 Lewis, *The Lion, the Witch and the Wardrobe*, 11, 20, 34, 36–38, 66, 71, 78–82, 84, 89, 98, 106, 108, 127–29, 132–33, 135, 182, 185–86.

70 Matt 18:5, 20; 24:5; Mark 5:9; 9:37, 39, 41; 13:6; 16:17; Luke 9:48; 21:8, 12; John 14:13, 14, 26; 15:16, 21; 16:23, 24, 26.

8. Analogical and Symbolic Narratives IV: Salvation, Encounters and Judgement

tell you, people can be forgiven all their sins and every slander they utter, but whoever blasphemes against the Holy Spirit will never be forgiven; they are guilty of an eternal sin" (Mark 3:28–30). Emeth is judged acceptable, but he is the only one out of an army of over one hundred thousand Calormenes, there is no evidence presented by Lewis for the salvation of the rest of the army, just this one! If we read Lewis carefully here (supported by those who transfer from hell to heaven through purgation in *The Great Divorce*—only one out of the teeming millions Lewis presents) he is not marginalizing faith: the overwhelming majority of followers of Aslan are saved, perhaps less than ten per cent are judged unacceptable; conversely the overwhelming majority of pagans and heathens are judged unacceptable, perhaps more than ninety per cent. Lewis is simply demonstrating that the *charity* of God, of God's love, *may* or *might* find a small number acceptable from the teeming hoards of non-Christians, anti-Christians, etc.

So what can we conclude: is this, by analogy, how God deals with humanity? There will be potential differences within differing realities but the closer matters get to judgment and salvation, the more alike encounters will be. This raises questions about salvation outside of the faith—amongst heathens and pagans, which we will turn to next.

5. THE ASLAN-CHRIST IV: JUDGMENT—A NARNIAN *ESCHATON*

How does Lewis present this? This existential crisis that has possessed humanity in the *fall* comes to a head when normal everyday life disappears. People who suffer, the afflicted and marginalized, know this; however, it will be in the *eschaton* that the delusions of humanity are stripped away and we will be judged, and God's judgment will be good: the saved, the elect, will be those who have "laid down their crowns;"[71] the damned will be those who hold out in their corrupt decisions (this is not a complete or definitive definition of Christ's criteria for last judgment, but part of it).

i. The Finality of Judgment

For Lewis the *eschaton* is final: of the four components (death, judgment, heaven, and hell) death is clearly final for humanity, but Lewis is highly orthodox. None of us can escape God's judgment, and the sifting into heaven and hell. In this Lewis is relatively Catholic: he subscribes to a doctrine of purgation (not necessarily purgatory, and there are difficult question here). All this will be examined from his apologetics and philosophical theology in the final part of this series; however, we may consider initially what he has to say on these matters in the Narniad.

Lewis presents something of this understanding in the final book of *The Chronicles of Narnia* entitled *The Last Battle*. As the world of Narnia comes to an end, all are resurrected, followed by judgment. All come face-to-face with the Aslan-Christ (whose form begins to change the further up and further in to heaven the redeemed

---

71 Rev 4:10.

travel). Each individual creature—human or animal—has to face Aslan, and as they do they look at his face, they either *love him*, or *loathe him*, they either turn one way or the other. Those who love Aslan and turn to him are not uniquely the Narnians; there are many creatures and humans who geographically and culturally have never heard of Aslan, or more pertinently had never known him *consciously*. As darkness falls over the remains of Narnia, as the destruction of the world gathers pace, the redeemed—including the Pevensie children—begin to notice something. Animals, creatures, were crawling and sliding—creatures they knew of, but also dragons and lizards, birds, even bizarre-looking creatures they had never dreamed of existing, all were being raised-up. This is accompanied by the sound of wailing and crying, howling and weeping: the sound of millions of creatures moving towards the door deafened them—"Talking Beasts, Dwarfs, Satyrs, Fauns, Giants, Calormenes, men from Archenland, Monopods, and strange unearthly things from the remote islands or the unknown Western lands."[72] These creatures turn one way or the other: to Aslan and into the new heaven and new earth, or they turn into the darkness, the decision is Aslan's and Aslan's alone, but the response of love or loathing in each creature *conforms* with Aslan's judgment—"All get what they want; they do not always like it."[73]

> As they came right up to Aslan one or other of two things happened to each of them. They all looked straight in *his* face, I don't think they had any choice about that. And when some looked, the expression of their faces changed terribly—it was fear and hatred: except that, on the faces of talking beasts, the fear and hatred lasted only for a fraction of a second. You could see that they suddenly ceased to be talking beasts. They were just ordinary animals. And all the creatures who looked at Aslan in that way swerved to their right, *his* left, and disappeared into *his* huge black shadow, which (as you have heard) streamed away to the left of the doorway. The children never saw them again. I don't know what became of them. But the others looked in the face of Aslan and loved *him*, though some of them were very frightened at the same time. And all these came in at the Door, in on Aslan's right.[74]

Love is the measure of judgment; love is the measure of the God of love that is love through-and-through. The beliefs and behavior, dictate what sort of response there is from each individual creature—whether they love or loathe him—but it is love that decides the fate of each when they face the God of love. It is altruistic love, *agape*, that drives and defines *faith*, the faith of a Christian; if not, then we must postulate that such faith is not faith, and underpinning all the churchly activities of such a loveless one (despite their church attendance, and apparent good works) is a sublimated hate (often driven by self-interest and self-aggrandizement), or even a disinterested indifference, of *the Christ*.[75] After this annihilation of Narnia many find themselves in

---

72   Lewis, *The Last Battle*, 174.
73   Lewis, *The Magician's Nephew*, 162.
74   Lewis, *The Last Battle*, 175–76.
75   This discussion rightly belongs in Lewis's *ecclesiology*—his doctrine of the church—which is discussed in the second part of this third book in the series: *C. S. Lewis—On The Christ of a Religious Economy. II. Knowing Salvation*, Pt. 2, Chs. 6–8.

8. Analogical and Symbolic Narratives IV: Salvation, Encounters and Judgement

heaven, the plains of heaven. Tirian, the last king of Narnia, "looked round again and could hardly believe his eyes. There was the blue sky overhead, and grassy country spreading from within."[76]

ii. A Shifting Puzzle?

The moment of judgment lasts but an instant (1 Cor 15:52), yet everything that had been the life and loves, actions and beliefs, is wrapped up in that moment and presented to the Aslan-Christ. Not all are perfect, in fact, none could be perfect, or perfectly acceptable before God's judgment. All will have something in their life that acts as a barrier between the judge and the judged. However, openness to the forgiveness of *the Christ* is essential, and is the king-pin to whether they loathe *him* in that moment of judgment, or *love* him. Ownership comes into this: those who belong to the Aslan-Christ; or those who belong to Satan, the devil, and his evil hoards—in Narnian terms, those who belong to Tash. Ownership decides; but ownership also reflects the beliefs and actions, the life, of the judged. Emeth, when he is confronted, in judgment, believes he is condemned because he assumes that having been in the service of the wrong religio-political belief system, he has served Tash. Therefore his beliefs and actions condemn him. Not so; because underpinning his life was *the good*, and the good issues from God in Christ. Therefore Aslan can say to him, "I take to me the services which thou hast done to him."[77] This is precisely because Aslan and Tash (God and the devil) are so utterly different: in honesty and goodness, Emeth could not have been claimed by any other. A minister or priest who oppresses and exploits in cruelty and self-interest may claim to be doing such acts in the name of Jesus (acts that by their very nature sin against the Holy Spirit—and the history of the churches is replete with such examples) but in a very real eschatological reality such a religious professional is doing such acts and belief in the name of Satan and his belief and acts are owned by Satan, though such a minister/priest may claim to be doing them in the interest of the church. Therefore, eschatologically, our religious categorization may be at odds with the judgment of Christ.

To elucidate we may look at two examples from the Narnian *eschaton*: Shift the Ape and Puzzle the Donkey. Both characters are complicit in triggering the Narnian *eschaton*, through the anti-Christ, yet one is saved, the other is condemned. Is this a shifting puzzle?—or a puzzling shift? Why is one saved and the other not? The answer lies in intention-led ownership: our will condemns or exonerates us, and what we will from the heart of our being dictates our *post mortem* ownership: "All get what they want; they do not always like it."[78] Shift the Ape takes on the role, out of self-interest, of the anti-Christ (though he does not see his actions in this light). He finds a dead lion's skin, makes it into a winter coat for Puzzle (who is a complying slave in many ways to Shift's malicious demands), once the coat is on Puzzle is trapped, shut away in a stable atop a hill, brought out at night for the Narnians to see—at a distance—being

---

76 Lewis, *The Last Battle*, 132.
77 Ibid., 154–55.
78 Lewis, *The Magician's Nephew*, 162.

presented as the real Aslan, with Shift the Ape speaking in his name and claiming his authority. The deception works; all is set for Shift's plan with the Calormenes—they invade, take over Narnia, putting it to the sword, and enslave the Narnians. Puzzle who hides behind being innocently stupid, is condemned to silence, shut away, except for the nightly presentation. As the story unfolds, the Calormenes begin to conquer, wasting the trees and enslaving the animals. They call on Tash, not believing him to be a real "god," yet Tash arrives. A small resistance by the King, along with Eustace and Jill from our world, and a couple of dozen Narnians unfolds. They attempt, at stable hill, to expose the Ape and the deception, but fail, and a battle ensues during which one-by-one, the Calormenes though superior force throw each member of the resistance into the stable, the entrance to which is now the gateway to the *eschaton*. As each of them passes through they either find themselves in the plains of heaven, or in the darkness of hell (devoured by Tash): an eschatological judgment.

As Shift is hurled through the stable door by the good Narnians, they catch a glimpse of a blinding greenish-blue light, and the screaming hoarse voice of Tash, who pounces and takes Shift.[79] Shift is taken by Tash, the demonic manifestation of evil, Satan (this is before Shift can face the Aslan-Christ in the Last Judgment, though there is a judgment here). Rishda Tarkaan (who has led the military operation, the take-over and subjugation of Narnia) finds himself with Tirian the last king of Narnia, thrown through the stable door together:

> Rishda gave a great wail and pointed; then he put his hands before his face and fell flat, face downward, on the ground. Tirian looked in the direction where the Tarkaan had pointed. And then he understood. A terrible figure was coming toward them. . . . It had a vulture's head and four arms. Its beak was open and its eyes blazed. A croaking voice came from its beak. "Thou hast called me into Narnia, Rishda Tarkaan. Here I am. What hast thou to say?"
> With a sudden jerk—like a hen stooping to pick up a worm—Tash pounced on the miserable Rishda and tucked him under the upper of his two right arms. Then Tash turned his head sidewise to fix Tirian with one of his terrible eyes . . .
> But immediately, from behind Tash, strong and calm as the summer sea, a voice said:
> "Begone, Monster, and take your lawful prey to your own place: in the name of Aslan and Aslan's great Father the Emperor-over-the-Sea."
> The hideous creature vanished, with the Tarkaan still under its arm.[80]

Tirian looks and the voice is from King Peter (the high king above all kings—from *The Lion, the Witch and the Wardrobe*), who speaks with the authority of Aslan. So, the question comes up again about condemnation before the Last Judgment. But the key is the question of ownership. It is a strange concept to today's modern, liberal, Western individuals who believe they belong to no one and are free to do as they wish, but all belong either to God in Christ, or to Satan. The key is in the propositional command: take your *lawful* prey with you. Our actions and beliefs betray us before we

---

79 Lewis, *The Last Battle*, 109.
80 Ibid., 124, and 125–26.

8. Analogical and Symbolic Narratives IV: Salvation, Encounters and Judgement

even come before God in judgment, and our beliefs and actions betray our allegiance, and—crucially—ownership. This allegiance and ownership draws them into hell: it is what they lived for, what they wanted. This is then the judgment of God. Judas confirmed this in his act of suicide, following on from his betrayal of the Christ.

Puzzle, by contrast, finds himself, *post mortem*, on the plains of heaven. He tries to avoid meeting Aslan, but this is impossible: "he walked up to Aslan, and he looked, beside Aslan, as small as a kitten looks beside a St. Bernard. The Lion bowed down his head and whispered something to Puzzle at which his long ears went down, but then he said something else at which the ears perked up again. The humans couldn't hear what he had said either time."[81] In judgment he is forgiven, because he has faced his sin and accepted in repentance how wrong he had been. Pertinently the question of ownership and allegiance sets him apart from Shift.

How do we compare Puzzle the Donkey and Shift the Ape. Both are involved in the same conspiracy. But Shift initiated, Puzzle followed out of stupidity (and a refusal to challenge Shift, having been brow-beaten and down-trodden by him for years) but Puzzle is not inherently evil and scheming, culpable and bad, and he is open to repentance and forgiveness. Shift has dug himself into a hole, he planned and initiated the deception, he accepts the rule given him by the Calormenes until he is too drunk and incapable, and believes not in God's compassion but only his own agenda, his own well-being.

iii. Neo-Kantian, Feuerbachian Dwarves?

Faith and Disbelief

After this Narnian *eschaton* there are a group of rebellious renegade dwarves who have lived in Narnia and know about Aslan but are cynical and skeptical, despite being amongst the saved, the redeemed.[82] When they are approached by Aslan in the new heaven and the new earth they fear him, perceive him as a monster, as a threat. Furthermore they do not perceive the wonders of this landscape of heaven which is more real than anything on earth, more wonderful and sweet that anything they could have seen or imagined. What is in reality *like* an early summer day, bright and beautiful, they perceive heaven as a dark, dark, rotten hole, a place without light, they sit in a huddle unaware of the wonders around them.[83] Lucy leads the others over to the dwarves. The dwarves can hear them, but can see but faint glimmers and outlines, like on a dark moonless night. They sense Lucy and the others are near and complain that they will bump into them, they describe where they are as a pitch-black,

---

81   Lewis, *The Last Battle*, 171.
82   Lewis, *The Last Battle*, Ch. 13, "How the Dwarves Refused to be Taken In."
83   Ibid., 135f. The odd thing, an inconsistency in Lewis's theology, is that the dwarves are in heaven when they have developed this hatred for Aslan, a rejection of Aslan, yet must have come face to face with him at the point of the Narnian last judgement: if they so loathed him, they surely would have gone off to the dark side into hell, whereas those in heaven had looked at Aslan (whether they had known him or not in this life) and loved him.

poky, smelly, little hole. They are oblivious to the goodness around them, perceiving kindness as a cruelty. When Lucy offers them a bunch of flowers, wild violets, they perceive them as filthy stable-litter. "'There is no black hole, save in your own fancy' cries Tirian the last king of Narnia to them."[84] Aslan comments to Lucy, "You see they will not let us help them. They have chosen cunning instead of belief. Their prison is only in their own minds, yet they are in that prison; and so afraid of being taken in that they cannot be taken out."[85] Despite the presence near them of the Aslan-Christ, the dwarves comment that Aslan has not come to help them, to save them. "'Well if that doesn't beat everything!' exclaimed Diggle. 'How can you go on talking all that rot? Your wonderful lion didn't come and help you did he? Thought not. And now—even now—when you've been beaten and shoved into this black hole, just the same as the rest of us, you're still at your old game. Starting a new lie! Trying to make us believe we're none of us shut up, and it ain't dark . . .'"[86]

"Oh Adam's sons, how cleverly you defend yourselves against all that might do you good."

These are neo-Kantian dwarves. And before we criticize Lewis for being prejudiced against dwarves, this is a point where we find—in the detail—some small elements of allegory in the Narniad. These dwarves,[87] and for that matter the Dufflepuds,[88] can be considered an allegory of *postlapsarian* humanity! Why neo-Kantian? The problem for the academy lies with the hermetic concept of reason adhered to in the West since the Enlightenment, enforced, it may be argued, by the philosopher Immanuel Kant's glass ceiling, philosophically installed between humanity and God whereby a philosophical barrage cuts humanity off from God (because the philosophers argued that there was no commerce, no connection between us and God, if there was a God). Though in effect the people who subscribe to this isolationism are merely creating a mental model that seals them off from God's Holy Spirit as they create a grey nihilistic world in their own image: just as these dwarves shut themselves off from the beauty and wonder, the freshness and purity, the joy and splendor of the new creation, the new heaven and the new earth. This allegory, which is veiled in the neo-Kantian dwarves, is made explicit in the character of Uncle Andrew in *The Magician's Nephew*. Near the end of the story we find Uncle Andrew having been imprisoned, like a zoo animal, by the talking creatures of Narnia. Andrew wants to destroy and exploit all that he sees in this new world: shoot the lion, harvest what he can and return to our world to be wealthy. However, when the animals speak to him enquiringly, he hears only roars and squeaks, clucks and baas—animal noises!—so they try to look after this ignorant creature, build a cage for him, offer him different foods, but he sinks into a stupor, a self-piteous torpor. Digory and Polly plead with Aslan to help him, explain to him the error of his ways. This, Aslan, explains, is not possible. Andrew would only regard

---

84   Ibid., 138.
85   Ibid., 140.
86   Ibid., 138.
87   Ibid., Ch. 13.
88   Lewis, *The Voyage of the Dawn Treader*, Chs. 9–11.

8. Analogical and Symbolic Narratives IV: Salvation, Encounters and Judgement

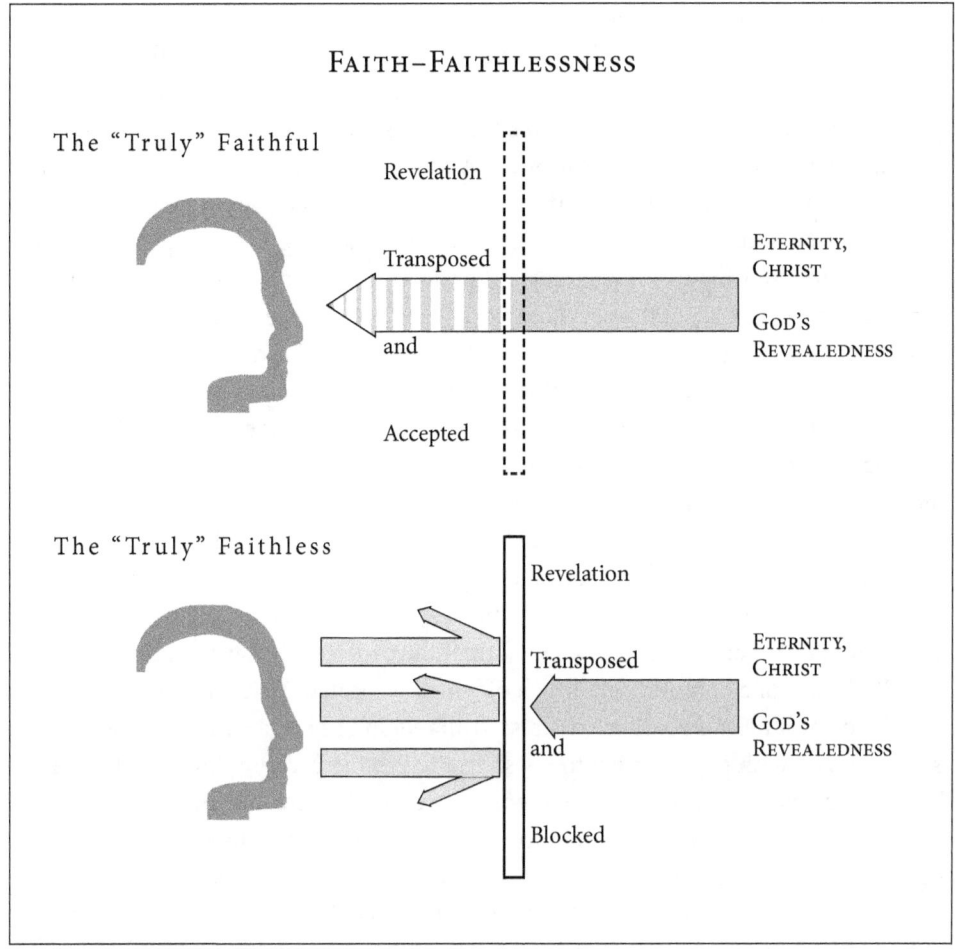

Figure 7 Faith–Faithlessness . . . and the neo-Kantian, Feuerbachian Dwarves

Aslan as a wild lion and hear nothing but roars instead of divine words of comfort. Aslan comments, "Oh Adam's sons, how cleverly you defend yourselves against all that might do you good!"[89] (See figure 7.) This is reminiscent of comments Lewis made in one of his most powerfully Platonic of sermons/addresses, "Indeed, if we consider the unblushing promises of reward and the staggering nature of the rewards promised in the Gospels, it would seem that Our Lord finds our desires not too strong, but too weak. We are half-hearted creatures, fooling about with drink and sex and ambition when infinite joy is offered us, like an ignorant child who wants to go on making mud pies in a slum because he cannot imagine what is meant by the offer of a holiday at the sea. We are far too easily pleased."[90]

---

89 Lewis, *The Magician's Nephew*, 158.
90 Lewis, "The Weight of Glory," (1st ed.) 21.

This raises questions about the veracity of our religious ideas, about the models we have constructed in our minds about God, salvation and humanity. Are these mental models entirely human-generated, a fantasy and illusion? Or is the pertinent question the degree to which these mental models coincide with the reality of God, and the triune reality of Christ's salvation. And, crucially, if these mental models that control our beliefs and actions differ too greatly from the God-given reality, then these very religious models may prevent us from knowing God and accepting the salvation proffered for us on the cross. Therefore in addition to Kant's glass ceiling, there may indeed be mental—psychological—barriers that we have created. To frame this in Feuerbachian terms, the religious ideas and mental models of such people as are allegorically represented by the neo-Kantian dwarves and Uncle Andrew, may not coincide and correspond with God's revelation, these ideas may not be from without, they may be no more than the heart-felt desires, the deepest longings, of the complex and manifold psyche of each individual projected onto the mind like a movie projected onto a screen. Dark depression and despair (the dwarves), selfishness and greed (Uncle Andrew) plays an important part in this. As the nineteenth-century German theologian Ludwig Feuerbach asserted, such experiences may simply be a projection: the mind may project the idea of a "god," then the experience may simply be from the deepest desires of a complex self, much of which is located in the sub-conscious. As a self-confessed atheist, Feuerbach dismissed all religion as mere wish fulfillment: "God is the realized wish of the heart, the wish exalted to the certainty of its fulfillment,"[91] furthermore the secret, he writes, of theology is that it is mere anthropology—religion and theology is the study of humanity. As with so many theologians in the Age of Reason and the Enlightenment Feuerbach grounded Christianity on human religious experience. Therefore he loses sight of God. Such a critique of religion loses much of its force when dealing with a divine encounter with humanity from outside, or, more pertinently, theologies which claim to deal with such an external encounter. That is, when humanity realizes that there is a God outside of all human expectations, a God that can be revealed to them, that can know them, seek them. Modern enlightened theology that secretly follows Feuerbach's "Freudian"[92] explanation of religion and appeals to atheism fails to follow through what it purports to believe. Robert Jenson the American Lutheran theologian commented:

> But just if Feuerbach is right, if there is in fact no antecedent one God, there also can be no one antecedent community of humankind. Feuerbach dreamed of a universal humanity and so of a shared eternal vision of human value, but therein he remained parasitic on the faith he debunked. Thus Western unbelief has since had to abandon that dream and now knows only classes and genders and races and cultures. Insofar as religion interprets itself by the resultant neo-Feuerbachian theory, religion is revealed as a struggle for metaphysical power, for each such group necessarily projects its ideal or compensatory vision of itself to be the final good. It is just so that scripture sees the gods of the peoples as idols

---

91 Feuerbach, *The Essence of Christianity*, 121 & 207.
92 Perhaps, *avant la lettre*.

8. Analogical and Symbolic Narratives IV: Salvation, Encounters and Judgement

and 'nothings'. Exactly as neo-Feuerbachian theory says, what each of the gods does is validate and enforce the particular human situation, with its structure of values, from which she/he/it is projected—in all the alienation and tyranny of every such situation.[93]

A Feuerbachian position is ultimately absurd—if there is no God then there is no truth, no morality and no meaning, if God is an illusion then so is certainty and meaning, which Feuerbachian and scientific atheists today rely upon; indeed their protestations of no "god" are grounded in a certainty which cannot exist according to their criteria. However, Feuerbach's observations are significant because they open up space between human religiousness and God. That is, space is opened up between the religious desire in humanity, the human capacity to invent gods and idols on the one hand, and the one true living God who we can only truly know in Christ on the other hand. God is ultimately transcendent, also triune; God is beyond all that we can conceive of and know, God is other, wholly other. Yet from this transcendence and otherness God comes to us from beyond the world of Feuerbachian religion, an imaginary world peopled by projected gods or idols. God comes to us in the incarnation: "The Word was made flesh and dwelt among us. And we have seen his glory, the glory of the only Son of the Father, full of grace and truth" (John 1:14). While humanity invents all manner of religions and "gods"/"idols," God comes to us in humility, divesting himself of much of his omnipotence and omniscience and omnipresence in the form of a vulnerable human baby. This is a concept or doctrine of God that humanity could never have dreamt up—God incarnate, dying for our self-inflicted sin, dying for our salvation.

So, God (in Christ; and analogically in Lewis's supposal, Aslan) dies to redeem the creation. So he has died for the neo-Kantian, Feuerbachian dwarves and Uncle Andrew. But they lack faith—primarily, faith in Aslan—but their lives, their values, their behavior betray this lack of faith (unlike Emeth and Shasta). Therefore it is our lives and our intentions, our *decisions*, that betray or confirm our allegiance, not necessarily our religious declarations:[94] the sovereignty and aseity of God in Christ will decide. This does not detract from the uniqueness of Christ, if anything it further denies a syncretistic approach to the world's religions. Lewis is therefore presenting his understanding of the eternally electing God who seeks the redemption of all creation, who seeks to be reconciled to his creatures, but it is also a picture of a creation and creatures that through the gift of free will can refuse salvation, can hold out against God by sealing itself into its own mental model of the world, of reality. This again relates to Lewis's neo-Arminian doctrine of atonement that will be dealt with fully later.

---

93 Jenson, *Systematic Theology* Vol. 1, 53.
94 "Not everyone who says to me, 'Lord, Lord,' will enter the kingdom of heaven, but only the one who does the will of my Father who is in heaven. Many will say to me on that day, 'Lord, Lord, did we not prophesy in your name and in your name drive out demons and in your name perform many miracles?' Then I will tell them plainly, 'I never knew you. Away from me, you evildoers!'" Matt 7:21–23.

ON THE CHRIST OF A RELIGIOUS ECONOMY. I. CREATION AND SUB-CREATION

A Baptized Imagination

Faith is crucial. Faith is our only legitimate response. Faith is manifested in our beliefs and actions. Hence Grace initiates; works (faith and actions) respond. Through the fall we have the ability, taken onto ourselves, of blocking out God's Grace and revealedness—the revelation of Christ—through the mental models we create essentially through our corrupt will. This is the "truly" faithless nature of disbelief, unbelief. This is presented analogically by Lewis in the neo-Kantian, Feuerbachian dwarves (*The Last Battle*), and the Dufflepuds (*The Voyage of the Dawn Treader*). Both may be considered an allegory of humanity. This is then presented explicitly in the character of Uncle Andrew (*The Magician's Nephew*). For the faithful, God's grace, through the Holy Spirit, should generate the ability in them to believe, that is, faith (the turning of the will away from self and to God) that allows God through to them and in that knowledge and understanding they can accept Christ's redemption. By comparison the faithless simply get what they want, but they may not be happy with this separation from God, particularly *post mortem*. A baptized imagination is the crucial event and component of the human here. Preveniently God will press on the human, who can accept or reject, even if they lack cognitive knowledge about the Christ event (Shasta and Emeth?). Once accepted, then the mind will be baptized by the Holy Spirit, and will be able to accept the free gift of salvation without blocking out what God offers. This prevenient action pressing on the human is a divinely-ordained preparation for the gospel to be received and believed. The mind, more pertinently, the imagination must be re-orientated, shaped, in a Christlike form, a godly direction, then it will be amenable to receiving the truth of the gospel with the intellect. If the imagination is not baptized then all manner of intellectual blocks from the will, the *fallen* and corrupt will, prevent the necessary openness to God's revelation. The neo-Kantian, Feuerbachian dwarves are locked into themselves but they are not in hell—nothing will press on them but the love of Christ. They are not condemned to hell; their personal pseudo-hell is of their own making. They are afforded a degree of protection in heaven even though they have built up this mental barrier to exclude the love of Christ. By comparison hell proper is defined by complete and utter freedom, therefore the most demonic and powerful dominate and exploit.

The degree to which the imagination can on the one hand be the object of divine inspiration and illumination and on the other hand an oracle of truth is debatable: many of the Reformers were dismissive of the imagination; the Reformed tradition regarded both the imagination and natural theology as suspect at best and of little consequence—the emphasis was placed on sin and fallenness. Lewis does address the question of sin and fallenness.[95] He places great emphasis in his spiritual autobiography and in his theological writings on the concept of a baptized imagination, where the imagination through a free and creative ordering of the contents of the mind is governed by the Holy Spirit: because of original sin an unbaptized imagination fails to

---

95 The question of a baptized imagination is examined in depth in the second book in this series: see, *C. S. Lewis—The Work of Christ Revealed*, Pt. 3, Ch. 11.

8. Analogical and Symbolic Narratives IV: Salvation, Encounters and Judgement

perceive the intrinsic value and meaning in stories and myths from a God-ward, and hence true, perspective. Lewis would have concurred with a Reformed position which proposed that the imagination was fallen and tainted by original sin, but he would have argued that it was not irredeemable in this life. Lewis does not necessarily tie the baptism of the imagination to an explicit liturgical practice: the Spirit blows where it wills (Gen 1:2b and John 3:8). Lewis sees a baptized imagination as an essential key in comprehending ultimate reality; this knowledge of reality is apprehended by acquaintance with and participation in the divine Logos. A person comprehending ultimate reality, a reality illuminated by the Logos (in the sense of an immediate, intuitive and imaginative capacity) has perception of God to the extent that such an acquaintance and perception is considered by Lewis to be revelatory; however, the rational interpretation of such an experience may be subject to distortion whilst communication of the experience may be flawed. Revelation of this kind is mediated through human faculties: it is human to err; to err is to be human. Lewis does not address whether epistemological baptism is permanent this side of eternity. Human epistemic limitations would seem to dismiss such a proposition; likewise the fact that we are still subject to the vagaries of sin—*simul iustus et peccator* (at the same time a sinner yet justified)—which is confirmed by Lewis's proposition of revelation transposed. Our sinfulness affects the degree of transposition.

iv. Matthew 25: Pagan Salvation?

By contrast with the neo-Kantian, Feuerbachian dwarves, Emeth's life, his desires, his actions, all that he was when alive, was evidence of faith in Aslan—preveniently engendered in him—even though he was culturally and geographically isolated from the Narnian "religion" centered on Aslan (in the same way that those who composed and heard the pagan myths that for Lewis and Tolkien prefigured, in literary content to a degree, Christ's atoning sacrifice, were isolated from the reality that took place in Palestine 2000 years ago). Emeth's faith was grounded in false, corrupt and wrong knowledge of the reality of God, leastwise, his faith in Tash did not accord with all that Tash was, but, ironically, this was what was required for faith in Aslan. Lewis's use of "account" (that is, when Aslan declares to Emeth that *he* accounts any *good* as service done to *him*) is comparable to Paul's use of *reckoned* in the context of Abraham's righteousness before God.[96] Pertinently, whereas King Peter declares to Tash—the demonic satanic god at the center of Calormen religion—"Begone, monster, and take your lawful prey to your own place [i.e. hell],"[97] it is the goodness (something of a Platonic form or norm, in intent) inherent in Emeth's faith and desire that links him to Aslan not to Tash: again, the question of ownership—do we belong to God, or to

---

96   "Abraham believed God, and it was reckoned [ἐλογίσθη, to charge to one's account, to keep a record of] to him as righteousness. Now to one who works, wages are not reckoned as a gift but as something due. But to one who without works trusts him who justifies the ungodly, such faith is reckoned as righteousness. So also David speaks of the blessedness of those to whom God reckons righteousness apart from works." (Rom 4:3–6).
97   Lewis, *The Last Battle*, 125

Satan? Otherwise Tash would claim him for his own because no desire or service, no faith or belief, which is vile can be done to Aslan, and none which is good and true, honest and *gracious* can be done to Tash.[98] Therefore, it is our lives and our intentions that betray or confirm our allegiance not necessarily our religious declarations, where allegiance issues from *faith*: the sovereignty and aseity of God in Christ will decide. These passages are Lewis explicitly trying to spell out to his readers the implications of the Parable of the Sheep and the Goats (Matt 25:31–46) for non-Christians. In this context Lewis wrote: "Then there's another thing that used to puzzle me. Isn't it frightfully unfair that this new life should be confined to people who have heard of Christ and been able to believe in *him*? Well, the truth is God hasn't told us what *his* arrangements about the other people are. We do know that no man can be saved except through Christ; we don't know that only those who know *him* can be saved through *him*."[99] Lewis has Aslan say, "I take to me the services,"[100] when confronting the pagan or heathen whose religiosity is not explicitly Christian; this is an analogy of Christ in judgment, his dictum spoken to those outside of the Judeo-Christian religious tradition, "Truly I tell you, whatever you did for one of the least of these brothers and sisters of mine, you did for me" (Matt 25:40). Faith therefore begets service (action, works) and service betrays our allegiance, and allegiance apportions ownership. When Lewis has Aslan say, "I take to me the services which thou hast done to him"[101] as justification of his *ownership* of Emeth and therefore of Emeth's redemption, is this an exposition of Matt 25:40, "The King will reply, 'Truly I tell you, whatever you did for one of the least of these brothers and sisters of mine, you did for me'"? If we help the poor the homeless, clothe and feed them, visit those in prison (Matt 25:35–36) even if we claim to be doing these faith-driven actions for ourselves or in the name of a false "god," Jesus in judgment will take them as having been done, *by proxy*, in his name? Surrogacy means that what we believe about the actions may not be a fair assessment of their context and value, *eschatologically*.

Does this detract from the uniqueness of Christ? On the contrary, if anything it further denies a syncretistic approach to the world's religions. Again, by no other name are we saved, where name equals authority. Lewis is therefore presenting his understanding of the *eternally electing* God who seeks the redemption of all creation, who seeks to be reconciled to his creatures. Aslan's sacrifice (in *The Lion, the Witch and the Wardrobe*) represents the overwhelming love of the absolute supreme transcendent God, who comes in infinite humility, meekness and modesty in Christ Jesus, gives himself to humanity in unconditional freedom and grace, despite the venomous hatred that humanity/creation heaped on him on the cross/Stone Table. There are numerous illustrations given by Lewis of encounters between creatures and humans in Narnia where the one thing the creature must do is repent of his/her sins, acknowledging in love the lordship of God incarnate (the Aslan-Christ): regarding her brother Edmund

---

98 Ibid., 154
99 Lewis, *Broadcast Talks*, II "What Christians Believe," 60
100 Lewis, *The Last Battle*, 154.
101 Ibid., 154–55.

8. Analogical and Symbolic Narratives IV: Salvation, Encounters and Judgement

(for whom Aslan allows himself to be sacrificed on the stone table because of Edmund's treachery), Lucy comments to her sister, "Does he know what Aslan did for him, does he know what the arrangement with the witch really was?"[102] As Lewis asserted, it is not necessarily only those who know him (in the manner of cognitive knowledge) who can be saved by him.[103] Do we truly know him? Do we fully understand what Christ did for us? We think we do, but is our knowledge any more definite, any more certain or complete than Emeth's or Shasta's? It is only in the *eschaton* that we will know as we our known (1 Cor 13:12).

---

102 Lewis, *The Lion the Witch and The Wardrobe*, 163
103 Lewis, *Mere Christianity*, 53.

9

Analogical and Symbolic Narratives V: Father Christmas in Narnia?— Intimations of Atonement and Salvation

SYNOPSIS:
How does Lewis's genre of "supposal" work, as a Christological exposition? How does the Narniad function as theologoumena? Does it make sense? Does what he presents in the Narniad cohere with, allowing for differences, the Christology that is at the heart of reality in our world? To answer these questions we can examine one of the more embarrassing characters in Narnia that just doesn't, on the surface, fit in with the logic of "supposal." The inclusion of the character of Father Christmas (the English equivalent of the American figure of Santa Claus) in *The Chronicles of Narnia* has consistently generated disapproval from numerous critics: what is a mythical person rooted in a uniquely this-world-religious-event doing in Narnia? Was Lewis right to include the character in *The Lion, the Witch and the Wardrobe*? Was he correct to retain him despite opposition from J. R. R. Tolkien and his fellow Inklings? There is justification for Father Christmas's inclusion precisely because of the incarnation in our reality, because of the cross-cultural relationship between Narnia and our world, but also because his presence is essential to the doctrine of atonement we can read from the Narniad. An explanation is here framed by identifying reasons within the coherence and rationality, the lucidity and consistency, of Lewis's sub-creation (the Narniad), the interaction of three worlds, three realities: first, the actions and beliefs of the people (the indigenous sentient creatures) of Narnia; second, the human migrants from earth who are in Narnia from its beginning; and third the imported evil from Charn (Jadis, the demonic queen, who becomes the White Witch).

This interaction is a form of cross-cultural fertilization, which explains why the words "Father Christmas" can be in Narnia—the concept being imported by the first humans (along with, we may speculate, other Victorian Christmassy ideas!), which is then applied to the gift-bearer. Any explanation of Father Christmas's presence is through an internal logic and by analogy, not by generating allegorical connections. The Father-Christmas-type-gift-bearer in Narnia and Bishop Nicholas of Myra (along with the assortment of Father Christmases, Santa Clauses, *et al*) are to be seen as manifestations of the same form (theoretically grounded in Lewis's Platonic Idealism). Therefore in this framework we can explicate a coherent reason and justification within the context of Narnian atonement theory; as such this Father-Christmas-type-gift-bearer is an eschatological harbinger of the loving judgement of God: Aslan's ultimate gifting of himself to redeem his creation.

ON THE CHRIST OF A RELIGIOUS ECONOMY. I. CREATION AND SUB-CREATION

1. INTRODUCTION: HOW DOES IT WORK?

How does Lewis's "supposal" work? Does it make sense? Does what he present in the Narniad cohere with, allowing for differences we would expect between two worlds, the Christology that is at the heart of reality in our world? We can answer this question by examining one of the more embarrassing characters in Narnia that superficially does not appear to fit in with the logic of "supposal." In C.S. Lewis's *The Chronicles of Narnia* there are many characters and creatures associated with our world—both real and mythological.[1] Many of these creatures, while not human, are people (for they are all characterized by personhood), and are from, for example, Greco-Roman and North European pagan mythology; many more issue from Lewis's imagination. As such they complement Lewis's aim in speculating what Christ would be like if he were incarnated into another world, outside and beyond our reality. However, there is one character that for many does not transfer into the world of Narnia. In *The Lion, the Witch and the Wardrobe*, Father Christmas makes what to many is an unusual, untimely, and out of place appearance—for many it is like an actor who has turned up at the wrong theater, on the wrong day, in the wrong costume, playing the wrong part, for the wrong play! Minotaurs play a satisfactory role; we can divorce them from any association we have with stories in this world and allow them to live a justified existence in Narnia because they do not generally have any connection with what we take to be reality in our world. There are those who will say that the Narniad is just a collection of children's stories and there is no need for children's stories to make sense—picture books for young children will have all sorts of seemingly contradictory and impossible events and characters in them. But Narnia is not, as we have established, just a childish story or a fantasy; it is dealing with an event that is at the heart of reality and human existence: the Christ event—the incarnation-cross-resurrection. If Lewis's aim was to explore an idea (what if Christ became incarnate in the flesh, the physical reality of another world, as another sentient life form, not another world within our universe but an entirely different universe, another reality) then we must ask whether this works on the micro level (individual characters and situations) as well as on the macro (the overall plan of the stories). This was Lewis's aim.[2] So, as we have established, Aslan is the deity, not necessarily an allegorical representation of our understanding of God; as such Aslan has divine qualities of power and authority, awe and holiness. He exudes love and the normal human response is to love *him*. But there is no one-to-one correspondence with Jesus: Narnia is not allegory. If supposition is not allegorical, but analogical we can, as we have seen, compare Aslan and Jesus and see similarities, but also, importantly, dissimilarities. The problem with Father Christmas's appearance is that he appears on the surface to be neither allegory nor analogical. He is indelibly associated with Christmas in our reality, which is more than a story, and can only transfer over to Narnia if there is a nativity story in Narnia—which, as we have seen,

---

1   For a description see, Gibson, *C. S. Lewis: Spinner of Tales*, 132.
2   See, specifically, Lewis writing to Mrs Hook, Dec 29, 1958. Lewis, *Collected Letters, Vol. III.*, 1004–5. For Lewis's aims and objectives in the Narniad see: Hooper, *C.S. Lewis A Companion and Guide*, 423–26.

9. Analogical and Symbolic Narratives V: Father Christmas in Narnia?

there is not. What is more the Christmas story is associated with transgression and redemption; however commercial and secular a modern Western Christmas becomes, the connection with sin, death, and atonement can never be fully eliminated. So what has this Father-Christmas-type-character got to do with atonement in Narnia? Did Lewis simply make a mistake by including him?

2. EXPLANATIONS AND CRITICISMS

To many readers the explanation for Father Christmas's appearance is Lewis's interest in these various mythological characters, hence we find—especially in *Prince Caspian*—a multitude of mythological characters from ancient European cultures. However, to say that Father Christmas is in Narnia because Lewis liked putting different mythological characters into a story, does not solve the difficulties, it simply rephrases the question into a circular argument, or answer: Father Christmas is in Narnia because Lewis put Father Christmas in Narnia. Michael Ward notes that while many of the Chronicles clearly have a biblical foundation, others do not and draw on widely disparate imagery and characterizations: "Father Christmas from popularized hagiography, a Snow Queen out of Hans Anderson, English children fresh from E. Nesbit, and a 'high style' diction reminiscent of Sir Thomas Malory."[3] So what are the criticisms?[4]

Lewis's colleague, friend, and fellow Inkling, J. R. R. Tolkien was highly critical of Father Christmas's appearance in Narnia. Tolkien spent many, many years making sure that everything within *The Lord of the Rings* made sense, cohered, and conformed to an inner logic, a logic internal to the story; by comparison he is attributed to have said, at an initial reading to the Inklings, that *The Lion, the Witch and the Wardrobe* was a mish-mash, a confused mixing of mythological creatures and ideas from widely disparate and contradictory sources.[5] Tolkien's criticism is important, for it raises questions not so much about Lewis's writing as about how readers respond to the Narniad. Tolkien's criticism is perhaps more to do with his subjective response than any desire to think through the problems and see whether there is an underlying coherence:

> Why then did Tolkien totally reject the Narnia stories? For reject them he did ... He disliked works of the imagination that were written hastily, were inconsistent in their details, and were not always totally convincing in their evocation of a "secondary world." *The Lion, the Witch and the Wardrobe* offended against all these notions. It had been very hastily written, and this haste seemed to suggest that Lewis was not taking the business of "sub-creation" with what Tolkien regarded as a proper seriousness. There were inconsistencies and loose ends in the story, while beyond the immediate demands of the plot the task of making Narnia seem "real" did not appear to interest Lewis at all. Moreover, the story borrowed so indiscriminately from other mythologies and narratives (fauns, nymphs, Father Christmas, talking animals, anything that seemed useful for the

---

3   Ward, *Planet Narnia*, 4.
4   For a brief summary of the salient criticisms of the presence of Father Christmas see, Brown, *Inside Narnia: A Guide to Exploring The Lion, the Witch and the Wardrobe*, 143–65.
5   Carpenter, *The Inklings*, 223.

plot) that for Tolkien the suspension of disbelief, the entering into a secondary world, was simply impossible. It just "wouldn't 'do,'" and he turned his back on it.[6]

Tolkien, like many others, gets confused by what he sees as a syncretistic amalgam of classical and medieval elements from diverse cultures, therefore he disliked the presence of Father Christmas. This led him to dismiss the story as beyond saving; as the series developed Tolkien had virtually nothing more to do with it: "Tolkien never changed his view. He so strongly detested Jack's assembling figures from various mythologies in his children's books that he soon gave up trying to read them. He also thought they were carelessly and superficially written."[7] A. N. Wilson commented further on this:

> Tolkien hated *The Lion, the Witch and the Wardrobe*. He regarded it as scrappily put together, and not in his sense a "sub-creation"; that is, a coherently made imaginative world. Moreover it was an allegory, a literary form which he never enjoyed. . . . Tolkien's aesthetic objection to the Narnia stories is a perfectly valid one if we attempt to judge Narnia by the standards of *The Silmarillion*. Lewis's books for children show signs of extraordinary haste in composition. . . . But it is a mistake to judge the Narnia stories as if they were a sort of slapdash *Lord of the Rings*.[8]

Was Tolkien's judgment hasty? The Narniad was written in relative haste without the years of considered labor Tolkien devoted to his imaginary world—Middle Earth—but this is not necessarily to the detriment of the Narniad. Roger Lancelyn Green, a friend and colleague also reacted immediately to the inclusion of Father Christmas, pressing Lewis to exclude the character.[9] Despite the opposition, particularly from Tolkien and others in his circle, Lewis insisted the character of Father Christmas stayed; he had ample opportunity to revise and delete the character, however, he believed it played a role and Father Christmas stayed.

Timothy Denham argues that Father Christmas is as much a mythical character as others in the Narniad, and as a figure of gift-giving he adds a spiritual dimension that could not have been achieved with any other character.[10] On the surface this spiritual dimension makes sense if the character of Father Christmas is divorced from his Christian milieu in this world and given entirely mythical-cultural status. In this context Father Christmas is to be seen as a spiritual gift bearer—whether this is seen in generally religious terms, or simply in mythological terms, is for the reader to decide. But is this possible, and was this Lewis's aim?

---

6 Ibid., 223–24.
7 George Sayer, *Jack: A Life of C. S. Lewis*, 313.
8 Wilson, *C. S. Lewis: a Biography*, 222, and 225–26.
9 Green and Hooper, *C. S. Lewis: A Biography*, , 301–29.
10 Dunham, "*The Lion, the Witch and the Wardrobe*: Summary," online at http://www.answers.com/topic/the-lion-the-witch-and-the-wardrobe-criticism.

9. Analogical and Symbolic Narratives V: Father Christmas in Narnia?

Many readers see Father Christmas in Narnia as representing the Holy Spirit—imparting gifts to fight evil with.[11] The gifts given to three of the Pevensie children are seen as representing the whole armor of God (Eph 6:11–17):

> Father Christmas distributes gifts to the children, which, in another blending, somewhat parallel the spiritual gifts given to the church. Peter is given a shield and a sword. In the familiar "whole armor of God" passage in Ephesians 6, the shield is faith and the sword is the Word of God. Susan receives a horn which can bring help, analogous to prayer, and Lucy receives a cordial with supernatural restorative powers, representing the gift of healing. . . . But with Lewis, unlike Tolkien and most other writers, the most common technique is to blend allusive and non-allusive elements. As Father Christmas is to some extent allied with Aslan, the gifts also have a Norse flavor. The most common poetic name for king in Anglo-Saxon and Old Norse poetry is "ring-giver" (sometimes "gift-giver"). Aslan, the Lord of Narnia, is distributing gifts to his followers.[12]

Marvin Hinten, writing here, generates an essentially allegorical interpretation that does not look for internal coherence within the story but simply looks at how the author's intentions and aims changed and developed, adapted and emerged, in the writing of a work. Allegorical interpretations do not look for explanations within the story but within the mind of the author, and the cultural and religious world the author, and importantly the reader, occupy. The story is not considered to have a life of its own, an inner coherence, rationality and logic. The story is not regarded as something that could have reasonably happened—the story is not granted a real existence *as if* (Lewis's "supposal") it could have come to pass. However, one interesting point Hinten does develop is the concept of the "gift-bearer"—Father Christmas's generosity is on behalf of the King, Aslan, the Lord of Narnia. But if this is a pneumatological "gift-bearer," why does the Holy Spirit take the form specifically of Father Christmas? Again, the problem remains. The context of these interpretations still relies upon allegory and there is an insufficient one-to-one correspondence between Ephesians 6 and the actual gifts. But whether this is how Lewis conceived of the inclusion of this character is another matter. Denham comments: "While some critics recognize the correlation between Father Christmas and the Holy Spirit, they tend to gloss over shared character attributes and focus on the individual gifts. In so doing, they end up over-spiritualizing the gifts and forcing parallels where they may not exist."[13] The pneumatological associations are taken further by some readers: Father Christmas in Narnia is seen as a helper who "performs a function in Narnia that is similar to the scriptural description of the Holy Spirit's function."[14] This is an allegorical interpretation drawn from John's Gospel (John 14:15–17). However, there does not appear to be sufficient one-to-one correlation between the gifts given to the Pevensie children and the scriptural evidence to sustain such an allegorical interpretation.

---

11   See, for example, Ford, *Companion to Narnia*.
12   Hinten, "'Deeper Magic:' Allusions in *The Lion, the Witch and the Wardrobe*," 9–21.
13   Dunham, "*The Lion, the Witch and the Wardrobe*: Summary."
14   Ibid.

Tolkien was not alone in seeking an eradication of Father Christmas from Narnia. John J. Miller, writing in *National Review*, commented that: "If ever there were a case for taking Christ out of Christmas, it's arguably in Narnia," furthermore he argues that Christmas should not be called Christmas in Narnia but "Aslanmas" and that "shouldn't Lewis have left Father Christmas out of his books entirely?"[15] Peter Schakel comments that the inclusion of Christmas itself is inconsistent since the Christmas holiday celebrates Christ's incarnation, so why is there no equivalent to our Christmas in Narnia?[16] Joseph R. Christopher perhaps summarizes this: "What is a symbol tied to a Christian celebration in the primary world doing in the secondary?"[17]

All of the criticisms approach the structure of the Narniad generally, the inclusion of this Father Christmas character specifically, in what can be argued is a superficial manner. Perhaps this is because of the childhood associations,[18] and the links with the superficiality of a secular Christmas celebration, but in rejecting Father Christmas in Narnia they are missing a fundamental element of the Narniad. Is it possible to find and invoke a hidden coherence? Is it possible, notwithstanding the criticisms, to find justification for Father Christmas in Narnia? There is justification for the inclusion of Father Christmas precisely because of the incarnation in our reality, the uniqueness of the Christ event, but also because of the cultural relationship between Narnia and our world, and because his presence is essential to the doctrine of atonement we can read from the Narniad. The clues given by Lewis for the inclusion of Father Christmas are in *The Lion, the Witch and the Wardrobe* and invoke his Platonic Idealism; but also the presence of this Father-Christmas-type-gift-bearer runs at the heart of the cross-cultural nature of Narnia, with its wealth of creatures and characters.

3. THE PROBLEM

The question then is, how do we explain Father Christmas's presence while not doing a disservice or injury to Lewis or the books? Can we systematically read a sound explanation out of *The Chronicles of Narnia* for Father Christmas's presence? To read out is to be exegetical, rather than eisegetical: can we draw out what is logically there, within the parameters of the Narnian reality set by Lewis, as distinct from reading into, projecting our solutions, into Narnia, which is the danger with readers/scholars conceiving of allegorical explanations? The problem is essentially one of cultural identity and names. Can we simply change Father Christmas's name. No; because the associations with the incarnation remain. Miller notes: "This is more than just a rose-by-any-other-name semantic dispute."[19]

---

15   Miller, "Xmas in Narnia."
16   Schakel, *Reading with the Heart: the Way into Narnia*, 140.
17   Christopher, *C. S. Lewis*, 118–19.
18   Donald Glover focuses on the childhood associations as a criticism: "Father Christmas, for all Lewis's attempts at his rehabilitation as a Christian figure, strikes the wrong note, reminding us all too forcefully of childish pleasures and frivolous fantasies." Glover, *C. S. Lewis: The Art of Enchantment*, 141.
19   Miller, "Xmas in Narnia."

9. Analogical and Symbolic Narratives V: Father Christmas in Narnia?

It is perfectly feasible and coherent within the reality of Narnia, as created by Lewis, for Aslan (God the Son) as the Son of the Emperor-over-the-sea (God the Father) to "send" a gift-bearer (through the Holy Spirit) into Narnia from beyond the world. The four Pevensie children are from another reality; likewise Jadis is from yet another utterly different reality. The Wood between the Worlds[20] indicates a positive infinity, a multitude, of different realities, a multiverse (parallel worlds, alternative universes, interpenetrating dimensions, alternative realities or timelines, etc.). The problem is therefore in the cultural identity generated by the name given to this Narnian gift-bearer. He is not called "Father Gift Bearer," or "Mother Bestower," or "Winter King," or some other name invented by the creatures of Narnia reflecting their unique cultural identity. We cannot escape the word "Christmas." The name Christmas represents something unique to our reality. So why do the Narnian creatures invoke the name? Narnia is a world that knows the name Aslan, but not the name Christ: this is a standard criticism against Father Christmas's appearance in *The Lion, the Witch and the Wardrobe*, but it is a deeply flawed criticism. It is not true. The various creatures of Narnia *do* know the word "Christmas," because the humans do. Humans are in Narnia from the point of its creation—the children Digory and Polly, but more pertinently, Frank the London cab driver and his wife, Helen, who will be Narnia's founding monarchs. We can assume that all four will know the name of Christ because of the religious traditions of late Victorian England, which Frank and Helen in particular would have absorbed culturally, through their upbringing and through the socio-religious nature of the Victorian education system, in addition to the evidence Lewis gives that they were Christians. So "Christmas" as a name and concept is in Narnia because humans are there—from the beginning.

4. *THE LION, THE WITCH AND THE WARDROBE*

Father Christmas's only appearance is in *The Lion, the Witch and the Wardrobe*. It is important to note that at no point does this Father-Christmas-type-gift-bearer declare who he is. Mr. Beaver identifies him as Father Christmas; as does Lucy.[21] But he is silent as to his precise nature, his ontological reality. The question therefore is why he is recognized as such. First of all we need to establish where, how, and in what context Father Christmas does appear in Narnia. There are two appearances; both are in *The Lion, the Witch and the Wardrobe*. The four Pevensie children with Mr. and Mrs. Beaver hide in an underground burrow-type-cave to escape the White Witch. Mr. Beaver leaves the cave to investigate the sound of a sledge. He returns to call out the children:

> "Come on!" cried Mr. Beaver, who was almost dancing with delight. "Come and see! This is a nasty knock for the Witch! It looks as if her power is already crumbling"... "Didn't I tell you," answered Mr. Beaver, "that she'd made it always winter and never Christmas? Didn't I tell you? Well, just come and see!" And

---

20 Lewis, *The Magician's Nephew*, Ch. 3, 33–40.
21 Lewis, *The Lion, the Witch and the Wardrobe*, 99.

> then they were all at the top and did see. It was a sledge, and it was reindeer with bells on their harness. And on the sledge sat a person whom everyone knew the moment they set eyes on him. He was a huge man in a bright red robe (bright as holly berries) with a hood that had fur inside it and a great white beard that fell like a foamy waterfall over his chest . . . "I've come at last," said he. "She has kept me out for a long time, but I have got in at last. Aslan is on the move. The Witch's magic is weakening."[22]

This is no anonymous gift bearer, it is a person everyone recognizes the moment they see him. How did Mr. Beaver know who this Father-Christmas-type-gift-bearer was meant to be?

The second appearance is *in absentia*. After Father Christmas has distributed gifts to an assortment of Narnian creatures that are then holding an outdoor celebratory meal, the White Witch comes across them and demands to know where the gifts came from. On hearing that they were from Father Christmas she immediately turns all the creatures to stone—kills them.[23] We do not see Father Christmas on this occasion, only the after-effect. He is a harbinger of Aslan's coming; the power of evil is weakening, which is why Father Christmas could come into Narnia. However, the stammering assertion by a fox, who bears witness to all that is implied in Father Christmas's appearing, especially in relation to Aslan, costs the creatures their lives—they are in effect martyred. Therefore, Lewis is asserting the link between sin and death, and the coming of redemption as a gift. The church used to emphasize this connection, but it has become lost in a secular, indulgent, Christmas. For centuries the day after Christmas Day was St Stephen's day, the joy of Christmas Day, the presents, the food, was followed by Stephen's feast day—Stephen being the first martyr of the church, who was stoned to death for bearing witness to God's redemption revealed in Jesus, the Christ.

The link with sin, death and redemption is taken further by Lewis in the significance of the gifts given out by this Father-Christmas-type-gift-bearer: a sword, a bow-and-arrow, a dagger—weapons of war—and a glass phial of magical liquid that will heal. Death is the common factor to the gifts—death to the enemies of Aslan, but more pertinently death to the children themselves. Their association with Narnia does lead eventually to their premature deaths (the train crash in *The Last Battle*). Death is also the teleology of the food, drink and joy given to the Narnia creatures by Father Christmas out of Aslan's good will—God's gracious gifts lead to death at the hands of evil.

5. ST. NICHOLAS, FATHER CHRISTMAS, SANTA CLAUS, KRIS KRINGLE, JUPITER, JOVE

Before we proceed further we need to decide who Father Christmas is, and what is implied by the cultural identity. The character is rooted in a real person—Saint Nicholas. Nicholas (270–346AD) was Bishop of Myra—part of modern-day Turkey.

---

22   Ibid., 97–101.
23   Ibid., 105–7.

9. Analogical and Symbolic Narratives V: Father Christmas in Narnia?

In the Greek patristic tradition Nicholas is known for numerous miraculous acts but he is revered and honored amongst many denominations, essentially for his generosity and in establishing the tradition of secret or anonymous gift giving. In the medieval church the gift-giving that had happened for centuries on his feast date (Dec 6) became associated with Christmas. In different European cultures this generates a mythical person who brings gifts into the homes of good children on Christmas Eve, and also on December 6. The emergence of Father Christmas, Sinterklaas,[24] Kris Kringle,[25] *et al.*, are related to, but develop a degree of independence from the historical figure of Nicholas of Myra. This degree of independence from the Christian roots led, in part, to the Puritans under Oliver Cromwell, during the period of the English Commonwealth, banning Christmas celebrations, though this was short-lived. Much that we associate with the cultural identity of Father Christmas developed in Victorian England, including the reintroduction of pagan associations—trees, decorations, indeed the very word, Yuletide. The jovial associations of Christmas are often seen as having been derived from pagan European culture—centered on the "god" Jupiter or Jove.[26] By the early twentieth century the Coca Cola drinks company had stripped Santa Claus of the last vestiges of his brown bishop's robe (with its grey ermine fur trim) and dressed him in a scarlet and white romper suit—the colors of the Coca Cola company—and employed him to advertise their products![27] Perhaps the commercialization of Christmas and its separation (divorce?) from its Christian roots, including the secularization of Father Christmas, was best expressed by that paradigm of postmodern youth, the cartoon character Bart Simpson, who commented: "Aren't we forgetting the true meaning of Christmas? You know, the birth of Santa."[28]

6. PLATONIC IDEALISM AND REALITY

Father Christmas is taken to be a mythical character unique to our reality, the planet Earth. As such Father Christmas is primarily related to God's revelation (the incarnation), then secondarily to Christianity (Nicholas, Bishop of Myra), and then, thirdly, to North European pagan myths and Greco-Roman "gods" (the various Father

---

24   The American name Santa Claus, developed from the Dutch name, *Sinterklaas* (in 1809, the New York Historical Society renamed Sinterklaas, Sancte Claus).

25   The name Kris Kringle is essential Germanic. It derives from Bavaria and Austria, "Christkind" or "Christkindl"—the mythical Christmas gift-bringer, however in modern Western culture the name has fallen into relative disuse, to be revived by the American film, *Miracle on 34th Street*.

26   See, Ward, *Planet Narnia*, Ch. 3 Jupiter, 42–76.

27   Santa, as a rotund figure dressed in a scarlet romper suit with cotton-wool-white trimmings all over was created for *The Coca-Cola Company* in 1931 by the advertising executive Haddon Sundblom (the campaign was used until 1964). While there is evidence that in the eighteenth and nineteenth centuries the apparel of the various Father Christmas characters was slowly changing from a brown full length coat, to maroon to red, with grey ermine trim, then white fur, the distinctive "Santa" romper suit was essentially an invention of *The Coca Cola Company*. The Sunblom Santas can be viewed at: http://www.thecoca-colacompany.com/heritage/cokelore_santa.html. Also:
   http://www.hymnsandcarolsofchristmas.com/santa/sundblom_santas.htm

28   The Simpsons, "Miracle on Evergreen Terrace," Season 9, No. 188/910, Production code: 5F07, original transmission, Fox: Dec 21, 1997.

Christmas/Santa Claus characters and the Roman "god" Jupiter), all of which relate to Nicholas Bishop of Myra as a gift-bearer, to a greater or lesser degree. The only clue Lewis gives us to his thinking is in a reflective passage added to the scene where Father Christmas hands out the gifts to three of the Pevensie children. Lewis refers to this character as Father Christmas obliquely: "Everyone knew him because, though you see people of his sort only in Narnia, you see pictures of them and hear them talked about even in our world—the world on this side of the wardrobe door."[29] Lewis comments that some of the pictures of Father Christmas in our world cast him as only funny and jolly, but that the character now before the children in Narnia was not at all comical. He was large, "and so real, that they all became quite still. They felt very glad, but also solemn."[30] So, a mythological figure in our reality becomes a real flesh-and-blood gift-bearer in a parallel universe. The clue here is, perhaps, in Lewis's Platonic Idealism, which explains something of the relationship.

i. Revelation and Myth-Making

If existence is judged by the effect a person has on other people, then judging by the profound impact Father Christmas has had on millions of people's lives, he is in one way very real. This brings us into Lewis's Platonic Idealism—that ideas, certainly for Lewis, are considered more important, in many ways, than so-called physical objects.[31] If what we take for reality is *perceivable* but not necessarily *intelligible*, but that the reality of forms in eternity is *intelligible* but not *perceivable*, the idea of Father Christmas as a gift bearer from God is more real (though not necessarily immediately perceivable), than the pale shadows perceivable in the multitudinous Santas and Father Christmases in the reality we occupy which we take to be perceivable. Ideas form the basis of humanity's attempt at creation—stories, for Lewis and Tolkien, were a form of sub-creation reflecting something of the refracted light of God's glory and truth. Tolkien is thought to have said, "We have come from God, and inevitably the myths woven by us, though they contain error, will also reflect a splintered fragment of the true light, the eternal truth that is with God. Indeed only by myth-making, only by becoming a 'sub-creator' and inventing stories, can Man aspire to the state of perfection that he knew before the Fall. Our myths may be misguided, but they steer however shakily towards the true harbor."[32] Lewis asserts in *The Lion the Witch and the Wardrobe* that Father Christmas is real in Narnia, but only talked about in our reality. In Narnia ideas become real.[33] This is part of the ontology of Narnia as a created

---

29   Lewis, *The Lion, the Witch and the Wardrobe*, 99.
30   Ibid.
31   See: Brazier, "C. S. Lewis: A Doctrine of Transposition," 669–88. See also, Patrick, "C. S. Lewis and Idealism," 156–73.
32   Carpenter, *J. R. R. Tolkien: A Biography*, 197–98. See also, Tolkien, "Mythopoeia," 85–90. Also, Tolkien, "On Fairy Stories," 38–89.
33   In terms of the relationship between reality and ideas, in particular Lewis's adoption of Berkeley's theory of immaterialism, or subjective idealism, encapsulated in the dictum, *esse est percipi* (the theory that we only know sensations or ideas of objects, we cannot know abstractions), see, Brazier, "C. S. Lewis: A Doctrine of Transposition," specifically, 671–72.

9. Analogical and Symbolic Narratives V: Father Christmas in Narnia?

reality; this is a "supposed" ontology with its own internal coherence. In our world only Nicholas, Bishop of Myra, is "real," all other Father-Christmas-type-gift-bearers are "ideas" related to Nicholas—this is part of the ontology of our reality. But then St Nicholas as a gift-bearer is only a shadow of the true form of the gift-bearer in eternity. As distinct from St Nicholas who was real, the popular mythological figures of Father Christmas, Santa Claus, *et al.*, do not exist in the generally accepted post-Kantian ontological sense we attribute to sentient existence (within a neo-Kantian single level closed universe), but Lewis as a philosopher was effectively, philosophically, a pre-Kantian Platonist. We may deduce that, for Lewis, the "idea" of a gift-bearer is on behalf of the King, the Lord, Yahweh, and that this gift-bearer is manifested in the shadowlands of our reality as Bishop Nicholas (and in a secondary sense in the multitudinous Santas and their ilk), but also in the shadowlands of Narnia (a potential parallel universe) as a real person making regular annual appearances.

ii. Transposition

A doctrine of transposition is the key to all of Lewis's work (literary, apologetic, and philosophical)—or, more exactly, a "flawed" doctrine of transposition, itself transposed platonically. If, as we have established, for Lewis, revelation proceeds eschatologically, from eternity and into our reality; this is primarily in the form of the incarnation, but secondarily in the modes of general and incomplete revelation. Reality, for Lewis, was simply a veil through which we might glimpse the source of this greater reality: eternity, heaven. But this is on God's terms and proceeds from eternity, drawing our gaze back to eternity. This other reality is at the heart of Lewis's Platonic Idealism. Lewis is at his most philosophically theological in invoking the concept of transposition[34] to explain how revelation operates, how God communicates and mediates truth and God's salvific intentions to us through various modes: from the general and incomplete (election—Israel and the law; good dreams—pagan premonitions of Christ; the universal ought—moral responsibility; the experience of the numinous—God's holiness; *Sehnsucht*—the hound of heaven; and the natural world), to the particular and perfect (the incarnation, and to a degree, Scripture).[35] Transposition is inevitably framed in Platonic terms. Lewis, like Berkeley and other Idealists and Platonists, saw that we can only understand the world around us through its relationship to a higher spiritual reality. Intimations of the higher realm, eternity, will inevitably be translated, transposed. But transposed revelation is more than a mere dilution, more than a watered-down version of the real thing. Revelation will give us intimations; the imagination then will conjure up images that help explain and draw us up to where we should be: eternity. The Bible, particularly the New Testament and specifically the parables of Jesus, are therefore often couched in symbolic—transpositional—language; more pertinently they are

---

34   Lewis, "Transposition," an essay first given as a sermon in Mansfield College, Oxford, on Whit-Sunday—no year is recorded—then published in, Lewis *Transposition and other Addresses* (1949), 9–20. A second, expanded, edition was published in, Lewis *They asked for a Paper* (1962), 166–82.

35   Modes of revelation are dealt with in depth in the second book in this series: *C. S. Lewis—The Work of Christ Revealed*, see, Ch. 2.

for Lewis analogical. There is no one-to-one correlation because this is simply not possible, in the same way that lines drawn on paper are a diminution of a solid object because they cannot be the real thing: they represent for us a fluid three-dimensional reality in an artificial two-dimensionality. (A pencil drawing of an oak tree is not an allegory of its solidity.) Therefore, we are forced to resort to images and concepts from this world to explain the world to come, the truly real world. There will inevitably be a diminution. This is why Lewis invokes the term "transposition." Ideas are a form of transposed revelation that is secondary to the primary revelation that is God in Christ Jesus. These ideas are pneumatologically imparted (the dove whispering into the mind) leaving the person to sub-create; therefore there will be an internal coherence to a story, there will be consistency and a logic of sorts, there will be unity, lucidity, rationality in the Narniad, but this may be hidden and needs to be exegetically drawn out.[36] These stories will reflect something of God's truth, but this will be transposed and therefore hidden to a degree. The Narniad is peppered with Lewis's understanding of platonically transposed revelation. For example, the Green Witch's attempt to seduce Jill and Eustace into believing that reality, the world of sense perception, is all there is, that their "ideas" about Aslan and the overworld (comparable to God and eternity) are a delusion.[37] In *The Last Battle* Lewis waxed Platonic and Berkeleyian. After the apocalyptically-charged end of the world in Narnia, Digory, having died and been raised in eternity, comments that: "'Of course it is different; as different as a real thing is from a shadow or as waking life is from a dream.' His voice stirred everyone like a trumpet as he spoke these words: but when he added under his breath 'It's all in Plato, all in Plato: bless me, what do they teach them at these schools!', the older ones laughed."[38]

iii. Illumination and Intimation

Perhaps Tolkien's criticisms that we encountered earlier were due to him adopting too tight, too contained and earthly an approach to inspiration and composition. Revelation leads to sub-creation; sub-creation must not be so tightly controlled so as to exclude what might on the surface be apparent contradictions and difficulties in a story. Middle Earth is a water tight, coherent and flawless creation; but is there sufficient space in the story for mystery, for invocation of the barely knowable as there is in the Narniad. It could be argued that there is insufficient room for God, perhaps Christian revelation, in Middle Earth as a sub-creation, though it can be acknowledge that Christ is hidden, pre-incarnational, and that the condition of all the creatures, dominated as they are by manifest evil, cries out for the redemption proffered by the Christ. Lewis started writing just the one book—*The Lion, the Witch and the Wardrobe*—without necessarily knowing that the other six books would follow. Yet it can be argued that they benefit from the lack of control over the detail that Tolkien identified because this leaves Lewis's imagination open to transposed

36 Lewis, *The Silver Chair*, 142–43.
37 For example, Ward, *Planet Narnia*.
38 Lewis, *The Last Battle*, 159–60.

9. Analogical and Symbolic Narratives V: Father Christmas in Narnia?

> **SALVATION HISTORY AND A CHRISTOCENTRIC RELIGIOUS ECONOMY IN THE NARNIAD**
>
> *The Magician's Nephew*—"tells the creation and how evil entered Narnia"
> ⬇
> *The Lion the Witch and the Wardrobe*—"the Crucifixion and Resurrection"
> ⬇
> *Prince Caspian*—"restoration of the true religion after a corruption"
> ⬇
> *The Horse and his Boy*—"the calling and conversion of a heathen"
> ⬇
> *The Voyage of the Dawn Treader*—"the spiritual life (specially in Reepicheep)"
> ⬇
> *The Silver Chair*—"the continued war against the powers of darkness"
> ⬇
> *The Last Battle*— "the coming of Antichrist (the Ape) the end of the world, and the Last Judgement"
>
> From Lewis's letter to Anne Jenkins, Mar 5, 1961.

Figure 8. A Comparison of Salvation History in Narnia and on Earth

ideas, intimations from the Holy Spirit. Transposition means that the hallmark of divine inspiration will be a flawed incompleteness—"rustling with the rumor that it will not always be so."[39] Perhaps Middle Earth, by comparison, is too complete and contained, when completeness is to be gifted in eternity. It could be argued that there is an element of circularity of argument here: that claiming the flaw at the heart of transposition simply covers a badly worked out philosophy. Not so. There is also the virtuous circle of consistency, and the deeper criterion of completeness or adequacy to the data. We are the object, not the subject; God is the verb. God initiates; God is the source and origin, the author of all revelation, and thus sets the terms. Only the incarnation is concrete in revelatory terms; sub-creation will necessarily be defined by intimation (illumined by the splintered fragment of the true light, the eternal truth of and from God) rather than eschatological completeness: thus, perhaps, the difference between Middle Earth and Narnia.

---

39   Lewis, "The Weight of Glory," first published in, *Transposition and other Addresses*, 21–33. Reprinted in, C. S. Lewis, *They asked for a Paper*, 208-9.

Given what we know of Lewis's understanding of imagination and inspiration, and how God's truth for humankind's benefit is transposed, then we must be able to postulate a reasonable explanation for the presence and use of the name Father Christmas in Narnia, likewise why this Father-Christmas-type-gift-bearer visits Narnia from beyond the world.

7. FATHER CHRISTMAS IN NARNIA: AN EXISTENTIAL THEOLOGICAL PROPOSITION

So, we may hypothesize—as Lewis did—that there are other realities, other universes and worlds—alien realities—all created and sustained by the one triune God, each with unique characteristics some of which would be beyond our comprehension. Moreover we may postulate that a loving God would seek to raise up sentient creatures—living, breathing, conscious life forms—created to praise and love God in freedom, with the implication that in this freedom they may choose to rebel, to sin, and to turn away to a greater or lesser degree (similar yet dissimilar to the nature of human rebellion in the ontological reality we occupy). Finally, if this triune God would seek the redemption of such alien creatures in ways similar, yet dissimilar, to the Christ event in our reality, then it seems fair to propose that something similar to the incarnation-cross-resurrection might (note the subjunctive) occur within the ontological parameters of such an alien reality. This is the analogical premise for Lewis's *The Chronicles of Narnia* (i.e., Lewis's "supposal"). What is more, if there is cultural exchange, commerce, between the worlds—as there is between earth and Narnia—and if creatures may travel, at the will of God between these worlds then something of the cultural norms that they have grown-up with, that form their identity, may, at the behest of God, travel with them.

i. The Gift Bearer

Such a religious economy happens within *The Chronicles of Narnia*. One such example must be this Father-Christmas-type-gift-bearer that appears in *The Lion, the Witch and the Wardrobe*, who greets three of the Pevensie children as the 100-year winter slackens and Aslan's arrival is perceived. What is more, the gift-bearers (here, and in Narnia, and arguably in many other realities) emanate from the same Platonic form (Lewis's Idealism); such a Platonic form is in itself a manifestation of the loving generosity of the one triune God and is in effect the working of the Holy Spirit. Platonism if it has any value or cogency illustrates the mechanism by which the Holy Spirit operates between the two realities: eternity and the created realm(s). Therefore, there is an intimate connection between the annual generosity of this Father-Christmas-type-gift-bearer in Narnia and the mythical figure of Father Christmas/Santa Claus in our reality (as there is also between our Father Christmas with all his pagan associations, and Nicholas, Bishop of Myra: the connection is pneumatological). The Narnian Father Christmas is then a precursor to the arrival of Aslan. But why does Aslan elect to send this Father-Christmas-type-gift-bearer into Narnia? The cultural connection must be with the humans, indeed with the first humans to settle in Narnia—the London cab

9. Analogical and Symbolic Narratives V: Father Christmas in Narnia?

driver Frank and his wife Helen who, as we have established, would have grown up with the cultural experience of a Victorian Christmas. The generosity of Aslan is such that this Father-Christmas-type-gift-bearer is sent from another world, perhaps even Aslan's own country, to give gifts to a worthy select within Narnia. Frank and Helen were meant to make the connection and perceive him to be *like* Father Christmas, and name him as such so that the Narnian creatures (right down the generations to Mr. and Mrs. Beaver) adopt the name without necessarily knowing or understanding the context and connection with the Christ event in our reality. Culturally the arrival of this Father-Christmas-type-gift-bearer would surely have been at or near the time of the winter solstice, the shortest day of the year, the time of year, the season, in which we celebrate Christ's birthday. As we noted earlier, at no point does this Father-Christmas-type-gift-bearer announce that he is Father Christmas (he is not the *form*, only a *shadow*) but being representative of the Earth festival of Christmas, implies that he is sent on behalf of the Lord of Christmas throughout all creations (in Trinitarian terms, God the Father). This exchange of cultural norms implies that though most Narnians will not have any conception of what Christmas is, they will happily accept the gifts, the joy, the celebration—in religious terms the meaning for them is apophatic. Therefore, the Beavers take him to be Father Christmas, a joyous figure associated with the world of the humans, and although the cultural meaning within Narnia will be apophatically de-Christianized, the relationship will stand for the humans (Frank and Helen, but also all their descendants[40]). Lucy recognizes, or so she believes, that he is Father Christmas, but that is after having been told by Mr. Beaver that it is Father Christmas. Susan and Peter will have been naturally skeptical due to their age (adolescent!).

ii. Cross-Cultural Fertilization

This exchange of cultural norms is in effect a form of multi-culturalism, which, although Lewis and Tolkien were writing before such a concept became commonplace in Western liberal societies in the later twentieth century, is found throughout their works. Father Christmas/Santa Claus is now, by and large, apophatically de-Christianized in the West, and even in Eastern societies. (In Matsue, Japan, penguins are dressed in Santa costumes and made to parade in the local park, daily, leading up to Christmas: children love them, but they have nothing to do with the gospel story of incarnation, merely recognition of the myth of a gift-bearer.[41]) This exchange of

---

40 When the Pevensie children arrive Narnia is bereft of humans. Mrs Beaver's comment that the four Pevensie children are the first humans ever in Narnia merely illustrates the success of the White Witch's ethnic cleansing. This would point to the fact that the White Witch has annihilated all of Frank and Helen's descendants, a holocaust of the Narnian humans, because of the prophecy regarding the four thrones at Cair Paravel. Many Narnians would probably have gone into exile in the surrounding lands, therefore they, along with say the Calormenes, or those living in the islands, would not be eligible to fulfil the prophecy.

41 Penguins dress as Father Christmas in Japan. BBC News: http://news.bbc.co.uk/1/hi/8400738.stm. Roast chicken and Christmas cake is now consumed by the majority of Japanese on Christmas Day: http://www.japaninc.com/node/2758

cultural norms is in effect a form of cross-cultural fertilization. Lewis's sub-creation (the Narniad) is defined in many ways by the interaction of three worlds, three realities: first, the actions and beliefs of the people (the indigenous sentient creatures) of Narnia; second, the human migrants from earth who are in Narnia from its beginning; and third the imported evil from Charn (Jadis, the demonic queen, who becomes the White Witch). Narnia is not a hermetic world, sealed-off from any other realities, and therefore cultures. The very lamp post that features so importantly in two of the books is, of course, imported from our world: the cross-bar from a Victorian cast iron lamp post is wrenched-off and taken into Narnia by Jadis, the lamp post growing from the cross-bar.[42] Generations of Narnian creatures would have looked at the illumined lamp post and been puzzled, what was this "lamm-ppow-st"? Edmund receives a battery-powered torch for his birthday days before the four Pevensie children are transported back into Narnia, where he uses it,[43] and then when they return to Britain he discovers from his satchel bag that it is missing—left in Narnia.[44] So what do the Narnians who discover it make of it? Do they attempt to produce their own design? If they discard it when its batteries fail this will cause pollution—chemicals leaking from the batteries which will change the environment. Knowledge of this "taw-ch" will have changed the locals: they will probably have learnt words like battery, bulb, aluminum, beam, switch, without having much understanding, meaning or cultural context. Then there are the school uniforms the Pevensie children are re-clothed in before they return to Britain at the end of *Prince Caspian*.[45] Would the preservation of these strange, bizarre and utterly foreign, clothes, have influenced Narnian fashion? Turkish delight is another thing imported into Narnia somehow in its past—or was the White Witch able to read Edmund's mind and know what his heart desired above all else?[46] Eustace and Jill Pole rescue King Tirian and give him sandwiches[47] to eat; very un-Narnian food and a word that would not have been in any Narnian language.[48] Later Jill talking to King Tirian about how they planned to get back into Narnia to help the king, explains about the complex sewerage and drainage system in London, the fact that London is a giant city like nothing in Narnia, also, she has to explain about trains, steam engines, carriages, and the railway network, including railway stations and platforms (utterly unknown in Narnia).[49] But for the fact that within days of this conversation Narnia is no more, subject to the apocalyptic Narnian *eschaton*, Tirian could quite easily, using the technological skills of the dwarves, be moved to invent a steam engine and railway network for Narnia, importing all kinds of words and concepts unknown to the local indigenous population. From what Jill told him about the drains and sewage system in

---

42   Lewis, *The Magician's Nephew*, 88.
43   Lewis, *Prince Caspian*, 27–28.
44   Ibid., 190.
45   Ibid., 189–90
46   Lewis, *The Lion, the Witch and the Wardrobe*, Ch. 4 Turkish Delight, 35–43; see also, 70, 88–89, 111–12.
47   Invented by John Montagu, 4th Earl of Sandwich, 1718–92; Sandwich is a coastal town in Kent, UK, in Sandwich Bay.
48   Lewis, *The Last Battle*, 48
49   Ibid., 50–52

9. Analogical and Symbolic Narratives V: Father Christmas in Narnia?

the metropolis of London, a similar system could have been dug by the dwarves and named "The Bazalgette"[50] by Tirian, from Jill's eager retelling of her school lessons! The name Bazalgette joining Father Christmas in Narnian vocabulary. Christmas is therefore also a word that clearly has been imported by humans—with no knowledge about its meaning to the local populace.

iii. Sin, Treachery, and Atonement

This Father-Christmas-type-gift-bearer may be divorced teleologically from the Christ event in our reality, but, the gift-bearing remains (and is implicitly an example of God's loving generosity in sending his only begotten Son into the world to die for humanity). The presence of this Father-Christmas-type-gift-bearer is a reminder to them that the Narnian humans are, in Lewis's often invoked-terminology, sons and daughters of Adam and Eve,[51] that in the reality in which their descendants were born, God descended to earth to die a criminal's death, in humility, to take their sin on his shoulders (the sin of Adam and Eve), to suffer and die in their place, so that the burden should be removed, so that they might begin to live as they were meant to be. Despite the commercialization of a Western Christmas, there is an indelible connection between what we take to be Father Christmas on the one hand, and the incarnation-cross-resurrection, and thereby atonement and human fallenness on the other. Even in our reality the sight of Father Christmas or Santa Claus *should* be a reminder of the Incarnation and all that issues from this central act of the relationship between God and human history.

Therefore, we cannot consider the presence of this Father-Christmas-type-gift-bearer in the consciousness of Narnians, and in the reality of an annual present-giving visit, without considering sin and atonement. Father Christmas's presence in Narnia points not to a nativity but to sin and fallenness in Narnia; the gift-bearer's presence points to Aslan's sacrifice (given that there is no nativity) to heal Narnia from sin, fallenness, and corruption. Atonement theory in *The Lion, the Witch and the Wardrobe* is not really explained or explicated; as it stands it may be considered as rather hollow and superficial—Edmund as traitor should die, but Aslan does so in his place. Why is one of the treacherous Narnians not selected as representative? It is not just Edmund who is a traitor: Tumnus the Faun who was a spy, Ginarrbrik the White Witch's dwarf, the wolves that formed her secret police, indeed all the creatures that have gone over to her side during the 100-year winter are guilty of treachery, treason, which brings judgment on Narnia once Aslan arrives. Has not the Aslan-Christ died for Edmund already in our reality, upon Calvary? Do we have the Aslan-Christ dying twice for humanity? Does not Edmund take the atonement won for him by Jesus on the cross with him to Narnia? Christ's sacrifice is complete and sufficient for all humanity. But why must Edmund die for his treachery in Narnia? Because of Calvary, Edmund's

---

50 Sir Joseph William Bazalgette (1819–1891), chief engineer of the London Metropolitan Board of Works creation of a fresh water supply and sewer network for central London.
51 Lewis, *The Lion, the Witch and the Wardrobe*, 11, 20, 34, 36–38, 66, 71, 78–82, 84, 89, 98, 106, 108, 127–29, 132–33, 135, 182, 185–86.

eternal life is not in jeopardy from his betrayal provided he repents, which he does.[52] However, the price must be paid to prevent all Narnia being consumed in fire and water. Traitors belong to Jadis, the White Witch, who is personified evil; treachery (Judas's sin) is evil and therefore as far from God as can be conceived. Treachery is not a private sin but has profound communal consequences. Hence, although through repentance Edmund's eternal salvation is assured, his mortal existence is threatened by the need for justice within Narnia. But, Aslan steps in to offer himself as sacrifice. The White Witch herself prepares to execute Edmund against the trunk of a tree, knowing that this is not the right place, because Aslan's forces have occupied the Stone Table.[53] Edmund is rescued and is brought before Aslan. He repents and Aslan forgives him. Aslan's righteousness is satisfied with repentance; it is then that the White Witch demands that the law be fulfilled. In religious self-righteousness she demands Edmund's blood because of the deep magic from the dawn of time written on the Emperor-beyond-the-Sea's scepter whereby all Narnia will be consumed in fire and water (an apocalyptic destruction of flood, earthquake, annihilation). Only God has the right to forgive; Aslan forgives Edmund, but personified evil demands the letter of the law be fulfilled. Knowing the consequences for Narnia once the White Witch has spoken her demand, Aslan must either hand Edmund over to be sacrificed or he must submit himself as the substitute sacrifice (Aslan will pay the ransom). Aslan's epiphany, his coming to Narnia, Edmund's treachery and the atonement achieved through the one perfect sacrifice are all intertwined: Aslan's sacrifice is a gifting. Therefore, the annual gift-giving by this Father-Christmas-type-gift-bearer is a precursory analogical representation of Aslan's self-sacrifice.

iv. A Narnian Fall

If Aslan's death is for all in Narnia, and not just Edmund's treachery, then there has to be a seed of sin, a Narnian fall that corrupts and condemns. This seed of sin must be seen as similar, but not the same, as the *fall* in our reality. This seed of sin enslaves all Narnians. The seed of sin may be considered to be Jadis's attempt to murder Aslan during the creation scene (recounted by Lewis in *The Magician's Nephew*[54]). This act writes the potential and ability to rebel and therefore to sin into Narnia. At some point early on the first murder would have been committed—the sin of Cain (and like Cain's murder of Abel, the act will have religious/sacrificial overtones—blood would have contaminated the land). In our reality the symbolic plucking of the fruit of the tree of the knowledge of good and evil is written into our very human consciousness, our wills; in the same way Jadis's attempt to murder Aslan germinates the seed of rebellion against Aslan's authority, which grows into the consciousness of all Narnians, and into the fabric of the created reality that is Narnia. With shed blood polluting Narnia it would have been only a matter of time until the tree of protection was destroyed (the tree is notable by its absence in subsequent books, and its uprooting explains

---

52   Ibid., 126.
53   Ibid., 123–24.
54   Lewis, *The Magician's Nephew*, 99–100.

9. Analogical and Symbolic Narratives V: Father Christmas in Narnia?

why the White Witch can reign with tyranny over Narnia for 100 years). These three acts (attempted murder; actual murder; and the destruction of the tree of protection), establish the need for righteous judgment and punishment, and thereby atonement for all Narnians. Given that treachery and treason are so great a threat to Narnia it is reasonable to assume that the destruction of the tree of protection occurs through treachery and treason, to be followed by the construction of the Stone Table for the act of sacrifice, a pagan rite—protectionist killing, in the place of true atonement.

Treachery is therefore the worst of all sins. In the context of Narnia for it destroys Aslan's creation and ultimately denies Aslan's righteous authority (in our reality it issues from the serpent—Lucifer, the fallen angel in disguise and his rebellion against God). Why has Narnia not been consumed in an eschatological vision of fire and water prior to Edmund's treachery? Why has this not happened within the previous 100-year winter when many Narnians committed treason by going over to the White Witch's side? This destruction is postponed by the White Witch's enchantments which keep Aslan (God's righteousness) and the Father-Christmas-gift-bearer out of Narnia, and freeze the land into perpetual winter: evil can thwart God's righteous aims, but not for ever. Tyrants rule, they may seem invincible but they will fail and pass, assuredly, always. Therefore, if the potential destruction of Narnia through fire and water is eschatological—it is of the end times—and if the White Witch's reign is as far as possible from Aslan's reign, which is why Narnia becomes a perpetual 100-year winter locked in snow and ice, then when Aslan comes his righteousness will thaw the White Witch's winter but his presence will bring sin to a head, to a crisis. As one of the chosen, one of the elect, one of the four human children who are pre-destined to re-found the Narnian monarchy, Edmund's treachery is the pinnacle of deceit, betrayal, duplicity and treason in Narnia: he must be executed on the Stone Table to prevent the eschatological judgmental crisis that will consume all Narnia in apocalyptic chaos. Edmund's treachery is the final trigger.

v. "Always Winter and Never Christmas"

Like the lamp post in Lantern Waste that "grew" out of Jadis's attempt to slay Aslan, Father Christmas stands as a witness to the loving judgment of God. His return prefaces Aslan's ultimate gifting—himself as the righteous sacrifice, to be killed on the Stone Table. The undying light that issues from the lamp post would not be there but for Jadis's attempt to extinguish Aslan, the light of Narnia. The weapon of attempted murder (the broken cross bar from the lamp post in London) rises to be a light to illumine Narnia, as the Narnian creatures become more and more entrapped, ensnared to sin and evil. The light is therefore an eschatological witness just as Father Christmas is an eschatological harbinger—which is why the White Witch sought so long and hard to keep him out during her century of tyranny, and why she had spies ever watching Lantern Waste. This Father-Christmas-type-gift-bearer was sent in the first place to be a sacramental sign of Aslan' love and righteous authority—in gracious favor the high king above all high kings sends gifts of good pleasure to Narnians.

This Father-Christmas-type-gift-bearer, like the lamp post in Lantern Waste, is a sacramental sign that all will one day be well, that atonement will be achieved, but the price will be high. Visits by this Father-Christmas-type-gift-bearer are to be seen as an eschatological herald of Aslan's authority, Aslan's righteous judgment, but they are also teleological, for they lead, cumulatively, year upon year to the end game: Aslan's return in the middle of time, the middle of Narnian time, to die on the Stone Table to redeem and set free all Narnians from the slavery of sin (sin being epitomized by treachery and treason). All of this, the economy of salvation in Narnia, is acted out of God's love for creation. This central event is set in motion by the visit of a little girl from our world that arrives at the lamp post of all places, who then introduces her siblings (with the exception, temporarily, of the treacherous Edmund) to Narnia, in time to meet the returning Father-Christmas-type-gift-bearer, and to meet Aslan and to accompany him, with her sister, to his sacrifice and resurrection. And perhaps this visitation at the end of the 100-year winter by the Narnian Father-Christmas-type-gift-bearer is the final visit. For with Aslan's sacrifice and resurrection, the visits by this gift-bearer, as a precursor, are no longer necessary. In our reality the gift-bearer follows on for centuries, millennia, after the incarnation-cross-resurrection; in Narnia, paradoxically, he is antecedent, although both are grounded in and are ontologically emanations from the one Platonic form, pneumatologically issuing from God's loving generosity and care for creation. Therefore the line, "always winter and never Christmas,"[55] refers to the coming of Aslan, the epiphany of his sacrifice. With the breaking of the White Witch's 100-year winter and the coming of Aslan any Narnian creature expecting a perpetual winter-solstice celebration and gift-giving (named "Christmas" because of the connection with the Narnian humans) is in for a surprise. Christ's-mas here equals Aslan's sacrifice, as Christmas in our reality (the incarnation) leads teleologically to Easter and the cross.

8. TOWARDS A NARNIAN ATONEMENT

Christ died for us, to save us from our sins: this is central to orthodox and traditional Christology. If Lewis's Narniad is a true analogy of human salvation, then we must be able to glean from the seven books generally, from *The Lion, the Witch, and the Wardrobe* specifically, a valid and comparable theory of atonement, but with unique characteristics to the supposed world of Narnia. Aslan dies to save Narnia and all its creatures, its inhabitants. We have established *why*, but the question remains *how*? How does Aslan's sacrifice of himself save Narnia? To ask such a question is to talk about atonement theories. So, in terms of systematic theology, what is a Narnian theory of atonement? How does such a theory compare with atonement in our reality? What follows here is an introductory sketch; a full analysis of Lewis on atonement theories is in the final part of this series.[56]

---

55   Lewis, *The Lion, the Witch and the Wardrobe*, 99.
56   Brazier, *C. S. Lewis—On the Christ of a Religious Economy. II. Knowing Salvation*, Pt. 2, Ch. 9.

9. Analogical and Symbolic Narratives V: Father Christmas in Narnia?

i. Freedom . . . under "The Law"

Invented in the sixteenth century by the Bible scholar and translator William Tyndale the word atonement ("at-one-ment") was coined to reflect the concept in the Hebrew Scriptures of *how* forgiveness takes place. In sixteenth-century early modern English there was no single word that could reflect and explain this Hebrew understanding of the process of forgiving or pardoning a transgression by and before God, an understanding from which issued the atonement theories of the disciples, the Apostle Paul, and the early church—post-resurrection. Christ's sacrifice reconciles as it forgives: therefore atonement must explain the simultaneous reconciliation of humanity to God, and the remission of sin, taking into account the question or need of propitiation and satisfaction. Atonement theories are therefore more than explanations of reconciliation because of an element of justice.

The *need* and *how* is conjectured by Lewis into the very nature of the reality that is the "supposed" world of Narnia: atonement relates to "the Law"—i.e., the Mosaic Law—and the ontology of reality (the very nature of the world that is Narnia). The law written on the scepter of the Emperor-beyond-the-Sea at the founding of Narnia is based on justice, ownership, and occupancy. The creatures have certain rights, where a right is a freedom enshrined in this law, in the nature of this creation. Sentient creatures, people who consistently act in an evil way, creatures who consistently immerse themselves in evil acts become evil and are therefore contrary to the very nature of their creaturely nature and to this law of creation. Such creatures are owned/possessed by the evil one and occupy an evil space: they are, to borrow Martin Luther's term, in bondage.[57] Therefore the White Witch claims ownership of Edmund for his treachery. If her ownership is not acknowledged, and her right under the "Law" to execute him, then the fabric of Narnia will collapse—the reality, the world of Narnia, will cease, it will be consumed in fire and water: the ontology (the nature of being) has been broken, rent asunder, which would usher in a premature *eschaton*. To avoid this destruction (though it happens eventually in the Narnian *eschaton*—in the seventh book, *The Last Battle*—thousands of years later) Aslan offers himself in exchange for Edmund; *he* will pay the blood price: but another "Law" from before the dawn of time states that when an innocent is sacrificed in the stead of the guilty death will turn backwards and the threat of destruction is lifted. But why does Aslan's sacrifice *satisfy* the "Law" and the need for justice? This is the question at the heart of all atonement theories.

ii. A Ransom Theory of Atonement

Lewis's atonement theory/model in the Narniad is essentially an adaptation of the ransom model. (Note, the Christlike hero of *The Space Trilogy* is named Elwin

---

[57] For example, the fate of Rishda Tarkaan in the Narnian eschaton, who is taken by Tash (the evil one, Satan); in response, Peter the High King order Tash, "Begone, Monster, and take your lawful prey to your own place: in the name of Aslan and Aslan's great Father the Emperor-over-the-Sea." Lewis, *The Last Battle*, 126.

Ransom. Ransom is an obvious clue to Lewis's atonement interests; Elwin, Elvin, is Anglo-Saxon meaning "elf," often "magical being," and "friend"). The ransom theory of atonement is patristic—it can be found as the framework for the drama of salvation, the working out of saving deliverance, salvation history, in the early church: Irenaeus (second century) and Origen (c. 184-253AD); in the writings of the Cappadocian fathers—specifically Gregory of Nyssa (332-95AD) and Basil the Great (330-79AD); also in Ambrose's (330-97) and Jerome's (347-420AD) works. The White Witch holds Edmund to ransom (from the Latin, *redemptio*; redemption, to redeem) she demands a blood price. The basic ransom model is summarized well by Taliaferro in his work analyzing the Narnian theory of atonement:

> In simplest outline, then, a Narnian-style version of the ransom theory is that evil-doers come to be in captivity to Satan, whether this captivity be considered legal in some sense or illegal. Satan claims he will release the captives if he receives Jesus Christ in exchange for them. Jesus gives himself over to Satan and the powers of darkness in the course of his passion and death. In the process of this self-donation Satan is overthrown. Death may be said to work backwards for Jesus himself rises from the dead and promises new life to all who renounce evil and seek harmony with God. Harmony with God is fully realized in a new life of fellowship with Christ, the Savior. The ransom theory formed part of the larger *Christus Victor* tradition which, in the words of Irenaeus, conceived of the purpose of the incarnation as a matter of Christ battling sin, death, and devil. Gustaf Aulén is an able 20th century exponent of this tradition.[58]

Reality is governed by law—not simple rules but the very fabric of creation has a particular character and so do the creatures (hence the phrase, natural law, or the law of nature), especially when they are sentient and conscious—then there is a deep law relating to the will, to conscious decisions, the responsibilities of the creature. The White Witch claims her right, where a right is a freedom enshrined in law, which reflects the very nature of being of the creatures and the creation. Blood spilt, shed in sacrifice—a blood price—will appease the Law; the means of sacrifice is variable (crucifixion, execution on a stone table, and so forth).[59] Aslan pays the ransom price, in Edmund's stead, clears the debt, with his own life. But the deeper magic, the law about righteousness relating to innocence and guilt causes the reversal: Aslan's resurrection. Ownership (by the White Witch) and occupancy (within the realm of evil) is abolished, bondage to personified evil is overcome, as death is reversed with the sacrifice and resurrection of the righteous one.

---

58   See, Taliaferro, "A Narnian Theory of the Atonement," 59. Taliaferro is referring to Gustaf Aulén, *Christus Victor*. Lewis laid out his theological masters and the education he received from them in a letter in response to an enquiry from a reader, in 1958 (Lewis writing to Corbin Scott Carnell, Oct. 13, 1958. Lewis, *Collected Letters, Vol. III*, 978-98). He only cites a handful of theological masters, but among them is Gustaf Aulén's seminal work on Christ's sacrifice, *Christus Victor*.

59   The question of the flexibility of the means of sacrifice and the centrality of the Hebrew tradition of blood spilt, shed blood, a blood price, was dealt with in depth in the first book in this series: *C. S. Lewis—Revelation, Conversion, and Apologetics*, see Pt. 3, Ch. 11, 205f., specifically §. 3.ii, "The Death of Jesus of Nazareth," dealing with the question of the means of death, the question of a debt paid, and Jesus's Hebrew heritage, 211-16; see also, §. 4 "The Blood of the Lamb," 217-26.

9. Analogical and Symbolic Narratives V: Father Christmas in Narnia?

iii. A Debt Theory of Atonement

There are, in keeping with Lewis's reading of the patristic, and also medieval theologians, deep similarities with a ransom theory of atonement and also the objectivist/judicial theory. The overcoming of evil, where law and reality are intimately intertwined, makes sense, though there are difficulties: how can one person being punished in the stead of another actually work—surely it simply creates further injustice? Can anyone rightfully claim or assume the guilt of another?[60] Lewis's answer is that Christ is not just another person, another creature: God is taking the guilt onto God's-self, drawing the human with him; furthermore, in his apologetics, Lewis subscribes to a debt model of atonement (which is implicitly part of the ransom model in the Narniad). If you get into financial debt and cannot repay, a wealthy neighbor or relative could give you the money to pay-off, or could take the debt over from you—and repay it. The neighbor could offer to pay for you, or s/he could simply purchase the debt from the bank and then write it off. The debt is absolved; the financial authorities are *appeased*. And there should be a much greater degree of friendship and co-operation, reconciliation and closeness (atonement) between you and the neighbor. You can stand aloof and proud and reject the neighbor's generosity, or you can prostrate yourself in thanks and ask what you may do in return: in both cases, this is a model of how people respond to Christ's sacrifice, and if we turn back to what we established about the Narnian Last Judgment, we can see such a choice of response in the creatures that pass through the gateway to face Aslan *post mortem*: some look at him in love (and thanks), and are saved; others loathe and hate Aslan, and are condemned.[61] The ransom and debt models together seem to work for Narnia: evil is overcome, justice is satisfied: "The ransom theory does not, then, face the difficulty of accounting for how an innocent person may bear another's guilt. Rather, its account of salvation is not too dissimilar to a tale of a morally innocent, spiritual warrior, a commando, breaking free captives."[62] There is a fabric and law to the very nature of reality (written on the Emperor-beyond-the-Sea's scepter), but there is a deeper law of love (the deeper magic from before the dawn of time).

There are many, many, more questions that need to be addressed on Lewis's atonement theory (generally and in the Narniad); and in his apologetics, what place is there for freedom in Christ? How is salvation internalized? How coherent is his understanding of atonement in the middle period works, and then in his mature period works? These questions, along with a much greater analysis of atonement in the Narniad and in his key apologetic works will take place in the final chapters of this series.[63]

---

60   See, Taliaferro, "A Narnian Theory of the Atonement," 81
61   Lewis, *The Last Battle*, 175–76.
62   Taliaferro, "A Narnian Theory of the Atonement," 82
63   Brazier, *C. S. Lewis—On the Christ of a Religious Economy. II. Knowing Salvation*, Pt. 2, Ch. 9–13.

9. CONCLUSION

Does this explain Father Christmas's presence in Narnia? This explanation does cohere with the internal logic of the story, rather than seeking allegorical coincidences; in the context of the internal coherence within the story this explanation does make sense. We may still ask, was Lewis simply mistaken; this was the first book in the Narniad and he may simply not have applied the internal logic of his "supposal" aim as consistently as in the later books in the Narniad. But then we may argue, what role have inspiration, illumination, and revelation if the story was divinely inspired? He may have appeared to have made a mistake, but the inspiration, pneumatologically, was sound. Is the work independent of Lewis and his aims and objectives? Lewis does not explain the presence of Father Christmas in *The Lion, the Witch and the Wardrobe*, in these terms. However, given the internal coherence and transposed meaning, in keeping with a Platonic doctrine of inspiration where the story, in effect, pre-exists, but is changed, diminuted, as Lewis is illumined by the Holy Spirit, and is inspired to write, and to structure the narrative, given that the stories are governed by Lewis's understanding of Idealism and his pneumatological doctrine of the imagination, it surely makes sense to extrapolate along these lines.[64] This explanation makes sense, phrased as it is in theological concepts. However, *The Lion, the Witch and the Wardrobe* is not a theological treatise, it is a story, originally a children's story. As a "supposal," as analogy—indeed it is an analogical and symbolic narrative—as such the Narniad is part of a long tradition that extrapolates profound theological truth in narrative form (the book of Job, Nathan's use of parable before the adulterous King David, etc., and the Parables of Jesus).

Father Christmas's presence in *The Lion, the Witch and the Wardrobe* may on the surface generate puzzlement and skepticism from adults who fail to see that this character is a Father-Christmas-type-gift-bearer sent by Aslan, but in Platonic terms he is ultimately a gift-bearer from God, Aslan's Father, the Emperor-beyond-the-Sea (perhaps there is substance, to a degree, in Trinitarian terms, to the Hinten-Denham hypothesis that this gift-bearer relates to the Holy Spirit[65]). In many ways what we are doing here is interpreting the story, extrapolating from the information given. But how would Lewis have responded? Should an author's work be ring-fenced? The book of Isaiah was written, according to Bible scholars, by several "Isaiahs" working in the tradition of the original Isaiah. The question of Father Christmas's presence did need explaining. By comparison we may ask, would a composer object to how a conductor interprets his/her composition? Often a conductor can bring out an understanding in a piece of music that the composer did not fully realize. Indeed, if we look at recording history, often a composer conducting his/her own composition

---

64   These theories about illumination, inspiration and Lewis's doctrine of transposition are dealt with in depth in the second book in this series: *C. S. Lewis—The Work of Christ Revealed*, see specifically Chs. 1, 3, and 11.

65   Hinten, "'Deeper Magic:' Allusions in *The Lion, the Witch and the Wardrobe*," 9–21; and Dunham, "*The Lion, the Witch and the Wardrobe*: Summary," online at http://www.answers.com/topic/the-lion-the-witch-and-the-wardrobe-criticism.

is not the best interpretation or recording of a work. Would Lewis have objected to scholars trying to sort out reasons behind what initially appear to be contradictions in *The Chronicles of Narnia*? I hope not. Lewis was humble enough to realize that he was a flawed human being who did not present sub-creation in as complete a manner as is desired by its target audience, that others might be able to help. During the Renaissance great painters worked in studios. Often they sketched out giant works, then the members of the studio painted in most of the scene in the artist's style, then the master would paint the faces and important detail. This was considered normal practice (it is from the early nineteenth century that we derive the idea of the artist as a Romantic and troubled individual who must produce everything without anyone else being involved). The presence of Father Christmas needed explaining. Lewis never offered an explanation, though, importantly, he refused to exclude the character, despite the scorn and pressure heaped on him. Given the coherence and rationality of his work, also how such stories as *The Chronicles of Narnia* have developed a life of their own away from the creator and author, it seems fair to postulate the explanation I have outlined here—whether what I have postulated works now lies with the reader!

So, in conclusion, why does Father Christmas appear in Narnia? Why is this eschatological harbinger of God's loving judgment recognized as a mythological figure related to our world, our reality?

1. Aslan, the Son of the Emperor-beyond-the-Sea, sent him, in and through the Holy Spirit (a deliberate invocation of Trinitarian concepts).

2. He is sent by Aslan as a gift-bearer in good pleasure and generosity of heart to reward those who have served Narnia, and therefore have served Aslan.

3. He is sent to remind, albeit often implicitly, the humans in Narnia of their soteriological heritage as sons and daughters of Adam and Eve. King Frank and Queen Helen cannot be divorced from their salvation history.

4. The name of Father Christmas for this gift-bearer may seem odd in a totally alien reality but this issues from the presence of humans in Narnia. In the early seventeenth century Native North Americans around Jamestown would have known the word "Christmas" but without the religio-cultural context the European settlers attributed to the word. Likewise the patchy presence of the Christian Church in Romano-Britain in the late fifth century would have led the native Celts to know the word "Christmas" as referring to a Roman religious festival, but with little or no understanding as to its meaning.

4. He is sent to be a sacramental symbol (along with the lamp post in Lantern Waste) that atonement *will* be achieved in Narnia. The lamp post's light is therefore an eschatological witness as Father Christmas is an eschatological harbinger.

5. He is sent as a reminder that sin has infected Narnia, issuing from evil brought into Narnia by the humans at the creation.

6. He is sent as a Father-Christmas-type-gift-bearer, a character in the role and tradition of Father Christmas, whom Aslan intended to be recognized and associated with Father Christmas, Santa Claus, Kris Kringle, *et al.*, and therefore ultimately the Christian saint, Nicholas of Myra, who was a living manifestation of the loving generosity of God.

7. The White Witch's ice age is characterized by "Always Winter and Never Christmas." Christmas here does not refer to a period of celebratory exchanging of gifts with accompanied binge-drinking and over-eating, but to Aslan's ultimate gifting: Christmas is referring to Aslan's sacrifice of himself to save all Narnia. With Aslan's death and resurrection there is no longer any need for the visits by this Father-Christmas-type-gift-bearer.

8. According to Lewis the gift-bearer we call "Father Christmas" in our reality issues from a Platonic form, pneumatologically authored, that now exists as an idea to us (*intelligible* but not *perceivable*), but in Narnia is a real flesh-and-blood person (as Nicholas, Bishop of Myra, the gift-bearer, was more real than the innumerable Santas we may encounter).

So "Father Christmas" as a "gift-bearer" is real both as a flesh and blood manifestation of a Platonic form within parallel realities and also as an idea (where ideas, for Lewis, are more real than physical reality).[66] Thankfully Lewis did not listen to the critics and he refused to exclude this character issuing from Platonic ontology and cross-cultural teleology. Therefore we need no longer balk at the presence of this Father-Christmas-type-gift-bearer in *The Lion, the Witch and the Wardrobe*, but see it as a sign of God's loving generosity to all creation. Indeed his presence is essential to the underlying doctrine of atonement that we can read from Lewis's Narniad, given the analogical "supposal" nature of these stories.

---

66   Lewis, *The Lion, the Witch and the Wardrobe*, 99.

9. Analogical and Symbolic Narratives V: Father Christmas in Narnia?

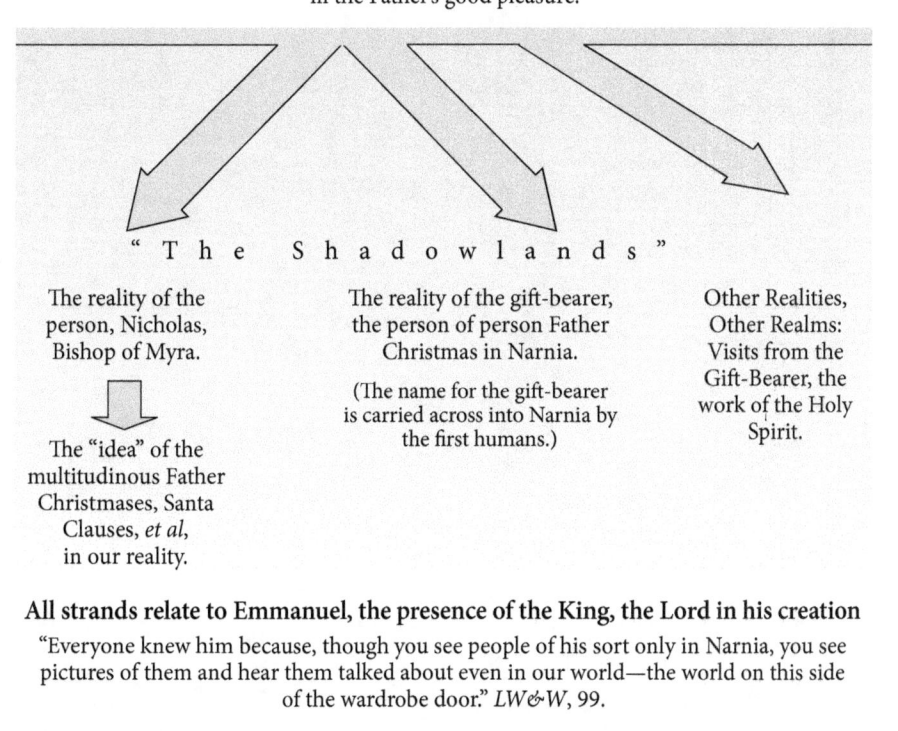

Figure 9. The Gift Bearer, the Work of the Holy Spirit

Bibliography

LETTERS AND ARTICLES BY C. S. LEWIS

Lewis, C. S., "Bulverism." In *Undeceptions: Essays on Theology and Ethics*, 223–28. London: Bles, 1971.
———. "Christian Apologetics." In *Undeceptions: Essays on Theology and Ethics*, 64–76. London: Bles, 1971.
———. "Christianity and Culture." In *Christian Reflections*, 12–36. London: Bles, 1967.
———. "Christianity and Literature." In *Christian Reflections*, 1–11. London: Bles, 1967.
———. "Cross-Examination." In *Undeceptions: Essays on Theology and Ethics*, 215–21. London: Bles, 1971.
———. "*De Descriptione Temporum*." In *They Asked for a Paper: Papers and Addresses*, 9–25. London: Bles, 1962.
———. "Dogma and the Universe." In *Undeceptions: Essays on Theology and Ethics*, 17–25. London: Bles, 1971.
———. "The Funeral of a Great Myth." In *Christian Reflections*, 82–93. London: Bles, 1967.
———. "The Future of Forestry." In *Poems*, 75. London: Fount, 2011.
———. "The Humanitarian Theory of Punishment." In *Undeceptions: Essays on Theology and Ethics*, 238–49. London: Bles, 1971.
———. "Introduction." In, *St. Athanasius: The Incarnation of the Word: Being the Treatise of St Athanasius, De incarnatione Verbi Dei*, 5–12. Translated by Sr. Penelope CSMV. London: Bles, 1944.
———. "Is Theism Important?" In *Undeceptions: Essays on Theology and Ethics*, 138–42. London: Bles, 1971.
———. "Is Theology Poetry?" In *They Asked for a Paper*, 150–65. London: Bles, 1962.
———. "It All Began with a Picture . . ." The *Radio Times, Junior Section*, CXLVIII, 15 July 1960.
———. "Letter to 'An American Lady,' Feb 20, 1955." In *Letters to an American Lady*, 38–39. Grand Rapids: Eerdmans, 1971.
———. "Letter to 'An American Lady,' Apr. 17, 1953." In *Letters to an American Lady*, 14. Grand Rapids: Eerdmans, 1971.
———. "Letter to a Former Pupil, Jan 4, 1941." In *Letters of C. S. Lewis*, edited by Walter Hooper, 2nd ed., expanded, 1988, 357–58. New York: Harcourt Brace, 1988.
———. "Letter to Anne Jenkins March 5, 1961." In *Collected Letters, Vol. III: Narnia, Cambridge and Joy 1950-1963*, edited by Walter Hooper, 1244–45. San Francisco: Harper San Francisco, 2007.
———. "Letter to Charles A. Brady, Oct 29, 1944." In *Collected Letters, Vol. II: Books, Broadcasts and War 1931-1949*, edited by Walter Hooper, 629–31. San Francisco: Harper San Francisco, 2004.
———. "Letter to Corbin Scott Carnell, Oct. 13, 1958." In *Collected Letters, Vol. III: Narnia, Cambridge and Joy 1950-1963*, edited by Walter Hooper, 978–98. San Francisco: Harper San Francisco, 2007.
———. "Letter to Dom Bede Griffiths OSB, April 16, 1940." In *Collected Letters, Vol. II: Books, Broadcasts and War 1931-1949*, edited by Walter Hooper, 390. San Francisco: Harper San Francisco, 2004.
———. "Letter to Dom Bede Griffiths OSB, April 24, 1936." In *Collected Letters, Vol. II: Books, Broadcasts and War 1931-1949*, edited by Walter Hooper, 187–90. San Francisco: Harper San Francisco, 2004.
———. "Letter to Dom Bede Griffiths OSB, Aug. 4, 1962." In *Collected Letters, Vol. III: Narnia, Cambridge and Joy 1950-1963*, edited by Walter Hooper, 1362. San Francisco: Harper San Francisco, 2007.
———. "Letter to Dom Bede Griffiths OSB, Dec 21, 1941." In *Collected Letters, Vol. II: Books, Broadcasts and War 1931-1949*, edited by Walter Hooper, 500–503. San Francisco: Harper San Francisco, 2004.

ON THE CHRIST OF A RELIGIOUS ECONOMY. I. CREATION AND SUB-CREATION

———. "Letter to Dom Bede Griffiths OSB, Jan 17, 1940." In *Collected Letters, Vol. II: Books, Broadcasts and War 1931–1949*, edited by Walter Hooper, 325–26. San Francisco: Harper San Francisco, 2004.

———. "Letter to Elsie Snickers, May 18, 1953." In *Collected Letters, Vol. III: Narnia, Cambridge and Joy 1950–1963*, edited by Walter Hooper, 329–30. San Francisco: Harper San Francisco, 2007.

———. "Letter to Genia Goelz, June 13, 1951." In *Collected Letters, Vol. III: Narnia, Cambridge and Joy 1950–1963*, edited by Walter Hooper, 126. San Francisco: Harper San Francisco, 2007.

———. "Letter to Jane Douglass, Dec 21, 1954." In *Collected Letters, Vol. III: Narnia, Cambridge and Joy 1950–1963*, edited by Walter Hooper, 545. San Francisco: Harper San Francisco, 2007.

———. "Letter to John Beversluis, July 3, 1963." In *Collected Letters, Vol. III: Narnia, Cambridge and Joy 1950–1963*, edited by Walter Hooper, 1437. San Francisco: Harper San Francisco, 2007.

———. "Letter to Mary Van Deusen, Feb 7, 1951." In *Collected Letters, Vol. III: Narnia, Cambridge and Joy 1950–1963*, edited by Walter Hooper, 91. San Francisco: Harper San Francisco, 2007.

———. "Letter to Mary Willis Shelburne, Apr 15, 1958." In *Collected Letters, Vol. III: Narnia, Cambridge and Joy 1950–1963*, edited by Walter Hooper, 935. San Francisco: Harper San Francisco, 2007.

———. "Letter to Mary Willis Shelburne, Jan 9, 1961." In *Collected Letters, Vol. III: Narnia, Cambridge and Joy 1950–1963*, edited by Walter Hooper, 1225. San Francisco: Harper San Francisco, 2007.

———. "Letter to Mary Willis Shelburne, July 21, 1958." In *Collected Letters, Vol. III: Narnia, Cambridge and Joy 1950–1963*, edited by Walter Hooper, 416. San Francisco: Harper San Francisco, 2007.

———. "Letter to Mary Willis Shelburne, May 30, 1953." In *Collected Letters, Vol. III: Narnia, Cambridge and Joy 1950–1963*, edited by Walter Hooper, 333. San Francisco: Harper San Francisco, 2007.

———. "Letter to Mary Willis Shelburne, Nov 26, 1962." In *Collected Letters, Vol. III: Narnia, Cambridge and Joy 1950–1963*, edited by Walter Hooper, 1383–84. San Francisco: Harper San Francisco, 2007.

———. "Letter to Mary Willis Shelburne, Nov 8, 1962." In *Collected Letters, Vol. III: Narnia, Cambridge and Joy 1950–1963*, edited by Walter Hooper, 1324. San Francisco: Harper San Francisco, 2007.

———. "Letter to Michael Edwards, June 27, 1958." In *Collected Letters, Vol. III: Narnia, Cambridge and Joy 1950–1963*, edited by Walter Hooper, 959. San Francisco: Harper San Francisco, 2007.

———. "Letter to Michael Edwards, Oct 20, 1956." In *Collected Letters, Vol. III: Narnia, Cambridge and Joy 1950–1963*, edited by Walter Hooper, 799–800. San Francisco: Harper San Francisco, 2007.

———. "Letter to Miss Breckenridge, Aug 1, 1949." In *Collected Letters, Vol. III: Narnia, Cambridge and Joy 1950–1963*, edited by Walter Hooper, 962. San Francisco: Harper San Francisco, 2007.

———. "Letter to Mrs D Jessup, 1 Dec, 1953." In *Collected Letters, Vol. III: Narnia, Cambridge and Joy 1950–1963*, edited by Walter Hooper, 380. San Francisco: Harper San Francisco, 2007.

———. "Letter to Mrs D Jessup, 5 Feb, 1954." In *Collected Letters, Vol. III: Narnia, Cambridge and Joy 1950–1963*, edited by Walter Hooper, 425. San Francisco: Harper San Francisco, 2007.

———. "Letter to Mrs Hook, Dec. 29, 1958." In *Collected Letters, Vol. III: Narnia, Cambridge and Joy 1950–1963*, edited by Walter Hooper, 1004–5. San Francisco: Harper San Francisco, 2007.

———. "Letter to Mrs Lockley, Jan 8, 1952." In *Letters of C. S. Lewis*, edited by Walter Hooper, 2nd ed., expanded, 1988, 416. New York: Harcourt Brace, 1988.

———. "Letter to Sheldon Vanauken, Apr. 6, 1955." In *Collected Letters, Vol. III: Narnia, Cambridge and Joy 1950–1963*, edited by Walter Hooper, 592. San Francisco: Harper San Francisco, 2007.

———. "Letter to Sr. Penelope CSMV, Feb 20, 1943." In *Collected Letters, Vol. II: Books, Broadcasts and War 1931–1949*, edited by Walter Hooper, 554–56. San Francisco: Harper San Francisco, 2004.

———. "Letter to Sr. Penelope CSMV, Jan 10, 1952." In *Collected Letters, Vol. III: Narnia, Cambridge and Joy 1950–1963*, edited by Walter Hooper, 156–58. San Francisco: Harper San Francisco, 2007.

———. "Letter to Sr. Penelope CSMV, July 29, 1942." In *Collected Letters, Vol. II: Books, Broadcasts and War 1931–1949*, edited by Walter Hooper, 525f. San Francisco: Harper San Francisco, 2004.

———. "Letter to The Church Times, Feb. 8, 1952." In *Collected Letters, Vol. III: Narnia, Cambridge and Joy 1950–1963*, edited by Walter Hooper, 164. San Francisco: Harper San Francisco, 2007.

———. "Letter to Tony Pollock, May 3, 1954." In *Collected Letters, Vol. III: Narnia, Cambridge and Joy 1950–1963*, edited by Walter Hooper, 466. San Francisco: Harper San Francisco, 2007.

———. "Letter to Wayne Shumaker, March 21, 1962." In *Collected Letters, Vol. III: Narnia, Cambridge and Joy 1950–1963*, edited by Walter Hooper, 1324. San Francisco: Harper San Francisco, 2007.

———. "Lilies that Fester." In *The World's Last Night and Other Essays*, 31–50. New York: Harcourt Brace, 1960.

———. "Man or Rabbit." In *Undeceptions: Essays on Theology and Ethics*, 82–84. London: Bles, 1971.
———. "Miserable Offenders." In *Undeceptions: Essays on Theology and Ethics*, 91–95. London: Bles, 1971.
———. "Must Our Image of God Go?" *The Observer*, Mar 24, 1963, 14.
———. "The Mythopoeic Gift of Rider Haggard." In *Of this and Other Worlds*, 128–32. London: Collins, 1982.
———. "The Novels of Charles Williams." Broadcast on BBC radio, the Third Programme, 11 Feb. 1949. In *Of This and Other Worlds*, 46–54. London: Collins, 1982.
———. "The Poison of Subjectivism." In *Christian Reflections*, 72–81. London: Bles, 1967.
———. "Preface to the Third Edition." In *The Pilgrim's Regress: An Allegorical Apology for Christianity, Reason and Romanticism*, ix–xx. 3rd ed. London: Bless, 1944. Note in some American reprints this "Preface" is placed at the end of the book and called an "Afterword."
———. "Rejoinder to Dr Pittenger." In *Christian Century* LXXV, Nov 26, 1958, 1369–71.
———. "Religion and Rocketry." In *The World's Last Night and Other Essays*, 83–92. New York: Harcourt Brace, 1960.
———. "Screwtape Proposes a Toast." In *Screwtape Proposes a Toast*, 1–18. London: Fontana, 1965.
———. "The Seeing Eye." In *Christian Reflections*, 167–76. London: Bles, 1967.
———. "The Sermon and the Lunch." (Expanded reprint.) In *Undeceptions: Essays on Theology and Ethics*, 233–37. London: Bles, 1971.
———. "The Sermon and the Lunch." *The Church of England Newspaper*, 2692, Sept 21, 1945, 1–2.
———. "Some Thoughts." In *The First Decade: Ten Years' Work of the Medical Missionaries of Mary*, 91–94. Dublin: Three Candles, 1948. Reprinted in *Undeceptions: Essays on Theology and Ethics*, 115–18. London: Bles, 1971.
———. "Sometimes Fairy Stories May Say Best What's to be Said." In *Of Other Worlds*, 35–38. London: Bles, 1966.
———. "Transposition." 1st ed. A sermon given in Mansfield College, Oxford on Whit Sunday, 28 May 1944. In *Transposition and Other Addresses*, 9–20. London: Bless, 1949.
———. "Transposition." 2nd ed. In *They Asked for a Paper*, 166–82. London: Bles, 1962.
———. "Two Ways with the Self." *The Guardian*, May 3, 1940, 215.
———. "We Have No 'Right to Happiness.'" In *Undeceptions: Essays on Theology and Ethics*, 265–69. London: Bles, 1971.
———. "The Weight of Glory." In *Transposition and other Addresses*, 21–33. London: Bles, 1949.
———. "Who was Right?—Dream Lecturer or Real Lecturer?" In *The Coventry Evening Telegraph*, 21 Feb. 1945, 4.
———. "Will We Lose God in Outer Space." *The Christian Herald*, LXXXI, April 1958, 7–10.
———. "The World's Last Night." In *The World's Last Night and Other Essays*, 93–113. New York: Harcourt Brace, 1960.

BOOKS BY C. S. LEWIS

Lewis, C. S., *The Abolition of Man: or, Reflections on Education with Special Reference to the Teaching of English in the Upper Forms of Schools*. University of Durham Riddell Memorial Lectures, fifteenth series. Oxford: Oxford University Press, 1943.
———. *Beyond Personality: The Christian Idea of God*. London: Centenary, 1944.
———. *Broadcast Talks*. Reprinted with some alterations from two series of Broadcast Talks "Right and Wrong: A Clue to the Meaning of the Universe" and "What Christians Believe" given in 1941 and 1942. London: Bles, 1942.
———. *Christian Behaviour*. London: Centenary, 1943.
———. *Christian Reflections*. Edited by Walter Hooper. London: Bles, 1967.
———. *The Chronicles of Narnia—Prince Caspian: The Return to Narnia*. London: Bles, 1951.
———. *The Chronicles of Narnia—The Horse and His Boy*. London: Bles, 1954.
———. *The Chronicles of Narnia—The Last Battle*. London: Bles, 1956.
———. *The Chronicles of Narnia—The Lion the Witch and the Wardrobe*. London: Bles, 1950.
———. *The Chronicles of Narnia—The Magician's Nephew*. London: Bles, 1955.
———. *The Chronicles of Narnia—The Silver Chair*. London: Bles, 1953.

———. *The Chronicles of Narnia—The Voyage of the Dawn Treader*. London: Bles, 1952.
———. *Collected Letters, Vol. I—Family Letters 1905-1931*. Edited by Walter Hooper. San Francisco: Harper, 2004.
———. *Collected Letters, Vol. II—Books, Broadcasts and War 1931-1949*. Edited by Walter Hooper. San Francisco: Harper, 2004.
———. *Collected Letters, Vol. III—Narnia, Cambridge and Joy 1950-1963*. Edited by Walter Hooper. San Francisco: Harper, 2007.
———. *The Dark Tower and Other Stories*. London: Collins, 1977.
———. *English Literature in the Sixteenth Century*. Oxford: Clarendon, 1954.
———. *Essays Presented to Charles Williams*. Oxford: Oxford University Press, 1947.
———. *The Great Divorce: A Dream*. London: Macmillan, 1945.
———. *A Grief Observed*. (Writing as N. W. Clerk.) London: Faber and Faber, 1961.
———. *Letters of C. S. Lewis*. Edited by Walter Hooper, 1st ed. London: Bles, 1966.
———. *Letters of C. S. Lewis*. Edited by Walter Hooper, 2nd ed. Revised and enlarged. New York: Harcourt Brace, 1988.
———. *Letters to an American Lady*. Grand Rapids: Eerdmans, 1971.
———. *Letters to Malcolm: Chiefly on Prayer*. London: Bles, 1964.
———. *Mere Christianity. A revised and amplified edition, with a new introduction, of the three books Broadcast Talks, Christian Behaviour and Beyond Personality*. London: Bles, 1952.
———. *Miracles. A Preliminary Study*. London: Bless, 1947.
———. *Miracles*. 2nd ed. London: Bless, 1960.
———. *Of Other Worlds: Essays and Stories*. Edited by Walter Hooper. London: Bles, 1966.
———. *Of This and Other Worlds*. Edited by Walter Hooper. London: Collins, Fontana, 1982.
———. *Out of the Silent Planet*. London: Bodley Head, 1938.
———. *Perelandra*. London: Bodley Head, 1943.
———. *The Pilgrim's Regress: An Allegorical Apology for Christianity, Reason and Romanticism*. London: Dent and Sons, 1933.
———. *The Pilgrim's Regress: An Allegorical Apology for Christianity, Reason and Romanticism*. 3rd ed. London: Bles, 1944.
———. *A Preface to Paradise Lost*. Oxford: Oxford University Press, 1942.
———. *The Problem of Pain*. London: Centenary, 1940.
———. *Reflections on the Psalms*. London: Bles, 1958.
———. *The Screwtape Letters*. London: Bles, 1942.
———. *Shall we Lose God in Outer Space*. London: SPCK, 1959.
———. *Surprised by Joy: The Shape of My Early Life*. London: Bles, 1955.
———. *That Hideous Strength: A Modern Fairytale for Grown-Ups*. London: Bodley Head, 1945.
———. *Transposition and Other Addresses*. London: Bles, 1949.
———. *Till We Have Faces*. London: Bles, 1956.
———. *Undeceptions: Essays on Theology and Ethics*. Edited by Walter Hooper. London: Bles, 1971. Published in the USA as, God in the Dock: Essays on Theology and Ethics. Grand Rapids: Eerdmans, 1970.
———. *Vivisection. A Pamphlet Published by The New England Anti-Vivisection Society*. Boston: New England Anti-Vivisection Society, 1948.
———. *The World's Last Night and Other Essays*. New York: Harcourt Brace, 1960.

OTHER BOOKS AND ARTICLES

Aeschliman, Michael D. *The Restitution of Man. C. S. Lewis and the Case against Scientism*. Grand Rapids: Eerdmans, 1998.
Alexander, Denis, "We are not descended from Adam and Eve—but still, Jesus was born to save us." *The Guardian*, 24 Dec 2011, 37.
Aquinas, Thomas, *Summa Theologiae*. 61 vols. Cambridge: Cambridge University Press, 1962-76.
Augustine. *The City of God (De Civitate Dei Contra Paganos)*. Edited by David Knowles, translated by Henry Bettenson. Harmondsworth, UK: Pelican, 1972.

———. *Confessions*. Translated by Henry Chadwick. Oxford World's Classics. Oxford: Oxford University Press, 1991.
Baker, John Austin. *Travels in Oudamovia*. London: Faith, 1976.
Balsbaugh, John. "The Pagan and the Post-Christian: Lewis's Understanding of Diversity Outside the Faith." In *Translated Theology: C. S. Lewis Light Bearer in the Shadowlands*. Edited by Arthur J. L. Menuge, 191–210. Wheaton, IL: Crossway, 1997.
Barrow, John, and Frank Tipler, *The Anthropic Cosmological Principle*. Oxford: Clarendon, 1986.
Barth, Karl. *Church Dogmatics*. 14 Vols. Translated and edited G. W. Bromiley and T. F. Torrance. Edinburgh: T. & T. Clark, 1936.
———. *Dogmatics in Outline*. London: SCM, 1949.
Bonting Sjoerd. L. "Theological Implications of Possible Extraterrestrial Life." *Zygon*, 38.3 (2003) 587–602.
Brazier, P.H., "C. S. Lewis: A Doctrine of Transposition." *The Heythrop Journal* 50.4 (2009) 669–88.
———. "The Pittenger-Lewis Debate: Fundamentals of an Ontological Christology." *The Chronicle of the Oxford University C. S. Lewis Society*, 6.1 (2009) 7–23.
———. "Why Father Christmas Appears in Narnia." *Sehnsucht* 3 (2009) 61–77.
Brown, Devin, *Inside Narnia: A Guide to Exploring The Lion, the Witch and the Wardrobe*. Grand Rapids: Baker, 2005.
Brunner, Emil. *The Mediator: A Study of the Central Doctrine of the Christian Faith*. Philadelphia: Westminster, 1947.
Calvin, John. *Institutes of the Christian Religion*. Edited by John T. McNeill. Library of Christian Classics. Louisville, KY: Westminster John Knox, 2006.
Campbell, Charles L. *Preaching Jesus: The New Directions for Homiletics in Hans Frei's Postliberal Theology*. Eugene, OR: Wipf and Stock, 2005.
Carpenter, Humphrey, *J. R. R. Tolkien: A Biography*. London: Allen & Unwin, 1977.
———. *The Inklings: C. S. Lewis, J.R.R. Tolkien, Charles Williams and their Friends*. London: Allen & Unwin, 1978.
Carretero-González, Margarita. "Sons of Adam, Daughters of Eve, and Children of Aslan: An Environmentalist Perspective on The Chronicles of Narnia." In *C. S. Lewis: Life, Works, and Legacy, Vol. 2 Fantasist, Mythmaker, and Poet*, edited by Bruce Edwards, 93–114. Santa Barbara, CA: Praeger, 2007.
Catechism of the Catholic Church. London: Burns and Oats, 2006
Christopher, Joseph R. *C. S. Lewis*. Boston: Twayne, 1987.
Crisp, Oliver, "Multiple Incarnations." In *God Incarnate: Explorations in Christology*, 155–75. London: T. & T. Clark, 2009.
Crowe, Michael J. "A History of the Extra-Terrestrial Life Debate." *Zygon* 32 (1992) 147–62.
Davidman, Joy, "The Longest Way Round." In *These Found the Way: Thirteen Converts to Protestant Christianity*, edited by David Soper, 13–26. Philadelphia: Westminster, 1951.
Dickerson, Matthew, and David A. O'Hara. *Narnia and the Fields of Arbol: The Environmental Vision of C. S. Lewis*. Culture of the Land. Lexington, KY: University Press of Kentucky, 2009.
Donahue, John R. *The Gospel in Parable: Metaphor, Narrative and Theology in the Synoptic Gospels*. 1959. Reprint. Minneapolis, MN: Augsburg Fortress, 1988.
Doolittle, Ford W. "Uprooting the Tree of Life." *Scientific American*, Feb. 2000, 72–77, 282–82. Online (subscription access):
http://www.nature.com/scientificamerican/journal/v282/n2/pdf/scientificamerican0200-90.pdf
Dostoevsky, Fyodor Mikhailovich, "Dostoevsky writing to his brother, April 15, 1864." In *Dostoevsky, a Self-Portrait*, edited by Jessie Coulson, 125–26. London: Oxford, 1962.
———. *The Brothers Karamazov*. Translated by Richard Pevear and Larissa Volokhonsky. London: Everyman's Library, 1990.
———. *Crime and Punishment*. Translated Richard Pevear and Larissa Volokhonsky. London: Everyman's Library, 1994.
———. *The Dream of the Ridiculous Man: A Fantastic Story* (1877). In *A Gentle Creature and Other Stories*, translated by Alan Myers, 108–28. Oxford World Classics. Oxford: Oxford University Press, 1995.
———. *Notebooks for Crime and Punishment*. Edited and translated Edward Wasiolek. Chicago: University of Chicago Press, 1967.

Downing, David, "Rehabilitating H. G. Wells: C. S. Lewis's *Out of the Silent Planet*." In *C. S. Lewis Life, Works, and Legacy, Vol. 2: Fantasist, Mythmaker and Poet*, edited by Bruce L. Edwards, 13–34. Santa Barbara, CA: Praeger, 2007.

———. "That Hideous Strength: Spiritual Wickedness in High Places." In *C. S. Lewis Life, Works, and Legacy, Vol. 2: Fantasist, Mythmaker and Poet*, edited by Bruce L. Edwards, 53–70. Santa Barbara, CA: Praeger, 2007.

Drees, William B. "Theologie over Buitenaardse Personen." *Tijdschrift voor Theologie* 27 (1987) 259–76.

Dunham, Timothy, "The Lion, the Witch and the Wardrobe: Summary." In *Novels for Students, Vol. 24*, edited by Marie Rose Napierkowski. Detroit: Gale, 1998. Online: http://www.answers.com/topic/the-lion-the-witch-and-the-wardrobe-criticism.

Fisher, Christopher L., and David Fergusson. "Karl Rahner and the Extra-Terrestrial Intelligence Question." *The Heythrop Journal* 47.2 (2006) 275–90.

Ford, Paul F. *Companion to Narnia: A Complete Guide to the Magical World of C. S. Lewis's The Chronicles of Narnia*. Grand Rapids: Zondervan, 2005.

Forsyth, Peter Taylor. *The Person and Place of Jesus Christ: The Congregational Union Lecture for 1909*. London: Hodder & Stoughton, 1910

Garland, Alex. *The Beach*. Harmondsworth, UK: Penguin, 1997.

Gibson, Alexander Boyce. *The Religion of Dostoevsky*. London: SCM, 1973.

Gibson, Evan. *C. S. Lewis: Spinner of Tales*. Grand Rapids: Christian University Press, 1980.

Glover, Donald, *C. S. Lewis: The Art of Enchantment*. Athens, OH: Ohio University Press, 1981.

Gluckman, Ron. "More Postcards from the Beach." www.gluckman.com/BeachGarland.html.

Golding, William. *Lord of the Flies*. London: Faber and Faber, 1954.

Green, Roger Lancelyn, and Walter Hooper. *C. S. Lewis: A Biography*. 2nd ed. London: Harper Collins, 2002.

Gunton, Colin E. *The Barth Lectures*. Transcribed and edited by P. H. Brazier. London: T. & T. Clark, 2007.

———. *Revelation and Reason Prolegomena to Systematic Theology*. Transcribed and edited by P. H. Brazier. London: T. & T. Clark, 2008.

Hauerwas, Stanley, Gerhard Sauter, and John Barton. *Revelations and Story: Narrative Theology and the Centrality of Story*. Farnham, UK: Ashgate, 1999.

Hebblethwaite, Brian. "Impossibility of Multiple Incarnations." *Theology* 104.821 (2001) 323–34.

Hinten, Marvin D. "'Deeper Magic:' Allusions in *The Lion, the Witch and the Wardrobe*." In *The Keys to the Chronicles: Unlocking the Symbols of C. S. Lewis's Narnia*, 9–21. Nashville: B. & H., 2005.

Hooker, Richard. *Of the Lawes of Ecclesiastical Politie* (1593–1662). Vols 1–9. Modern edition: Richard Hooker, *Of the Laws of Ecclesiastical Polity*. Edited by A. S. McGrade. Cambridge: Cambridge University Press, 1989.

Hooper, Walter. *C. S. Lewis: A Companion and Guide*. London: Harper Collins, 1996.

Hunt, W. H. *Pre-Raphaelitism and the Pre-Raphaelite Brotherhood*. London: Macmillan, 1905.

Jenson, Matt. *The Gravity of Sin*. London: Continuum, 2006.

Jenson, Robert. *Systematic Theology*. 2 vols. Oxford: Oxford University Press, 1997.

Law, William. *Serious Call to a Devout and Holy Life and The Way to Divine Knowledge* (1729). Alachua, FL: Bridge-Logos, 2008.

Lawton, Graham. "Uprooting Darwin's Tree of Life." *New Scientist*, 24 Jan. 2009, 34–39. Online (subscription access): http://www.newscientist.com/article/mg20126921.600-why-darwin-was-wrong-about-the-tree-of-life.html.

Lindbeck, George A. *The Nature of Doctrine: Religion and Theology in a Postliberal Age*. Louisville, KY: Westminster John Know, 2009.

Lindqvist, C., et al. "Transmission of stress-induced learning impairment and associated brain gene expression from parents to offspring in chickens." *PloS One (Public Library of Science)* 2.4, 11 April 2007.
Online: www.plosone.org/article/info%3Adoi%2F10.1371%2Fjournal.pone.0000364

Lindsay, David. *Voyage to Arcturus*. London: Metheun, 1920.

Mascall, E. L., *Christian Theology and Natural Science*. London: Longmans Green, 1956.

Bibliography

Maximus the Confessor. Centuries, 1108A–B. In *St. Maximus the Confessor: The Ascetic Life, The Four Centuries on Charity*, edited by Polycarp Sherwood. Ancient Christian Writers. Mahwah, NJ: Paulist, 1955.

Meacham, Steve. "The Shed where God Died." *Sydney Morning Herald Online*, 13 Dec. 2003. Section: "Spectrum", 8. Online: http://www.smh.com.au/articles/2003/12/12/1071125644900.html.

Meynell, Alice. "Christ in the Universe." In *The Oxford Book of English Mystical Verse*, edited by D. H. S. Nicholson and A. H. E. Lee, 463–64. Oxford: Clarendon, 1917.

Miller, John J., "Xmas in Narnia." *The National Review* 57.24, 22 Dec 2005. Online: www.nationalreview.com.

Milton, John. *Paradise Lost*. Oxford: Oxford University Press, 2008.

More, Thomas. *Utopia*. Penguin Classics. London: Penguin, 2004.

Mueller, Stephen P. "Translated Theology: Christology in the Writings of C. S. Lewis." In *Translated Theology: C. S. Lewis Light Bearer in the Shadowlands*, edited by Arthur J. L. Menuge, 279–302. Wheaton, IL: Crossway, 1997.

Parsons, Andrew. "On the Judges and the Christian Conscience." *Kensington Parish News*, Spring 2011, 5–6.

Patrick, Meriel. "Letting In and Shutting Out: Themes in the Thought of C. S. Lewis." *The Journal of Inklings Studies* 2.2 (2012) 27–46.

Pearce, Joseph. *C. S. Lewis and the Catholic Church*. San Francisco: Ignatius, 2003.

Pecknold, C. C. *Transforming Postliberal Theology: George Lindbeck, Pragmatism and Scripture*. London: T. & T. Clark, 2005.

Pittenger, W. Norman. "Apologist versus Apologist: A Critique of C. S. Lewis as 'Defender of the Faith.'" *Christian Century* LXXV, 1 October 1958, 1104–7.

Pullman, Philip. *His Dark Materials*. A trilogy consisting of: *Northern Lights*. New York: Scholastic Point, 1995; *The Subtle Knife*. New York: Scholastic Point, 1997; *The Amber Spyglass*. New York: Scholastic Point, 2000.

Rahner, Karl, *The Trinity*. New York: Crossroads, 1997.

Rayment-Pickard, Hugh. *The Devil's Account: Philip Pullman and Christianity*. London: Darton, Longman and Todd, 2004.

Ross, Charles. "C. S. Lewis, Augustine, and Rhythm of the Trinity." *Journal of Inklings Studies* 2.1 (2012) 3–22.

Sammons, Martha C. *A Guide through Narnia*. London: Hodder and Stoughton, 1979.

Sayer, George. *Jack: A Life of C. S. Lewis*. London: Hodder & Stoughton, 2005.

Sayers, Dorothy. *The Mind of the Maker*. New York: Harcourt, Brace, 1941.

Schakel, Peter. *Reading with the Heart: The Way into Narnia*. Grand Rapids: Eerdmans, 1979.

Sickler, Bradley L. "Infernal Voluntarism and 'The Deep Courtesy of Heaven.'" In *The Problem of Hell: A Philosophical Anthology*, edited by Joel Buenting, 163–78. Farnham, UK: Ashgate, 2010.

Solzhenitsyn, Aleksandr Isaevich. *Warning to the West*. New York: Macmillan, Hill & Wang, 1976.

Stroup, George W. *The Promise of Narrative Theology: Recovering the Gospel in the Church*. Reprint. Eugene OR: Wipf and Stock, 1997.

Taliaferro, Charles A. "A Narnian Theory of the Atonement: Ransom Theory in C. S. Lewis, 'The Lion, the Witch, and the Wardrobe.'" *Scottish Journal of Theology* 41.1 (1988) 75–92.

Temple, William. *Nature Man and God*. London: Macmillan, 1934.

Terry, Justyn. *The Justifying Judgement of God: A Reassessment of the Place of Judgement in the Saving Work of Christ*. Paternoster Theological Monographs. Milton Keynes, UK: Paternoster, 2006.

———. "Recovering the Christian Mind: Educating the Anglican Ministry Today." Address given at the Mere Anglicanism 2012 Conference, St. Philip's Church, Charleston, South Carolina. Video recording of conference online: http://anglican.tv/content/mere-anglicanism-2012-very-revd-dr-justyn-terry

Tolkien, J. R. R. "Mythopoeia" (written 1931). In *Tree and Leaf*, edited by Christopher Tolkien, 85–90. London: Allen and Unwin, 1978.

———. "On Fairy Stories." In *Essays Presented to Charles Williams*, edited by C. S. Lewis, 38–89. Oxford: Oxford University Press, 1947.

———. *The Lord of the Rings*. London: Allen & Unwin, 1954–55.

Toynbee Polly. "Narnia Represents Everything that is most Hateful about Religion." *The Guardian*, Monday 5 Dec. 2005). Online: http://www.guardian.co.uk/books/2005/dec/05/cslewis.booksforchildrenandteenagers

Vidu, Adonis. *Postliberal Theological Method: A Critical Study*. Paternoster Theological Monographs. Milton Keynes, UK: Paternoster, 2005.

Walsh, Chad. *C. S. Lewis Apostle to the Skeptics*. New York: Macmillan, 1949.

Ward, Keith. *God, Faith and the New Millennium*. Oxford: Oneworld, 1998.

Ward, Michael. *Planet Narnia: The Seven Heavens in the Imagination of C. S. Lewis*. Oxford: Oxford University Press, 2008.

Watson, Francis. *Text, Church and World: Biblical Interpretation in Theological Perspective*. Edinburgh: T. & T. Clark, 1994.

Whittaker, Edmund Taylor. *The Beginning and the End of the World*. Riddell Memorial Lectures, 14th series. Oxford: Oxford University Press, 1942.

Williams, Rowan. "Judas Betrayed his Brother with a Kiss." *The Guardian Weekly*, 22 Apr. 2010, 38–39.

Wilson, A. N. *C. S. Lewis: A Biography*. London: Collins, 1990.

Wolfe, Judith. "C. S. Lewis and the Eschatological Church." In *C. S. Lewis and the Church: Essays in Honour of Walter Hooper*, edited by Judith Wolfe and Brendan N. Wolfe, 103–16. London: T. & T. Clark, 2011.

Wolterstorff, Nicholas. "C. S. Lewis on the Problem of Suffering." *The Chronicle of the Oxford University C. S. Lewis Society* 7.3 (2010) 3–20.

Wright, John, editor. *Postliberal Theology and the Church Catholic: Conversations with George Lindbeck, David Burrell, and Stanley Hauerwas*. Grand Rapids: Baker Academic, 2012.

Wright, N. T. "Simply Lewis: Reflections on a Master Apologist After 60 Years." *Touchstone Magazine* 20.2, Mar 2007, 39–40.

———. *The Resurrection of the Son of God*. London: SPCK, 2003.

Index of Names

Abel 13, 256
Adam 18, 21, 34, 36, 39, 47–50, 52, 55, 59, 69, 76–77, 85, 98–100, 105, 107, 135, 147, 159, 162, 176, 195, 206, 210, 224, 230–31, 255, 263
Adonis 44, 144
Ambrose, of Milan 50, 260
Aquinas, Thomas 22, 124,–25, 150–51, 161
Aristotle 22
Arminius, Jacob 64, 207
Athanasius 142, 160, 211
Augustine of Hippo 6, 36, 47–48, 50–55, 57, 62, 70–71, 90, 97–98, 102, 114, 128, 147, 157, 159, 192, 202, 223

Baker, John Austin 72
Balder 128, 144
Barleycorn, John 43
Barth, Karl 19, 124, 189, 198
Basil the Great 260
Baxter, Richard 125
Bazalgette, Sir Joseph William 255
Bede Griffiths, Dom 36, 54, 92, 147, 182–83
Beethoven, Ludwig 11
Beversluis, John 63
Bonting, Sjoerd L. 141, 159, 160–61
Brunner, Emil 19

Cain 13, 256
Campanella, Thomas 159f.
Carpenter, Humphrey 241, 248
Coca-Cola Co., The, 247f. *see Father Christmas*
Constable, John 11
Crisp, Oliver 141, 163–65
Cromwell, Oliver 247
Cyprian of Carthage 50

Damascene, John 170
Daniel 13
Dante (Durante degli Alighieri) 13
Darwin, Charles 102–3
David 2, 130–31, 148, 158, 165, 235, 262

Donahue, John R. 126–27
Donne, John 185
Dostoevsky, Fyodor Mikhailovich 67, 71, 73–76, 80, 97, 108, 110–12, 115
Drees, William B. 141, 159

Eliot, T. S. (Thomas Stearns) 81
Elisha 85
Erskine, Thomas, of Linlathen 74
Esau 13
Eve 18, 34, 39, 47–50, 52, 55, 59, 69, 76, 77, 81–82, 85, 98–100, 105, 107, 135, 147, 164, 176, 210, 224, 247, 255, 263
Ezekiel 43

Father Christmas 135, 196, 198, 239–49, 252–53, 255, 257, 262–65
   Kris Kringle 246–47, 264
   Nicholas of Myra (St Nicholas) 239, 247, 264
   Santa Claus 239, 246–49, 252–53, 255, 264
   Sinterklaas 247
   Sancte Claus 247f.
   Jupiter 246f.
   Jove 246f.
Fergusson, David 141, 158, 160, 165
Feuerbach, Ludwig 232–33
Fisher, Christopher L. 141, 158, 160, 165
Frei, Hans Wilhelm 124

Gabriel 1
Garland, Alex 79–80
Gethsemane 61, 178, 204, 215
God 1–10, 13, 15, 17–30, 32–35, 39–45, 46, 48–60, 61–65, 67–71, 73–83, 85–90, 92–95, 97–101, 103–8, 110–19, 123–28, 130–33, 135–39, 142–43, 145–49, 151–67, 169–85, 187–95, 198–210, 212–15, 217–20, 222–36, 239–40, 243, 245–53, 255–63, 265
   Advocate 201 *see Narnia, Pneuma the Holy One*

Christ 1–10, 12–13, 15, 17–20, 23–24, 27, 31–32, 33, 35–36, 38, 40, 42–50, 52–54, 57–58, 62– 65, 67, 69–70, 73, 75–77, 81–83, 86–87, 89, 93–95, 97, 99, 101, 106–7, 110–12, 114–15, 118–19, 121, 123–24, 126–27, 128–29, 131–36, 138, 139, 141, 142, 143, 144, 145–54, 156–60, 162, 164–65, 169–71, 173, 175–82, 186–89, 191–93, 196–200, 202–13, 215, 217–18, 220–37, 240, 244–45, 246, 249–50, 252–53, 255, 258–62 *see Narnia, Aslan*

Father 12–13, 17, 20, 27, 30–31, 34–35, 77, 86, 135–36, 142–43, 161, 163, 165, 167–73, 175, 177, 182–83, 184–86, 188, 189–93, 196, 198–202, 210, 215–16, 221–23, 228, 233, 239, 240–49, 252–53, 255–59, 262–65 *see Narnia, Emperor-beyond-the-Sea, and, Emperor-over-the-Sea*

Holy Ghost 34, 183, 185, 190, 192 *see Narnia, Pneuma the Holy One*

Holy Spirit 4, 13, 17, 20, 24, 27, 33, 35–37, 48, 54, 62, 64–65, 69–70, 86, 88, 93, 97–98, 106, 111, 119, 128, 135–36, 138, 142–43, 150–51, 163, 167–73, 175–76, 179, 183–84, 186, 190–202, 209, 215–16, 218–19, 221, 224–25, 227, 230, 234, 243, 245, 251–52, 262–63, 265 *see Narnia, Pneuma the Holy One*

Jesus 1–10, 13, 20–21, 23–24, 31, 35, 41–44, 46, 48, 53–54, 55, 61, 63, 65, 75, 99, 100–1, 106–7, 119, 124, 126–29, 135, 136, 142, 143–44, 148, 159, 161–62, 165, 168–71, 175, 179–184, 186–82, 201, 203–5, 208, 212–13, 215, 222–24, 227, 236, 240, 246, 249–50, 255, 260, 262 *see Narnia, Aslan*

Lord 4–5, 23, 38–41, 48, 49, 71, 78–79, 85–86, 112, 138, 145–46, 148, 184, 192, 196, 199, 222–24, 231, 233, 241–43, 249, 253, 265

Messiah 1–3, 77, 126, 135
Yahweh 43–44, 249, 265
Yeshua 1 *see God, Jesus*

Golding, William 67, 71, 78, 80
Green Lady, The (*Perelandra*) 82–83, 147, 149, 151, 164
Gregory of Nazianzus 170
Gregory of Nyssa 260
Gunton, Colin E., 7, 19–20, 189

Hauerwas, Stanley 124, 126
Hebblethwaite, Brian 141, 160–61, 162–65
Hoyle, Sir Fred 22
Hunt, William Holman 181

Isaiah 262

Jacob 13, 64
Jenson, Matt 51
Jenson, Robert 199, 232–33
Jerome 32, 83, 260
Job 28, 31, 33, 70, 262
John (Gospel) 13, 17–20, 27, 42–43, 53, 168–69, 176, 178, 180, 189, 191–92, 193, 195, 200–201, 203–4, 205, 213–14, 217, 221–22, 224, 233, 235, 243
Judas Iscariot 13

Kant, Immanuel 230, 232–33
Karamazov, Ivan (The Brothers Karamazov, Братья Карамазовы) 111, 117
Keats, John 11
King's College London 101
Kreeft, Peter 11–12

Lindsay, David 130–31
Longfellow, Henry Wadsworth 11
Lubac, Henri de 124
Luke (Gospel) 33, 43, 63, 76, 123, 126, 169, 176, 217–18, 224
Luther, Martin 52, 259

MacIntyre, Alasdair 124
Maleldil (The Space Trilogy) 82–83, 173–74, 191
Malory, Sir Thomas 241
Mark (Gospel) 43, 127, 149, 169, 176, 215, 218, 224–25
Marx, Karl 72
Mary 1, 13, 61
Mascall, E. L. 141, 159–60
Matthew (Gospel) 179, 203, 235
Maximus the Confessor 19–20
Meynell, Alice Christiana Gertrude, Thompson 141, 153–54, 165, 188
Miller, John J. 244
Milton, John 57, 67, 71, 76–77, 80– 81
Montagu, John, 4th Earl of Sandwich, 254
More, Henry 67, 72, 79
Moses 126

Index of Names

Napoleon 110, 115–16
Narnia 12, 17, 20, 27, 38–40, 43, 67, 80–81, 84–85, 108, 117, 123, 127–29, 131, 132–39, 141–42, 150, 153–54, 157, 167, 169, 172–80, 183–99, 202–4, 206–10, 212,–13, 215–19, 221–30, 236, 239–58, 259, 261–65
    Aravis 215–16, 218–21
    Aslan 24, 27, 38–39, 43, 70, 84–85, 127, 129, 133–36, 141, 144, 148, 150, 153, 167, 173–75, 17–80, 183–90, 193–222, 224–31, 233, 235–37, 239–40, 243, 245–46, 250, 252–53, 255–64 *see God, Christ*
    Beaver, Mr and Mrs 184, 210–11, 245–46, 253
    Bree 187, 208, 215–16, 218–19, 220–21
    Caspian, Prince and King 132, 148, 179–80, 186, 191, 194, 196–97, 205–6, 208, 211, 241, 251, 254
    Digory 39, 84–85, 108–9, 176–77, 180, 195, 212, 230, 245, 250
    Dufflepuds 205, 208, 230, 234
    Emeth 195, 203, 213, 222–25, 227, 233–37
    Emperor-beyond-the-Sea 175, 183–86, 190, 193, 195, 198–99, 211, 216, 256, 259, 261–63
    Emperor-over-the-Sea 135, 184, 186, 190, 193, 217, 219, 228, 245, 259
    Eustace 178, 180, 186, 194–95, 196, 198, 205, 207, 214, 228, 250, 254
    Frank, King 245
    Ginarrbrik 255
    Helen, Queen 38, 245, 253, 263
    Hwin 215, 218–19, 220–21
    Jadis 39–40, 70, 84, 97, 109–12, 117, 135, 213, 239, 245, 254, 256–57 *see White Witch*
    Jill 178, 180, 194–98, 205, 207, 228, 250, 254–55
    Nikabrik 196, 206
    Pevensie 174–75, 178–80, 184, 190, 194–96, 206–7, 210, 215, 226, 243, 245, 248, 252–54
        Edmund, King 70, 135–36, 139, 148, 174–75, 178, 184, 186, 194, 197, 206–7, 209–10, 213–15, 236–37, 254–60
        Lucy, Queen 43, 136, 148, 178, 180, 186, 195, 197, 198–200, 205–15, 229–30, 237, 243, 245, 253
        Peter, King 12–13, 148, 178, 186, 206–7, 210–11, 218, 228, 235, 243f., 253, 259
        Susan, Queen 178, 185, 194, 206–7, 210, 212, 243, 253
    Pneuma the Holy One 191–97, 198, 199, 215–16, 218–19 *see God, Holy Spirit*
    Polly 39, 84, 109, 139, 180, 207, 230, 245
    Puddleglum 205
    Puzzle 203, 227–29
    Rabadash 207, 219
    Shasta 43, 186, 194, 200–201, 203, 209, 212–13, 215–21, 233–34, 237
    Shift 175, 203, 227–29
    Tash 186, 219, 222–23, 227–28, 235–36, 259
    Tirian, King 196, 198, 227–28, 230, 254–55
    Trumpkin 205
    Tumnus 195, 255
    Uncle Andrew 39, 97, 108–12, 117, 180, 195, 206, 230, 232–34
    White Witch 39, 70, 84, 109, 129, 134–35, 174–75, 176, 184, 194–95, 196, 208, 210, 213–14, 239, 245–46, 253–60, 264 *see Jadis*
Nathan 262
Nicodemus 42, 53, 203, 213

Origen 260
Orual 211
Osiris 144
Owen, Robert 72
Oxford 6, 8, 11, 39, 77, 98, 153, 181, 206, 249

Paul, the Apostle 27, 33, 46, 49–50, 55, 57, 106, 148, 155, 169, 181, 187, 235, 259
Pelagius 98–100
Pittenger, William Norman 98, 144
Plato 7, 26, 72, 128, 129, 144, 250
Psyche 141, 144–45, 211
Pullman, Philip 67, 72, 80–82, 86, 139

Rahner, Karl 141, 158, 160, 165, 176, 198
Ransom, Elwin 82–83, 141, 144, 145, 147, 149, 151, 173–74, 259–60
Raskolnikov, Rodion Romanovich (Родион Романович Раскольников) 97, 110–12, 117
Rider Haggard, Sir Henry 129–30

Sammons, Martha C., 175–80
Satan 40, 49–50, 65, 70, 76, 78, 80–81, 107, 111, 115, 148–50, 211, 227–28, 236, 259–60

277

Screwtape 12, 29, 32, 44, 67, 74, 80, 87–89, 92, 115, 123, 127, 132, 138, 141–42, 145–46, 172, 182, 209–10
Shakespeare, William 99, 136
Simon Peter 13, 147–48
Simpson, Bart 247 *see Father Christmas*
Socrates 63, 99

Temple, William 159, 219
Tertullian (Quintus Septimius Florens Tertullianus) 50
Thomas (doubting) 187, 205
Thomas the Rhymer (Thomas Learmouth) 157–58
Tolkien J. R. R. 12, 32, 37–38, 39–40, 123–24, 138–39, 158, 235, 239, 241–44, 248, 250, 253
Turner, Joseph Mallord William 11
Tyndale, William 259

Vidu, Adonis 125

Wagner, Richard 11, 83, 130
Ward, Keith 141, 160–62, 165, 241, 247, 250
Watson, Francis 18–19, 24
Wells, H. G. (Herbert George) 130, 146, 152
Wittgenstein, Ludwig Josef Johann 124–25
Wolterstorff, Nicholas 71
Wordsworth, William 11
Wright, N. T. (Nicholas Thomas) 3, 11, 42, 124

Index of Subjects

academic 11, 103, 128
Age of Reason 6, 7, 9, 11, 124, 232 see Enlightenment
agnus Dei 214-15
allegory 123, 129, 131-32, 134, 137-39, 172, 175, 230, 234, 240-43, 250
    allegorical 123, 127-29, 134, 137, 141, 144, 175, 239-40, 243-44, 262
analogy 5, 103, 109, 123-24, 129, 131-32, 142, 145, 155, 173, 175-76, 179, 182, 192, 205-6, 211, 223, 225, 236, 239, 258, 262
    analogia 129
    analogical 5, 17, 20, 39, 42-43, 49, 65, 68, 83, 87, 117-18, 123-24, 127-29, 131-33, 138-42, 144, 149, 152, 166-67, 169, 172-73, 175, 189, 190, 197, 212, 224, 240, 250, 252, 256, 262, 264
    analogically 142, 145, 178, 183, 201-3, 207-9, 221, 233-34
    analogous 129, 176, 243
angel(s) 1, 49, 76, 77, 257
animate 30
anthropocentrism 33
apokatastasis 58
apologetic(s) 5, 8, 12, 17, 20, 24-26, 38, 45, 47, 54, 65, 68, 70-71, 87, 92, 97, 111, 125-26, 131, 143-45, 146, 152, 177, 181, 192, 211, 213-14, 225, 249, 260-61
    a/Apologist 8, 10, 48, 62, 98, 144
apophatic 149, 193, 209-210, 253
apostate 69, 99, 128, 152, 154, 206
apostle(s) 2, 3, 7-8, 13, 46, 50, 106, 169, 218
    apostolic 7
Arminian(ism) 64, 207, 233
arrogance 68, 86, 92, 155, 219
Aslanian 223
atheist 81, 128-30, 139, 148, 154, 232
    atheism 130, 148, 232
    a/Atheistic 11, 46, 48, 69, 71-73, 81, 99, 108, 113, 118, 129-30, 141, 146, 148, 152
atonement 8, 19, 47, 55, 58, 61, 64, 65, 70, 75, 99-100, 135, 138, 141, 150, 152-59, 162, 163, 169, 173, 178, 203-4, 233, 239, 241, 244, 255-61, 263-64 see redemption, and, theory
atone 8, 20, 48, 143
atoning 12, 63, 75, 114, 119, 135, 235
    debt 65, 260, 261
    ransom 65, 82, 83, 141, 144-45, 147-49, 151, 173-74, 256, 259-61
autonomy 60
axiom 17, 20-21, 25, 27, 40
    axiomatic 17-18, 167

banished 49, 76
Baptist 3
    baptized 103, 150, 166, 173, 234-35 see imagination
    baptism(al) 150-51, 169, 218, 235
    unbaptized 234
beauty 11, 24, 37, 45, 68, 74, 141-44, 170-71, 203, 211-12, 217-18, 222, 230
behavior 9, 53, 71, 87, 97-100, 102, 104-6, 109, 110, 111-13, 117, 192, 226, 233
belief(s) 4-10, 18, 22, 25, 30, 32, 35, 52, 54-5, 61, 65, 72-73, 75-77, 81, 86, 100, 107-8, 110, 113, 123, 132, 147-49, 160, 167-68, 173, 198, 213, 221, 223, 226-29, 230, 232-34, 236, 239, 254 see faith
believer 4, 77, 139, 172
Bible 3, 8, 11, 25, 27, 33-34, 37, 131, 134, 147, 177, 191-92, 249, 259, 262
    biblical(ly) 8, 18, 20, 25, 31-32, 39, 47, 48, 50, 67, 69, 76, 97, 123-27, 146, 152, 164, 175-80, 188, 204, 224, 241
    New Testament 2-3, 6-8, 43, 45, 168-69, 177-78, 191, 249
    Old Testament 2, 31, 75, 168, 177-78, 183, 187, 191, 214
    scriptural 49, 57, 85, 118, 123, 125-27, 162, 169, 181, 243
    Scripture 2, 9, 12, 19, 31, 45, 48, 63, 98, 104, 123-24, 126-27, 159, 162, 164, 201, 232, 249
blissful 59, 69, 76

blood 15, 43, 70, 74–75, 91, 95, 99, 106, 148, 177–79, 185, 187, 194, 219–21, 248, 256, 259–60, 264

Calormenes 39, 222, 225–26, 228–29, 253
Calvinism 62
   Calvinist 64
character(s) 17, 20–21, 23, 27–29, 30, 40, 42, 49, 88, 97, 102, 110–12, 123, 128–29, 132, 141–49, 152, 172, 175, 184, 188, 196, 203–4, 211, 215, 230, 227, 234, 239, 240–48, 260, 262–64
Christian(s) 1, 3–11, 13, 17–18, 21–23, 25–26, 32, 35, 41, 43, 47–50, 54–59, 61, 63–64, 68–71, 77, 80–81, 87, 90–95, 113, 115, 117, 126, 128–29, 130–32, 135, 137, 139, 141–42, 144, 146–48, 152–54, 156, 160, 162, 164, 167–69, 172, 174–75, 177, 181–85, 190, 192, 195, 202, 214, 222–26, 236, 242, 244–45, 247, 250, 263, 264
   Christendom 12
   Christianity 3, 4, 10–11, 13, 29, 32–33, 35, 37, 44, 58, 62, 63, 81, 87, 89, 93, 99, 114, 119, 125, 139, 142, 153, 169, 172, 181–83, 190, 202, 232, 237, 247
Christlike 93, 128, 143, 144, 147–48, 173, 211–12, 234, 259 *see imago Christi, imatatio Christi, and, imago Dei*
   Christlikeness 82, 112, 124, 141–45, 147–49, 150, 167, 212
Christology 3–5, 17, 48, 98, 134, 141, 144, 145, 161, 167–68, 173, 189, 208–9, 239, 240, 258
   Christological 24, 77, 123, 128, 132, 138, 144–45, 158, 204, 218, 239
churches 1–10, 12–13, 18–19, 25, 34, 50–59, 78, 81, 92–93, 98, 107, 124–26, 128, 131, 133, 135, 143, 147, 149, 159, 168, 175, 181–82, 184–85, 192–93, 205–7, 223, 226–27, 243, 246–47, 259–60, 263
   denominations 4, 6, 124, 192, 247
Church of England 4, 10, 52–53, 57, 78, 98, 126, 185
   Anglican(s) 3, 4, 6, 12, 41, 51–52, 57, 72, 79, 98, 105, 124, 160, 163
   Thirty-Nine Articles 52
civilization 78–79, 98, 110
communion 27, 35, 55, 69, 82, 142, 170, 193, 217
concupiscence 47, 53–54, 77, 97, 102–4, 106
condemn(ation) 49, 51, 53, 56, 59, 62, 81, 85, 89, 92, 116, 175, 203, 207, 227–28
consciousness 67–68, 69, 75, 80, 88, 93, 130, 175–76, 208, 255, 256

convert/conversion 4–6, 10, 47, 50, 53–54, 73, 128, 134, 141, 148, 160, 170, 192, 203, 213, 218, 221, 223, 251
corruption 40, 41, 48–49, 52, 58, 62, 68, 75, 93, 104, 119, 134, 148, 162, 251, 255
   corrupted 42, 53–55, 60, 67, 74–75, 83, 87, 94, 97, 99, 104, 153–55, 218
   corrupting 47, 58, 85, 100, 127, 147
Creation(s) 1, 8–9, 12, 17–29, 30, 31, 32–45, 46–49, 51, 55, 59–60, 67, 69, 71–72, 75–77, 84–85, 86, 97–98, 100–4, 117, 118, 123, 124, 130, 132, 134–35, 137–39, 143, 147, 149, 151, 154–55–57, 159–60, 167–68, 173–78, 179, 183–84, 186, 187–88, 192, 194, 196, 199, 201–2, 204, 208, 213–14, 217, 221, 230, 233, 236, 239, 241–42, 245, 248, 250–60, 263–65 *see sub-creation*
   beginning 13, 22, 25–27, 29, 32, 38, 40, 62, 114, 116, 126, 168, 182, 184, 211, 239, 245, 254 *see ex nihilo*
   create(d) 8–9, 12, 17–30, 32–33, 35, 37, 42, 46–47, 50–51, 53, 55, 57, 59–60, 63, 67–68, 71–73, 79–81, 90, 99–103, 107, 111, 114–17, 134, 136, 138, 145, 147, 151, 155, 157–58, 176, 184, 197, 203–4, 208–10, 214, 216–17, 219, 232–34, 245, 247–48, 250, 252, 256
   creationism 25
   creationist 25f.
   creativity 19, 24, 37, 38, 165, 167, 202, 212
   creator 17, 19, 20–25, 28, 30–32, 34–38, 42, 44, 54, 83, 146, 151, 175, 189, 208, 216, 248, 263
   creature 15–17, 25, 28, 30–32, 34–36, 48–49, 51–52, 56–60, 67–73, 80, 83, 88, 100, 102–4, 114–15, 138, 142, 144, 146, 151–54, 156, 174, 178, 188, 194, 197, 200, 216, 221, 226, 228, 230, 236, 258, 260–61
   design 26, 28, 254
   ex nihilo 18, 20–23, 26, 37, 174
   fabrication model 18
   matter-energy 30
   primary creation 37
   speech-act model 17, 19
   steady state theory 22
   time and space 26, 33, 117, 201
   universe 8, 12–13, 18–19, 22, 24–25, 26–30, 33, 34, 38, 58–59, 69, 95, 107, 111, 115, 130, 134, 138–39, 141, 148, 150, 153–54, 156–59, 161–64, 173, 203, 240, 248, 249
   web of life 103

world 4, 6-8, 10-13, 17, 19, 20, 22, 24-31, 35, 37-38, 40-46, 50, 52, 55-59, 67-68, 73, 77, 80-84, 92-93, 100, 105, 107, 109, 112, 115-19, 126-27, 128, 131-38, 143, 148, 150, 154, 157-58, 160, 167-69, 172-74, 176, 179-81, 183-84, 186, 189, 193, 196-99, 202-3, 205, 211, 214, 217-19, 222, 225-26, 228, 230, 233, 236, 239-45, 248-49, 250-55, 258-59, 263, 265
creed(s) 3-4, 8-9, 55, 68, 72-73, 124, 129, 168
crisis 64, 79, 94, 108, 112, 139, 146, 174-75, 203, 213, 225, 257
crucifixion 8, 48, 60, 99, 106, 129, 169, 175, 184, 187, 199, 212, 251, 260
    c/Cross 2, 12, 17, 20-21, 33, 39, 40-41, 44, 45-47, 48, 55, 58, 61, 65, 70, 76, 87, 95, 99-100, 114, 128, 130, 135, 139, 141-42, 146, 150, 155, 162-64, 173, 180, 196, 199, 204, 215, 232, 236, 239-40, 244, 252-55, 257-58, 264
    crucified 8, 20, 47, 99, 154, 199
culture(s) 9-11, 49, 79-80, 86, 108, 124, 155, 158, 232, 241-42, 247, 254
    cultural 1, 7, 11, 22, 69, 87, 93, 110, 165, 239, 242-47, 252-54, 263-64
custodianship 17, 21, 37, 38-40, 59, 83, 97, 114, 117-18, 149

damnation 42-43, 52, 65, 99, 147, 224
    damned 13, 43, 145-46, 179, 210, 225
Darwinian 69, 102, 104
death 8, 12-13, 20-21, 26, 27-28, 31, 38, 40-41, 43-46, 48-52, 55-58, 62-65, 76, 82-84, 99, 106, 108, 111, 128-29, 133-34, 142-43, 152-54, 156, 158, 160-61, 175, 177-78, 185-86, 210, 213-14, 216, 222, 225, 241, 246, 255-56, 259-60, 264
decisions 34, 36, 49, 86, 88, 97, 99, 102, 105-7, 111, 119, 146-47, 175, 219, 224-25, 233, 260
Deity 41, 45, 134, 183
delusion 36, 78, 86, 91, 110, 115, 250
depravity 40, 47, 50, 61-64, 108, 110, 153, 214
    depraved 56, 62-64, 110
dialectic 45, 67, 80, 86, 133
    complementary dialectic 45
    dialectical 45, 74
    supplementary dialectic 45
disease 59, 67, 84, 90, 155
disobedience 18, 49, 50, 52, 54-55, 57, 67, 77, 80, 82, 85-86, 115, 159
    disobeying 100, 138
Docetic 167, 187, 208

Docetists 187
doctrine(s) 3-6, 8, 12, 17-28, 30-31, 35, 37-39, 40-52, 54-64, 73, 77-78, 80-81, 97-100, 107, 112, 114-17, 123, 128, 132, 138, 142, 147, 152-56, 159, 167-68, 172-74, 181-82, 184, 186, 192, 201, 218, 225-26, 233, 239, 244, 249, 262, 264
door/gateway 179-80
dualism 51, 53

Eastern Orthodox 12, 192
ecclesiology 6, 226 *see Church*
    ecclesial 6, 129
    ecclesiastical 6, 45
economic 13, 126, 168-69, 172-73, 198, 200
ego 111, 114-43, 206
    egotism 33-34, 114
elect 13, 50, 224-25, 252, 257
    election 13, 19, 65, 249
encounter(s) 3, 5-7, 43, 109, 126, 142, 156, 173, 201, 203-4, 207, 212-19, 221-22, 225, 232, 264
Enlightenment 6, 7-9, 59, 119, 123-25, 230, 232 *see Age of Reason*
entropy 27, 41
environmental 38, 40, 71, 100, 105, 119
eritis sicut Deus 97, 108, 110-11, 113, 135, 147
eschatology 9, 223
    eschatological 13, 71, 161, 162, 170, 179-80, 203, 213, 227-28, 239, 251, 257-58, 263
    eschaton 8, 42, 55, 72, 118-19, 136, 167, 174-75, 181, 188-89, 196, 198, 211-12, 225, 227-29, 237, 254, 259
    end of all things 42, 162, 175, 179, 189
    four last things 8, 55
eternity 22, 25, 29, 34, 37-38, 42, 44-45, 51, 89, 136-38, 157, 161, 172, 175, 179, 189-90, 197, 202, 205, 212, 235, 248-52
Evangelical(s) 3-7, 12, 81, 126
evidence 2, 22, 25-26, 33, 44, 62, 71, 82, 104, 128, 136, 155, 167, 168, 172-74, 190, 225, 235, 243, 245, 247
evil 23, 36, 38-39, 42, 48-56, 60, 65, 67, 70-71, 76, 80-88, 92, 94, 98, 106, 109-11, 118, 127, 130-31, 134, 139, 147-51, 158, 174, 176-78, 186, 195-96, 198, 200, 206-7, 209-10, 213, 218-19, 223-24, 227-29, 239, 243, 246, 250-51, 254, 256-57, 259-61, 263
existential 15, 73, 111, 139, 146, 173, 193, 203, 212, 220, 225, 252
    exist(s) 19, 20-21, 23-24, 26, 28-29, 31-32, 36-37, 41, 58, 63-64, 68, 81-82,

281

87, 92, 107, 111, 114, 117, 136, 149, 155, 157–58, 160, 164, 205, 233, 243, 249, 262, 264
existence 9, 13, 15, 18, 20, 23–27, 36–37, 51, 56–58, 64–65, 71–72, 85, 88, 99, 105, 108, 111–12, 114, 116, 146, 153, 156, 158–59, 161–62, 165, 168, 176, 186, 200, 210, 240, 243, 248–49, 256
extra-terrestrial(s) 158, 159–61, 163, 165

faith 3–5, 6, 8, 11, 53, 62, 65, 74, 87, 97, 110–11, 117, 126, 129, 131, 145, 147, 156, 162, 169–70, 179, 196, 199–200, 205–6, 210, 222–26, 232–36, 243 *see belief*
fall, the *see original sin*
fantasy 123, 129, 137, 138, 232, 240
    fantasies 123, 244
felix culpa 58, 81
Feuerbachian 203, 229, 231–35
flesh 13, 42, 50–53, 85–86, 88, 92, 133, 137, 148, 160, 168, 186–87, 189, 191, 197, 217, 221, 233, 240, 248, 264
forgiveness 63, 65, 75, 77, 90, 93, 95, 99, 107, 112, 119, 202–3, 205, 207, 214, 227, 229, 259
    forgiver 111
    forgives 70, 91, 99, 256, 259
    forgiving 167, 214, 216, 259
form 2–3, 5, 7, 10, 17, 19, 21, 23, 26, 31–33, 37–39, 41, 46, 53, 59, 61–64, 67–68, 70, 73, 75–76, 80, 87, 93, 97–98, 102, 113, 123, 126–27, 131–32, 136–37, 139, 142, 144, 147, 149, 151, 156, 161–62, 165, 169–70, 173, 175–77, 185–86, 188, 189–90, 198, 200, 203–4, 208–9, 212, 215, 218–19, 225, 233–35, 239–40, 242–43, 248–50, 252–54, 258, 262, 264, 265
Freudian 48, 232
fulfillment 10, 17, 19, 20, 29, 40–41, 45, 83, 114, 169, 232

genetic 39, 100, 102, 104–5, 170 *see creation, sub-creation. Naturalism, Scientism, reality, and, teleology*
    DNA 71, 97, 100–105
    evolution 8, 18, 32, 37, 56, 68–69, 71, 102–7, 158, 163
    evolutionary 22, 46, 63, 104, 130
    gene(s) 71, 97, 100–105
    genetics 71, 102
    genome 97, 100–104
    hereditary 61, 75, 98, 100, 104, 106

horizontal gene transfer/HGT 71, 102–5, 107
species 15, 39–41, 56, 59, 68, 71, 82, 85–86, 102–5, 125, 130, 138, 141, 146–47, 152–53, 155–57, 162, 164–65, 167, 172–74, 188
genre 31–32, 79, 123, 128–29, 131–32, 136, 149, 212, 239
glory 13, 18–19, 29–30, 35, 45, 52, 104, 126, 142, 160, 169, 180, 217–18, 222, 233, 248
Gnostic 81, 103, 136, 201, 187
good 4, 17–18, 20, 27–28, 34, 36, 48–49, 50–53, 56, 58–59, 60, 62–64, 67–68, 72, 76, 80–90, 98, 99–100, 102, 106–13, 115, 117–18, 127, 130–31, 142, 144, 147, 156–57, 158–59, 163–65, 173, 174, 176–77, 181, 191, 195, 197, 199, 205–7, 211, 218, 222–28, 230, 231, 232, 235–36, 246, 247, 249, 256–57, 263, 265
gospel 4, 7–8, 11–13, 18–19, 42–44, 93, 111–12, 125–29, 131–32, 135, 141, 147, 153, 168, 191, 203–5, 212–14, 222, 234, 243, 253
grace 13, 19, 35–36, 45, 47, 50, 52–53, 55, 62–65, 75, 77, 80, 83, 90, 97–98, 105–6, 128, 138, 141, 143, 145, 162, 169–70, 202, 218, 223, 233–34, 236
    dis-graced 99
    gracious 19, 164, 236, 246, 257
    resistible 65
Greek 1, 2, 6–8, 10, 13, 26, 32, 50, 58, 72, 129, 144, 148–49, 168, 170, 187, 189, 191, 247
guilt 15, 54, 74, 77, 87, 89, 90–91, 95, 217–18, 260, 261

heathen 203, 218, 236, 251
heaven 4, 8, 13, 18, 20–21, 25, 29, 32, 34, 41–43, 46, 55, 57, 62, 65, 68, 72, 76, 80, 86, 111, 116–17, 145–46, 157–58, 165, 167, 175, 179, 181, 187, 189, 192, 194, 196, 210, 212, 223, 225–30, 233, 234, 249
hell 8, 13, 42–43, 55, 62, 65, 76, 80–81, 89, 93, 99, 114–17, 145–46, 150, 158, 172, 175, 179, 181, 209–10, 225, 228–29, 234–35 *see infernal voluntarism*
    Hades 51, 58
    Sheol 51, 58
heresy 72, 77, 81, 98–99, 182, 187
    heterodoxy 77
history 3, 5, 10, 12, 20–21, 44–46, 56, 68–69, 86, 104, 106–8, 110, 125–28, 131, 134–35, 149–50, 155, 161, 165, 167, 173–74, 203–5, 227, 255, 260, 262–63
    historical 3, 5, 12, 31, 62, 12–28, 165, 247

human 2-4, 6-9, 11, 13, 18-19, 20-21, 23-24, 26-29, 31-39, 41, 42, 45, 46, 47-60, 63-65, 67-71, 75-76, 78-80, 85-90, 92-93, 97-100, 102-8, 110-19, 128, 130, 132, 135, 13-8, 141, 143-49, 151-55, 157, 159, 160-65, 168-70, 172-76, 179-80, 182, 186-89, 191-92, 195-98, 201-5, 209, 211, 217, 219, 22-24, 226, 229, 232-36, 239-40, 245, 252-58, 261, 263, 265
homo sapiens 68
human-centered 3, 159, 170
humanity 1-3, 5, 7-8, 12-13, 17-21, 24, 28, 30-35, 37-44, 46, 47-52, 54-55, 57-65, 67-73, 75-88, 91-93, 95, 97-100, 104-14, 117-19, 123-24, 127-28, 132, 138-39, 141-42, 145-65, 168-70, 173-74, 187-88, 203, 205, 210, 224-25, 230, 232-34, 236, 248, 255, 259
human nature 9, 34, 36, 52, 56, 59, 64-65, 75, 78, 98, 104, 106, 115, 151, 161, 162-65
humility 63, 86, 103, 143, 215, 221, 233, 236, 255

Idealism 239, 244, 247-49, 252, 262 *see Platonism*
illumination 48, 128, 234, 262
illumined 48, 87, 211, 251, 254, 262
imagination 21, 29, 31, 37, 48, 103, 128, 141, 166, 173, 200, 234-5, 240-41, 249-50, 252, 262
imaginative 37, 121, 130, 138, 165, 167, 193, 235, 242
Imagining 123
imago Christi 21, 33, 142-45, 171
image of Christ 33, 142, 143, 170-71
imago Dei 21, 32, 34, 37
imitatio Christi 142-43
imitation 7, 44, 142-43
immeasurable 23, 24
immeasurability 24
inanimate 17, 30, 31, 155
incarnation 2, 6, 8-9, 17, 19, 20-21, 24, 29, 31, 33, 40-41, 43-44, 46, 48, 55, 58, 99, 114, 119, 128, 129, 133, 134, 136-38, 141, 143, 150-54, 156-68, 172, 186, 187-89, 190, 204-5, 208, 211, 215, 217, 233, 239-40, 244, 247, 249, 251-53, 255, 258, 260 *see multiple incarnations*
descend(ed) 2, 43, 100, 107, 160, 221, 255
descent to reascend 13, 211
incarnate(d) 4, 8, 20, 23-24, 43, 47, 58, 123, 131, 133-34, 138, 141, 150-51, 153, 156, 161-63, 168, 186, 188-89, 204, 208, 215, 217-18, 233, 236, 240
incarnational 137, 217, 250
nativity 167, 180, 187-88, 240, 255
reascend 13, 43, 160, 169, 211
independence 35, 36, 108, 147, 247
infernal voluntarism 42 *see hell*
infinity 22, 23, 24, 73, 151, 245
finite 19, 23-24, 151, 160-61, 165
infinite 19, 23-24, 37, 151, 160-61, 162, 165, 185, 188, 231, 236
infinitum capax finiti 24 *see Trinity*
inheritance 49, 58, 99, 102, 104
Inklings 40, 42, 123, 239, 221, 241
innocent 48, 54-55, 73-74, 90, 155, 157, 177-78, 207, 259, 261
innocence 58, 73, 82, 155, 260
innocency 74, 85
in potentia 65
intellect 6, 103, 234
intelligible 7, 28, 137-38, 157, 162, 165, 167, 193, 248, 264
interpretation 3, 7, 34, 50, 63, 68, 87, 94, 137, 235, 243, 263
intimation(s) 29, 42-44, 46, 62, 128, 130, 132, 137, 139, 213, 249, 251
Israel 2, 19, 85-86, 133, 249
Hebrew 1-3, 23, 32, 44, 48-49, 85, 106, 133, 191, 222, 259, 260
Jewish 2, 3, 10, 18, 21
Jews 2, 22, 24, 135
Judaic 26, 128
Judaism 1, 25, 48, 139

joy 29, 30, 84, 143, 146, 167, 193, 201-2, 207, 230-31, 246, 253
judge(s) 2, 8, 20, 28, 46, 56, 60, 63, 75, 77, 97, 107, 119, 170, 214, 222-24, 227, 242
judgment 8, 13, 29, 36, 42, 45, 55, 62-65, 89, 107, 112, 129, 134, 162, 167, 170, 175, 177, 179, 200, 202-3, 207, 210, 213-14, 217, 222-29, 236, 239, 242, 255, 257-58, 261-63
justification 8, 49, 53, 110, 112, 115, 138, 148, 207, 236, 239, 244

Kantian 123, 124, 203, 229, 230-35, 249
kenotic 160, 215
kenosis 23, 143, 169, 215
kingdom 42-43, 65, 80, 114, 123-24, 127, 145, 186, 191, 195, 223, 233
knowledge 1, 19-20, 48-49, 54, 56-57, 67, 76, 80-81, 83-85, 87-89, 93, 95, 109-10, 118,

126, 128, 134, 147, 154, 162, 165, 172, 177, 182, 203–5, 212, 216, 220, 224, 234–37, 255–56
  know 5, 6, 9, 18, 19, 23, 25–29, 34, 38, 41, 43, 45, 50, 56, 59–60, 62, 64, 69, 74–75, 84, 92–94, 99–100, 108, 113, 130, 136, 139, 146–47, 153–56, 165, 172–74, 176, 182, 184–85, 192, 195–96, 198, 203, 205–7, 209, 211–13, 215, 217, 219–20, 222–23, 225–26, 229, 232–33, 236–37, 245–48, 252, 254, 263
  knowable 17, 21, 25, 31, 183, 250

language 6, 9, 21–22, 24, 26, 31, 48, 55, 57, 123–25, 127, 149, 188–90, 212, 249, 254
Last Judgment 65, 162, 213, 228, 261
Latin 1, 6, 50, 54, 129, 147, 168, 185, 192, 260
law(s) 12–13, 28, 49, 50–51, 56, 63, 70, 86–89, 97, 105, 107–13, 118, 133, 149, 168, 177, 185, 249, 256, 259–61
l/Liberal 4, 9, 13, 67, 73, 81, 87, 97, 98, 105, 123–25, 137, 139, 149, 228, 253
  l/Liberalism 9, 10, 98, 113, 124–26, 149
  liberals 9, 86
light 6, 9, 19, 41, 62, 69, 83, 87, 89, 106, 115–16, 128, 132, 135, 138, 143, 148, 153, 157–58, 181, 198–99, 201, 209, 214, 217, 224, 227–29, 248, 251, 257, 263
lion 131, 134, 136, 141, 184, 187–90, 197, 203–5, 208–9, 211–12, 216, 219–21, 227, 230–31, 242, 262
  lionized 43, 188–89, 204
literature 6, 10, 35, 37, 45, 57, 77, 128–29, 158, 163
logic 32, 47, 64, 131, 136, 139, 141, 162, 166, 213, 215, 239–41, 243, 250, 262
  logical 6, 61, 64, 113, 126, 161–62, 164
love 4, 13, 18, 26, 28, 30, 33–36, 45, 59, 62, 74–75, 90, 94–95, 114–15, 118, 129, 132, 143, 146, 154, 156, 165, 167–72, 177–78, 182–83, 185, 190, 193, 195–96, 199, 202, 204, 207, 210–12, 217–19, 225–27, 234, 236, 240, 252–53, 257–58, 261
  agapē 169
  Deus caritas est 169

magic 57–78, 84, 109, 177–78, 184–85, 208, 219, 243, 246, 256, 260–62
  magical 86, 246, 260
martyr 246
mercy 91, 94, 99
messiahship 1–3

metaphor 43, 49, 54, 123, 127, 131
  metaphorical 54, 177
  metaphors 123, 127
metaphysics 9, 163
  metaphysical 51, 53, 163–64, 232
Methodist 3
Modalism 168, 198–200 *see Trinity*
  modalistic 24, 199–201, 217
modern 6, 8, 10, 12–13, 22, 45, 57, 63, 65, 79, 91, 110, 113, 123–25, 138, 149, 152, 169, 185, 192, 228, 241, 246, 247, 259
  Modernism 6, 9–10, 123–25
  Modernist 4, 9, 10
modes 102, 168, 198, 249
moral(s) 65, 102, 110–13
  amoral 23, 40, 109, 148
  ethical 9, 111, 158, 190
  ethics 5, 9, 49, 65, 81, 102, 110–11, 113, 130
  morality 9, 81, 92, 97, 107–8, 111–13, 149, 233
  moralizing 132, 135
multiple incarnations 138, 141, 150–53, 156–66, 188–89, 204
mystical 54, 216
myth 17, 21–22, 31–32, 44, 55, 57, 78, 83, 103, 128, 130, 132, 144–45, 147, 248, 253
  mythical 31, 61, 132, 239, 242, 247, 252
  mythological 48, 55, 57, 76, 159, 240–42, 248–49, 263
  mythology 10, 81, 129, 144, 240
mythopoeic *see sub-creation*

Narnia 12, 17, 20, 27, 38–40, 43, 67, 80–81, 84–85, 108, 117, 123, 127–29, 131, 132–39, 141–42, 150, 153–54, 157, 167, 169, 172–80, 183–99, 202–4, 206–10, 212–13, 215–19, 221–30, 236, 239–58, 259, 261–65
  Narniad 123, 127, 13–39, 141–42, 146, 154, 157, 167, 173–77, 179–81, 183–84, 186, 188–93, 198–200, 202, 205, 212–13, 214, 225, 230, 239–42, 244, 250–51, 254, 258–59, 261–62, 264
  Narnian 70, 121, 123, 133–34, 136, 142, 167, 183, 184–85, 189, 196, 202, 208, 216, 218, 220, 225, 227, 229, 235, 239, 244–46, 252, 253–61
  Narnians 157, 179, 199, 213, 221–22, 226–28, 253–58
narrative(s) 5, 12, 17, 20, 27, 42–44, 59, 65, 68, 73, 83, 87, 117–18, 121, 123–24, 126–29, 131–33, 136, 138–39, 141–42, 144–45, 147, 149, 152, 166–67, 172–73, 175, 181–82, 189–90, 203–4, 212, 218, 241, 262

Index of Subjects

naturalism 130, 147, 149
    naturalist 130, 148
    naturalistic 138, 148
Natural Law 111-12
nature 2, 3, 7, 9, 18-46, 49-50, 52-59, 61, 63-65, 69-71, 73-75, 78, 84-85, 90, 97-99, 102-7, 115, 117-18, 123, 126, 130-31, 135-36, 138, 142-43, 147-48, 151-52, 155, 157, 160-63, 165, 170, 172, 174, 182, 184, 186-89, 191, 193, 198, 202-3, 208-9, 217-18, 227, 231, 234, 244-45, 252, 259-61, 264
neighbor 45, 107, 169-71, 219, 261
nihilism 51, 110, 169
    nihilistic 58, 110-11, 117, 130, 230
    nothing(ness) 8, 11, 18, 20-23, 26, 37, 38, 43, 46, 50, 53, 56, 58, 62, 74-75, 77, 87, 93, 95, 99, 102, 104, 112, 115-18, 133, 137, 155, 160, 165, 169, 199, 205-7, 210, 217, 231, 234, 242-54

obedience 19, 34, 45, 49, 51, 54, 59, 63, 67, 80, 83-86, 147, 184, 218
    obeying 36, 83, 100
ontology 9, 114, 170, 174, 187, 248-49, 259, 264
    ontological(ly) 9, 28, 35, 43, 53-54, 57, 75, 82, 97, 117-18, 152, 159, 161, 163, 170, 186, 189, 204, 212, 245, 249, 252, 258
originality 32, 37, 38
original sin 8, 12, 15, 17-20, 30-31, 36, 40-41, 45-55, 57, 59, 60-62, 64-65, 67-68, 70, 72-73, 75, 78-80, 83, 85-88, 90, 93-94, 97-100, 102, 104-19, 139, 144-45, 147, 149-50, 152-53, 156, 158-59, 162-63, 164-65, 176, 234, 235
    fall 8, 9, 12, 15, 17-18, 20-21, 25-26, 28-29, 31-36, 40, 46-52, 54-82, 85-88, 90, 93, 97-100, 105-8, 110-19, 132, 135-38, 139, 144-45, 147, 149-50, 153, 157-59, 164-65, 167, 170, 174, 176, 183, 198, 206, 207, 210, 224-25, 234, 248, 256
    fallen(ness) 12-13, 30, 36-37, 41, 43, 46, 49-51, 53, 55-56, 58-64, 70, 73, 76, 79, 82, 85, 87, 93, 104, 107, 110, 138, 141, 143, 147, 150-58, 164, 169, 211, 234-35, 247, 255, 257
    fell 2, 36, 49, 55, 56, 69-70, 83, 113, 217, 228, 246
    freedom 9, 18, 23-24, 30, 37, 50, 52, 67, 73, 79-80, 83, 86, 97, 108, 110, 112, 117, 118, 124-25, 147, 167, 173-74, 190, 217, 234, 236, 252, 259-61

f/Free will 28, 31, 51, 53, 55, 58, 60-61, 65, 75, 82-83, 85, 90, 98, 105, 107, 117-18, 159, 224, 233
homo incurvatus in se 54, 70, 85, 108
insubordination 54
inverted 62, 88
lapsed 2, 55, 206
own volition 52, 83, 86, 98, 103, 224
postlapsarian 47-48, 55, 60, 61, 71, 73, 79, 80, 82, 107, 118, 124, 230
prelapsarian 47-49, 55, 58-60, 69, 72-73, 82, 93, 138, 173
pride 36, 57-58, 69-70, 75, 86, 90, 92, 94, 108-9, 114, 207, 219, 221
proud 40, 85, 86, 92, 105, 149, 178, 221, 261
rebellion 17, 21, 29, 32, 46-50, 54, 57, 59, 72, 81, 83, 85-86, 93, 97, 104, 111-12, 119, 124, 130, 135, 167, 174, 197, 252, 256-57
rebellious 70, 145, 156, 229
total depravity 47, 50, 61-64
treachery 70, 135, 174-75, 178, 185, 237, 255-59
treason 70, 184, 214, 255, 257-58
trespass 49
unfallen 47, 55, 59-60, 155
will 6-9, 13, 20, 22-23, 25-43, 45-51, 53, 55-77, 80-86, 88-91, 93-94, 97-100, 102-19, 124, 126-27, 129-31, 134, 141-43, 145, 147-50, 152, 155-57, 159-63, 165-66, 169-70, 172-73, 175-78, 180-81, 183, 185, 188, 191, 195-97, 201-2, 204-8, 210-12, 214-15, 217-25, 227, 229-30, 233-34, 236-37, 240, 245-46, 248-61, 263
willful 48, 61, 69, 79, 85, 105-6, 110, 192, 197
wilful 13
wilfulness 13
orthodox 1, 3, 5, 7, 9, 12, 17, 28, 30-31, 47-48, 54, 71, 73, 76-78, 80, 97, 99, 112, 123, 125, 147, 152-53, 160, 163, 165, 167-68, 172, 174, 181, 188, 199, 201, 214, 225, 258

pagan 8, 10-11, 18, 25-26, 32, 59, 128, 133, 135-36, 144, 148, 203, 211, 213, 215-18, 220, 235-36, 240, 247, 249, 252, 257
paganism 10, 59, 185
p/Pain 15, 24, 28-31, 34-39, 41, 44, 54, 56-60, 62-63, 64, 67-68, 70-71, 75, 82, 85, 87, 89-95, 105, 114-17, 154, 182-83, 187, 207
    affliction 28, 207

285

painful 15, 36, 54, 57, 59–61, 63, 70, 94, 116–17, 145, 149, 172, 208, 210
    suffering 28, 58, 71, 74, 94, 118, 128, 143–45, 161, 187, 199, 204, 207
Panentheism 21, 28, 30, 183
    Panentheistic 201, 217
Pantheism 21, 28, 30, 41
p/Parable(s) 33, 34, 65, 73, 75, 92, 94, 123–24, 126–27, 131, 149, 166, 181, 190, 205, 207, 236, 249, 262
    parabolic 123, 127
paradise 67, 68, 79–80, 82, 86, 105, 211
paradox 26, 42, 45, 111, 117, 157, 189, 203, 211
particularity 23–25
patristic 7, 13, 47, 54, 81, 123, 125, 142, 160–61, 165, 170, 247, 260–61
Pelagian 72, 99, 105, 108, 141, 145
    Pelagianism 97–99
    Pelagians 52, 99, 100
perception 2, 6, 13, 18, 29, 40, 43, 47, 148, 167, 168, 173, 201, 205–13, 217, 235, 250
    perceivable 7, 138, 248, 264
person 2–6, 10, 13, 20, 25, 30, 34, 41, 52–54, 60–61, 69, 82–84, 86, 90–91, 93–94, 106, 111, 116, 127–28, 131, 139, 142–45, 147, 151, 161–63, 165, 167–75, 180–84, 186–93, 195, 197, 198–99, 200–5, 209, 211–14, 216, 222–24, 235, 239, 246–50, 261, 264–65
    personal 3, 5–7, 13, 49, 74, 85–86, 93–94, 107–9, 111–12, 139, 148, 161, 178, 181–82, 201, 204, 217, 222, 234
    personality 151, 161, 165, 182
    personhood 163, 170, 176, 194, 202, 240
perversion 53, 68, 94, 105
philosophy 5–7, 9–10, 26, 81, 124–25, 131, 251
    philosopher(s) 5, 6–8, 11, 50, 71, 99, 123–24, 141, 151, 159–60, 162, 230, 249
    philosophical(ly) 5, 12, 17, 20, 22, 32, 38, 47–48, 68, 87, 111, 124–26, 142–43, 148, 149, 152, 158, 163, 182, 192, 211, 214, 225, 230, 249
physics 22 *see* science
Platonism 7, 25, 41, 136, 169, 223, 252
    Platonic 7, 24–27, 29, 37, 42, 44, 123–24, 136, 139, 189–90, 231, 235, 239, 244, 247–50, 252, 258, 262, 264–65
    Platonist(s) 7, 51, 249
Pneumatology 35, 192, 243, 252, 262
    breath 24, 43, 176, 186–87, 191, 193–96, 200–201, 216, 250
    breathe 193, 194, 200, 206
    chastiser 195, 196
    comforter 195f.
    courage 145, 195, 198, 199, 209–10, 216

    disquieting presence 191
    enabled 119, 135, 195–96
    enabler , 196
    filioque 192–93
    gift-bearer 239, 242–46, 248–49, 252–53, 255–58, 262–65
    guide 83, 129, 134, 173, 175–80, 196, 198, 240, 241
    haunting 183, 192, 200, 209
    holiness 52, 73, 87, 148, 173, 240, 249
    Holy Ghost 34, 183, 185, 190–92
    Holy Spirit 4, 13, 17, 20, 24, 27, 33, 35–37, 48, 54, 62, 64–65, 69–70, 86, 88, 93, 97–98, 106, 111, 119, 128, 135–36, 138, 142–43, 150–51, 163, 167–73, 175–76, 179, 183–84, 186, 190–202, 209, 215–16, 218–19, 221, 224–25, 227, 230, 234, 243, 245, 251–52, 262–63, 265 *see Narnia, Pneuma the Holy One*
    hope 121, 138, 193, 196, 198–200, 263
    Pneuma, the Holy One 191–199, 215–16, 218–19
    pneumatological 35, 243, 252, 262
    presence 21, 27, 31, 53, 67–68, 87, 93, 105, 142, 145, 165, 167f., 173, 182, 187, 190–94, 200–201, 203–4, 208–10, 215–16, 230, 233, 239–44, 252, 255, 257, 262, 265
    prevenience 98, 126
    prevenient 37, 47, 53, 55, 62, 63, 64, 98, 128, 141, 143, 145, 218, 234
    preveniently 62, 70, 106, 173, 175, 196, 218–19, 224, 235
    process(ion) 26, 57, 94, 125, 129, 131, 141–45, 150–52, 188, 193, 201, 259–60
    sanctification 63, 145, 170, 175, 179, 190
political 2, 6, 31, 68, 69, 72–73, 75, 80, 85, 108, 110, 203, 227
postliberal(s) 12, 123–26, 142
postmodern(ism) 6, 81, 107, 124–26, 247
post mortem 13, 42, 51, 58, 115, 145, 151, 190, 195, 210, 227, 229, 234, 261
potential 2, 20, 28, 33, 37, 40, 42, 50, 64, 65, 77, 104, 128, 152–53, 156, 158, 162–63, 213, 215, 225, 249, 256, 257
praise 29, 30, 35, 115, 139, 252
prefigure 135
    prefigurement 123, 128, 132–34, 135, 218
Presbyterian 3
proposition 24, 39, 58, 75, 97, 111, 128, 142, 156, 158, 160, 163, 188, 190, 221, 235
Protestant(s) 7, 12, 35, 52, 72, 164, 192

Index of Subjects

purgatory 4, 5, 117, 209, 210, 225
    purgation 210, 225
Puritanism 52

reality 7, 12–13, 18, 19, 20–21, 24, 27–28, 32, 35, 43–44, 46, 54, 56, 62, 64–65, 68–69, 72, 77–81, 87, 89, 93, 104–5, 107–8, 112, 119, 123, 127, 131–39, 141–42, 144, 146, 148–49, 150, 153, 157–58, 162–63, 165, 167–70, 172–73, 176, 180–83, 186–87, 189, 190, 193, 196, 198, 200, 203–6, 208–10, 212–13, 215, 217, 220–21, 227, 229, 232–33, 235, 239–40, 244–45, 247–50, 252, 253, 255–59, 261, 263–65
realization 2, 6, 55, 59, 61, 88, 94, 112, 131, 168, 200
reason 3–4, 7, 31, 45, 48, 60–61, 64, 87, 94, 100, 107, 112–13, 124, 131, 133, 136, 141, 154, 159–60, 162–63, 166, 190, 192, 230, 239
rebirth 44, 45, 145
redemption 2, 19–20, 49, 50, 53, 55, 57, 59, 77, 138, 142, 149, 152–56, 162–64, 167–68, 174, 180, 206, 233–34, 236, 241, 246, 250, 252, 260
    redeem(s) 13, 44, 46–48, 138, 146, 154, 165, 169, 179, 188, 215, 233, 239, 258–60
    redeemer 2, 17, 111
Reformed 7, 64, 198, 234–35
relation 6, 21, 30, 32–33, 35–36, 38, 40, 45, 47, 50, 54–56, 58, 105–7, 118, 128, 132, 145–46, 163, 170, 186, 193, 209, 246
    relationship 4–5, 7–8, 25, 32, 34–36, 45, 48–50, 73, 79, 82–83, 87, 112, 114, 124, 129, 131, 146–47, 167, 172–73, 177, 182–86, 189, 208, 216–17, 219–20, 239, 244, 248, 249, 253, 255
religion(s) 1–5, 8, 10, 13, 18, 25–26, 32, 44–45, 49, 52, 57, 59, 73–75, 78–79, 81, 93, 108, 114, 128, 131–34, 139, 141, 144–45, 148, 160–62, 174, 192, 219–20, 222–23, 232–33, 235, 251, 236
    religious 1–5, 10, 13, 22, 32, 44, 53, 57, 59–60, 73, 75–78, 81, 87, 99, 103, 111, 123, 125–26, 128, 133–36, 137–39, 148, 154, 157–59, 167–68, 173–75, 189–91, 202–4, 206, 211, 213, 216, 218–24, 227, 23–33, 236, 239, 242–43, 245, 252–53, 256, 263
    religious economy 1, 12–13, 64–65, 123, 125–26, 134–36, 137, 139, 157, 167, 173–75, 190, 191, 202–3, 213, 226, 251–52, 258, 261, 265

repentance 15, 87–91, 93–94, 95, 148, 170, 203, 207, 214, 221, 229, 256
responsibility 17, 21, 35, 37–38, 40, 56, 63, 67, 77, 100, 149, 249
resurrection 2, 7–9, 12, 17, 19–21, 31, 33, 35, 40–46, 48, 55, 111, 117, 128–29, 133–35, 141–42, 150, 160–62, 170, 174, 177–79, 194, 204–5, 208, 214, 240, 251–52, 255, 258–60, 264
    resurrected 8, 20, 42–43, 47, 74, 117, 123, 143, 150, 162, 175, 204, 208, 214, 225
revelation 1–10, 13, 19–20, 24–25, 45, 48, 50, 62, 64, 74–75, 86, 112–13, 123–26, 128, 133–35, 139, 141–43, 145, 153, 162, 167, 177, 184, 187, 198–99, 200–3, 205–9, 211–13, 217, 231–32, 234–35, 247–49, 250–51, 260–62
    reveal 93, 104, 124, 145, 149, 161, 192, 209, 218
    revealed 2, 5–7, 48, 75, 88, 93, 145, 168, 182, 184, 193, 199–201, 209, 217, 232, 246
    revelatory 42, 123, 235, 251
reverential 80
righteous 13, 23, 49, 53, 92, 112, 162, 175, 223–24, 257–58, 260
    righteousness 13, 49, 52, 57, 74–76, 157, 235, 256–57, 260
Roman 3–4, 6, 8, 10, 12, 19, 50–53, 57, 61, 126, 198, 207, 240, 247–48, 263
Roman Catholic 3–4, 51, 52–53, 198
Romantic 11, 263
    Romanticism 11, 124

sacramental 5, 159, 257–58, 263
sacrifice(d) 20, 35–36, 47–50, 53–55, 61, 65, 70, 75–77, 100, 110–11, 114–15, 118–19, 134–35, 139, 143–44, 146, 150, 164–65, 167, 169, 174–75, 176–79, 184, 187, 188, 205, 207, 211–12, 214, 218–19, 235–37, 255–61, 264–65
    sacrificial 43, 169, 209, 256
saint 94, 139, 264
salvation 1, 2, 5–6, 12, 19–21, 32, 42, 44, 46, 47, 52, 55, 65, 89, 93, 95, 98–99, 106, 123, 125–28, 131, 134, 141, 145, 150–51, 159, 162, 164–67, 172–74, 177–78, 188–89, 203–4, 212, 222–25, 232–34, 256, 258, 260–63
    salvific 12, 100, 123, 128, 165, 173, 213, 224, 249
    saved 2, 13, 47, 65, 118, 150, 153, 162, 180, 186, 198–99, 203, 213, 222–25, 227, 229, 236–37, 261
    soteriology 162, 214

science 8, 22, 25, 26, 38, 97, 104–5, 118, 129–30, 133, 138, 146, 150, 153, 182
  scientific 11, 18, 22–28, 31, 39, 40–41, 48, 56, 59, 71, 94, 97, 100, 119, 130, 149, 158–59, 233
  scientifiction 130–31
  Scientism 149
  scientist(s) 22, 25, 81–82, 102–3
Scripture *see* Bible
Sehnsucht 53–54, 249 *see Pneumatology*
self 1, 4–5, 7, 13, 15, 22–23, 26, 40, 43, 49, 53, 56, 58–61, 62–63, 67, 69–71, 73, 77, 80–81, 83, 85, 88, 90–94, 99, 105–9, 111, 114, 115–18, 125–27, 130, 137, 139, 143, 146, 148–49, 167–69, 172, 175, 182, 187, 192, 194, 198–99, 201, 207, 226–27, 230–34, 256, 260–261
  selfish 35, 49–50, 54, 58, 62, 79, 94, 100, 105–6, 108, 116, 143, 178
  selfishness 79, 86, 108, 114, 178, 232
separation 17, 19, 21, 30–31, 51, 53, 69, 186, 198, 234, 247
shadows 44, 83, 87, 248
shriven 91
sin(s) 4, 8, 12–13, 15, 17–20, 30–31, 36, 40–41, 45–46, 47–57, 59–62, 64–65, 67–68, 70, 72–76, 78–81, 83, 85–95, 97–100, 102, 104–19, 138–39, 143–45, 147, 149, 150, 152–53, 156–59, 162–65, 167, 174–78, 188, 197, 205, 210, 213–14, 217–18, 221, 223–25, 227, 229, 233–36, 241, 246, 252, 255–60, 263 *see original sin*
  sinful(ness) 53–54, 75, 87, 89–90, 93–94, 106, 110, 202, 206, 235
  sinned 15, 71, 88, 105, 152
  sinner(s) 15, 49, 67, 77, 87–89, 90–91, 95, 159, 175, 178, 217, 235
society 9, 40, 43, 49, 60, 67, 72, 78, 108, 115, 124, 135, 155, 182–83
spiritual 31, 35, 45, 48–51, 53–54, 58, 64, 67, 69, 75, 82, 83, 90, 92, 97, 102, 104, 106, 115, 117, 130, 134, 143, 148–49, 155, 162, 175, 178, 182–83, 187, 201, 211–12, 219, 234, 242–43, 249, 251, 261
sub-creation 1, 8, 12, 17, 21, 37, 38, 40, 104, 123–24, 173, 204, 239, 241–42, 248, 250–51, 254, 263 *see creation*
  mythopoeic 123, 130–31, 173, 204
  mythopoeically 147
  stories 5, 31–32, 37, 71–72, 108, 110, 118, 121–24, 128–31, 133, 134, 136, 138, 141–42, 144, 146, 172, 186, 204–5, 217, 235, 240–42, 248, 250, 262–64
  story 8, 12, 21, 25, 31–33, 43, 47–49, 55–59, 67–68, 70–73, 75–76, 79, 80–82, 87, 97, 103, 108, 118, 124, 126, 128–29, 131, 133–34, 137, 142, 145, 147, 154, 157, 188, 197, 201, 210, 215–16, 220, 228, 230, 240–43, 250, 253, 262
secondary creation 37
sub-creators 37–38
supposal 132–34, 136–39, 167, 173, 192, 213, 215, 233, 239–40, 243, 252, 262, 264
supposition(s) 123, 132, 134, 136–39, 141, 146, 151, 172, 175, 199, 203, 240
supposition 138
subjective 2, 4, 7, 9, 11, 12, 203, 208, 241, 248
supernatural 10, 81, 88, 111, 130, 137–38, 148, 173, 191, 243
symbolic 123–24, 127–29, 131–33, 138–39, 141–44, 147, 149, 167, 173, 176, 189, 212, 249, 256, 262
  symbolize 123, 129, 179, 185
systematic 3, 5–6, 17, 21, 50, 57, 59, 125–27, 131, 145, 163, 167, 174, 258
  systematician 5
  systematize 12, 17, 137

teleology 41, 246, 264
  telos 29, 40–41, 58
temptation 55, 59, 67, 76, 80–82, 84, 86, 90, 109, 147, 151, 176, 215
theodicy 97
theology 3–9, 12, 17–18, 20, 22, 26, 29, 38, 47, 55, 57, 63–64, 68, 75, 77, 81, 85, 87, 90, 97–98, 123–28, 142, 149, 152, 158, 160, 163, 167, 173–74, 176, 181, 183, 189, 192, 199, 211, 214, 225, 229, 232–34, 258
  theologians(s) 3–8, 11–12, 41–42, 54, 72, 77, 87, 103, 123–26, 141, 144, 151, 159–60, 163–64, 169, 189, 198–99, 232, 261
  theological 5–6, 8–12, 17, 21, 47, 58, 64, 67–68, 71–73, 76–77, 80, 98, 103, 106, 110–11, 118, 121–27, 129, 131, 138, 155, 157–58, 160, 162–64, 168, 190, 234, 249, 260, 262
theophany 172, 174, 186–87, 190, 208 *see epiphany*
  theophanic 136, 151, 153, 167, 187, 199
theory 7–8, 18, 22, 25–26, 32, 37, 64–65, 97, 102–4, 107, 110, 158, 165, 232–33, 239, 248, 255, 258–61
tradition(s) 1–3, 10, 19, 21, 25–26, 32, 34, 50, 55, 59, 64, 81, 98, 133, 135, 149, 157–59, 183, 190, 192, 201, 218, 234, 236, 245, 247, 260–62, 264

Index of Subjects

traditional 3–5, 8–9, 30, 89, 99, 110, 112, 124, 170, 181, 214, 258
transcendent 7, 23–24, 32, 148, 233, 236
  transcendence 23–24, 62, 127, 233
translation 1, 54, 78, 144, 190
  translates 144
transmission 49–51, 53, 75–76, 97–98, 100, 104–5, 247
  transmitted 71–72, 75, 98, 100, 105–6
transposition 71, 131, 190, 235, 248–51, 262
  transposed 41, 44, 136, 172, 235, 249–50, 252, 262
  transposing 131
Tree of Life 102–4, 176, 180
trial 82, 83, 84
Trinity 2, 13, 20–21, 25, 30, 33–35, 54, 82, 126–27, 131, 135–36, 139, 142–43, 146, 151, 162–63, 167–69, 172–74, 176, 181–93, 195, 198–4, 209, 212–13, 216–17, 222, 224 *see Chrislike(ness), Christology, incarnation, infinitum capax finiti, Pneumatology, and Word*
  divine 2–3, 9, 17–19, 31, 36, 43, 51, 54, 57, 59, 64, 91, 98–99, 114–15, 118, 148, 151, 154, 161–65, 169–70, 173–74, 176, 181, 183, 187–88, 191, 195, 198, 200, 204, 207–8, 211, 231–32, 234–35, 240, 251
  divinized 52
  economic Trinity 13, 126, 168–69, 172–73, 198, 200
  epiphany 135
  Father 12–13, 17, 20, 27, 30–31, 34–35, 77, 86, 135–36, 142–43, 161–63, 165, 167–72, 173, 175, 177, 182–86, 188–93, 196, 198–99, 200–2, 210, 215–16, 221–23, 228, 233, 239–49, 252–53, 255–59, 262–65
  I am 10, 23, 26, 28, 29, 56, 91, 136, 169, 180, 200–201, 207, 214–16, 220–22, 228
  immanence 24, 168–69
  immanent 13, 24, 136, 167–69, 172, 198, 200, 203, 217
  immanent Trinity 13, 136, 167–69, 172, 200, 203, 217
  Immanuel 30, 230
  monotheism 168
  persons (trinitarian) 13, 25, 142f., 167–72, 181–86, 189–193, 198–201, 205, 214, 217, 222,
  Son 21, 27, 34–35, 41–42, 114–15, 133, 135, 151, 153, 161–62, 164, 167–70, 172, 175, 182–88, 190–93, 198–99, 201–2, 211, 216, 222–24, 233, 245, 255, 263, 265
  three-in-one 168, 185
  Trinitarian 2, 5, 20, 24–26, 167–68, 169–73, 175–76, 181–84, 186, 190, 193, 198–200, 215, 217, 253, 262–63
  triune 13, 17, 20, 22, 24, 34–35, 82, 112, 142, 165–70, 172–74, 181–82, 184–86, 190, 193, 199–202, 209, 215, 217, 219, 232–33, 252
truth(s) 8, 12–13, 17–18, 21, 31–32, 45–46, 55, 57, 59, 62–63, 68, 74, 94, 97, 111–13, 118, 121, 124–25, 126, 132–33, 138–39, 141, 144–45, 147, 149, 167–69, 172–73, 175, 184, 190–91, 201, 205, 207, 209, 221–24, 233–34, 236, 248–49, 250–52, 262

understand 2–3, 6, 18, 23, 27–28, 39, 44, 47, 50, 61, 103, 108–9, 113–14, 128, 141, 174, 178, 182, 195, 205–6, 210–11, 237, 249
  understanding 1–7, 10, 12–13, 17, 20, 31, 38, 40–44, 47–48, 50, 52, 54–55, 62, 64, 67, 71, 81, 88–89, 93, 97, 100, 107–8, 114, 123–24, 127–28, 137, 139, 141–42, 145–46, 150, 167–70, 172–73, 181–82, 184, 189–90, 197, 204–5, 208–9, 211, 217–18, 225, 233–34, 236, 240, 250, 252–54, 259, 261–63
  understood 5, 7–8, 19, 26, 38, 48, 62–63, 113, 171, 199, 228
universal 3, 11, 19, 23, 25, 49, 55, 64–65, 104, 108, 152, 154, 156, 159, 232, 249
  universalist 159
unknown 44, 146, 184, 226, 254
Utopia 67, 72

via negativa 149

wisdom 37, 85, 99, 109, 149, 155
  wisely 85
witness 2–3, 20, 28, 67, 76–77, 79, 85, 108, 125–26, 135, 178, 246, 257, 263, 265
  Witness 135, 265
w/Word 13, 24, 42, 101, 109, 126–27, 137, 142, 160, 168, 176, 189, 198, 207, 211, 233, 243
  asarkos 189
  enfleshed 187–89, 208
  ensarkos 189
  logos 17–19, 189
  unfleshed 189

Index of C. S. Lewis's Works
An index of Lewis's works cited or quoted

Beyond Personality 24-25, 27, 29, 35-36, 93, 114-15, 142-44, 161, 169, 181, 183, 204
Broadcast Talks 23-25, 55, 57-58, 73, 86, 89-90, 93, 108, 111, 143, 236
"'Bulverism' or The Foundation of Twentieth Century Thought," 28, 37

"Christian Apologetics" 25, 92
Christian Behaviour 13, 35, 90-91, 93-95
"Christianity and Culture" 89
The Chronicles of Narnia 12, 38-39, 67, 80-81, 84-85, 108, 118, 123, 128-29, 131-32, 135, 138, 141-42, 150, 167, 172, 196, 225, 239, 240, 244, 252, 263
   The Horse and His Boy 43, 132, 167, 180, 186-87, 191, 194, 200, 203, 207-9, 215, 218-19, 251
   The Last Battle 39, 132, 177, 179-80, 186, 189-91, 195-96, 198, 203, 207, 211-12, 222-23, 225-29, 234-36, 246, 250-51, 254, 259, 261
   The Lion, the Witch, and the Wardrobe 39, 43, 70, 84, 109, 111, 129, 132, 139, 148, 178-80, 184, 188, 191, 193-96, 204, 208, 211-15, 224, 228, 236-37, 239-45, 248, 250, 252, 254-55, 258, 262, 264
   The Magician's Nephew 24, 38, 39, 42, 67, 80, 84, 86, 97, 108, 109, 111, 116, 132, 154, 157, 176, 177, 180, 188-89, 191, 194-95,
   Prince Caspian 132, 148, 180, 186, 191, 194, 196, 205-6, 208, 211, 241, 251, 254
   The Silver Chair 39, 43, 132, 134, 178-80, 191, 194-95, 197, 205, 250-51
   The Voyage of the Dawn Treader 132, 136, 167, 178-80, 184, 186, 191, 195, 197, 198-99, 205, 208-9, 211, 214, 230, 234, 251
"Christianity and Literature" 35, 37
Collected Letters, Vol. I 92
Collected Letters, Vol. II 92, 131, 183

Collected Letters, Vol. III 8, 25, 27, 29, 34, 37, 55, 57-58, 61, 63, 65, 90-92, 132, 134, 138, 142, 218, 240, 260
"Cross Examination" 76, 95, 267

The Dark Tower and Other Stories 146 *see The Space Trilogy*
"De Descriptione Temporum" 10, 125
"Dogma and the Universe" 22, 25, 32-33, 156

English Literature in the Sixteenth Century 45

The Four Loves 36, 90, 115
"The Funeral of a Great Myth" 44, 130
"The Future of Forestry" 39

The Great Divorce 12, 17, 42-43, 99, 115-118, 123, 127, 132, 138, 141-42, 144-45, 172, 196, 206, 209-10, 212-13, 225-27, 230-31, 234, 245, 251, 254-56
A Grief Observed 25, 45, 63

"Is Theism Important?" 10
"It All Began with a Picture" 133

"Letter to 'An American Lady,' Apr. 17, 1953" 183
"Letter to "An American Lady," March 4, 1953" 35
"Letter to "An American Lady," Nov 26, 1962" 38
"Letter to Anne Jenkins, Mar 5, 1961" 121, 142, 218, 251
"Letter to Anne Jenkins, Mar. 5, 1961" 134
"Letter to Charles A. Brady, Oct 29, 1944" 131
"Letter to Dom Bede Griffiths, April 24, 1936" 54, 147
"Letter to Dom Bede Griffiths, Aug. 4, 1962" 182
"Letter to Dom Bede Griffiths, Dec 21, 1941" 183
"Letter to Dom Bede Griffiths, May 23 1936" 54, 147
"Letter to Dom Bede Griffiths OSB, April 16, 1940" 36

"Letter to Elsie Snickers, May 18, 1953" 61
"Letter to Genia Goelz, June 13, 1951" 61
"Letter to Jane Douglass, Dec 21, 1954" 61
"Letter to John Beversluis, July 3, 1963" 63
"Letter to Mary Van Deusen, Feb 7, 1951" 61
"Letter to Mary Willis Shelburne, May 30, 1953" 91
"Letter to Mary Willis Shelburne, Apr 15, 1958" 62
"Letter to Mary Willis Shelburne, July 12, 1958" 90
"Letter to Mary Willis Shelburne, Jan 9, 1961" 91
"Letter to Mary Willis Shelburne, Nov 8, 1962" 58
"Letter to Mary Willis Shelburne, Nov 26, 1962" 92
"Letter to Michael Edwards, June 27, 1958" 55
"Letter to Michael Edwards, Oct 20, 1956" 55
"Letter to Miss Breckenridge, Aug 1, 1949" 56
"Letter to Mrs D. Jessup, 5 Feb, 1954" 61
"Letter to Mrs D. Jessup, Dec. 1, 1953" 27
"Letter to Mrs Hook Dec. 29, 1958" 132, 134
"Letter to Mrs Hook, Dec 29, 1958" 240
"Letter to Mrs Johnson, July. 17, 1953" 29
"Letter to Sr. Penelope CSMV, Feb 20, 1943" 37
"Letter to Sr. Penelope CSMV, Jan 10, 1952" 34
"Letter to The Church Times, Feb. 8, 1952" 8, 25, 55
"Letter to Tony Pollock, May 3, 1954" 121, 138
"Letter to Wayne Shumaker, March 21, 1962" 55, 57
Letters of C. S. Lewis 90, 183
Letters to an American Lady 35, 38, 183
Letters to Malcolm: Chiefly on Prayer 25–30, 35–36, 38, 41, 60, 89–91, 94, 98, 145

"Man or Rabbit" 44
Mere Christianity 3, 4, 13, 29, 32, 35, 44, 58, 114, 125, 142, 169, 172, 181–83, 190, 202, 237
Miracles 22–25, 27, 29, 32, 38, 41, 43–44, 57–59, 74, 90, 130, 142, 152, 154, 161, 165, 169, 182, 188, 192
"Miserable Offenders" 91, 93
"Modern Theology and Biblical Criticism" (aka "Fern Seed and Elephants" 98
"The Mythopoeic Gift of Rider Haggard" 130

"The Novels of Charles Williams" 136–37

The Pilgrim's Regress 45, 129, 133, 144
"The Poison of Subjectivism" 56, 62, 183
A Preface to Paradise Lost 77

The Problem of Pain 15, 24, 28–31, 34–36, 37–38, 44, 54, 56–60, 62–64, 67–68, 70, 75, 82, 85, 87, 89–95, 105, 114–15, 118, 182–83

Reflections on the Psalms 22, 25–27, 29, 30, 32, 34, 44, 91–92, 94, 145
"Rejoinder to Dr Pittenger" 98, 144
"Religion and Rocketry" 152, 155, 157, 159
"Religion Without Dogma?" 44

The Screwtape Letters 12, 29, 32, 44, 80, 87–89, 92, 115, 123, 132, 138, 141–42, 145, 172, 182, 209–10
"Screwtape Proposes a Toast"/*Screwtape Proposes a Toast* 32, 88–89, 115
"The Seeing Eye" 155
"The Sermon and the Lunch" 57, 73, 78
"Shall We Lose God in Outer Space" 152
"Some Thoughts" 25, 28, 59
"Sometimes Fairy Stories" 131, 133
The Space Trilogy 12, 40, 82, 123, 128–30, 132, 138, 141–42, 146, 148, 150, 153–54, 167, 172, 173, 191, 259
    The Cosmic Trilogy 146
    "The Dark Tower" 146
    Out of the Silent Planet (*The Space Trilogy*, Bk. 1) 40, 55, 59, 130, 144, 146–47, 149, 167, 173–74
    Perelandra (*The Space Trilogy*, Bk. 2) 55, 59, 67–68, 80, 82– 83, 85–86, 131, 138, 144, 146–47, 149–51, 156, 158, 164, 173
    That Hideous Strength (*The Space Trilogy*, Bk. 3) 146, 148–49, 173
Surprised by Joy 29, 45, 69–70, 79, 92, 130, 143, 213

They Asked for a Paper 249, 251
Till We Have Faces 12, 123, 141–42, 144, 148, 211
"Transposition" 249–50, 269
Transposition and other Addresses 249, 251

Vivisection 38

"We Have No 'Right to Happiness' " 73, 112
"The Weight of Glory"/*The Weight of Glory* 45, 231, 251
"The World's Last Night" 22, 59, 152
"Who was Right—Dream Lecturer or Real Lecturer" 22, 26
"Will We Lose God in Outer Space" 152

Index of Greek, Latin, and Derived Terms, and Works

Theological concepts and terms listed as they appear in the text, rather than the usual dictionary forms

ἀγάπη 169–72, 202
ἀναλογία 129
ἀνάλογος 129
ἀποκατάστασις 58
ad infinitum 49, 69
agnus Dei 214–15
a posteriori 2, 193

Christus 1, 65, 260
Christus Victor 65, 260
corpus 42, 47, 172

De Civitate Dei 50, 54
De Diversis Quaestionibus Ad Simplicianum 50
Deus caritas est 169
doctrina 6
δοκέω 187

ἐλογίσθη 235
ἔσχατον 8
    eschaton 8, 42, 55, 72, 118–19, 136, 167, 174–75, 181, 188–89, 196, 198, 211–12, 225–29, 237, 254, 259
eritis sicut Deus 97, 108, 110–11, 113, 135, 147
ex nihilo 18, 20–23, 26, 37, 174

felix culpa 58, 81
filioque 192
φρόνημα τῆς σαρκός 53

homo incurvatus in se 47, 54, 70, 85, 108

imago Christi 21, 33, 142–45, 171
imago Dei 21, 32, 34, 37
imitatio Christi 142–43
immanere 168
in absentia 246
infinitum capax finiti 24
in potentia 65

lapsarian 47, 48, 60
λόγος 17–19, 18–89, 101, 235
λόγος ἄσαρκος 188–89
λόγος ἔνσαρκος 188–89

ὁ θεὸς ἀγάπη ἐστίν 169
οἰκονομία 13, 168

πατήρ 7
περί 170
περιχώρησις 170
πίστις 170
πνεῦμα 191
    pneuma 191f., 218
postlapsarian 47–48, 55, 60–61, 71, 73, 79–80, 82, 107, 118, 124, 230
post mortem 13, 42, 51, 58, 115, 145, 151, 190, 195, 210, 227, 229, 234, 261
prelapsarian 47–48, 49, 55, 58–60, 69, 72–73, 82, 93, 138, 173

redemptio 260

simul iustus et peccator 235
σύμβολον 129

τέλος 58
timeo danaos et dona ferentes 26
triquetra 185

via dolorosa 204
via negativa 149

Χριστός 1, 2
χώρησις 170

Sectional Contents

Foreword | xiii

Introduction. C. S. Lewis—On The Christ of A Religious Economy. I. Creation and Sub-Creation | 1

1. Who or What is the Christ | 1
2. Why C. S. Lewis | 3
3. Aims and Objectives | 4
4. Explanations, Qualifications | 6
    i. Revelation and Reason | 6
    ii. Patristic | 7
    iii. Platonism | 7
    iv. Apologist/Apologetics | 8
    v. Creation, Fall, Incarnation, Resurrection, Second Coming, and the Four Last Things | 8
    vi. Ontology | 9
    vii. Liberal/liberal, Modernism | 9
    viii. Pagan | 10
    ix. Romantic | 11
5. "... and the Collected Works of C. S. Lewis" | 11
6. The Christ of a Religious Economy | 12

PART ONE THE FALL, ORIGINAL SIN, AND AN EXISTENTIAL CRISIS

Chapter 1. Creation and The Fall I: C. S. Lewis—A Doctrine of Creation | 17

1. Introduction | 18
2. "And God said..." | 18
3. Lewis on Creation: The Work of Christ | 20
4. First Axiom: God the Triune Creator | 20
5. Second Axiom: The Actuality of Creation | 25
6. Third Axiom: Purpose, Character, and Nature | 27
    i. Theological Principle A: Creation as Separation | 30
    ii. Theological Principle B: The Myth of Creation | 31
    iii. Theological Principle C: Humanity's Relation to God and Creation | 32

        Why the Human? | 33
        Purpose | 35
        Relation and Obedience | 36
        The Fall | 36
   vi. Theological Principle D: Sub-Creation and Sub-creators | 37
7. Fourth Axiom: The New Creation | 40
   i. Cause and Cross, Creation and Consummation | 40
   ii. Lewis: Markers of the New Creation | 42
   iii. Nature and Grace | 45
8. Rebellion | 46

Chapter 2. Creation and The Fall II: Lewis's "Augustinian" Account | 47

1. Introduction | 47
2. The Fall: The Biblical Account | 48
3. Augustine's Doctrine | 50
   i. A Judeo-Christian Anthropology | 50
   ii. A Roman Catholic and Anglican Perspective | 51
   iii. Concupiscence | 53
4. *homo incurvatus in se*: What does Lewis have to Say? | 54
   i. The Fall . . . and the Unfallen | 54
   ii. *postlapsarian*: The Fallen | 55
   iii. *prelapsarian*: The Unfallen | 59
   iv. *lapsarian*: Original Sin | 60
5. A Doctrine of Total Depravity | 62
   i. An Inverted Understanding | 62
   ii. A Doctrine of Limited, or Pseudo-Depravity | 64
6. Whither Atonement? | 65

Chapter 3 Creation and The Fall III: Innocence and Sin Re-Interpreted | 67

1. Introduction | 68
2. The Fall: Re-Told | 68
3. The Fall: Variation on a Theme | 71
   i. An Idealistic Inversion? | 72
   ii. Dostoevsky: *The Dream of a Ridiculous Man,* | 73
        Innocence Corrupted | 73
        Religion as the Result of the Fall | 74
   iii. Milton, *Paradise Lost* | 76
   iv. Golding: *Lord of the Flies* | 78
   v. A Hedonistic Paradise | 79
4. Lewis-Pullman: The Fall Re-Visited, or Re-Defined? | 80
   i. An Unholy Inversion | 80
   ii. Paradise Retained | 82
   iii. "All get what they want; they do not always like it." | 84
   iv. Obedience-Disobedience: A Dialectic | 85
5. In the Shadow of Christ: Sin and Sinners | 87

i. A Consciousness of Sin | 88
     Screwtape's Inverted Understanding | 88
     An Orthodox Teaching | 89
     Disorder and Responsibility | 90
     Personal Responsibility | 91
     "The more important sins" | 92
  ii. Sinfulness and Desperation | 93
6. The Answer: The Christ | 94

Chapter 4 Creation and The Fall IV: The Human Condition before God | 97

1. Introduction | 97
2. Creation, Neo-Pelagianism, and Transmission | 98
   i. Solving the Problem for Ourselves | 98
   ii. Lewis: Grace and Free Will | 98
   iii. Born this Way? | 100
   iv. Inheritance? | 102
   v. Graceless Stress in a Hostile World | 105
3. The Independence/Interdependence of Decisions | 106
4. *eritis sicut Deus*: "The Idea" | 108
   i. The Fall: The Freedom Taken to Redefine | 108
   ii. "I deduced from all of this the utter necessity of faith in Christ." | 110
5. Reason and Natural Law | 111
6. Created Freedom and Custodianship: The Human Condition | 114
   i. Lewis on the Hell of the Self: Condemnation and Destruction | 114
   ii. What If?—Ontological Custodianship | 117

PART TWO CHRIST REVEALED THROUGH ANALOGICAL AND SYMBOLIC NARRATIVE

Chapter 5 Analogical and Symbolic Narratives I: Narrative Theology, Supposition and Genre, Mythopoeic Theorizing—Imagining The Christ | 123

1. Introduction | 124
2. Theology after "Modernism" and "Liberalism" | 124
3. Narrative Theology | 126
4. Lewis: Analogical-Symbolic Narratives | 128
   i. A Veiled Understanding Outside the Church | 128
   ii. Genre and Source | 128
5. Narnia: Lewis's "Supposal" | 131
   i. Mythopoeic Theorizing | 131
   ii. "The Whole Narnian Story is about Christ" | 133
   iii. Aslan ... or Christ? | 136
   iv. "The Probable and the Marvelous" | 136
6. How Successful is Lewis's Supposition? | 138

ON THE CHRIST OF A RELIGIOUS ECONOMY. I. CREATION AND SUB-CREATION

Chapter 6 Analogical and Symbolic Narratives II: Christology and Christlikeness—Hiddenness and Multiple Incarnations | 141

1. Introduction | 142
2. Christ, Translated and Transposed | 142
    i. The *imago Christi* and the *imitatio Christi* | 142
    ii. Christlike—and the Christ | 144
    iii. Christlikeness—Ransom and Psyche | 144
3. The Hidden Christ I: By Analogy | 145
4. The Hidden Christ II: The Space Trilogy | 146
    i. Christ's Servants | 146
    ii. The Anti-Christ | 147
5. The Question of Multiple Incarnations | 150
    i. The Limits of Atonement? | 150
    ii. Aquinas Poses the Question | 151
6. Lewis on Multiple Incarnations | 151
    i. The Doctrine of Universal Redemption | 152
    ii. Quarantine, Cosmic Implications and Atonement: Wither Humanity? | 152
    iii. Created Diversity | 157
7. The Argument Extended | 158
    i. Rahner and Fisher and Fergusson on Multiple Incarnations | 158
    ii. Bonting, Drees, and Mascall on Multiple Incarnations | 159
    iii. Hebblethwaite on Multiple Incarnations | 160
    iv. Crisp on Multiple Incarnations | 163
    v. Ward on Multiple Incarnations | 165
8. The Argument Resolved? | 165

Chapter 7 Analogical and Symbolic Narratives III: Christology and Christlikeness—Trinitarian Considerations | 167

1. A Doctrine of God | 168
    i. God is Triune | 168
    ii. Immanence and Economic Action | 168
    iii. God is Love | 169
        Deus caritas est—ὁ θεὸς ἀγάπη ἐστίν—God is Love | 169
        The Eschatological Direction of the Love of God | 169
        Ever-Focusing on the Other | 170
2. A Christian Analogy? | 172
3. The Trinity in The Space Trilogy | 173
4. A Triune Salvation History? | 174
5. Trinitarian Considerations | 175
    i. Christian Concepts | 175
    ii. Creation | 176
    iii. The Tree and the Garden | 176
    iv. Sacrifice and Resurrection | 177
    v. Salvation | 178
    vi. End Times and Final Judgment | 179

vii. Resurrection Life | 179
viii. The Stable, Door, and Garden | 179
6. A Doctrine of the Trinity | 181
7. A Narnian Trinity | 183
   i. The Triune God: Father, Son, and Holy Spirit | 183
   ii. The Father: The Emperor-beyond-the-Sea | 184
   iii. The Son: Aslan—An Epiphanic Enfleshed Theophany | 186
   iv. The Son: Aslan—an Enfleshed Logos—Corporeal and Creaturely | 187
      Incarnation or Theophany | 187
      λόγος ἄσαρκος/λόγος ἔνσαρκος | 188
      "He no longer looked to them like a lion." | 189
   v. The Holy Spirit: The Spirit of the Emperor-beyond-the-Sea and of Aslan | 190
8. Pneuma The Holy One: I. A Disquieting Presence | 191
   i. A Haunting | 192
   ii. "Who Proceeds from the Father and the Son" | 192
9. Pneuma The Holy One: II. Action and event | 193
   i. The Breath of Aslan | 193
   ii. The Comforter | 195
   iii. The Enabler | 196
   iv. The Chastiser and the Moral Guide | 196
   v. The Guide and a Symbol of Hope | 198
10. A Triune Statement of Self-Revelation | 198
    i. Trinitarian Language | 198
    ii. A Trinitarian Revelation: Courage and Hope | 199
    iii A Trinitarian Revelation: "I am that I am" | 200
11. Conclusion: A Narnian Doctrine of God? | 202

Chapter 8 Analogical and Symbolic Narratives IV: Salvation, Encounters, and Judgment—the Work of the Aslan-Christ | 203

1. Introduction | 203
2. The Aslan-Christ I: Lewis's Mythopoeic Sub-Creation | 204
   i. Aslan | 204
   ii. Perception: A Human Model | 205
      Dread and Wrath, Terror and Amazement | 205
      A Troubling Presence, An Enfleshed Form | 208
      Fear and Trembling, Hidden and Apophatic | 209
      Beauty and Love, Grief and Intensity | 211
3. The Aslan-Christ II: Encounters | 212
   i. The Nature of the Encounters | 212
   ii. Encounters: An Awesome Meeting | 213
4. The Aslan-Christ III: Pagan Encounters | 215
   i. Encounters: Shasta and Aravis, Bree and Hwin | 215
      Shasta—The Conversion of a Pagan? | 215
      Aravis—The Conversion of a Religious? | 218
      Bree and Hwin—The Conversion of Sentient Beings? | 220
   ii. Encounters: Emeth | 222

5. The Aslan-Christ IV: Judgment—A Narnian Eschaton | 225
      i. The Finality of Judgment | 225
      ii. A Shifting Puzzle? | 227
      iii. Neo-Kantian, Feuerbachian Dwarves? | 229
         Faith and Disbelief | 229
         "Oh Adam's sons, how cleverly you defend yourselves against all that might do you good." | 230
         A Baptized Imagination | 234
      iv. Matthew 25: Pagan Salvation? | 235

Chapter 9 Analogical and Symbolic Narratives V: Father Christmas in Narnia?—Intimations of Atonement and Salvation | 239

   1. Introduction: How Does It Work? | 240
   2. Explanations and Criticisms | 241
   3. The Problem | 244
   4. *The Lion, the Witch, and the Wardrobe* | 245
   5. St. Nicholas, Father Christmas, Santa Claus, Kris Kringle, Jupiter, Jove | 246
   6. Platonic Idealism and Reality | 247
      i. Revelation and Myth-Making | 248
      ii. Transposition | 249
      iii. Illumination and Intimation | 250
   7. Father Christmas in Narnia: An Existential Theological Proposition | 252
      i. The Gift Bearer | 252
      ii. Cross-Cultural Fertilization | 253
      iii. Sin, Treachery, and Atonement | 255
      iv. A Narnian *Fall* | 256
      v. "Always Winter and Never Christmas" | 257
   8. Towards a Narnian Atonement | 258
      i. Freedom . . . under "The Law" | 259
      ii. A Ransom Theory of Atonement | 259
      iii. A Debt Theory of Atonement | 261
   9. Conclusion | 262

www.ingramcontent.com/pod-product-compliance
Lightning Source LLC
Chambersburg PA
CBHW060508300426
44112CB00017B/2586